WEB 2.0
and
BEYOND

Principles and Technologies

CHAPMAN & HALL/CRC
TEXTBOOKS IN COMPUTING

WEB 2.0
and
BEYOND

Principles and Technologies

Paul Anderson

CRC Press
Taylor & Francis Group
Boca Raton   London   New York

CRC Press is an imprint of the
Taylor & Francis Group, an **informa** business

A CHAPMAN & HALL BOOK

Cover Image: Makoto Uchida and Susumu Shirayama. Formation of patterns from complex networks. *Journal of Visualization*, Vol. 10, No. 3, pp. 253--256, (2007). http://www.race.u-tokyo.ac.jp/~uchida/blogdata/ Used with permission.

CRC Press
Taylor & Francis Group
6000 Broken Sound Parkway NW, Suite 300
Boca Raton, FL 33487-2742

© 2012 by Taylor & Francis Group, LLC
CRC Press is an imprint of Taylor & Francis Group, an Informa business

No claim to original U.S. Government works

Printed in the United States of America on acid-free paper
Version Date: 20120521

International Standard Book Number: 978-1-4398-2867-0 (Hardback)

Library of Congress Cataloging-in-Publication Data

Anderson, Paul (Paul David), 1964-
   Web 2.0 and beyond : principles and technologies / Paul Anderson.
      p. cm. -- (Chapman & Hall/CRC textbooks in computing ; 7)
   Includes bibliographical references and index.
   ISBN 978-1-4398-2867-0 (hardback)
   1. Web 2.0. 2. Internet--Social aspects. I. Title.

TK5105.88817.A53 2012
004.67'8--dc23   2012009449

**Visit the Taylor & Francis Web site at
http://www.taylorandfrancis.com**

**and the CRC Press Web site at
http://www.crcpress.com**

Dedicated to my mother and father, Ruth and David Anderson

Contents

SECTION II **Web 2.0 Services**

SECTION III **Framework for the Future**

CHAPTER 14 ■ Technology and Standards   251

Preface

The Web is no longer the sole preserve of computer science. Web 2.0 services have imbued the Web as a technical infrastructure with the imprint of human behaviour, and this has consequently attracted attention from many new fields of study including business studies, economics, information science, law, media studies, philosophy, psychology, social informatics and sociology. In fact, to understand the implications of Web 2.0, an interdisciplinary approach is needed, and in writing this book I have been influenced by Web science—a new academic discipline that studies the Web as a large, complex, engineered environment and the impact it has on society.

The structure of this book is based on the iceberg model that I initially developed in 2007 as a way of thinking about Web 2.0. I have since elaborated on this and included summaries of important research areas from many different disciplines, which have been brought together as themes. To finish off, I have included a chapter on the future that both draws on the ideas presented earlier in the book and challenges readers to apply them based on what they have learned.

READERSHIP

The book is aimed at an international audience, interested in forming a deeper understanding of what Web 2.0 might be and how it could develop in the future. Although it is an academic textbook, it has been written in an accessible style and parts of it can be used at an introductory undergraduate level with readers from many different backgrounds who have little knowledge of computing. In addition, parts of the book will push beyond the levels of expertise of such readers to address both computer science undergraduates and post-graduate research students, who ought to find the literature reviews in Section II to be particularly useful reference resources.

OVERVIEW

The structure of the book is based on the iceberg model of Web 2.0, which I developed as a way of separating Web 2.0 services (the tip of the iceberg) from the technologies and principles that underpin them. Accordingly, the book is in three sections; the Six Big Ideas, Web 2.0 Services, and Framework for the Future. Students who are new to the subject should start with the *What Is Web 2.0?* chapter that precedes Section I, as it presents background information and key concepts, and provides context for the rest of the book.

Context

What Is Web 2.0?: Sets the scene for the rest of the book by looking at the events around the dot-com boom and bust in the mid- to late-1990s and the role they had in the origins of Web 2.0 as an idea. It goes on to examine some of the controversy around Web 2.0 and explains the key ideas as they were expressed in Tim O'Reilly's (2005b) seminal paper, *What is Web 2.0: Design patterns and business models for the next generation of software*. From here, the chapter presents and explains the iceberg model and the concepts it depends on, which are loosely based on O'Reilly's seven principles.

Section I

The Six Big Ideas: Six chapters covering user-generated content, the architecture of participation, data on an epic scale, harnessing the power of the crowd, openness, and the network effect and Web topology (what size and shape the Web is and why it matters). These chapters have been constructed as a coherent, cumulative argument that ought to be read sequentially by all levels of readers. However, parts of the last chapter may pose difficulties for students who do not have a working knowledge of statistics.

Section II

Web 2.0 Services: A further six chapters, arranged roughly chronologically, that cover the main types of Web 2.0 services, namely blogs, wikis, online social networks (Facebook, MySpace etc.), media sharing sites (podcasts, photo and video sharing sites), social bookmarking (e.g., Delicious), and micro-blogging (e.g., Twitter). Each chapter begins with an overview of the service and how it is used, followed by a brief history of how it came to be developed and the technology involved. The second half of each chapter is given over to looking at important research themes and a summary of key findings from the literature. These should be particularly relevant to post-graduate students who are embarking on a period of in-depth study into an aspect of Web 2.0, Web science or social media. These chapters provide a guide to the state of the art, attempting to tease out key research themes and agendas.

Section III

Framework for the Future: The book's final section covers the technologies and standards that underpin the operation of Web 2.0 and considers ways in which these will develop in the future.

In the first chapter there is a summary of how the Web works, which leads into an explanation of the developments that have made Web 2.0 services possible. It also explains the critical role that standards play in the development of new technologies and analyses the ways in which standards are produced. Although nonexperts may gain a superficial understanding of the main developments, much of this chapter is aimed at computer scientists with a working knowledge of code and markup languages. The second chapter in this section covers various possibilities for future developments. It challenges readers to consider what, if anything, might be meant by the term 'Web 3.0' and how they would interpret it based on what they have learned so far.

USING THE BOOK

The book has been designed as a teaching resource as well as a general reference work. At the end of each chapter is a set of questions and points to ponder, where each of the three main audiences should find something relevant to their field of study. In addition, for those students who wish to pursue some of the topics in more detail, I have provided a list of further reading.

Introductory Level

The non-expert reader will get the most benefit from starting at Chapter 1 (*What Is Web 2.0?*) and reading Section I sequentially, as the chapters have been constructed as a coherent, cumulative argument. Whilst each chapter *can* be read independently (significant sections of related content from other chapters are cross-referenced), this will not give the reader the same sense of the inter-relatedness among the ideas, principles and technologies that is so important to understanding Web 2.0.

Computer Science

Most of the material relating to Web technologies has been brought together in Chapter 14, although the chapters in Section II also cover the technologies that relate specifically to each of the Web 2.0 services. In addition, there is detailed coverage of technology standards and the processes of standardization in Chapter 14. This is important, not only as context for the development of the technology, but also as an explanation of the first principles that are used to assess how 'open' standards and the resultant technologies are deemed to be.

Research Students

Research students who have a particular focus or agenda, say investigating an individual Web 2.0 service, should find the material in Section II especially useful. In particular, the second half of each chapter provides a detailed breakdown and review of the current state of the art within the academic literature, identifying key ideas and themes that emerge time and again. For example, the repeated presence of the power law, small-world effects and various other aspects of complex networks are rapidly emerging as major themes in the research of Web 2.0.

However, to fully appreciate the context in which this research has been carried out and to help make sense of the results and what they might tell us about the Web in general, the reader is also advised to read Section I first.

HOW TO READ THIS BOOK

From the very beginning of the commissioning process, this book was designed to appeal to a broad audience. The challenge for me was to maintain the rigour of the academic method whilst communicating in a way that could be understood by non-engineers.

My main focus was to keep the text as clear and uncluttered as possible. Website Uniform Resource Identifiers (URIs) presented me with a particular problem in this respect, so I have developed a pragmatic approach for dealing with these. For example, where a website or webpage constitutes part of the evidence base, say to support a potentially contentious statement or to reference a specific idea or opinion, I have turned it into a standard citation with a full entry in the reference section. However, where a website or webpage has been included, say, to provide a representative sample of a debate or opinion, to illustrate something quickly or easily, or to provide further information, I have included it as a footnote. When it comes to providing URIs for Web 2.0 services or company websites that can be found easily through a search engine, I rely on the reader's initiative to find them for themselves.

In a similar vein I have had to be equally pragmatic when dealing with quotations. Throughout the book I have used double quotation marks, along with a citation and page number, to indicate a direct quote from someone else's text. However, where an author has used a one- or two-word expression that is particularly apt, I have quoted without using a page number in the interest of keeping the text moving as much as possible. I have used single quotation marks to differentiate specific terms, or those that have disputed meanings or are neologisms from these short quotes. The reader should therefore be able to distinguish between the two types of terms on the basis of the punctuation alone.

In computer-related writing, placing a full stop/period inside quotation marks can introduce inaccuracies or ambiguity into the text (Boolean search, which considers everything inside the quotation marks as part of the search term, provides an example of this type of problem). I have therefore placed the full stop/period at the very end of sentences so as to be consistent and to avoid creating errors.

Too many capital letters can also disrupt a text, so I have tried to keep them to a minimum where to do so would not create errors or confusion. Whereas 'the Web' and 'the Internet' are both proper nouns and therefore need to be spelled with a capital letter, using compound nouns in their open form (e.g., 'Web page' and 'Web site'), although helpful for novice readers, creates a visual barrier in a book like this where the terms are used often. With this in mind I have used the closed forms of these compound nouns (e.g., 'webpage' and 'website'), which anyone reading this book should be sufficiently familiar with.

In terms of point of view, I have also tried to keep things simple. In order to avoid the clumsy 'he or she' structure I have tended to use the gender-neutral plural 'they'—except where this would cause confusion. I have also used the active voice wherever possible even when this means using 'I'—a practice that is sometimes frowned upon in scientific writing.

Finally, I hope you enjoy reading this book. My overall aim was to make Web 2.0 as interesting as possible, and to not only appeal to students from a wide variety of disciplines outside computing, but also to offer something broad and stimulating to the computer scientist. Too often, in my opinion, computer science has a tendency to focus on developing vocational skills such as programming, to the detriment of wider considerations that make for a well-rounded scientist practising in the modern world. I hope that I may have contributed something towards putting the science back into computer science.

Paul Anderson
Nottingham

Acknowledgements

A work of this nature is a demanding task and there are a number of people whom I would like to heartily thank for their encouragement, support and assistance during the research and writing processes.

Two people in particular are deserving of my gratitude. Firstly, I would like to thank Randi Cohen, acquisitions editor at CRC Press, who had the initial idea for this book and who has provided invaluable advice along the journey. Secondly, I want to thank Gaynor Backhouse from Intelligent Content (undoubtedly the 'Neil Young of editing'), who has done a masterful job of massaging my rough drafts into a coherent and consistent text whilst exercising immeasurable patience.

Many thanks are also due to the book's two technical reviewers, Nitin Agarwal at the University of Arkansas, Little Rock, and Rich Gazan at the University of Hawaii at Manoa. Their feedback and corrections have been extremely valuable.

I am indebted to Dr Robin Evans of the Statistical Laboratory, Cambridge University, for his expert advice on some of the Web's statistical properties. I also owe a huge debt of thanks to my first readers, Dr Tim Anderson, Dr Andrew Ashworth, Alan Carter-Davies and Raza Rizvi. Their feedback on the readability and pitch of the material early on in the process proved particularly enlightening. I would also like to thank Iris Fahrer, project editor at Taylor & Francis. There are also several people and organisations who have assisted with figures and diagrams, especially Dr David Millard of Southampton University, Marcus Freeman and Dr Akshay Java of Microsoft.

About the Author

Paul Anderson is a writer and technology forecaster for Intelligent Content Ltd and until recently was technical editor for JISC TechWatch, a horizon scanning service for United Kingdom universities. A graduate in computer science from the University of Leeds, he has worked for more than 25 years in industry and academia as a software developer, technology transfer officer and technology futures specialist. He has also written extensively for a range of education, trade and current affairs publications and in 2007 was awarded the EPSRC's Computer Science Writer of the Year prize.

(Photograph By Richard Wain. Copyright: Intelligent Content, Ltd)

Introduction

The Web is already so much a part of our lives that familiarity has clouded our perception of the Web itself.

SIR TIM BERNERS-LEE
Inventor of the World Wide Web (1999, 2)

The Web is an artificial creation a technical infrastructure, a network of documents created bit by bit, link by link by millions of people. Being able to visualize this infrastructure is big business and companies such as Microsoft and Bell Labs have created enormous, coloured topological maps, not unlike the star charts that astronomers use to depict distant galaxies.[*] Plotting the distribution of the millions of hypertext links that constitute the network produces intense white circles that show where there is the most interest, where the concentration of information burns the brightest. Bright pinks, blues and greens mark the less active galaxies of the information universe. Long, coloured streaks link one concentration of information with another (Figure 0.1).

Somewhere on that map, most likely, will be you: a node, connected to millions of other nodes. It might be just a few fragments, a set of photographs you published on Flickr after a family celebration or a blog that you've been writing for a couple of years. It might be something more substantial, maybe a Facebook profile and your social networking history. Each of these acts has added to the structure of the Web. They are all tiny points of light in the information firmament.

The reason you are there is almost certainly something to do with Web 2.0, an umbrella term for a group of user-oriented Web-based services such as blogs, wikis and online social networks, which started to become popular in the mid-2000s. Although the Web had been around since the mid-1990s, it was Web 2.0 services that provided the easy-to-use tools that enabled millions of people to publish their own media and interact with each other in new ways. These services have now been taken up to such an extent (Facebook, for example has over 750 million users) that some people believe they are changing the way we as a society communicate and interact.

---

[*] *MIT Technology Review* magazine has an article outlining some of the visualization techniques used to show the information links and flows on the Web and in Web 2.0 services. This includes the work of Microsoft's Matthew Hurst (Naone 2008). The work of Bell Labs (now also being undertaken by its spin-off Lumeta Corporation) is described in Cheswick et al. (2000).

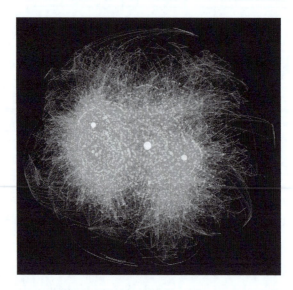

FIGURE 0.1   (See colour insert.) Internet blog map. Computer generated map showing relationships between Internet weblogs (blogs). (From Matthew Hurst/Science Photo Library. With permission.)

However, to fully understand what Web 2.0 is all about we need to go on a journey. This will take us from the beginning of the World Wide Web, a simple tool that Tim Berners-Lee invented to help him manage projects at CERN—the European physics laboratory—to its explosion in popularity towards the mid-1990s, made possible by the release of the Mosaic Web browser. Then we will explore the dot-com boom and subsequent crash, a time when confidence in the power of the Web to change society and to be a source of highly successful businesses was profoundly questioned. This prepared the ground for 'Web 2.0', introduced as a catchy term to describe a group of companies with ideas and business models for deploying a new breed of Web services. By commercializing the Web they promised to deliver a renewed period of growth to the computer industry.

From this vantage point we will look at the developments that have come to be associated with the term and, importantly for students, analyse what current research is telling us about them. We will then look at where this is likely to take us next—into a future of connected data and ubiquitous computing.

Many complain that Web 2.0 is all hype and no substance, and although the term is still widely used in computer science and related disciplines, many people outside of academia are starting to say that the Web 2.0 moniker is passé—that what we are talking about is social media: software applications that allow people to interact online in a social manner. Others focus on the Web as an evolving technical infrastructure, arguing that "Web 2.0 … is no longer something entirely new, but it is generally accepted as the current 'version' of the Web" (Vossen 2011, 67).

For me, neither of these descriptions is entirely accurate. Whilst I would agree that the technologies and standards that underpin Web 2.0 services are due to the ongoing evolution of the Web, overseen by the World Wide Web Consortium (W3C), I would question whether or not to go as far as to say that Web 2.0 can be reduced solely to a description of a stage in the Web's technical development. Similarly, to rename Web 2.0 as social media is to privilege the users' perspective of Web 2.0—as a set of services that facilitates online social interaction. Whilst neither of these descriptions is wrong per se, it might be fair to say that on their own they are not sufficient to encapsulate the full *implications* of Web 2.0.

What both of these interpretations tend to obscure is the point that Tim O'Reilly was making when he adopted the term: that is, following the dot-com boom and bust of the early 2000s, there are emerging, Web-based business models that are going to generate huge wealth for a new generation of technology companies. This should perhaps orientate our perspective: that the starting point for understanding Web 2.0 is, in the jargon, the search for ways to successfully monetize the crowd; that is, to develop successful business models that harness the huge numbers of people participating online through social media and the free-to-use Web 2.0 services, which in turn rely on the open standards and technologies of the World Wide Web.

This distinction, between the technologies and standards of the Web and the Web 2.0 services that depend on them, is at the heart of the iceberg model I have developed for thinking about Web 2.0 and understanding its implications. At its core are the six big ideas, key concepts that explain and critique the Web 2.0 discourse. What I have therefore tried to achieve is something that is grounded in an understanding of the technical nature of the Web but communicated in a way that can be understood by non-engineers. It is in this spirit, then, that the first chapter begins in Silicon Valley in the mid-1990s at the beginning of the dot-com boom, with the best opening day for a new stock in Wall Street's history that sent shock waves through the investment community.

## CHAPTER 1

What Is Web 2.0?

W EB 2.0 IS A SLIPPERY CHARACTER TO PIN DOWN. Is it a revolution in the way we use the Web or just another technology market 'bubble'? The short answer, for many people, is to refer to a group of services that have become deeply associated with the term: blogs, wikis, podcasts, Really Simple Syndication (RSS) feeds etc., which facilitate a more socially connected Web where everyone is able to add to and edit the information space. The longer answer is rather more complicated and pulls in economics, technology and new ideas about the connected society. To some, however, it is simply a time to invest in technology again—a time of renewed exuberance after the dot-com bust.

Indeed, it is market failure that is the backdrop for the emergence of Web 2.0. After the dot-com bust in the early 2000s, a general sense of inertia descended over Silicon Valley. Despite this, there was a small number of Internet services that had not simply survived, but appeared to be thriving. In 2004, a group of technology publishing executives from O'Reilly Media and MediaLive International met to develop ideas for a business conference that would capture this feeling that the Web was more important than ever. During the discussion the idea of a second, reborn Web was debated and the term *Web 2.0* was coined to describe it.

In this chapter we will look at how the idea of Web 2.0 came about and why it is so difficult to be precise about what it means. We will also look at the iceberg model, a way of thinking critically about Web 2.0, which is the basis of the structure of this book. To begin with, however, we will go right back to the beginning of the story, to technology markets and the dot-com boom and bust.

1.1 THE DOT-COM BOOM AND BUST

During the late 1990s there was an enormous boom in technology-related stocks and shares, most notably anything that was connected to the Internet—a technology that was just beginning to impinge on the general public's awareness. Many commentators trace this boom to 9th August 1995 when a Web browser company called *Netscape* floated its shares (i.e. made an initial public offering, or IPO) on the NASDAQ technology stock market. Netscape's core product was a repackaging of *Mosaic*, an early Web browser developed by a team at the University of Illinois Urbana–Champaign, which had two important features that differentiated it from other early browser products: it supported the display of graphics and it ran on the highly popular Microsoft *Windows* operating system. Before Mosaic, browsers had been purely text-based and ran on academic computing systems that used the Unix operating system. Netscape gave their browser away to the general public for free and this enabled millions of people to access the embryonic World Wide Web and to engage in activities that we would recognize today such as e-commerce, posting product reviews and discussion groups.

Thanks to Mosaic's ubiquity, it was felt there would be a lot of interest in the company's IPO and the stock was offered at a fairly high valuation of US$28. Nobody expected what happened next: within a few hours the price had more than doubled, valuing the fledgling company at US$2.2 billion—as much as some of the giant industrial companies that had been listed on the stock market for decades. It was the best opening day for a new stock in Wall Street's history and sent shock waves through the investment community (Cassidy 2002).

The IPO kick-started five years of financial frenzy in which hundreds of millions of dollars were invested in start-up Internet companies. It was, as many economic commentators have noted since, a classic economic bubble in which benign economic conditions, such as low interest rates, coincided with the development of a new technology and a widespread belief that the technology would change the way the world worked. This 'Internet bubble' took place across the world, but was most acute in the United States, where many of the technology companies had their headquarters and where the economy had already been growing rapidly in what would later become known as the Clinton economic boom. Cheered on by market analysts and the media, ordinary savers across the world invested money in any stock that had a whiff of the Internet about it.

It was, in the words of Alan Greenspan (1996), chairman of the US Federal Reserve (FED), a period of "irrational exuberance" and like all bubbles it had to burst. The NASDAQ peaked on 10th March 2000 and over the next few days it headed downhill, fast. It had grown nearly five times in the intervening half decade, but within a couple of years it had almost returned to its pre-Netscape level, leaving thousands of start-up companies bankrupt and much of Silicon Valley—the spiritual home of the computer industry—out of work.

1.2 THE EMERGENCE OF WEB 2.0

A general sense of inertia descended over the Valley during the first years of the new century and it was in this atmosphere that a group of technology publishing executives from O'Reilly Media and MediaLive International gathered in the spring of 2004. The purpose of the meeting was to develop ideas for a business conference that would help lift the gloom that hung over Silicon Valley's Internet and Web industry. The premise was that out of the wreckage of the dot-com bust a small number of Internet services had not simply survived, but appeared to be thriving. Those at the meeting felt that these companies had some essential features in common and demonstrated more than technical prowess: they were grappling with how to develop novel ways of working and new business models using Internet technologies. During the discussion the idea of a second, reborn Web was debated and history records that one of those present, Dale Dougherty, a vice president of O'Reilly (and co-founder of O'Reilly Media Inc.) coined the term *Web 2.0*.* Thus it is important to note that the term was not coined in an attempt to capture the essence of an identified group of technologies, but rather something far more amorphous.

Initially, the conference was planned as a one-off event[†] and was held between the 5th and 7th of October 2004 in San Francisco with the theme The Web as Platform. About a year later Tim O'Reilly laid out his thinking behind the concept of Web 2.0 in what might be considered to be its founding document: *What Is Web 2.0: Design Patterns and Business Models for the Next Generation of Software* (O'Reilly 2005b). This document, together with the now annual conference, kick-started a frenzy of activity. It seemed that O'Reilly and his colleagues had been right: what Silicon Valley and the rest of the Internet industry needed was something to refresh their confidence in the world-changing capability of the Web.

Over the next two years or so, thousands of Web company start-ups either formed or re-branded under the Web 2.0 moniker. The bust was over, indeed, and some even began to wonder whether they were witnessing the start of another bubble. There was a flood of conferences, workshops and exhibitions and the marketing teams of the computer industry went into overdrive. The mainstream media took up the story and saturated the general public with newspaper and magazine articles about Web 2.0 and the Social Web. New, and now iconic, services such as YouTube were founded and others, such as Facebook and Flickr that had begun as tiny start-up companies in the early 2000s, suddenly experienced exponential growth.

However, it is important to remember that Web 2.0 was not the cause of the up-turn in the computing industry. In fact, it was more of a reflection of what was happening 'on the ground'. Despite the gloom in Silicon Valley, millions of new users were becoming familiar with the Web and, having found their feet, were happily engaging in a range of new activities based around the production and sharing of online content. Widespread, grassroots participation bubbled up, enabled by the availability of cheap consumer electronics such as digital cameras and the mass adoption of broadband, and this meant that ordinary users played a much bigger role in the Web's development than they had before (Fu et al. 2008).

Web 2.0 can therefore also be thought of as a kind of social movement (Birdsall 2007; boyd 2006). As Maximilien and Ranabahu (2007, 480) have written: "The success of this movement is not only due to the various new social applications that it enables but also due to the grassroot community that govern its evolution".

1.3 CONTROVERSY AROUND THE WEB 2.0 MONIKER

Since its inception the very idea of Web 2.0 has suffered an existential crisis. In the months following the first conference there was much discussion amongst technology developers as to the appropriateness of the moniker (or as it is often called, *meme*[‡]) and, indeed, there

---

* In fact, the phrase had been used prior to 2004 and there is a documented example in an article for *Print* magazine by writer and interface designer Darcy DiNucci in which the term is used in the context of how the Web might become available through everyday objects like TVs and microwaves (DiNucci 1999).

[†] http://www.web2con.com/web2con/

[‡] The term 'meme' was coined by Richard Dawkins in his 1976 book, *The Selfish Gene*, to refer to a cultural idea that is transmitted between humans.

are echoes of these debates to this day. At the nub of this is the use of '2.0', which has specific connotations in software development, implying that this is a second 'version' of the Web, which is in some manner superior to what went before.*

SOFTWARE VERSIONING

When developing software, programmers usually add a version number to the name of a software product. Each time an update is made to the code, either to provide new features or to fix bugs, a new number is assigned. This is usually done in an ordered fashion, so that version 2.0 follows version 1.0 and so forth. Many software companies also like to distinguish between a major release that changes many features of the software and a minor one that simply fixes a few small problems. They indicate a minor release by incrementing the digit after the decimal point, so that 2.1 is a minor update on version 2.0. It is because of this that the choice of 'Web 2.0' at the initial 2004 meeting signalled to the world of software development (possibly unintentionally) that they thought a major new version of the Web had in some sense been 'released'.

In a well-read blog post, Tim Bray, inventor of Extensible Markup Language (XML), explained how he disliked the "'Web 2.0' *faux*-meme" arguing that it could not be right since he felt the Web—in terms of what the user was capable of experiencing—was at least at version 3.0 (Bray 2005, blog). He also argued that Usenet (a 1980s Internet discussion forum) should perhaps be called version 1.0, reflecting a view that if version numbers were to be used at all, they should start with pre-Web applications and services. Others, such as developer Sam Ruby, also got involved: should it be 3.0? (Ruby 2005) Or perhaps we are only at 2.0 since computer scientists index things from zero.

For Sir Tim Berners-Lee (Figure 1.1), the inventor of the Web, the debate was moot. While there are a number of Web-based applications that demonstrate the ideas behind Web 2.0, these are not really technologies as such, but services (or user processes) built using the building blocks of the technologies and open standards that underpin the Internet and the Web. As we shall see later on, Berners-Lee is quite clear that Web 2.0 uses so-called Web 1.0 standards and technologies. From this perspective, changes to the Web as a technical infrastructure are the product of evolution rather than revolution. Web 2.0 applications and services should not be held up in opposition to 'Web 1.0', but instead should be seen as a consequence of a more fully implemented Web.

Needless to say Tim O'Reilly (Figure 1.2) robustly defended his company's brainchild, arguing that it was not productive to get involved in detailed debates about version numbering but, rather, it was more meaningful to concentrate on the bigger picture since the meme "capture[s] the widespread sense that there's something qualitatively different about today's web" (O'Reilly 2005a, blog). As long as the name points in the right direction, he argued, then it has served its purpose.

---

* To get a flavour of what O'Reilly meant by the differences between Web 1.0 and Web 2.0, see his original paper (O'Reilly 2005b).

FIGURE 1.1 (See colour insert.) Sir Tim Berners-Lee (From Flickr, photo by Silvio Tanaka, Creative Commons Attribution 2.0 Generic (CC BY 2.0) See: http://www.flickr.com/photos/tanaka/3212373419/)

O'Reilly's comment about direction is interesting. Most technically literate people are sufficiently aware of what Web 2.0 means, that when presented with some new service, they can say 'ah, a Web 2.0 service'. However, they might struggle to articulate precisely why this should be so, and a number of academics and technology writers have questioned whether the term really means anything at all (Birdsall 2007; Dalsgaard and Sorensen 2008; Sankar et al. 2008; White 2007; Allen 2008).

FIGURE 1.2 (See colour insert.) Tim O'Reilly (From Flickr, photo by Robert Scoble, Creative Commons Attribution 2.0 Generic (CC BY 2.0). See: http://www.flickr.com/photos/scobleizer/2228299097/sizes/l/in/photostream/)

Trebor Scholz (2008) describes Web 2.0 as a Foucault-ian épistémè, that is, something grounded in, and conditioned by, the time it was developed as a concept. On a more practical note, Google staffer Joe Gregorio compares Web 2.0 to a psychiatrist's Rorschach inkblot test into which anyone can "pour their own thoughts and ideas" (2005, blog). Cisco staff who are experienced in designing Web 2.0 systems are blunt: "[I]t is almost impossible to define Web 2.0 without hand waving and a lot of animation" (Sankar et al. 2008, 3). Bebo White (2007) argues that the term "borders on hype" (p. 3) and that this is often the case with new terms associated with the leading edge of technology.

Felicia Song (2010) believes that the term is "murky" and "theoretically anaemic" (p. 250) and has been overused to the point where it is applied to virtually any new application or digital start-up business, and that this results in "conceptual vagueness at best and absolute meaninglessness at worst" (p. 249). She argues that many of the key ideas associated with Web 2.0, for example increased user participation and social interactivity, have always been a feature of the Web, and notes the difficulty of identifying a transition moment when the Web moved from version 1.0 to 2.0. Cormode and Krishnamurthy (2008) agree, writing: "A precise definition is elusive and many sites are hard to categorise with the binary label 'Web 1.0' or 'Web 2.0'" (p. 1). Others argue that we have to accept that the term is intended to hold a number of different concepts. As Allen (2008, webpage) writes: "Web 2.0 is a shorthand term for many different things … In short Web 2.0 is about ideas, behaviours, technologies and ideals all at the same time".

1.4 O'REILLY'S WEB 2.0

What can we conclude? O'Reilly's 2005 paper is largely conceptual and sometimes quite confused.* First-time readers will probably struggle to understand the subtle differences between patterns and principles, and, indeed, in some places principles are repeated as patterns. However, this is not necessarily unintentional. Rather than having a "hard boundary", O'Reilly argues that Web 2.0 has a "gravitational core" around which revolves a solar system of sites and services that to varying degrees demonstrate various principles, lessons and competencies. This rather fluid approach to describing Web 2.0 means that it can be subject to change as ideas mature. What is important for the student, however, is to realize that although much work has been done since to refine what is meant by the term Web 2.0, its roots as a rather vague collection of thoughts, examples and business jargon has undoubtedly affected its ensuing history.

In order to develop a clearer understanding of what O'Reilly was describing we will begin by examining the seven 'principles' outlined in his original paper (O'Reilly 2005b). I have organised these so that the ideas flow into and build on one another. From here I will outline my own thoughts, in response to O'Reilly's principles, ending with an overview of the iceberg model, which forms the conceptual framework for this book.

---

* In 2009, Tim O'Reilly issued an update to the 2005 paper in conjunction with John Battelle (O'Reilly and Battelle 2009).

1.4.1 The Web as Platform

Fundamental to Web 2.0 is the idea that these companies were all working, at some level, with a new technology paradigm: the *Web as Platform*.

Essentially, a *platform technology* is a coherent infrastructure upon which other technologies can operate.* The most widely known example is a computer's operating system, which provides an infrastructure for software programs to run on. Prior to 2005 the PC was considered to be the most important platform technology, consisting of hardware, which was fairly tightly specified (originally by IBM), and Microsoft's *Windows* operating system. This combination was so stable that many other companies could develop software—following the platform's specifications—and be confident not only that their code would run successfully but also that it would have a worldwide market of millions of potential users.

Releasing software for the platform involved selling and physically distributing code, usually on a CD-ROM disc. The user would load the CD-ROM into their PC and copy the code across to the operating system, which in turn would run the code. This kind of distribution, which still exists today but is increasingly anachronistic, is known colloquially as 'shrink-wrapped' since the CD-ROM is usually supplied wrapped in plastic film, with a licence note attached to it.

With the Web as Platform however, the vision was that the browser would no longer simply be a window into a world of hypertext information, but a place where users could carry out tasks and run applications. Although the technology at the time dictated that the browser itself would need to run on some kind of desktop PC, what was important was the potential of the browser, since it was understood that, in the near future, browser technology would be available on all sorts of devices (e.g. smartphones). Developing online 'services' that worked through the browser would therefore allow for a kind of universality and remove many of the limitations of PC software (such as the need to upgrade software by CD-ROM).

1.4.2 End of the Software Release Cycle

The move to a services model meant a number of changes to the way that software companies worked. The most important was that the staged process of releasing software updates with a new version number was ending as, when software is accessed as a service it can be updated whenever the developer likes: there is no need to physically distribute a new version. In this way the traditional idea of a regular cycle of software release has been replaced by the idea that software is permanently in a state of 'beta' testing (the testing stage before software is formally released) popularly known as *perpetual beta*. As O'Reilly noted, many of the successful online services had been in beta for years and remained effectively unfinished.

---

* For more on this, see Evans et al. (2006).

The advantage of this way of working is that the software development process can benefit from user feedback at an earlier stage. That is, a company will set up an online service and make it available to users as soon as is practicable. The users then interact with the new system and the developers obtain feedback, either indirectly by monitoring the site or directly by asking for it. The service can then be tweaked and new changes introduced on a daily or even hourly basis. Proponents argue that this way of working enables these companies to develop online services that are highly responsive to their users. Indeed, one way of looking at this style of development is to see the user as a co-developer, helping the service to continually improve. As O'Reilly writes: "It's no accident that services such as Gmail, Google Maps, Flickr, del.icio.us, and the like may be expected to bear a 'beta' logo for years at a time" (O'Reilly 2005b, 12).

1.4.3 Lightweight Programming Models

In order to be able to develop software in this way, O'Reilly pointed out that many of the successful Web services companies were making use of 'lightweight' and 'open' software development techniques. We will have more to say on this when we discuss openness in Chapter 6 and technology and standards in Section III of this book, but essentially this involves working in ways that allow other developers to re-use and build upon a service. Such an approach values simplicity of design over complex infrastructure and emphasizes building systems that encourage others to hack and re-mix the data being provided. The significance of this was, according to O'Reilly, that this style of working allowed users to take the services in new directions, unimagined by their creators.

1.4.4 Software above the Level of a Single Device

Another advantage of designing systems that use the Web browser as a platform is that the browser can act as a kind of universal client, allowing the service to be run anywhere that supports a browser. Since, in 2005, online services were being delivered over the Web via the browser they could be accessed from a wide variety of platforms including desktop PCs, smartphones and gaming consoles. Drawing on the ideas of long-time Microsoft developer Dave Stutz (now retired), O'Reilly urged designers to develop systems that rose above the level of a single device, i.e. that were not designed solely for desktop PCs. He cited Apple's iTunes as a primary example of a company embracing this concept by seamlessly integrating the handheld iPod, the desktop computer and Apple's back-end servers (which provide the online service).

1.4.5 Rich User Experiences

One of the most obvious characteristics of what many people label as Web 2.0 is the provision of slick, easy-to-use and responsive user interfaces. As the ideas behind the Web as Platform have developed, online services increasingly resemble the sophisticated functionality of traditional PC-based applications. O'Reilly highlighted this development citing Web-based services, such as Google's Gmail, that resembled and competed with pre-existing PC applications. Although this had been going on for some time (for example, e-commerce systems had been around for many years and even some of the earliest Web browsers allowed for applets—small chunks of computer code that undertook user tasks), O'Reilly predicted that the pace of change in this area would rapidly accelerate and that there would be: "an unprecedented period of user interface innovation" (O'Reilly 2005b, 16). Again, there have been a number of technological developments that have allowed this to happen and these will be covered in detail in Section III.

1.4.6 Harnessing Collective Intelligence

In the original paper, O'Reilly argues that one of the key principles demonstrated by companies that had made the transition from Web 1.0 to Web 2.0 successfully was that they "embraced the power of the web to harness collective intelligence" (O'Reilly 2005b, 6). The Web, through the interactions of millions of users, was in effect being turned into a form of "global brain" in which services like blogs and Wikipedia would make good use of the so-called wisdom of crowds.

O'Reilly did not define precisely what he meant by collective intelligence, preferring to rely on a series of examples to demonstrate the concept. Many of the services that we discuss in detail in this book are presented by O'Reilly as examples of using collective intelligence, including blogs, Wikipedia and the social bookmarking site del.icio.us (now Delicious.com). However, to truly understand what O'Reilly was alluding to we must first acknowledge the problems inherent in bandying about terms like 'intelligence', 'brain' and 'wisdom'. We also need to understand the roots of the idea of collective intelligence. This is a complex discussion and we will return to it in much greater detail in Chapter 5 of this book.

1.4.7 Data Is the Next 'Intel Inside'

O'Reilly also talked about data being the next 'Intel Inside'. This comment is now becoming dated as it refers to an advertising campaign run by microprocessor company Intel between 1991 and the mid 2000s[*] so I will attempt to put it into context.

By the end of the 1980s, as microprocessor supplier to IBM and its competitors, Intel was well placed to take advantage of the burgeoning market in personal computers. However, it wasn't the only microprocessor supplier in the market and it was also aware that everyday users of a PC might imagine that all the components were made by the PC company. In order to secure its position, Intel wanted to differentiate itself from the competition. The problem was how to raise the company's profile and create brand loyalty for a product that was essentially just a component of a larger product and which most people would never see. So Intel ran the 'Intel Inside' marketing campaign as a badge of quality. The implication was that if a PC had an Intel processor inside, it would be a cut above other computers. In order to get their message out, Intel paid half the cost of other companies' advertise-

---

[*] http://www.logoblog.org/intel-logo.php

ments if they used the Intel logo (Elliott 2007). This resulted in the new logo becoming widely recognized and led to the introduction of the famous 'four note jingle'.

Tim O'Reilly noted that, increasingly, it was a Web service's underlying database that provided critical functionality in a way that was similar to a PC's core microprocessor (under a PC as Platform model). He wrote: "Data is indeed the Intel Inside of these applications, a sole source component in systems whose software infrastructure is largely open source or otherwise commodified" (O'Reilly 2005b, 10). He gave the example of one company that had even adapted the slogan to their own use. Navteq, a company that had spent US$750 million building a detailed database of American city streets, used the slogan "NavTeq Onboard", on their car navigation systems.

1.5 SO, WHAT IS WEB 2.0?

What can we conclude from our discussion of Web 2.0 and its myriad definitions? It emerged from a discussion about how to describe, using business models and technology developments, observable and successful grassroots activity within the computer industry following the dot-com bust. These 'green shoots' were hailed as the beginning of a revolution not just in technological terms, but also in human terms, as more and more people became producers as well as consumers of content.

However, before we get too excited by this, we need to remember that the Web itself is an evolving technical infrastructure—a collection of documents connected by a skein of hypertext links. The Web has grown because we continue to add more and more content to it, and Web 2.0 services depend on this infrastructure.

In the rest of this section we will examine some of the details of these two perspectives and introduce what I call the remorseless logic of the link. This is my attempt to encapsulate the power of the fundamental unit of the Web—the hypertext link. From here I will explain how these discussions feed into the iceberg model of Web 2.0 that will form the supporting structure for the rest of this book.

1.5.1 Evolution versus Revolution

One could argue that attitudes to Web 2.0 form a kind of a spectrum. At one end is Tim O'Reilly, promoting his company's idea of a new, invigorated Web, dusting itself down after the dot-com bust. At the other is Tim Berners-Lee, implementing his vision of a shared information space.

The problem with this line of thinking is that it assumes that both sides are talking about the same thing. In fact, it is important to emphasize that much of what O'Reilly outlined was based on discussions about a revolution in business strategy, marketing and brand positioning. There is much talk in the paper of 'market dominance', 'competitive advantage' and 'business models'. However, for many people the short answer to the question 'What is Web 2.0?' is to refer to a group of services that have become deeply associated with the term: blogs, wikis, podcasts etc., that facilitate a more socially connected Web where everyone is able to add to and edit the information space.

What both of these perspectives highlight is a focus on the services, but these are just the visible tip of the iceberg. Berners-Lee's first priority is with the Web as an evolving technical infrastructure: the technologies, standards and protocols on top of which the services sit. This ongoing development is more of a perpetual beta than 'Web 2.0' and is invisible to most of us.

1.5.2 The Remorseless Logic of the Link

There is one final aspect of the Web that needs to be taken into account when trying to understand Web 2.0. Whereas the six big ideas of the iceberg model could be envisioned as vertical concepts, drawing out the relationship between the services and the technologies of the Web, the logic of the link is a horizontal force that cuts across the big ideas.

The logic of the link is rooted in the idea of the Web as a technical infrastructure (remember that the Web consists of millions of HTML documents connected by hyperlinks) and I call it remorseless because of the relentless way it continues to reach out to more and more content: from text through photos, video and sound files, and now to people. This last is of particular significance. Although barely mentioned in O'Reilly's 2005 document, connecting people is now considered to be one of the most important characteristics of Web 2.0. For this reason, in the mind of the general public and in much media commentary, the terms *social Web, social media* or *social software** have become interchangeable with 'Web 2.0' (Constantinides and Fountain 2008; Rowe and Ciravegna 2010).

The remorseless logic of the link is a theme that will emerge time and again throughout this book. As Web 2.0 has evolved over the last half-decade the link has incorporated more, and different, types of content, which in turn has led to an explosion in data collection and reuse in applications and services. This will come to the fore when we finally consider what might be beyond Web 2.0.

1.6 THE ICEBERG MODEL

I have used the iceberg metaphor, introduced earlier, as the basis for my model of Web 2.0 (see Figure 1.3). This helps to untangle the issues and present the technologies and standards of the Web as the evolving bedrock for an ecosystem of services. Joining the two together are the six big ideas, based loosely on O'Reilly's seven principles, which provide a structure for thinking critically about the relationship between the two.

---

* The idea of social software is not particularly new and can be traced back to at least the 1970s (Hochheiser and Shneiderman 2010).

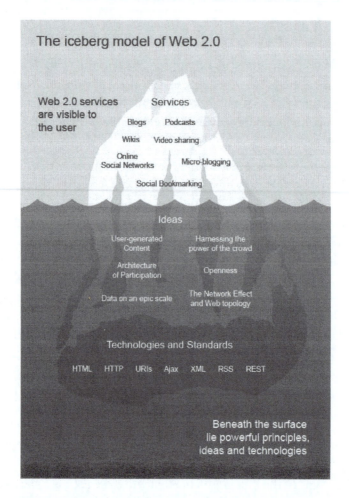

FIGURE 1.3   (See colour insert.) The iceberg model of Web 2.0. (Illustration © 2011 by Intelligent Content Ltd Licensed under a Creative Commons Attribution-NonCommercial-NoDerivs 3.0 Unported license (CC BY-NR-ND 3.0))

The iceberg model provides the structure for the rest of the book, which is divided into three sections to reflect the layers in the model. We will begin by considering the ideas and principles that form the middle layer before reviewing the different services that form the component the user sees. Finally, in Section III, we will discuss the technologies and standards that underpin the Web's evolution, and look to the future, beyond Web 2.0.

I

The Six Big Ideas

By the end of 2006, Web 2.0 had gone from being a conference buzzword to front-page news on *Time* magazine. It had only taken two years to capture the public's imagination—a testament to the power of the central idea it encapsulated, that of a new, improved, 'second version', of the Web that promised to deliver a new period of growth to the computer industry. However, this has been controversial, and Section I explains the source of some of this controversy and provides a critical framework for thinking about it.

In the following six chapters I articulate six big ideas, based on concepts originally outlined by Tim O'Reilly, both to explain and problematize the ideas behind Web 2.0. The key to understanding the role of the big ideas is to separate the Web as a technical infrastructure—a global information space—from the services and applications that most people are familiar with. I have used different techniques to help with this process—historical context, for example, is used to explain the mis-match between established technology principles and the way they have been interpreted in the context of Web 2.0. For this reason, each chapter should be read in sequence the effect is cumulative, and without it, the inter-relatedness of the ideas will be compromised.

## CHAPTER 2

User-Generated Content

AT THE END OF 2006, TIME MAGAZINE'S PERSON of the Year was 'You'. On the cover of the venerable US news magazine, underneath the title of the award, was a picture of a computer with a mirror in place of where the screen would normally be, in order to reflect the face of the reader. Since the 1920s kings, presidents and popes had graced the cover, each selected for their unique contribution to statesmanship or world history during the preceding year. In 2006 however, the editors decided that the person who had contributed most was 'everybody', the ordinary people who were flocking in the millions to emerging, Web 2.0 services and making mass contributions to the Web. This was the year, it was felt, in which the Web was "bringing together the small contributions of millions of people and making them matter" (Grossman 2006, webpage).

The *Time* article reflected the widespread belief that something fundamental had happened to the Web in the mid-2000s. Whereas in the past users were considered to be rather passive, surfing the Web by following hypertext links and either reading or downloading content written by others (the *read-only Web*, also known as *Web 1.0*), in the 'new' Web that was emerging the user was an active participant. In an important conceptual change, not only were users becoming producers of content rather than simply consumers (Allen 2008; Bruns 2008), but there was also a step-change in the range of what users could do: share media (photos, videos etc.) post reviews of products and services (e.g. book reviews on Amazon or seller reviews on eBay), enter into a dialogue with others (e.g. blogging and online social networking), and tagging (either for personal use or to share with others) (Dalsgaard and Sorensen 2008). This level of involvement gave rise to another term that is often associated with Web 2.0: the participatory or *read-write Web*.

How had this come about? In part it was a result of ongoing technical developments. Previously, a knowledge of Hypertext Markup Language (HTML) and other technical skills were required in order to create and publish Web-based content and it was thus left mainly to specialist webmasters, Web design companies and major content providers, with their comprehensive content management and publication tools (Ding et al. 2009). To some, Web 2.0 marks the widespread adoption of lightweight, easy-to-use Web publishing tools such as blogs and wikis, which have freed the production of content from the Web's underlying technology. This resulted in an explosion of self-published material and allowed users to interact in new ways, contributing all sorts of content to the Web's structure. The collective name for all these contributions is *user-generated content* (UGC).

2.1 WHY PEOPLE DO IT

The Organisation for Economic Co-operation and Development (OECD)* has reported a number of reasons why UGC has emerged as such a major focus of activity on the Web, and the report clusters them into four categories (OECD 2007):

Technological: increased broadband availability and home computer processing capabilities (and later, smartphone technology); low-cost and high-quality video and photographic equipment widely available; improvements in software and Internet infrastructure.

Social: rise of a younger, digitally aware generation; popular interest in the Internet from all age groups driven by curiosity; ongoing improvements in ease-of-use and increasing media interest in the Web.

Economic: lower costs and decreased barriers to entry for the creation of UGC; improvements in techniques to host and distribute Web-based advertising and therefore provide a business model for investment in Web 2.0 services.

Legal and Institutional: development of new forms of copyright and other licences (e.g. Creative Commons) and influence of the open source software movement (see Chapter 6).

In particular, the OECD notes the importance of the rise in broadband Internet access and its wide availability in many countries at reasonable cost, saying: "the global transition to broadband drastically altered the environment in which users could create, post and download content" (OECD 2007, 13).

However, these broad-brush categories do not capture the individual, personal decisions made by users as to whether they produce UGC or not. The OECD (2007) noted a number of *motivational factors* including connecting with peers, achieving a certain amount of online fame or notoriety and the creative desire simply to express oneself. This concurs with what several research projects have found, with Kim (2010) stating that for many users, especially the young, self-expression and the desire for online fame are both aspects associated with UGC. Lee (2008) found that often, UGC has become increasingly entwined

---

* Organisation for Economic Co-operation and Development (OECD) is one of the world's largest sources of economic and social data. Part of its remit is to collect and aggregate economic and social statistics from different countries so they can be used in comparative studies. In 2006 the OECD was involved in organising *The Future Digital Economy: Digital Content Creation, Distribution and Access* conference that took place in Rome and which led to the commissioning of the UGC report. It was felt that Web 2.0 and UGC in particular would have considerable economic impact, especially on national media industries, and therefore warranted further study.

with online social network sites and thus there are strong social reasons why users engage with this type of content.

Other findings include those of Shao (2009), who has argued that we can understand why people create UGC by looking at it through the lens of uses and gratifications theory. This presents media use in terms of the gratification of the psychological needs of the individual. He outlines three aspects of UGC: consumption (simply viewing or downloading others' work), participation (either through ranking or rating others' work, posting comments, or interacting with other users to discuss it) and finally, production. He concluded that people undertake these different activities for different psycho-social reasons: they consume the content for information and entertainment, participate for social interaction and community development, and produce their own content for self-expression and self-actualization (seeking peer recognition or fame).

2.2 SCALE OF ACTIVITY

There is no doubt that the Web 2.0 services that provide opportunities to produce UGC are popular and increasing in popularity. In August 2011, a glance at the top 20 sites provided by Internet traffic analysts Alexa, showed Facebook, YouTube, Wikipedia and various blogging systems leading the field.* This is not the same however, as knowing how many users produce content. Complicating factors include the spread of identical content across more than one site or service, the fact that not all registered UGC service users are active contributors, and difficulties defining UGC precisely.

One of the few sources, at least for the United States, is the Pew Internet & American Life project, which undertakes annual surveys into users' online habits. In late 2009 it presented figures to the effect that 30% of Internet users in the United States regularly share online something they have created themselves (such as a video), 26% post comments on blogs or other sites, 15% take online content and remix it and 11% work on their own blog or homepage (Smith 2009). They also report that on a typical day in America, 15% of Internet users post something online for others to see.

Although there does seem to be evidence of generational differences, with Pew reporting in 2006 that 35% of adults and 57% of teenagers aged between 12 and 17 created online content (Lenhart 2006), these differences may be declining as time passes (in 2009 there was evidence of increased activity by older adults) (Lenhart et al. 2010a). There may also be movement between the types of content that people are creating over time with blogging falling out of favour amongst the young as they have moved over to online social networking.

Apart from this, there has been little research that takes an overall view of UGC. However, this is not to say that there has been no research into the use of individual types of service, and we will cover this in Section II.

---

* http://www.alexa.com/topsites

2.3 THE PROBLEM WITH USER-GENERATED CONTENT

Unfortunately, there is no generally accepted definition of UGC. The OECD (2007) has produced a widely quoted definition, based on three characteristics, which I shall use to demonstrate the inherent difficulties:*

- Content that is made publically available over the Internet

- Content that reflects a certain amount of creative effort

- Content that is, in general, created outside professional practices and routines

The first characteristic is what the report calls a publication requirement: there must have been a process of making the material available to others via a website, blog, online social network etc. The OECD specifically rules out e-mail and Short Message Service (SMS) text as a form of UGC since these are forms of communication between individuals rather than public acts. However, they do classify social network site content, which is perhaps only visible to a small group of friends, as 'publication' under this definition. This is a subject of debate and Stöckl, Rohrmeier and Hess (2008) for example, point out that a social network like MySpace can be considered to be purely a communication tool, or a UGC platform, or indeed can be considered to be both.

The second characteristic is even more difficult. There is a requirement for a process whereby users "add their own value" (OECD 2007, 8) and under this definition, merely copying a TV show clip and placing it on YouTube does not count as UGC, whereas uploading one's own home video of a family gathering does. So far, this requirement for creative effort conforms to what we normally consider when we think of 'content'. However, it does not help us when we consider what is normally considered UGC. Under this definition, can we include activity such as ranking a seller on eBay, whereby the buyer has only to click the number of stars they wish to award the seller? It is easy to see why this would fail the requirement for some kind of creative effort, and yet this kind of activity is clearly considered UGC. While it may have been relevant in the early days of Web 2.0, the requirement for creative effort is clearly a difficult, even redundant distinction in the general understanding of UGC, and poses a problem for anyone trying to undertake research into UGC.

The third characteristic is in some ways easier to define but more difficult to apply in a real-world context. Although the practices and routines of professionalism are not defined in detail, the OECD argues it is important to distinguish UGC from content produced by commercial organisations. This includes the idea of the 'publishing value chain': the series of steps and the people involved when a traditional item of content such as a book is created, edited, printed and distributed. Each step in the chain involves some kind of hurdle, usually to ensure product quality and commercial value. In contrast, UGC involves little or no gatekeeping and the barriers to entry have been significantly lowered. In this sense it is outside the normal practices of professional content production. This aspect of UGC also

---

* Note that this discussion is not meant to provide a comprehensive review of the subject but rather coverage of a particular sub-set of issues connected with the difficulties inherent in the OECD's definition.

includes the idea of a professional as someone who makes a living and therefore needs to charge for content in some manner. The OECD points out that the vast majority of UGC is produced by non-professionals without the expectation of profit or remuneration and it is in this way that UGC is decoupled from the idea of professionalism.

However, many professional content producers also produce content for Web 2.0 services in their spare time, for example, their family videos. Can this content be said to have been produced outside professional practices and routines? A professional journalist may have a personal blog, which might well be considered UGC in the OECD definition, and yet it will be produced to the same level of journalistic skill and professional training that the author employs in their paid-for work. The lines are blurred even further when you look at how some Web 2.0 platforms, built for UGC, are used to publish professionally produced work. Kruitbosch and Nack (2008) note how YouTube, for example, attracts large amounts of professionally produced content as well as the do-it-yourself, or 'DIY' material and they found that 30% of randomly selected videos were professionally generated, which translated to 80% of the most popular videos.

This distinction is further complicated by the technology used to create UGC. Apart from the development of freely available Web publishing tools such as blogging software and wiki systems, a significant driving force behind UGC has been the availability of low-cost, fairly high-quality consumer digital media technology such as hand-held, high-definition video cameras: this sometimes makes it difficult to ascertain whether the content was produced using professional practices or not (Hagemann and Vossen 2009). Indeed, Kim (2010) argues that, at least in the case of YouTube, UGC is starting to influence professional practice.

Blurring the lines between the professional and the amateur has led to the rise of what might be called professional-amateurs or *pro-ams*, a new breed of amateur content producers who work to professional standards (Leadbeater and Miller 2004). Tapscott and Williams (2007) describe this overlap between amateur and professional in economic terms—as a merging of producer and consumer—that results in a grey area called the *prosumer* (although the term itself was coined by futurist Alvin Toffler back in 1980).

For some, the solution is not to rely too much on the distinction between professional and amateur. Fraser and Dutta (2009) point out that the demarcation between the amateur and the professional is a fairly recent development that only became clearly articulated in the twentieth century, and that anyway: "cultural production is the one sphere where the traditional distinction between amateur and professional is the hardest to defend" (p. 216).

Kim (2010) supports these views and argues that we should consider UGC to be an evolutionary rather than revolutionary phenomenon, in the sense both that the Web technology that supports it has evolved, but also that the general idea of the practice of amateurs getting involved in the development of content and media actually has a long history. He notes, for example, the popularity of pamphleteering in the late eighteenth century[*] and the development of DIY fanzines and grass roots media during the 1960s and 1970s

---

[*] Pamphlets were printed, unbound books or leaflets, usually of a polemic or political nature, which were distributed by hand. They were popular in 18th-century America and Western Europe following the widespread introduction of low-cost printing presses.

counter-culture movement. One might add to this the rise of DIY music in the late 1970s through the punk rock movement.

2.3.1 The Roots of UGC

For Sir Tim Berners-Lee, the Web's inventor, UGC is what the Web was always intended to be. If we look at the history of the development of the Web we can see that his original vision was very much of a collaborative workspace where everything was potentially linked to everything in a "single, global information space" (Berners-Lee 1999, 5) and, crucially for this discussion, the assumption was that "everyone would be able to edit in this space" (Laningham 2006, 12:20).

The first development, Enquire, was a rudimentary project management tool, developed while Berners-Lee was working at CERN*, which allowed pages of notes to be linked together and edited. A series of further technological and software developments led to the creation of the World Wide Web and a browser or Web client that could view *and edit* pages of marked-up information (see Chapter 14, Figure 14.2). However, during a series of ports to other machines from the original development computer, the ability to edit through the Web client was not included in order to speed up the process of adoption within CERN (Berners-Lee 1999). This attitude to the 'edit' function continued through subsequent Web browser developments such as ViolaWWW and Mosaic. Crucially, this left people thinking of the Web as a medium in which a relatively small number of people published and most browsed, but it is probably more accurate to picture it as a fork in the road of the technology's development, one which has meant that the original pathway has only recently been rejoined. Tim O'Reilly later agreed, and in a 2006 update on the meaning of Web 2.0 he writes: "Tim Berners-Lee's original Web 1.0 is one of the most 'Web 2.0' systems out there—it completely harnesses the power of user contribution, collective intelligence, and network effects" (O'Reilly 2006a, webpage).

This is important because when we think about what the Web is (all those HTML documents linked together) we can see that all 'content' forms a constituent part of what the Web is. The Web as a technical infrastructure is not interested in who produced the content or how much creative effort they put in, rather it is concerned with how much there is and whether or not it is being linked to. If it had not been for the fork in the development of browser technology there would have been no concept of UGC—everything would have been 'UGC' from the outset. As Lee (2008, 1500) notes wryly: "To some people, 'user-generated content' may seem just a fancy, if not confusing, term to describe *authors* who are creating works like others have before" (my italics).

2.3.2 User-Generated or Content?

This discussion provides insight into why it is so hard to define UGC. I am going to propose that part of the problem is that most definitions attempt to give equal weight to

---

* The European Organisation for Nuclear Research based near Geneva.

both parts of the phrase, 'user-generated' and 'content'. If we put aside the significance of 'user-generated' for the moment, then this frees us up to think about the nature of content.

Shirky (2008) has argued that a significant proportion of UGC is not content in the usual sense, intended for a general audience, but is niche material, "just the ordinary stuff of life—gossip, little updates, thinking out loud" (p. 86). People have always undertaken this kind of behaviour, the difference now is that it takes place in the same public online medium as professional activity. Much of what gets posted online is "in public but not for the public" (p. 90). Shirky goes on to argue that this boils down to a change in the nature of our patterns of communication. In the past it was very clear what was broadcast media (TV, newspapers etc.) and what was communications media (telephone calls, telegrams etc.). The former was one-to-many communication and the latter was one-to-one. With the Internet came e-mail and instant messaging (IM), which allowed many-to-many (group) communication. His point is that these divisions are being broken down by Web 2.0 services and we have yet to understand or get used to the consequences.

By deconstructing what we mean by 'content' in this way, Shirky provides us with a way of thinking about Web content that is *scalable*, i.e. it can withstand change, in terms of new Web 2.0 services that may emerge and the new types of content that will inevitably emerge with them. However, there is a distinction to be made: between 'explicit' content, where the user knowingly contributes to a Web 2.0 service, and 'user data', which are collected implicitly in the course of the user making use of the service—something we will discuss further in the next chapter.

2.4 THE VALUE OF UGC AS A TERM

Does this mean that UGC has no value in our discussion of Web 2.0? While the term itself has caused problems, what it brings together is a set of developments that have undoubtedly had a significant impact on our understanding of Web 2.0. This includes the wide availability of broadband and, more recently, smartphones, along with a combination of lightweight, easy-to-use Web publishing tools and low-cost, digital technology, which has triggered a huge increase in the amount and diversity of content being produced. This is probably the key point to make about the user-generated side of UGC: not who creates the content (their professional status or how much creativity is involved) but that there are so many of them. It is highly unlikely that any commercial company would have produced Wikipedia, because the cost of paying so many content producers would have been beyond any possible model of return on investment. Likewise, no company could have created, and be constantly modifying, the personal profiles of hundreds of millions of people (as happens on online social network sites such as MySpace or Facebook).

If we accept Shirky's (2008) concept of 'scalable content', then one way of thinking about the value of UGC as an idea is as a shorthand term for the huge increase in the scale and variety of contributions to the Web we are currently seeing. However, we have to be careful not to adopt the all-encompassing nature of scalable content uncritically. In fact, to understand how Web 2.0 works we need to distinguish between explicit and implicit contributions, linked together in ways that were not necessarily intended or imagined when their creators contributed them. In the next two chapters we will see why these distinctions are important and look at the implications for how we think about Web 2.0.

EXERCISES AND POINTS TO PONDER

1. Think about what you have read in this chapter concerning the Web as a technical infrastructure and the excitement generated about UGC. Is such excitement justified? Is UGC an aspect of the 'revolutionary' nature of Web 2.0 or a product of the Web's evolution?

2. Broadly speaking, what are the problems inherent in the OECD's definition of UGC? Can you list them as a series of bullet points?

3. Based on what you have read so far, what do you imagine will be the benefit to your studies of thinking about content as explicit and implicit?

FURTHER READING

For more on the scale of user activity in UGC, see Pew Internet reports on how different generations use the Internet: http://pewinternet.org/Reports/2010/Generations-2010.aspx

More discussion of consumer of media becoming the producer of content under Web 2.0 is provided in Axel Bruns's (2008) book.

The original Enquire software is documented in an online manual: http://infomesh.net/2001/enquire/manual/#editorial

## CHAPTER 3

Architecture of Participation

<p>T</p>HE ARCHITECTURE OF PARTICIPATION IS ONE OF THE MORE subtle founding principles of Web 2.0. It builds on the idea of user-generated content and feeds directly into the enormous scale of data that Web 2.0 services are collecting. The key to understanding it is to give equal weight to both words: this is about technical architecture as much as participation, and at the most basic level this means that a service can be designed to facilitate mass user participation and improve its own performance as a consequence. As Allan Vermeulen, Chief Technology Officer at Amazon, told the founding Web 2.0 conference: the architecture of participation concept is based on the premise that a lot of information is "locked up" inside their customers and that they could build technology which channels that information into the system so that it can be used by others (O'Reilly et al. 2004).

O'Reilly (2005b) gave the example of Napster, which operated as a free, online music sharing service between 1999 and 2001.[*] The system used peer-to-peer (P2P) file sharing techniques which meant that every user contributed to the service by allowing their own PC to act as a node in the file distribution network. Napster kept a central database of where music could be located in the distributed system of PC nodes and set its defaults so that whenever a user downloaded the Napster software to access music on other people's PCs they too, by default, became another node, and any music they had on their own PC became part of the service. A user had to specifically opt out if they didn't want to share (Governor et al. 2009). In this way, each new person who used the service also automatically helped to build the shared, centralized database. O'Reilly contrasted this way of building such a database with more traditional methods, for example by paying people to add data or asking for volunteers.

An important side effect of Napster's (and other P2P systems such as Gnutella) built-in architecture of participation was that tens of millions of users around the world found they could very easily 'share' music with each other as well as access it. This represented a considerable threat to the established audio industry and, when combined with what was then

---

[*] Napster was closed down for legal reasons, but the ideas around peer-to-peer that it promoted are still used today and O'Reilly thought that it still provided a powerful example of what he was describing. The brand name survives as a paid service for music downloads.

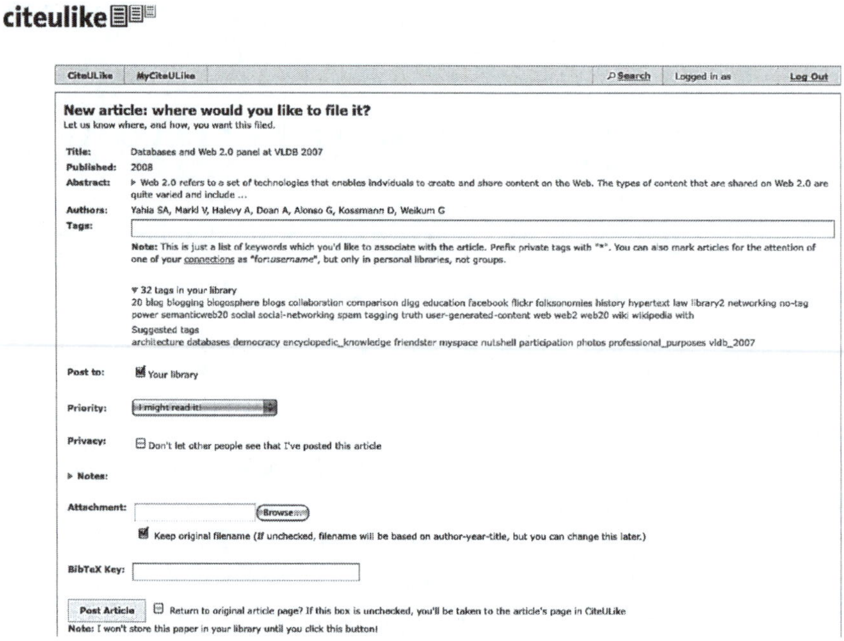

citeulike

FIGURE 3.1   The CiteULike service. (Reproduced with the kind permission of CiteULike.org).

the emerging MP3 player technology, provided the ammunition for a grassroots rebellion against music companies (Mock 2004; Boyle 2008). This in turn raised questions about intellectual property rights (see Chapter 6) and resulted in a famous law case between A&M records and Napster in 2001—which resulted in the service being closed down by the court. However, the ease with which Web technology could facilitate users working together to achieve a common goal had been demonstrated and the same technological concepts have been used in a number of other Web 2.0–style services, most notably the Skype telephony service.

Another example that might be of particular interest to students is the academic book-marking service, CiteULike (Hammond et al. 2005). Here, users can upload reference details of academic papers that they either have read or plan to read. The user can add their own personal metadata say, by tagging the papers with keywords they would like to associate with that paper. By default the service makes this information available to all other users, although there is a privacy setting so that the paper and the metadata can be made only available to that user in their own private library (the 'post to' tick box in Figure 3.1).

3.1 HISTORY OF ARCHITECTURE OF PARTICIPATION

The idea and the term seem to have originated in the *open source software* movement. O'Reilly (2004, 2003) describes how he came to use 'architecture of participation' to describe systems designed for user contribution. Note that this was before the coining of 'Web 2.0' as a term. He was heavily influenced by Larry Lessig's book *Code and Other Laws of Cyberspace* and by discussions with Linus Torvald (the originator of Linux) and other open source software developers. These developers argued that the way a system's code is internally structured, i.e. its architecture, is as important for the long-term sustainability of an open source software product as making the code open source. The code must be conducive to being worked on by many developers, thus its architecture must be modular with loosely coupled layers, so that discrete units of code can be modified and/or added to by disparate groups of developers (Baldwin and Clark 2006).

Web 2.0 continues this tradition by designing services that can be extended by third-party developers either by creating plug-ins or by re-using data through what is known as an open *Application Programming Interface* (API). We'll have a lot more to say on this in Chapter 6, but in brief, an API provides a mechanism for programmers to make use of the internal functionality of a piece of software without having access to the source code. Widely used in Web 2.0, APIs allow an existing software module or service to be built upon and extended by others without the new software being tightly coupled into the existing system.

There is however, another way in which the Web took hold of the idea of participation. Pointing out that both the open source and the early Internet communities had long traditions of architecture of participation, O'Reilly (2006b, 267) argues that the Web took "the idea of participation to a new level, because it opened that participation not just to software developers but to all users of the system". This refers to the original hypertext concept: that anyone could create a link to anything else, without the need to ask permission or to have too much technical knowledge. Hypertext and Hypertext Markup Language (HTML) encouraged users to join in and build the Web. He goes on to write: "The architectures of Linux, the Internet, and the World Wide Web are such that users pursuing their own 'selfish' interests build collective value as an automatic byproduct" (p. 268). These projects, O'Reilly argues, have a 'natural' architecture of participation, whereas others may have to work to overlay such a participation-based structure over a system that would not normally possess it.

3.2 DESIGNING FOR PARTICIPATION

O'Reilly (2005b) observes that one of the key lessons that Web 2.0 has to teach us is that users add value to a service by contributing information. However, only a small percentage of the total number of users of a service will ever feel engaged to the extent where they *explicitly* add new data to an application through some kind of formal feedback mechanism. To illustrate this, consider the case of eBay. The online auction site has built an enormous following, in part because of its reputation rating system. After every purchase a buyer is given the opportunity to rate the purchase process and this rating is aggregated to provide a broadly accurate feedback signal to other potential purchasers—it is technology's response to the age-old expression: *caveat emptor*. Adding a rating is easy thanks to slick graphics and a responsive user interface and it is certainly encouraged, indeed seen as part of the etiquette of being a well-mannered eBayer, but it is voluntary. Nothing about the system's behaviour forces the user to leave feedback. They are simply nudged in that direction.

Contrast this with the way in which a system such as Google works. Google has enormous, and unique, search-log data files, culled from the vast clickstreams of its own and its partners' websites. Every time someone uses Google's search box, data are collected about the search terms entered, the results list produced and the results the user finally clicks on.

The data can be used to find patterns, to serve advertisements, to compare data from different variants of the algorithm and to see what works.

However, unlike the eBay example, these data are collected *implicitly*, as a side effect of using the service: the user is unaware of the data collection process and is not asked to do anything other than the behaviour they need to undertake in order to carry out a search. Google's founders, in the course of trying to solve the problem of how to build a search engine that could cope with the scale of the Web, learned so much about its 'deeper nature', that they have been able to use this knowledge to leverage the architecture of participation to build a system that constantly improves itself.

3.2.1 Patterns for Participation

Developing Web services that make the most of their users and their associated data is a source of continuing competition within the computer industry and has driven innovation in software design, user interface systems and community site building. As Gavin Bell (2009, 77) has written, designing sites that "people use socially is quite different from building desktop software or service-based websites". Web 2.0 services not only allow users to carry out tasks (e.g. share a photograph, publish some text), but are also designed to engender and nurture social community and interaction. Crucially, the way sites work also facilitates the collection and reuse of data gained through that social interaction. Developing sites that achieve this involves considerable attention to the way that humans behave and has drawn on the ideas of interaction design, a branch of computer science and psychology. As Web 2.0 has developed, various techniques and strategies have been trailed, perfected and reused in varying ways.

Patterns are particularly important in this respect. They are reusable 'building blocks', consisting of worked-out, successful solutions to common design problems. They take the form of abstract software architecture patterns which guide the structure of the site's underlying software, and design patterns that support the function and behaviour of the user interface (Park et al. 2011; Schmidt et al. 1996).

The basic concept has its roots in building architecture and the ideas of Christopher Alexander (Governor et al. 2009). In the 1980s Kent Beck and Ward Cunningham began to experiment with transferring the concept across to software development and it has since become a well-used technique in the industry. Web 2.0 software design engineers make considerable use of these ideas (see the Further Reading section at the end of this chapter).

Leveraging the full power of the architecture of participation, however, requires huge amounts of user contributions, both explicit and implicit. As Evans (2006, slide 33) states, successful Web 2.0 companies have become the ones who use it to collect and aggregate "the best data". In the following chapter we will look at the epic scale of data that is being produced and learn how the collection and curation of vast databases of user information has become the defining characteristic of Web 2.0.

EXERCISES AND POINTS TO PONDER

1. The introduction of Web 2.0 has the potential to change the way that libraries operate, a process that has become known as Library 2.0. Using recently published papers and books, explore how Web 2.0, and in particular the idea of the architecture of participation, has changed the library landscape.

2. Pick a well-known Web 2.0 service that you are familiar with (e.g. eBay, Amazon, Facebook, YouTube, LastFM etc.). Analyse the user interface and the way in which the user is guided to use the service as they participate. Make a list of the ways in which the site 'encourages' the user to add and share content and to participate in the service.

3. Imagine that you and your classmates are running a business start-up and are creating a new Web 2.0 service. Undertake a discussion as to how you could design the site to ensure that there is an architecture of participation, i.e. that users will not only use the site on a regular basis, but will also contribute and share content as much as possible.

FURTHER READING

For more on the practical use of design patterns in the development of Web 2.0 sites and services see Mahemoff (2006), Governor et al. (2009) and Olsen (2007). The classic text on the general idea of patterns in software is *Design Patterns: Elements of Reusable Object-Oriented Software* (Gamma et al. 1994).

For more on Napster, its effect on the music industry, intellectual property rights (IPR) and so forth see McCourt and Burkart (2003), Chapter 4 of Boyle (2008), and Lessig (2004).

Data on an Epic Scale

Increasingly … everyone in the world casts an 'information shadow,' an aura of data which, when captured and processed intelligently, offers extraordinary opportunity and mind-bending implications.

TIM O'REILLY AND JOHN BATTELLE (2009, 2)

In the overview of Web 2.0 at the beginning of this book we explored Tim O'Reilly's (2005b) article, which introduced the idea of 'data as the next Intel Inside'. Without revisiting the detail here, the essence of the discussion was that a Web service's database (under a Web as Platform model) provides the critical functionality for a Web service in a similar way to a computer's microprocessor (under a PC as Platform model). In fact, he went as far as to say: "the value of the software is proportional to the scale and dynamism of the data it helps to manage" (p. 4). He emphasized this in a more recent paper on Web 2.0 technologies, writing that: "We see the era of Web 2.0, therefore, as a race to acquire and control data assets" (O'Reilly and Battelle 2009, 3).

However, O'Reilly's slogan was very much of its time and is only really meaningful to those who understand the story behind it. Because of this I have chosen to call this idea *data on an epic scale*, partly because it is self-explanatory and partly because O'Reilly's metaphor does not fully envisage the 'epic scale' of data that the Web is producing.

To get a sense of just how big the Web has become and how much data it generates, we will take an illustrative (rather than comprehensive) look at the history of search on the Web. This will demonstrate how quickly and to what extent the Web has expanded as well as providing context for the development of data collection and management tools. In addition, this should help our understanding of the Web as an evolving infrastructure of content and hyperlinks and tie in another one of the six big ideas: harnessing the power of the crowd. By examining the history of search we will see that:

- The scale and speed of the Web's growth caused problems for early Web innovators in their attempts to map new content as it appeared and make it easy to find

- Two main approaches were developed to deal with this: advanced, automated indexing techniques (to cope with the ever-expanding scale of the Web) and human intelligence-based systems to make the information easy to find

- The impact of commercial interests on what had previously been a very science-oriented Web meant that search techniques became a source of new tools for collecting data on individual user's actions.

We will then go on to explore just how big the scale of data collection has become, and show how the collection and curation of vast databases of user information has become the defining characteristic of Web 2.0 services.

4.1 A SHORT HISTORY OF SEARCH

As we saw in the Introduction to this book, in the early days of the Web there was no need for a search engine. Of the thousands of servers that were connected to the Internet, only a handful had the additional software needed to provide Web facilities. Tim Berners-Lee maintained a hypertext list of every Web server that was hosting webpages, and you can still see a snapshot of it as it stood in March 1992.* It has about twenty-five entries, mainly academic and research institutions, including the likes of University of Graz (Austria), Denmark's Technical Library, Helsinki Technical University, the High Energy Centre (Netherlands), IN2P3 (France), the Italian Physics Institute, Hebrew University (Israel), and the Stanford Linear Accelerator.

However, it wasn't long before things started to change. With the increase in the number of Web servers coming online, the number of webpages also increased. Berners-Lee recognized early on that there were two different types of information that would appeal to two different audiences and he did something that was to prove very important in the history of search: he split his list of Web servers into two (Berners-Lee 1999). The first carried on as before, listing the servers and their geographical locations, whilst the second list focused on the content of the pages that were hosted on these servers, and grouped it according to subject matter. This was to be the beginning of the very first Web directory—a list of the Web's content that used human intelligence to create a structure that would make it easier for people to find what they were looking for.

Things didn't stop there. The Web was still growing and, aware of the problem of keeping track of it all, Berners-Lee asked for resources for what he called a 'virtual librarian', someone to keep the directory up to date. In March 1993 he found the resource in the person of Arthur Secret, the engineer son of the French Consul in Geneva (Gillies and Cailliau 2000). At CERN, Secret set about organising the content of the Web. He used hierarchical tree structures and replicated human thought processes so that people could find what they were interested in by drilling down through a series of linked pages. This became the *WWW Virtual Library*,† a list of webpages categorised by subject such as History,

---

* See: http://www.w3.org/History/19921103-hypertext/hypertext/DataSources/WWW/Servers.html
† http://vlib.org/

Education and Agriculture. At first the task was manageable, but it wasn't long before the number of new servers was doubling every few months and the amount of new content was increasing exponentially.

4.1.1 Wandering the World Wide Web

Meanwhile, others outside CERN had begun to think about the same problem. Matthew Gray, a physics undergraduate at the Massachusetts Institute of Technology was one of several people who had started to play with the idea that there needed to be some sort of automated solution (Knoblock 1997; Couvering 2008). He had been experimenting with something called a *Web spider*, a small piece of software that collected data about how many Web servers there were by following the hypertext links between them.* In June 1993, his spider, which he called the *WWW Wanderer*, or W4, uncovered 125 individual Web server computers and counted 17,000 documents on its first search of the Web. As more and more of these servers came online, Wanderer systematically 'crawled' the links between the documents looking for the new ones that had been added since its last visit. Gray ran the service every couple of months or so and found that a Web server was being added every day.

But Gray inevitably hit the same problem that had occurred to Tim Berners-Lee: simply counting and listing the available Web servers did not help people find particular content (Battelle 2005). Rather than throwing human brainpower at the problem, Gray instinctively sought an automated solution and developed Wandex, a piece of Web indexing software. Wandex listed the Uniform Resource Identifiers (URIs) (or Web 'addresses') of the webpages on each server.† This meant that there was now an extra level of information that could be used to find webpages on a particular topic. It wasn't necessarily very intuitive—the URIs were really just file names like the one Berners-Lee used for his very first webpage—but it was better than nothing.

4.1.2 Web Crawler, Page Ranking, and the Full Text Search

By the end of 1993 there were two key approaches to mapping the Web: a human-generated directory that provided a high-quality and intuitive way to find webpages but which was inevitably out of date; or a comprehensive, automated index that was quite hard to navigate. Both methods had their own set of problems and as the Web continued to expand this could only get worse. However, just around the corner there was a third way emerging, one that attempted to imbue an automated indexing system with some basic human intelligence.

---

* A snapshot of the results that the spider produced is still available on MIT's webserver. See: http://www.mit.edu/~mkgray/net/.

† A source of continuing confusion in articles, papers and other documentation is the use of Uniform Resource Identifier (URI) and Uniform Resource Locator (URL) to refer to the mechanism that identifies Web resources (i.e. the Web 'address'). In fact, URL is a sub-set of URI and in older documentation about the Web both terms were used in context to distinguish between the two usages. However, following reviews of this practice by the World Wide Web Consortium (W3C) and Internet Engineering Task Force (IETF) in the mid-2000s it was recommended that future specifications and related documentation should use the general term 'URI'.

Brian Pinkerton was an undergraduate student at the University of Washington when he created *Web Crawler,*[*] another Web spider (Pinkerton 1994, 2000). On its first 'crawl' Pinkerton's spider produced an index of 6,000 Web servers, nearly fifty times more than Wanderer's first crawl. However, Crawler had a twist. Not only did it create a database to collect and index the URIs of the webpages it found, it also stored a copy of the full text of each webpage.

Using a database in this way—essentially to store a copy of the Web—was a huge leap forward towards the development of the kind of search engine that we would recognize today. Web Crawler could search the database of text and compare the keywords in the search query with the words contained in the Web documents. It could work out which webpages featured the keywords more often and rank the results list accordingly. It was a fairly crude form of ranking—frequency of search term does not necessarily equate to the best, most relevant results—but it was more useful than no ranking at all. Crawler was the first automated attempt at providing some of the human intelligence of Arthur Secret's directory and it was a huge success.

Initially the system ran on a single, standard PC of the time (a 486 processor, with an 800-MB hard disk), which held the index in a simple database. This meant that a copy of the entire text of the Web was capable of being stored on a single computer. However, as the Web continued to grow, the amount of data being collected soon overwhelmed the simple database. Improvements were made, including a sophisticated, commercial database system from Oracle (with 100 gigabytes of hard disk space) which was connected to multiple PCs, but even this wasn't enough and Pinkerton soon found that adding new hardware was almost a monthly occurrence.

Round about this time there was another development that was taking the Web by storm: the release of the Mosaic Web browser (Reid 1997a). Although not a search technology, Mosaic was important because for the first time ordinary people, using home computers, were able to install a browser and get on to the Web easily. Mosaic was the Web's first 'killer app'[†] and all of a sudden, hundreds of thousands of new people started to arrive on the Web, ready to browse webpages, create their own, and, increasingly, to search.

This was important for Web Crawler because, all of a sudden, as well as indexing the Web it had to deal with huge numbers of people wanting to search it, and at its peak this reached around 300,000 user queries a day (Pinkerton 2000). The speed at which such queries could be processed and results returned became a major problem and eventually the demand for Crawler devastated the network resources at the University of Washington (Pinkerton 2000). Once again the growth of the Web had defeated any attempt to manage it.

---

[*] http://www.webcrawler.com/
[†] A 'killer app' is a term used to describe any application that is so compelling it drives adoption rates at breakneck speed, along with the uptake of any technologies associated with it.

4.1.3 Alta Vista and the Application of Computational Brawn

Pinkerton's daily battle with the hardware and database resources required to keep pace with the growth of the early Web is just one example of a serious struggle that was starting to emerge. In fact, it was symptomatic of the beginning of the end of an era in which university undergraduates and researchers had been able to deploy their brains and a handful of desktop computers to crack the problem of indexing the Web. Things had hit a wall, and from the middle of 1994 a power shift began to take place.

The success of Mosaic had launched the Web out of its niche and given it mass-market appeal. With the influx of large numbers of new Web visitors, big companies started to become interested. The difficulty of the problem and the potential prize on offer began to attract the attention of serious software developers in established computer companies.

One such company was DEC (Digital Equipment), a computer company that no longer exists but which was well-known and successful in the 1970s and 1980s. DEC had been struggling commercially in the late 1980s and was looking for new markets and opportunities (Battelle 2005; Comerford 1992). It was in the process of introducing a new computer processor called Alpha, which had been designed for parallel processing. Each processor had up to four chips on it and these chips could work together, co-operating on a bit of code execution. Alpha was also designed to work well with large databases of information.

What better way to demonstrate the power of their new system than to tackle the problem of indexing the Web? DEC staff estimated that to index the Web completely, as it stood in late 1995, would need a database of just under a terabyte (1,000 GB). To demonstrate the power of the new processor they developed a search engine, Alta Vista, which sent out a 'brood' of up to a thousand spiders across the Web. All this extra computational power meant that Alta Vista could start collecting significant amounts of extra data, creating a far more complete index of the Web and therefore a better search engine.

Alta Vista was launched in December 1995 with an initial index of sixteen million documents and was a phenomenal success. Yet still the Web grew. By 1998 the AltaVista service was being run on twenty DEC Alpha machines, each with a 500-GB hard disk—a long way away from Brian Pinkerton and his 800-MB, 486 processor.

4.1.4 Yahoo! and the Value of the Clickstream

By the mid-1990s the race to build a perfect search engine was hotting up and the Web directory, pioneered by Arthur Secret, was not yet out of the running. In 1993, Jerry Yang, a Ph.D. student at Stanford University, was experimenting with the then newly launched Mosaic Web browser, and was creating a list of all the sites he visited. His friend and fellow Stanford researcher, David Filo, wrote a small piece of software to automatically keep track of the list and publish it back to the Web.

In 1994 *Jerry and David's Guide to the WWW* took off through word-of-mouth and became an early Web phenomenon. It was renamed *Yahoo!* but was not a search engine in the sense of Web Crawler or Alta Vista. It had no automatic crawl but instead used the intelligence of human editors to group websites into categories and sub-categories. However, much more than this, Yang and Filo latched on to the idea that the people visiting their site and clicking on links were telling them something. They worked out that if there were three websites listed under the sub-category 'pizza making', but users nearly always chose the last one, then perhaps the list should be re-ordered to make it the first. The act of clicking—the tiny bit of information that it imparted—said something about that person's preferences. It marked a choice, a vote of confidence, a bit like Ask the Audience on the popular TV show *Who Wants to Be a Millionaire*. Yahoo!'s first CEO, Tim Koogle, said that: "people came to our servers and they'd leave tracks … We could see every day exactly what people thought was important on the Internet" (Battelle 2005, 62).

Yahoo! became an early pioneer of what is now known as the *clickstream*— aggregating and making use of information about what the user chooses to click on and read (Nissenbaum 2010). Collecting this kind of information substantially added to the amount of data collection that was taking place. But even more importantly, the idea of watching what people do online and learning from what the majority choose established what was to become one of the defining concepts of the Web—popularity.

4.1.5 Google, Popularity and the PageRank Algorithm

No examination of the history of search would be complete without a look at the company that now dominates the search landscape: Google. In 1996, two Stanford University Ph.D. students, Larry Page and Sergey Brin, and their tutor Terry Winograd, alighted on what seemed to be a very clever solution to the problem of how to rank a user's search results: imagine that all the pages of the Web are like academic papers (Brin and Page 1998; Langville and Meyer 2006).

In the academic world, a paper's worth is largely measured by the number of other papers that cite it. The citations provide a kind of popularity metric that also assumes a measure of quality, i.e. that better papers get cited more often. The trio called this *importance* and argued that this same metric could be applied to a webpage. Its importance could be gathered, in part, from the number of links from other webpages that connected to it. Strictly speaking, this had been done before (it was known as *link analysis*) but they added a twist by saying that not all incoming links were equal, and worked out a way of weighting the links so that some counted for more than others. The two students applied their knowledge to Web searching by developing a search engine based on their citation algorithm, *PageRank*.

Brin and Page were not the only ones to come up with the idea of analysing the link structure of the Web in order to help with search. In particular, Jon Kleinberg's *HITS* algorithm was published independently at around the same time (Langville and Meyer 2006). However, although similar, it was Google's founders who decided that their solution could be the basis for a company.

With the PageRank algorithm at its core, the Google search engine outstripped its competitors when it was introduced in 1999. It had wider coverage and provided more accurate results. It gathered praise from technology reviewers and users alike, who marvelled at its uncanny accuracy. The secret was that right from the beginning Google's founders were determined that their solution would be able to keep pace with the continuing growth of the Web—at all costs, it would scale.

The amount of data required to power the Google algorithm is phenomenal. Google 'crawls' the Web and calculates a PageRank number for every single page it can find and keeps track of all the links between pages, in itself a huge data collection and processing task. Google also records a log for each and every Web search. They represent the records of millions and millions of search terms, the results produced, and the choices that each one of us makes when we decide what to click on next. These data can be used to find patterns, to compare data from differing variants of the algorithm and to see what works.

4.2 THE WEB GOES COMMERCIAL

From the mid-1990s, commercial interests began to lay the foundations for a new industry based on the Web, and the geographical axis for this new economy was the United States. The Web became the 'unsettled land' of the Internet and with it came the sense of unlimited opportunity and optimism of the dot-com boom that turned its back on tried and tested business models in favour of building market share over the bottom line. The 'Get Big Fast' motto reflected the dot-com plan to operate at a sustained net loss in order to establish a brand, dominate a market and see off competitors so that they could charge profitable rates for their services later on (Oliva et al. 2003).

With the battle for market share came the battle for 'mind share'. There were now millions of eyes on the Web and channelling them in one direction or another became the focus of a great deal of effort. Some of the big names of the Web of today emerged such as Amazon, eBay and LastMinute.com, but although e-commerce sites were good for selling things, search engines and browsers carried out more fundamental activities—helping people see what was available—and therefore received considerable commercial interest.

Driving this was the language of marketing, which started to dominate what had been a very science-oriented Web. As in the offline world, the ultimate goal was to be able to profile customers, track and manage customer relationships and anticipate their future wants and needs. In the online world, however, there was a new breed of electronic tools and performance indicators becoming available that could improve and help track the data collection needed to do this (Goldfarb et al. 2011):

Cookies: At the most basic level, cookies are tiny files that contain arbitrary pieces of data that act as a unique ID. When you visit certain websites the server that hosts the site will store a permanent cookie on your computer so that if you revisit the site, it can recognize your computer. This works because at the same time as the server stores its cookie on your computer it will set up a corresponding file, often in the website's database, with a matching ID. This file can be used to store information such as the last time your computer visited the website, which pages were looked at and in what order, and how much time was spent browsing. However, cookies were controversial. They first hit the headlines around 1996 because of the potential for them to be used to infringe on privacy and track people's behaviour (Mercado Kierkegaard 2005). Six years later, rules about the use of cookies became part of the 2002 European Union Telecommunication Privacy Directive.

Web Bugs: Tiny images, just one pixel by one pixel in size, buried within the HTML code of a webpage and invisible to the user (Goldfarb et al. 2011; Murray and Cowart 2001). They can be used by advertisers to detect when users move from one page to another, how far they scroll down or when they leave a site. They differ from cookies in that nothing additional is stored on the user's computer and so they are far harder to detect. Also known as *clear GIFs*, *1x1 GIFs, pixel tags* or *Web tags*. Murray and Cowart (2001) reported that over 90% of websites that made mention of a top-50 consumer brand used Web Bugs.

Click-Through Rate (CTR): Search engines, most notably Google and Bing, as well as many Web 2.0 services use a business model based on presenting advertisements as a user browses results or pages of content (Richardson et al. 2007). The main method for this is known as *pay-per-performance*, in which an advertiser only pays when a user clicks on an advert and follows the link through to the advertiser's own pages. Thus, the CTR is an important metric and trying to predict it for a particular advertisement is an important function of modern marketing.

Impressions: An alternative to CTR is for an advertiser to pay whenever their advertisement is delivered to a webpage (McCandless 1998; Chatterjee et al. 2003). Advertisers are charged based on the basis of the cost-per-thousand-impressions.

These clues can be collected, stored and analysed, and although their usefulness is often questionable, the idea of gathering information about what people do online has gained traction.

4.3 WORKING AT THE INTERNET SCALE

What the history of search shows us is how big the Web has become and therefore how critical it is for companies to design systems that can handle *Internet-scale* levels of data collection and processing. *Scalability* is an important concept in this respect. Generally, when we talk about scalability we mean that adding resources to a system allows it to cope with an increased workload in a well-understood and predictable manner. That is, an increase in resource x, will result in an increase in performance or abilities, y.

In simple terms, there are two types of scalability: vertical and horizontal (Sankar et al. 2008; Mei et al. 2008). Vertical scalability is the more traditional form and involves adding faster computers, or ones with more memory, to cope with an increase in workload requirements, i.e. we increase the resources available at each computational node. Horizontal scaling is the form taken by the majority of Web 2.0 services and involves increasing the number of computers or servers involved in a problem, rather than increasing their individual power, i.e. we increase the number of nodes.* The computational problem is then distributed across more computers, often spread over a number of different data centres.

---

* In this scenario, ordinary commodity PCs are usually used as computing nodes (rather than specialist servers), which are more prone to hardware failure. This means that the software has to handle individual node failure within its data processing algorithm. This technique is reminiscent of the packet-switched nature of data transfer on the Internet, which allows for individual routers etc. to fail and be by-passed.

To give some idea of the scale of these data processing infrastructures one only needs to look at the industrial-scale collections of computers that power Web 2.0. When it opened in 2006, Google's largest data centre, at The Dalles, had three buildings, each roughly 6,380 square metres (68,680 square feet) (Gilder 2006; Carr 2008; Strand 2008). Although shrouded in commercial secrecy, Google has admitted that each of these buildings contains 6,000 computers, bolted together in dozens of racks, each of which holds 40 machines (Shankland 2008). This many computers will consume over 100 MW of electricity per day, which is enough to power a small British town like Chester or Burnley. This partly explains the location of the new server farm at The Dalles, on the bank of a large river, with its own dam providing the hydro-electric power needed to run it.

The Dalles data centre, although large, is just one of many, possibly dozens spread across the world. It is a small part of what has become known as the Googleplex, a world-wide network of data collection and processing systems (Iyer and Davenport 2008). Estimates vary as to the true scale of the Googleplex. Despite considerable interest no one from outside the company is entirely sure. Websites such as Data Center Knowledge try to keep a watching eye on developments and they estimate that Google spent more than US$1.4 billion on data centre infrastructure in the first three quarters of 2010 alone (Miller 2010a). They estimate that Google has at least 36 major data centres, spread across four continents.

Google is not alone. Microsoft is also building the data centre infrastructure to handle information processing at the Internet scale, and smaller companies such as Amazon, Yahoo!, eBay, Facebook, MySpace and LinkedIn are also joining in. Facebook, for example, maintains nine data centres across the United States (Miller 2010b) and is in the process of building another one in the Pacific Northwest. The company runs at least 60,000 servers (see Chapter 10 for more details). Amazon, for its part, believes it has so perfected the art of running its own data centres that it sells its spare capacity to other Internet-based businesses. Yahoo! also likes the Pacific Northwest of America and has a 13,000 square metre (140,000 square feet) data centre in Quincy, Washington, another similar centre in New York, and is in the process of building one in Switzerland (Miller 2010c).

What the giants of Web 2.0 have built is an impeccable infrastructure for the collection of data on an epic scale. This is also referred to as working at the level of the petabyte, where the amount of data is measured on the peta-scale (or 1,000,000 GB). These firms have perfected the technological art of handling data on this Internet scale, where there are literally millions of users reading, linking to, sharing, uploading, following, searching billions of documents, photos, files and other snippets of information around the world and around the clock. The number of users and the amount of data that is being channelled through one or other of these big companies is staggering—billions of visits per month and hundreds of millions of individual users. In a world where information, in the evocative phrase of Hans Christian von Baeyer, "drizzles around us like rain" (Baeyer 2003, 3), these companies collect millions of droplets which cumulatively form mighty rivers—which can be fished.

4.4 USING THE EPIC SCALE OF DATA

By examining the history of search we can see how data collection became the key tool in the battle to manage the scale and reach of the expanding Web. However, when commercial entities began to take an interest in the Web's potential, interest in this data, and the techniques used to collect it, took a new turn. These developments have led to a new generation of Internet infrastructure that can handle working at the peta-scale, constantly collecting, aggregating and mining the daily deluge of real-time data and transient online content. In developing this infrastructure, these companies have, according to O'Reilly (2005b), understood something deeper about the nature of the Web.

This understanding of the Web's 'deeper nature' has led to new insights such as the architecture of participation and how to harness the power of the crowd. O'Reilly (2005b) has described how Amazon annotated a simple database of book ISBNs by adding new information, and most importantly, by getting customers to add their own data in the form of reviews and personal wishlists. By creating the infrastructure for users to contribute in this way, Amazon harnessed the 'work' of a willing crowd of volunteers who helped to create a unique database that is much less open to competition from other companies, since to re-create large amounts of user-generated content is difficult and time consuming.

It is this kind of collection, aggregation, enhancement and reuse of data that O'Reilly has identified as one of the defining characteristics of Web 2.0 services.

By using some of that data to provide a free and interesting service, Web 2.0 companies keep users engaged and prepared to keep on participating, which in turn continues to improve their data.

We are almost certainly at the beginning of what can be achieved by the companies who have built up vast datasets of information created at least in part by their users. Indeed, new technology such as smartphones with location capability, have brought new classes of data to the Web. These new data, which can be linked to existing data, enhance existing datasets and therefore increase their value. The cycle of data acquisition and linking, therefore, starts again and has even stimulated a race to acquire and control particular data assets (O'Reilly and Battelle 2009).

Increasingly, however, attention is being focused on how these data stores can be leveraged to extract the potential 'intelligence' that may be contained within the huge amounts of user-generated content being produced. In particular, there is a race to own what has become known as the Social Web, data about individuals, their relationships and their interests, garnered from online social networks (a topic we will return to in Chapter 10). I call this 'harnessing the power of the crowd', although it is probably more familiar to most people as 'collective intelligence' and it forms the subject of the next chapter.

EXERCISES AND POINTS TO PONDER

1. Web 2.0 services are notoriously secretive about the scale of their server operations, but information does make its way into the public domain. What can you find out about the latest state of play of these company's operations?

2. In Section 4.1.4 we discussed the idea of human-edited search listings. A project which still pursues this approach is the Open Directory Project (ODP), also known as Dmoz. Explore this service and find out about its history and current status. What are the advantages and disadvantages of this approach? Find out what the research literature has to say on this.

3. Over the course of a period of time, say a week or a month, assiduously record the search terms that you use every time you use a search engine. At the end of the time review the list. How much information about you as a person and your interests could be gleaned from this data? Having done this, read John Battelle's thoughts on what he calls the 'Database of Intentions' and reflect on what you have learned (Battelle 2005) (see Chapter 1).

4. Write a short essay on cookies and their implications for users' privacy. Include discussion of the European Union's 2009 directive on the use of cookies, the forthcoming changes in HTML5 and the views of developers who make use of the technology.

FURTHER READING

For detailed discussion of the issues surrounding personal privacy and data collection see Nissenbaum (2010), Solove (2007) and Abelson et al. (2008).

For more on Web Bugs and other invisible web-based surveillance methods see Martin et al. (2003) and Harding et al. (2001).

More information on the Web's early history and, in particular, the story of the WWW virtual library (including an interview with Secret) can be found at: http://vlib.org/admin/VLresources

The mathematics of Google's search algorithm are explored in detail in Langville and Meyer (2006).

## CHAPTER 5

Harnessing the Power of the Crowd

I would suggest that collective intelligence be taken seriously as a scientific and societal goal, and that the Internet is our best shot at seeing it happen in our lifetimes.

TOM GRUBER
(*2008, 2*)

It's a mistake to romanticize all this more than is strictly necessary. Web 2.0 harnesses the stupidity of crowds as well as its wisdom.

LEV GROSSMAN
Writing for Time Magazine (2006, Webpage)

In his bestselling business book of 2004, *New Yorker* magazine columnist, James Surowiecki, begins by taking the reader to an English country fair at the turn of the twentieth century. The scientist Francis Galton is wandering around the stalls and comes across a weight-judging competition, in which members of the public are waging six-penny bets on guessing the weight of an enormous ox. Since large numbers of people had entered the competition it pricked Galton's curiosity as he had long held an interest in the intellectual capabilities of the average person. His agenda was dark, at least by modern sensibilities, since he was keen to scientifically prove that the average person was capable of very little and was, frankly, quite stupid. After the competition was over and the prizes awarded, Galton borrowed the tickets from the organisers and ran a series of statistical tests on them. Expecting the average guess to be wildly off the mark, he was surprised to discover that it was, in fact, correct to within one pound. Although disappointing from the point of view of Galton's scientific agenda, the results enabled him to write a paper for the science journal *Nature*.* Surowiecki argues that the implications of what Galton found that day have yet to be fully understood. He calls the effect, and his book, the *Wisdom of Crowds* and it has been very influential on Web 2.0–style thinking, with several writers adapting Surowiecki's ideas to fit their observations on Web and Internet-based activities.

The idea of some kind of 'sixth sense' that operates within large crowds of people was attractive to the commentators who were exploring the idea of a second wave of Web development in the mid-2000s. In his 2005 article, Tim O'Reilly argued that one of the central principles of companies that had made the successful transition from Web 1.0 to Web 2.0 was that they "embraced the power of the web to harness collective intelligence" (O'Reilly 2005b, 6). He gave the example of Cloudmark, a collaborative spam filtering system, which aggregates "the individual decisions of e-mail users about what is and is not spam, outperforming systems that rely on analysis of the messages themselves" (p. 2). O'Reilly argued that the Web, through the interactions of millions of users, was in effect being turned into a form of "global brain" (p. 9) that made good use of the wisdom of crowds.

One can see the attraction of the argument. Through the power of the network effect (see Chapter 7) millions of users were engaged in a frenzy of content production, driven both explicitly by the urge to contribute, and implicitly by the architecture of participation. If crowds of people could deliver some form of collective intelligence then surely the Web, with its user-base constituting the largest crowd in human history, was the crucible for something spectacular. While it is possible that this may turn out to be the case, we must first acknowledge the problems inherent in bandying about terms like 'intelligence', 'brain' and 'wisdom'.

5.1 THE WISDOM OF CROWDS

Let us begin with Surowiecki's book (2004). First of all it is important to note that Surowiecki does not use the Web to demonstrate his concepts† and that the ideas come with caveats as to their limitations. It is perhaps rather unfortunate that the book's publisher used a strapline that glossed over the subtleties of Surowiecki's explication ("why the many are smarter than the few and how collective wisdom shapes business, economies, societies, and nations") as it could be argued that this has led to a rather uncritical adoption of his ideas with respect to our understanding of Web 2.0, and this should give us cause to pause for thought.

In the book he outlines three different types of problem, which he calls cognition, co-ordination and co-operation. He goes on to demonstrate his idea of how these types of problems can be solved more effectively by groups, operating according to specific

---

* See: http://galton.org/essays/1900-1911/galton-1907-vox-populi.pdf?page=7
† Although Surowiecki told *Newsweek* magazine that the Web is 'structurally congenial' to the wisdom of crowds. See: http://www.thedailybeast.com/newsweek/2006/04/02/the-new-wisdom-of-the-web.html

conditions, than even the most intelligent individual member of that group. According to his definition, cognition problems are those that require a single, definitive answer (e.g. who won the FIFA World Cup in 1966?) or those to which there is more than one answer but where some answers are better than others (e.g. what is the best place to build a public swimming pool?). Such problems need answers that are not entirely random (e.g. guess whether a tossed coin will land on heads or tails). Co-ordination problems require members of a group to work out how to organise their behaviour with each other, e.g. how do buyers and sellers find each other and agree a fair price in the marketplace? Finally, co-operation problems involve getting people, each with their own self-interest at heart, to agree on something for the collective good (e.g. at what level to set a tax on carbon dioxide production). Through a series of case studies and examples from economic history, Surowiecki shows how crowds of non-experts have provided better solutions than isolated experts, provided that four key criteria are present: diversity of opinion, independence of opinion, that the group is decentralised (and therefore each member can draw on some form of local, grassroots knowledge) and finally that a process of aggregation takes place (Wagner et al. 2010).

How is it possible that, under certain conditions, the wisdom of the crowd is greater than that of the most well-informed expert within that crowd? Surely the process of aggregating a wide variety of answers will dilute the predictions or suggestions of those who know a lot about a problem. Well, Surowiecki admits that for most types of problems, 'average' leads to mediocrity. However, he posits that with certain types of decision-making problems, and if the group involved is sufficiently large and diverse, then overall the errors made by individuals cancel each other out.

However, even this is not without its detractors. For example, Wagner et al. (2010) disagree, arguing that while one aspect of having a large crowd is the reduction of errors and 'noise', this is not the main effect the crowd has. They believe the diversity of the crowd is the key factor because it ensures that a number of different individuals are independently applying their own way of solving the problem (formerly known as a *heuristic* in the field of artificial intelligence). Their insight is that it is the collation of the results of these different heuristics that leads to the crowd's capacity for certain types of problem solving.*

What this debate allows us to see is that the term 'wisdom of crowds' as used by Surowiecki is highly nuanced, specific to particular scenarios and not without its detractors. Having established more precisely what Surowiecki meant we can see that it is often unclear whether or not the aspects of Web 2.0 under discussion conform to Surowiecki's definitions and four criteria. This should make us more careful about using the term uncritically, particularly when it is being used to ascribe merit to Web 2.0 more generally.

---

* Readers interested in the statistical and theoretical basis for why the wisdom of crowds might work are directed to Chapter 1 of Cass Sunstein's book, *Infotopia* (2006) and his discussion, amongst other interesting things, of the Condorcet Jury Theorem.

5.2 COLLECTIVE INTELLIGENCE

Now that we have established more precisely what Surowiecki meant by wisdom of crowds, let us turn our attention to another phrase that is often used interchangeably with it. The term 'collective intelligence' has tended to replace wisdom of crowds in recent years, but this too has several problems associated with it. Firstly, what kind of intelligence are we referring to? If we equate information to intelligence then many of the examples in O'Reilly's paper stand up to scrutiny. However, if your understanding of intelligence more naturally focuses on the idea of having or showing some kind of intellectual ability, then the phrase becomes more problematic—after all, after more than fifty years of experimentation, computer science has yet to deliver a form of artificial intelligence than can pass Alan Turing's famous test.[*]

5.2.1 A Philosophy of Collective Intelligence

So far we have been skirting around some fairly substantial material connected to epistemology (the study of knowledge). Halpin (2008) notes that a fundamental assumption in analytical philosophy has been the idea that intelligence resides in the individual. However, recent empirical work in psychology and cognitive science has increasingly challenged the assumption that intelligence is irreducibly individual. The emergence of collective intelligence facilitated by the Web has not, therefore, escaped the attention of philosophers, who have begun to wonder what this means for traditional views of the nature of human cognition (Halpin 2008; Halpin et al. 2010). Indeed, it was a philosopher, Pierre Lévy, who coined the term collective intelligence and he defined it as: "A form of universally distributed intelligence, constantly enhanced, coordinated in real time, and resulting in the effective mobilization of skills" (Lévy 1997, 13).

However, the idea of harnessing *distributed human intelligence* pre-dates both Lévy and the development of the Web. Gregg (2010) and Gruber (2008) note that as long ago as the 1960s computer scientists were speculating on the ability of computers to help groups of people work cooperatively to solve problems. An early pioneer in this, as in so much else, was Doug Engelbart, who not only invented the computer mouse but also set out the BootStrap Principle, a concept for human–computer interaction that harvested distributed knowledge. Heylighen (1999) points out the increasing interest in collective intelligence long before the emergence of Web 2.0 in areas such as simulated societies, robotics and studying how swarms of bees behave in the wild.

What is important for our discussion is to be aware that some of the debate centres around the role of what are called *representations*: models or maps of the world and its behaviours, which in some ways represent our internal cognitive states. Researchers in this area posit that the Web has provided a mechanism whereby everybody is allowed access to the *same* set of representations. Indeed, Halpin noted that Tim Berners-Lee set out to create a universal information space and has argued that the Web has produced "a veritable explosion of representations" (Halpin 2008, 1). What is interesting

---

[*] For details of the Turing test see the annual Loebner AI prize website: http://www.loebner.net/Prizef/loebner-prize.html

about the emergence of Web 2.0 is that not only can anyone access the representations, but increasingly anyone can *modify* them. In this way representations become the result of collective work which harnesses the fact that, in the words of Lévy: "no one knows everything, everyone knows something, all knowledge resides in humanity" (Halpin 2008, 7).

We should also take account of the *extended mind* hypothesis. This proposes that not all human cognition takes place entirely within the brain, but instead draws on an extended network of external, physical props and aids. A classic example would be the way that most of us reach for pen and paper when asked to do long multiplication (Smart et al. 2009). Thus it can be said that in some senses the machinery of the human mind is not solely located within the human head. If that is the case then surely, the argument goes, the Web might lead to powerful effects, perhaps even creating what might be termed a Web-extended mind. Many Web technologists think so. Joshua Schachter for example talks of his Delicious.com bookmarking system as an "amplification system for the memory" (Weinberger 2007, 165).

This is not the place to go into a detailed discussion of the philosophical issues, but those who are considering the idea of some form of collective intelligence operating on the Web should be aware of the existence of such debates. However it is also important to bear in mind that even if one accepts the idea of an extended mind, there needs to be another act of critical thinking before believing that Web 2.0 services provide some kind of mental prosthetic.* As Halpin et al. (2010) note, although the idea of the Web providing a form of extended mind seems to be widely accepted by the Web development community, it is not so within the philosophy community where it is the subject of vigorous on-going debate.

5.3 HARNESSING THE POWER OF THE CROWD

Using terminology such as collective intelligence to describe Web 2.0 services in general, disguises their differences and ascribes a positive quality to them. Whilst this may have been important when the term was originally being deployed as a marketing slogan, we need to think a little more deeply about it if we are to use the term as a tool for understanding Web 2.0. Examining some of the detail behind the ideas of wisdom of crowds and collective intelligence is therefore helpful as we start to see that, in order to understand Web 2.0, these terms should not be used uncritically. In the academic literature these debates are writ large. Tapscott and Williams (2007) defined collective intelligence as: "the aggregate knowledge that emerges from the decentralised choices and judgements of independent participants" (p. 41). Others prefer the term *collective knowledge* which, according to Vossen and Hagemann (2007, 329), "refers to the capacity to provide useful information based on human contributions, which is genuinely social in the sense that it gets better as more people participate in it, contribute to it and use it". This is a

---

* In terms of the nature of knowledge, its provenance and its reliability.

nuanced position, but takes us away from the more problematic use of the word 'intelligence'. Gruber (2008) takes the view that it is perfectly acceptable to refer to the idea of collective intelligence, but that, in so doing, one needs to accept that at present Web 2.0 does not exhibit something that might deserve that label. He prefers the term *collected intelligence*, indicating that what we mainly have to date is vast collections of user-generated content that exhibits certain properties but which, firstly, does not conform to the criteria set by Surowiecki and, secondly, has yet to be aggregated and recombined in ways that generate something that could be labelled 'artificial intelligence'. Gregg (2010) has argued that working with collective intelligence is a fundamentally different way of viewing how computers can support human decision making, moving away from an emphasis on helping the individual problem solver, towards harnessing the power of the group.

In practice, all of these definitions offer something towards the ongoing effort to describe just what is going on with user participation in Web 2.0 services. Music recommendation services that aggregate and mine the 'collected opinion' of large numbers of users in order to make suggestions to other users are more clearly an attempt to use computers to replicate some kind of collective human intelligence as described by Lévy. A service like Wikipedia, on the other hand, perhaps corresponds more closely to Vossen and Hagemann's definition of collective knowledge. It is because of the need to talk about what is happening on the Web in an inclusive way, but to allow specificity where necessary, that I prefer to talk about *harnessing the power of the crowd*. With this in mind there are two key questions that help us to unlock some of features that characterise how Web 2.0 services utilize the power of the crowd and to identify some of the specifics:

1. Is the service primarily a tool to facilitate collaboration or to aggregate individual, independent actions?

2. Is the service's 'product' created explicitly or implicitly?

5.3.1 Explicit Collaboration

Wikipedia has been held up by many as a primary example of the way in which Web 2.0 can harness the power of the crowd (Swarts 2009; Sunstein 2006; Suh et al. 2009; Almeida et al. 2007). As we will discuss in detail later on in this book, huge numbers of individuals from across the world have worked together to develop a free, online encyclopaedia consisting of millions of articles, and in this sense it can be seen as utilizing some of the techniques of crowdsourcing.* The content produced by Wikipedia editors is licensed under Creative Commons, which allows contributions to be made by anyone but provides some protection for the content's future use (Bruns 2008). Medelyan et al. (2009) have argued that such a way of working draws on the ideas of a nineteenth-century philosopher, Charles Sanders

---

* The term crowdsourcing was coined by *Wired* journalist Jeff Howe (2006) to conceptualize a process of Web-based out-sourcing for the procurement of media content, small tasks, even solutions to scientific problems, from the crowd gathered on the Internet.

Peirce, who argued that knowledge had a public character and should be converged upon by participants in what he called a 'community of inquiry'.[*]

More recently, Kittur and Kraut (2010) have begun to explore similarities and differences between what is known about Wikipedia and the wider wikisphere. It is early days in this emerging line of enquiry, but their work suggests that there may be common laws that apply to how co-ordination works, with patterns emerging for how contributors communicate, how workload is distributed and how conflict is resolved, and the Wikimedia software (that generates the Wikipedia website) provides tools that support these collaborative practices. Many of these behavioural patterns are found not only in other wiki projects but also in open source software development.

5.3.2 Explicit Aggregation

Tagging is another area of Web 2.0 that is often cited as demonstrating the power of the crowd. A tag is a keyword that a user attaches to a digital object (e.g. a blog post, picture or video clip) to describe it, usually so that they can find it again at a later date. A tag is thus a form of what are called *metadata*, i.e. data that describe a resource (Morville 2005; Mathes 2004; Alag 2009). Metadata are usually produced and added to a resource by information scientists in order to help other people find what they are looking for and there are two key concepts that are very important. Firstly, the use of taxonomies: hierarchical systems for structuring a classification.[†] Secondly, the use of controlled vocabularies, which try to take account of ambiguity in language (so, for example, there might be strict rules on the use of plurals and what to do about synonymy).[‡]

However, as tags are increasingly being created outside formal classification systems, and by ordinary users rather than information scientists, there is a certain amount of messiness that comes with the territory. When I add a tag to my Flickr photostream, I am free to add whatever words I like. So, for example, whilst a lot of people might tag photos of San Francisco with the obvious tag, 'San Francisco', I might use the shorthand 'SF'. Tags are therefore a form of user-generated content and there are two main types of tagging that Web 2.0 services support (Marlow et al. 2006; Golder and Huberman 2005). Firstly, there is *folksonomy* (or *self-tagging*) where the owner of an item tags that item with their descriptive keywords that will be easy for them to recall later. Flickr is a prime example: a user can upload a photograph and add tags to the photo, but other users cannot by default add additional tags.[§]

---

[*] There remains, however, serious academic debate over the precise nature of such a community. For example, as we will see later on, it is not entirely clear whether Wikipedia is mainly edited by a small number of what might be called 'elite' users or whether it is a genuine expression of the 'power of the crowd'.

[†] Primary examples include the Dewey Decimal classification system for books and the Linnaean system for categorising living creatures.

[‡] There are a number of other issues with the way words are used for describing resources. For a further discussion of some of them, see Golder et al. (2005).

[§] In certain circumstances other users, who have been designated 'friends' of the owner of the photographs, can also add tags, but the vast majority of tagging on the site is by the owner. See Chapter 11 for more details.

FOLKSONOMY VERSUS PERSONOMY

The term *folksonomy* is generally acknowledged to have been coined by Thomas Vander Wal in July 2004 (Morville 2005; Guy and Tonkin 2006; Mathes 2004). His ideas stem, in part, from his experience of building taxonomy systems in commercial environments and finding that successful retrieval was often poor because users could not 'guess' the right keyword to use. He has, however, expressed concern in the recent past about the way the term has been mis-applied and his definition, taken from a blog posting, attempted to clarify some of the issues:

"Folksonomy is the result of personal free tagging of information and objects (anything with a URL) for one's own retrieval. The tagging is done in a social environment (shared and open to others). *The act of tagging is done by the person consuming the information*" (my italics)

(VANDER WAL 2005, BLOG).

Although folksonomy tagging is done in the social environment of a Web 2.0 application, Vander Wal emphasizes that it is *not* collaborative and it is not a form of categorization. He makes the point that tagging done by one person on behalf of another ('in the Internet space' is implied here) is *not* folksonomy* and that the value of a folksonomy is derived from people using their own vocabulary in order to add explicit meaning to the information or object they are consuming (either as a user or producer). However, in much of the academic literature, the term *personomy* has been used to describe an individual's tag collection, with folksonomy being used to describe the combined set of all the personomies within an application or Web service (Hotho et al. 2006).

---

* He describes this as 'social tagging'.

Secondly, there are some Web 2.0 services that provide what is usually called *collaborative tagging* or *free-for-all tagging*, i.e. more than one person can add tags to an item of content. The prime example, and one of the first to do this, is the Delicious bookmarking site. Users who bookmark the same Uniform Resource Identifier (URI) can share in the process of adding tags to that bookmark.

One of the important distinctions between folksonomies and collaborative tagging is the motivation that the user has for engaging in tagging. In folksonomy production, users tag items so that they can find them easily at a later date. Thus, I might tag all the photos in my photostream of family gatherings as 'family'. This is fairly meaningless to others, but at the time I am not particularly interested or motivated to consider the wider potential uses of that tag across the service I am using. Others may, however, deliberately tag their photos to attract the attention of other users or to help other people (Marlow et al. 2006). The issue of motivation is important for our use of terminology—for example, should tags generated to attract attention from others be called 'collaborative'?

In both folksonomies and free-for-all tagging, the tags are generated again and again. By collating information about the frequency with which particular tags are used it is possible to spot emerging trends of interest. This information is often visualised as *tag clouds*, in which tags that are used more often are displayed in larger text. It is the large number of people contributing that leads to opportunities to discern contextual information when the tags are aggregated

(Owen et al. 2006), and Web 2.0 service providers make use of the data held in the mass of tagged objects in their systems through a process often known as *tag gardening* (Governor et al. 2009).

5.3.3 Implicit Aggregation

A term used widely in discussions about harnessing the power of the crowd is *collaborative filtering*. Unfortunately, like many of the concepts discussed in this chapter, it is problematic. The term pre-dates Web 2.0 and was coined by Xerox in 1992 to describe their Information Tapestry software—an experimental mail system developed at their Palo Alto research centre (Goldberg et al. 1992; Terry 1993). They were interested in how to help their research staff filter useful documents from the large volume of individual e-mails and e-mail lists they received. A basic tenet of the work was that information filtering would be more effective if humans could be involved in the process. By this they meant that users should be able to help each other by recording their reactions (such as level of interest) to the documents they read, in what were called *annotations*. Other users could then filter their incoming e-mail stream based on what other readers had said in their annotations. One of the key aspects of this form of filtering was that users were participating for the general good, whilst understanding that they would also benefit personally (Terry 1993; Goldberg et al. 1992).

Later additions to the Tapestry software included an e-mail client that had 'LikeIt' and 'HateIt' buttons and this points us in the direction of the way the term collaborative filtering has come to be used more recently: to describe a type of system that aggregates information about human users, both explicitly and implicitly, irrespective of the level of active 'collaboration' they support. O'Reilly's (2005b) example of the Cloudmark e-mail system is a case in point. The only action that the user needed to take was to highlight those incoming e-mails that they considered to be spam. By sharing these decisions with the Cloudmark system the aggregated data could be used to detect and eliminate the user's spam as well as providing benefit for others. However, although there is an explicit action, can this level of activity really be described as collaborative? Is the primary motivation one of acting for self-interest or the interest of other users?

Where Cloudmark required an explicit action on behalf of the user, other systems aggregate data that is implied. For example, by tracking and recording what a user watches or listens to it is possible to build up a profile of the individual. When this data is aggregated for many users, valuable information can be generated about any particular user in relation to the group. Many music or film recommendation sites work this way, relying on the architecture of participation to constantly update and refine their data. When a user makes a query the software uses a similarity metric to determine a sub-group that most closely matches the preferences of the user. It then analyses the preferences of the sub-group and infers options to recommend to the user. In this example it is much more difficult to justify the term 'collaborative' as these types of service use an architecture of participation model: a user adds to the collection of data about preferences and opinions as a side effect of using the service rather than as a deliberate action. In these latter examples, in sharp contrast to the Wikipedia model, the ownership of the data 'product' belongs to the owners of the service. Although the user can take advantage of the aggregated database they have no rights to the content they have added.[*]

5.4 HARNESSING THE POWER OF CRITICAL THINKING

By analysing different types of Web 2.0 service in this way we begin to see various features emerge. I have presented an illustrative sub-set here as a way of critiquing some of the values that have a tendency to influence the discussion around Web 2.0 but in doing so, do I also run the risk of creating another set of values? Does Wikipedia's collaborative, commons-based peer production paint a picture of it being 'the good guy'? Has the debate become polarised around collaboration/aggregation?

Perhaps it is more helpful to think of a spectrum of different activities with characteristics that can be combined in many ways (where, for example, would eBay's recommendation system sit in a rigidly polarised system?). The important thing, as with many aspects of Web 2.0, is to be prepared to take apart ideas that are uncritically held to be truths in order to reveal new questions that help us with the thinking and research processes. For example, what do we mean by collaboration? What role does motivation play? Who owns the products of the activity of the crowd? What implications do issues of ownership have for the "universally distributed intelligence, constantly enhanced, coordinated in real time, and resulting in the effective mobilization of skills" postulated by Lévy (1997, 13)?

Some of the key Web 2.0 concepts have been described using terminology that has been borrowed from earlier technology contexts or even different knowledge domains and the transfer has not always resulted in an accurate application of the old concept to the new scenario. Being able to understand and critique this will become more and more important as studying the Web becomes increasingly inter-disciplinary.

This is particularly true for openness—the subject of the next chapter. Openness is one of the most complex and nuanced Web 2.0 ideas and by examining some of its complexity we can see how, once again, positive qualities have been ascribed to Web 2.0 through the use of a term that has been applied uncritically. The following chapter will attempt to unravel some of these issues and provide a framework for thinking about what it means to describe something as 'open'.

EXERCISES AND POINTS TO PONDER

1. Wagner et al. (2010) assume that individuals are 'independently' applying diverse ways of solving problems. However, on the Web it is often true that people in the crowd are aware of, and can be influenced by, others' ideas. Consider this distinction and its implications in the context of the quote from Lévy: "no one knows everything, everyone knows something, all knowledge resides in humanity".

2. What does understanding the history of 'collaborative filtering' tell us about how such terms have become distorted when applied to discussions of Web 2.0? What other terms have been distorted? Why is this kind of distortion a problem?

---

[*] For an example see Last.fm's terms and conditions: http://www.last.fm/legal/terms#para3

3. The tag cloud is an important concept for developing Web-based software that exhibits some of the ideas of collective intelligence discussed in this chapter. A fuller discussion of tag clouds is provided in Chapter 12. When you have read these two chapters, develop a software program to display tag clouds. In order to do this, set up an account on the Delicious social bookmarking site and populate it with content and suitable tags. Develop a software program that uses the Delicious Application Programming Interface (API) to extract details of these tags and then displays a tag cloud. Details of the Delicious API are provided at: http://www.delicious.com/help/api and you may also find this Web Monkey article on the API of use: http://www.webmonkey.com/2010/02/using_the_delicious_api/. There is also a detailed discussion of different programming approaches in Chapter 3 of Satnam Alag's book (Alag 2009) which you may find helpful.

FURTHER READING

A more detailed analysis of the dynamics of crowds, flows of information and decision making can be found in Chapters 16 and 22 of Easley and Kleinberg (2010).

For far more detail on the mechanism of collaborative tagging and discussion as to whether it fits a power law, see Halpin et al. (2007).

MIT's Centre for Collective Intelligence is a good source of additional material (http://cci.mit.edu/). Their resources include a review of evidence, Malone et al. (2009), from an analysis of 250 examples of 'collective intelligence' on the Web.

Psychologists are exploring how intelligence resides in human groups in order to learn lessons for using the power of online groups. See for example the work of Anita Williams Woolley.[*]

Two useful introductions to some of the issues of developing software that exhibits some aspects of collective intelligence theory are Segaran (2007) and Alag (2009).

A related area, which is gaining interest within the research community, is the study of *games with a purpose*. These are games that require human participation to complete a task that would otherwise be computationally difficult for the computer to undertake. For example, a game in which images are labelled. Ahn and Dabbish (2008) provide an introduction.

---

[*] See: http://public.tepper.cmu.edu/facultydirectory/FacultyDirectoryProfile.aspx?id=282

## CHAPTER 6

Openness

Web 2.0 is the popular name of a new generation of Web applications, sites and companies that emphasise openness, community and interaction.

DAVID E. MILLARD AND MARTIN ROSS
(*2006, 1*)

Because of their inherent sociality and openness, Web 2.0 capabilities can stimulate a particularly reciprocal relationship between the technology and its users.

HERTOGH ET AL.
(*2011, 127*)

In his exposition on Web 2.0, O'Reilly (2005b) emphasized openness as a key characteristic. This ranged from using open source software to develop Web 2.0 services, to the role of mass participation in the development of online resources such as Wikipedia. He also outlined the sharp contrast between the open ways of working through the Web as Platform concept (using open standards, protocols and software) compared to the 'closed' world of the centralised, monolithic, proprietary operating system. From this point of view, Web 2.0 practices such as involving users in the development of the software (made possible by the perpetual beta development cycle) and providing services that are free of charge can also be presented as badges of openness: users are being treated in an 'open' way and the product is also being developed in the open.

These ideas have manifested themselves in other ways. Walker (2005), for example, equates openness in Web 2.0 with the idea of the untamed, free nature of wild animals by arguing that mass participation, user-generated content and a lack of centralising control has meant that hypertext has, in effect, 'gone feral'. Others point to a highly developed social norm within many Web 2.0 user communities that champions sharing and collaboration (Palfrey and Gasser 2007).

However, we should say at the outset that ascribing openness to Web 2.0 in this uncritical way is problematic, and susceptible to vagueness and confusion (Murray-Rust 2008).

It reinterprets the history of a particular, technology-mediated notion of openness in such a way that 'Web 2.0' is associated with 'good'. In this chapter we will see how this has come about by examining the roots and culture of openness, which emerged out of early Internet technology developments; the principles of openness on the Web and how these are being undermined; the practices of openness, particularly with respect to the real-world practices of standards bodies, open source software production, Creative Commons and open data. This will provide the tools to understand the different ways in which openness can be interpreted and to critique how it is ascribed to Web 2.0.

Finally, we will explore how the Web 2.0 theme of maximizing financial return from monetizing unique datasets is at odds with the idea of openness, based on existing business models. We will look at how the Web's economic value has been calculated in the past and where it has gone wrong, and I will argue that what is fundamentally important, before trying to calculate monetary value, is to understand the size and shape of the Web, and how fast it is growing.

6.1 THE ROOTS OF OPENNESS ON THE WEB

The Web's propensity for openness is in large part due to its inventor, Sir Tim Berners-Lee, who resisted the temptation to make money out of asserting and exploiting intellectual property rights (IPR).* When asked about this in an interview at the Web 2.0 Summit conference in 2009, he replied that he had seen too many promising documentation systems fail because of attempts to control what was allowed to be added to the system (O'Reilly and Berners-Lee 2009). He knew that to gain widespread acceptance the system had to be "really, really flexible" [1:00] and to his mind, releasing the Web with as few restrictions as possible was the only way he could achieve this.

Berners-Lee went on to explain that in order to give his online document system a global reach he was effectively asking every owner of a document or other publishable content to put it on the Web by labelling it with a URI, and this was a big thing to ask. Requiring payment as well would have been too much. However this was not the only reason: Berners-Lee had, as a scientific researcher, spent many years immersed in the culture of the early Internet—and the dominant culture of the Internet was one of openness.

6.1.1 A Short History of the Internet

The Internet had been around for a good many years by the time the Web was invented in 1989. Indeed, Tim Berners-Lee was just a small child when the event that catalysed the development of ARPANet, the forerunner of the Internet, took place.

In 1957, at the height of the Cold War, the Soviet Union's launch of Sputnik—the first ever satellite—sent shock waves through the American public. The government panic that ensued, eventually resulted in the foundation of a special research division of the American

---

* See Section 6.3.1 for more on IPR.

Defense Department, called the Advanced Research Projects Agency (ARPA). One of this agency's projects was to develop a communications network that would join up various computing centres and research groups spread across the country.

One of the key goals of this new network was that it should be able to survive a nuclear attack and provide improved 'second strike' capability (Baran 2009). This was seen as very important because in the late 1950s, US military planners ran simulations as to what would happen to the nation's telecommunications and military networking capability during a major attack and the results showed that although large parts of the wiring between different centres might survive, key switching and routing centres would be lost and this would cause the whole network to fail.

At the time, computer networks and the main telecommunications system were vulnerable because they were too centralised: there was too much reliance on key hubs or control points in the network. What was needed was a distributed network—one with many points and no hierarchy or centralised control—in order to minimize vulnerability. Making such a distributed system work was difficult and involved a number of new concepts in network communications, many of which were developed by Paul Baran at the RAND Corporation. Three engineering *principles* were introduced on which the Internet still operates today: decentralised network structure; distribution of the network's control processing across the individual points of the system; large-scale redundancy so that if some of the points are broken or congested the overall system still functions.

In order to get these principles to work in a real network, a number of new ideas and technologies needed to be introduced. The most important development was to make use of digital communication as digital signals can pass through a large number of intermediate points without degrading, unlike the analogue networks in use at the time, which had a limit of around five such steps.

PACKET SWITCHING

A NEW IDEA FOR THE DIGITAL NETWORK

Perhaps the best-known innovation was *packet switching*, a concept that still underpins the Internet today. Packet switching allowed engineers to design the distributed and flexible digital network that was envisaged, by breaking messages into a number of small, discrete packets.

The packets are sent individually over the decentralised network and are free to travel by whatever route becomes available. At the other end, the whole message is re-constructed from the individual packets. In this way, if a particular link in the network chain is damaged or working slowly due to congestion, packets can be diverted around the problem. In the late 1950s this was a very different way of thinking about communication: existing, analogue networks worked by creating a circuit between two nodes that wished to communicate. Such a circuit had to be maintained for as long as it took to make a telephone call or send data and were therefore particularly susceptible to disruption.

The embryonic network, ARPANet, was launched in September 1969 and connected four nodes: the University of California, Los Angeles; Stanford Research Institute; University of California, Santa Barbara; and the University of Utah. By the early 1970s, discussions were taking place about how to connect this military research network with others such as the research network at University College London. Thus was borne the Internet's founding concept: a *network of networks* (Kirstein 1999). This was consolidated by the work of Vint Cerf, Robert Metcalfe, Jon Postel, Robert Kahn and others who developed the Internet's basic architecture and the communication protocols: TCP/IP (Leiner et al. 2009; Mowery and Simcoe 2002). At this time the word 'internet' was coined to refer to a network that made use of the new protocols.

In the early 1980s ARPANet was split into two: a secret military network and ARPA-Internet, dedicated to research in general. By the mid 1980s the National Science Foundation had become involved in running the latter and over the following few years it was opened up to give access to corporations and the general public and it became the Internet as we know it today. By the late 1980s this network was commonly referred to as 'The Internet'.

PROTOCOLS

Just as diplomatic protocols are an agreed way of behaving between countries, a computer or communications protocol is a set of rules about how a piece of software or equipment should behave. They are especially prevalent in organising how different software components or hardware systems communicate with each other through various messaging systems. Although diplomatic protocols tend to be informal, consisting of unwritten rules and centuries-old forms of common courtesy, computer-related protocols are formal and well documented. It is for this reason that many people confuse standards with protocols.

In terms of the Internet, the *Transmission Control Protocol* (TCP) and the *Internet Protocol* (IP) were the first two networking protocols in the *Internet Protocol Suite*, the set of communications protocols used for the Internet.[*]

What is important to remember is that it is highly unlikely that these developments would have taken place in a commercial arena—the risks were too great and the potential benefits far too long-term for any acceptable return on investment (Castells 2001). Indeed, the large telecommunications companies of the day resisted this new paradigm and the largest, AT&T, turned down a number of opportunities to commercialize the research work (Baran 2009). According to the eminent sociologist Manuel Castells (2001), early developments took place in the "twilight zone of the resource-rich, relatively free spaces created by ARPA, the universities, innovative think-tanks, and major research centres" (p. 23), and this resulted in the emergence of a particular culture based around the Internet.

---

[*] See: http://tools.ietf.org/html/rfc1122

6.1.2 Ethos of Early Internet Development

We reject: kings, presidents, and voting. We believe in: rough consensus and running code.

DAVID D. CLARK, 1992[*]

As we have just seen, although the Internet was driven initially by the military and by military planning, the engineering innovations were carried out in rather different environments. In particular, Castells (2001) has argued that much of the work was carried out by (post-) graduate students who were "permeated with the values of individual freedom, of independent thinking, and of sharing and co-operating with peers—all values that characterised the campus culture of the 1960s" (p. 24). He has argued that these factors shaped the technological development of the early Internet to the extent that the idea of freedom, which is so important to the Web today, was "culturally determined". He has also argued that a number of cultural layers came together on the early Internet with the most important for our discussion of openness being the Techno-meritocratic and the Hacker.

The *techno-meritocratic* culture is rooted in academia and science in the sense that, in the academic world, merit arises from the publication of papers. In this respect, publication is a form of openness in that it comes from the wider emphasis in science of sharing data, being reviewed by your peers, and producing results that can be replicated.

As the early pioneers of the Internet's technologies were often academics or researchers, these values were transferred across. Much as academics accrue respect through peer review and publishing, the techno-meritocratic culture places value on achieving merit through the development of ingenious and well-constructed technical ideas and software code that is admired by others and, crucially, which contributes in some way to "a technological system that provides a common good for the community ..." (Castells 2001, 39). Merit can only be achieved through one's peers and so clear communication of new ideas, particularly through the sharing of software, was important.

The *hacker* culture Castells refers to is not the one represented by the popular media (i.e. breaking into secure systems and spreading viruses and malware). The original hackers were a group of programming pioneers who liked to interact online through the early computer networks, working together on joint projects and adhering to a common set of cultural values that were essentially techno-meritocratic.[†]

---

[*] Internet pioneer and MIT professor David D. Clark coined the phrase 'we reject kings' during a presentation to the Internet Engineering Task Force (IETF) in July 1992 (Clark 1992, 543). The idea was to capture the essence of what counted to the Internet pioneers: that an idea or new technology must work well, rather than being imposed because it had been championed by a corporate lobbyist or a charismatic leader within a standards committee (for more on this see Chapter 14).

[†] It is often forgotten that until the late 1960s most computer software was provided for free by hardware manufacturers and there was also another type of freedom: to use, adapt, re-purpose and redistribute the software at will. Universities were actively involved in the development of this software and members of staff wrote and shared their own education and research-based applications in a process that we now recognise as the forerunner of open source software.

What was important in this early hacker culture was that code could be shared, examined by programmer peers, modified and then shared again. There was also a culture of *gifting*—of freely contributing help to other people's software development projects in the expectation of help with one's own projects.

These values of sharing and gifting fed into something quite concrete in the development of the early Web. The earliest browsers developed by Tim Berners-Lee and his colleagues at CERN and other research establishments all featured a 'View Source' facility which allowed the reader of an HTML document to easily see the underlying tag code. As Vint Cerf noted in a panel discussion to mark the twentieth anniversary of the Web, this early feature meant that people in effect trained each other: "it was almost like a medieval apprentice arrangement where you could learn from other people—if you liked their webpage you could copy them and this notion of learning by doing and learning by sharing, I thought was one of the most powerful engines behind the spread of the Web" (Cerf 2009, 11:50).

Finally, there is one more strand to the story of the early development of the Internet—a last hurdle for it to overcome. In the 1980s and 1990s the Internet was competing against proprietary networks from companies such as AOL, CompuServe and Prodigy. These provided Internet-like communications networks and access—for a price—to online content and to tools such as e-mail and bulletin board messaging. Although these were based on the same technologies that had been developed in Castell's non-commercial 'twilight zone', they were separate networks being run by companies for profit.

Ultimately these networks did not survive. They were too reliant on centralised control and, although arguably for good commercial reasons, had developed what became known as *walled gardens*: information spaces in which content was kept away from other networks so that, for example, one could only send an e-mail to a person in the same network. Although a veritable minnow in the early 1990s, the Internet ultimately triumphed as the global communications network solution, in large part because its open philosophy offered so many more possibilities, both commercial and non-commercial.

6.2 PRINCIPLES OF OPENNESS

The Web was built on egalitarian principles to be a system in which: "any person could share information with anyone else, anywhere" (Berners-Lee 2010, 1). There are four core principles, underlying the way the Internet and Web have been constructed, that underpin this open architecture: net neutrality, universality, decentralisation and layered architecture.

6.2.1 Net Neutrality

Net neutrality holds that all communications traffic should be treated equally. That is, anyone who wishes to use the Internet to communicate should be able to do so and there should not be systems in place that prioritize one type of traffic or a particular company's content over another. This is sometimes also referred to as the *best effort approach*, i.e. a best effort is made by the network provider in all cases and for all types of traffic. It has its roots in one of the key architectural principles of the early Internet known as the *end-to-end principle* (Saltzer et al. 1984) which states that the complexity in the network should be concentrated at the ends, where the users connect devices such as PCs and printers. The middle part of the network—the Internet 'cloud'—should be as simple as possible, carrying out its basic task of transferring communications traffic. To give priority to one sort of data over another adds complexity, which needs to be avoided if the Internet is to remain a decentralised and resilient system.

Since 2003, net neutrality has been the subject of some debate, particularly with the advent of bandwidth-intensive tasks like video streaming, and has been threatened on a number of occasions by government policy makers and large telecommunications companies. Some companies would like to prioritize traffic since it would help them deliver a better quality of service for these traffic-heavy tasks and would also allow them to prioritize access to content for commercial gain (for example, a website owner could pay its Internet Service Provider a kind of 'speed tax' to make sure that users trying to connect to their site can do so faster).

Tim Berners-Lee has remarked on the continuing debate as to whether exceptions should be allowed to the principle of net neutrality, in particular debates about a proposal by Google and Verizon that Web traffic from mobile devices should be treated differently (Berners-Lee 2010). He wonders aloud whether it is time to consider some legal enforcement of net neutrality and in fact, a number of countries, including Canada, France, Norway, UK and US, are considering doing just that (Ofcom 2010).

6.2.2 Universality

The principle of *universality* (or more simply *Web for All*) means that there should be no restriction on the type of information the Web can incorporate, with all information linked simply by hypertext and a Uniform Resource Identifier (URI). There should be universal access with no restrictions on the type of computer hardware or software, the human language used, or either the physical or mental abilities of the user. Where the Internet created a network of networks, which meant that users did not need to worry about how to communicate with another computer, the Web added a further layer of abstraction: it prioritized the resource, signified by the universality of the URI, rather than the computer it happened to be located on.

However, certain Web 2.0 services are beginning to challenge the principle of universality. Sites such as MySpace and Facebook are becoming walled gardens in a similar way to the proprietary networks of the 1980s and 1990s. The technical concern is that each piece of information does not have a URI and thus is only accessible from within the site itself. This is a fundamental break with the underlying architecture of the Web and Berners-Lee warns: "The more this kind of architecture gains widespread use, the more the Web becomes fragmented, and the less we enjoy a single, universal information space" (Berners-Lee 2010, 2).

---

* See: http://www.w3.org/Consortium/mission

The corollary of this is that the data that users put in to a social networking site become 'locked in' to that particular service (because they do not have a URI and cannot be linked to from other parts of the Web). This means that some services are creating 'silos' of data that have been closed off from the rest of the Web (W3C Incubator Group 2010).

Another form of walled garden is being created by the increasing popularity of Web 2.0 *apps*, applications that only run on a smartphone or a tablet computer (such as the iPad). We will return to this in more detail in Chapter 14, but for now we should note that Berners-Lee is concerned because apps are small client programmes running on the phone or tablet's operating system and not within a Web browser. One cannot link to the pages within a magazine app in the same way as a webpage within a magazine's website. Apps are therefore not part of the wider Web even though they use some of the underlying Web standards to communicate.

6.2.3 Decentralisation

The Web also has a principle of *decentralisation*—there is no central authority deciding what is allowed or whether or not a certain user can add a hypertext link. As Berners-Lee (1998) has argued, it is commonly accepted in systems design that any single, central controlling point that is involved in an operation tends to limit the way the system scales, and produces a single potential point of failure. The lack of a single controlling point is therefore very important to how the Web has been conceived. It is reinforced by the Web's technical standards, which are open and royalty-free (see Section 6.3.1) so that people can create applications without making a payment or requiring permission from a centralised authority.

6.2.4 Layered Architecture

The fourth principle is the *layered architecture.*[*] The Internet and Web are often represented as an hourglass in order to demonstrate that there are a number of technology layers, each one building on top of the one below[†] (Zittrain 2008; Deering 2001). The bottom half of the glass represents the various ways of physically connecting to the Internet, which is itself made up of layers (see Figure 6.1). The top half represents what might be termed the 'uses' or applications of the Internet. The hourglass waist is the layer that handles the IP, on which all uses are built and to which all the various connection technologies lead. The size and pinched shape of this layer makes visible the idea that the IP is as simple and feature-free as possible, making no restrictions on what can be built on top of it. It also reflects the lack of any alternatives for this layer of the network. As we can see from the diagram, the Web runs on top of the Internet and indeed is just one of a variety of possible applications.

---

[*] Architecture is used here to refer to the way a software system is structured internally.
[†] The basic idea of an hourglass shape describing networks was first outlined in a report in 1994 called *Realizing the Information Future*, although the idea has been refined over the years. See: http://books.nap.edu/ openbook.php?recor d_id=4755&page=53 #p200063459960 053001

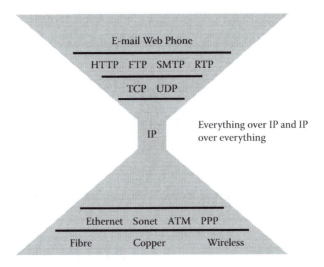

FIGURE 6.1 The Internet hourglass. (Illustration © 2011 Intelligent Content Ltd Licensed under a Creative Commons Attribution-NonCommercial-NoDerivs 3.0 Unported license (CC BY-NR-ND 3.0)).

This layered structure means that the two can develop independently. Thus, the underlying network has been speeded up enormously since the Web was introduced in 1990, but there have been no changes needed to Web protocols to handle this.

6.2.5 The Implication of Openness

Zittrain (2008) has noted an important implication of openness: generality. By this he means that because the Internet and Web have been engineered to be open systems, they can be extended in new and innovative ways. Formally, he defines this as: "[a] system's capacity to produce unanticipated change through unfiltered contributions from broad and varied audiences" (Zittrain 2008, 70). He argues that generality is under threat from moves that may affect openness such as efforts to undermine net neutrality.

6.3 OPENNESS IN PRACTICE

As stated earlier, there is a general sense in which openness has been ascribed to Web 2.0 in such a way as to assign positive qualities to it. However, by looking at the technological development of the Internet and the Web we have been able to see that, far from being a benevolent influence, some Web 2.0 services create walled gardens and undermine net neutrality.

However, this is not the end of the story. Next, we will look at some of the ways that openness manifests itself as a set of practises—within standards bodies, open source software, Creative Commons and open data—in order to understand where the idea of 'open' as 'good' originates. We will see how, once we start to look at some of the detail, there are different degrees of openness that have different implications. This should make us more thoughtful about how we interpret claims of openness and, hopefully, when someone describes something as 'open' our response will become: "what do you mean by 'open'?"

6.3.1 Open Standards

In a general sense, standards are commonly accepted agreements on ways to do or make things. Imagine how much easier life would be if we only needed one electricity charger for all our different gadgets. Establishing standards is therefore partly about ensuring compatibility (or *interoperability*) between products but it also has additional benefits. Standards may establish a minimum level of quality, or reduce the amount of variety, allowing for economies of scale (imagine how difficult and expensive life would be if each charger needed to be plugged into its own type of wall socket).

Open standards are the bedrock of the Internet and Web. They allow different groups of technologists to work on different areas of the Internet and Web in parallel, confident that when systems are put together they will interoperate. Open standards also help to avoid the anti-competitive nature of *vendor lock-in*, where one company has too much power over a market because it controls a proprietary (or 'closed') standard.*

While it is fairly easy to identify a closed standard, it is more difficult to be sure about what constitutes openness (Cerri and Fuggetta 2007; Kelly 2006), although it is important to be clear that, in a general sense, open standards are seen as a good thing and have been very important in the Web's success (Herman 2006)—something I shall explain in more detail in Chapter 14. For now, all we need to know is that how open a standard is perceived to be depends on a combination of different factors, including:

- The process: the mix of people involved in creating the standard, the stages the standard goes through before it is approved and the extent to which a wide range of opinions has been taken into account

- The speed by which the standard is created: too fast and there is the danger that not enough care has been taken or that the processes have not been sufficiently democratic; too slow and the standard risks being irrelevant before it has even been published

- The cost of accessing and using the standard

- Any copyright or IPR impediments to implementing the standard

If we use just these criteria, we can begin to define an open standard as a standard that is produced through careful, democratic processes and is either free of charge or has a very low cost associated with using it. From this we can start to see how openness has become associated with 'good', or at least better than average. Providing products free of charge or at very low cost is a theme that recurs throughout the discussion of openness.

---

* Proprietary standards are created and owned by individual companies for use within their organisation and by their customers, who may be charged a fee to use them.

INTELLECTUAL PROPERTY RIGHTS

In the broadest sense, *intellectual property rights* (IPR) is the name given to a group of legal rights that confer exclusive control over the products of human creativity or ingenuity, for a fixed amount of time (the *term*), to their creators. Once the term of the right has expired, the creative work passes into the public domain where it can be copied, adapted and distributed. Intellectual property rights subsist in a range of creative/inventive endeavours, are manifested in different forms (from copyright through to patents) and encompass areas of law as diverse as trademarks and plant breeders' rights.

Although a good deal of legal and economic theory underpins the idea of IPR, at the heart of the matter is an attempt to solve a simple dilemma: how can the people who invest time and resources in solving a particular problem or creating a work of art or entertainment, make a living from their work? Granting rights to the creators ensures that they can maintain some form of exclusive market—an artist can sell her own paintings—or sell the rights to that market for someone else to exploit, such as a writer to a book publisher (Boyle 2008; Korn and Oppenheim 2007; Lessig 2004). This is at the heart of the IPR-based business model: the ability to licence, for a fee, certain rights in the protected work. Traditionally, an IPR-based business model has been seen as more lucrative than a service-based business model as a licensor can issue many licences and make money several times over from the same invention.

The quid pro quo for this protected status is that once the term of the right expires the work becomes public property, ensuring that new ideas permeate society. In addition, and crucially with patents, the ideas generated in the course of creating the patented product, are available for the rest of society to see, throughout the life of the right, although no one else can exploit them commercially. In this way, patents are supposed to act as a form of protected disclosure and provide a stimulus for further innovation and creation.

However, IPR has been a cause of considerable controversy within the computer industry, not least because the main technical building block, software, is subject to different treatment in different legal jurisdictions. In the UK, for example, software is treated as a text (it is the 'expression' of the idea that is protected rather than the idea itself) and is therefore protected using copyright. In the US, however, software can be patented, which prohibits the unauthorized use of the technical solution itself (the idea) contained within the software. This latter approach is particularly problematic since software can also be seen as an algorithm—a type of mathematical formula—and it is widely accepted that the idea contained within an algorithm cannot be restricted by any form of IPR.*

6.3.2 Free and Open Source Software

In a nutshell, 'free' (in the sense of both 'freedom' and 'free of charge') and open source software (FOSS) is software code that is open to scrutiny, modification and reuse, and which can be redistributed in its new form. As O'Reilly makes clear in his original article, FOSS plays a major role in the infrastructure of Web 2.0 services and applications. Indeed, FOSS has been critical in the development of the Internet and Web in general, including the provision of key items of infrastructure such as the Apache HTTP Server and the Mozilla Firefox browser.

---

* This is a distinction that has been noted by people such as Richard Stallman, a software pioneer who has developed the idea of 'free software'.

Usually FOSS is created by peer production through the collaborative efforts of disparate individuals who come together to complete a project. In terms of IPR this means that no one, particular individual or company has exclusive rights to the code. This is why, in commercial terms, it is often seen as the poor relation to proprietary software—one of the common misconceptions is that 'you can't make money out of something that's free of charge'. In fact, there are many companies operating successful business models based on FOSS, and there is a lot of innovation taking place in service-based business models.[*]

However, as with open standards, there are different interpretations of both freedom and openness that are accepted by different organisations. Open source software, for example, is software that has been released under a licence that has been certified by the *Open Source Initiative* (OSI), which describes in legal terms what can and cannot be done. These licences are certified to meet the criteria of the Open Source Definition (OSD).[†] Free software, however, must meet the criteria of the *Free Software Foundation* (FSF) and conform to the Free Software Definition (FSD).[‡] As one example, software produced by the *Apache Software Foundation* (ASF) meets the criteria of the OSI, but does not necessarily meet the requirements of the FSF. So one way to understand the differences is to look at how the different organisations interpret notions such as 'open' and 'free'.

The ASF is quite clear that its use of 'freedom' focuses on the freedoms of software developers, who should be completely free to develop code as they wish with no impediment, legal or otherwise (Anderson 2009). One of the implications of this is they emphasize openness in the software development method. Every decision is made in public and recorded so that there is always a clear record as to how the code came to be the way it is. Other open source projects, whilst they may make the code public, do not necessarily make all records from the development process open.

However, whilst the ASF's code is open source at the point of publication, what happens to it after that is of less concern. So, if for example a company wanted to build ASF code into a proprietary product, the ASF licence allows them to do it (as does the OSI licence). This is quite different to, say, the FSF, which insists that code which carries their licence can only be used in other software that meets the FSD. This is fundamentally an issue of freedom—the ASF's primary concern is that developers should have the freedom to develop code as they wish. For the FSF however, it is the *users* that should have complete freedom to view, use, modify and redistribute code, something they cannot do if open source code is running in a proprietary product.

This worldview is often considered to be personified by one the earliest hackers, Richard Stallman, the founder of the Free Software Foundation and a constant critic of 'closed', proprietary software. To Stallman, software is an issue of free speech—the right to access and inspect source code to see what it is doing should be a fundamental right in the information age.[§]

---

[*] See: http://www.oss-wat ch.ac.uk/resources/businessandsustainability.xml

[†] http://www.opensource.org/docs/osd

[‡] http://www.gnu.org/philosophy/free-sw.html

[§] For more on these debates see: http://www.oss-wa tch.ac.uk/resources/Stallman.xml and http://www.oss-watch.ac.uk/resources/erenkrantz.xml

6.3.3 Creative Commons

Copyright is a form of IPR that prohibits unauthorized copying of original works such as books, maps, films etc. Generally speaking, existing copyright rules mean that as soon as an author creates an original work, restrictions are instantly, and automatically, applied. However, not everybody wants this level of restriction, particularly if they are interested in sharing their content with others and allowing them to repurpose it. *Creative Commons* provides a simple mechanism for getting around this formality and for being clear about what the author will allow. However, it is important to understand that it does not challenge the existing system of copyright, rather it builds upon it: the author does not give up their copyright, they refine it. There are, for example, rules about how the originator of the work is attributed when a copy is made and whether or not copies can be used for commercial purposes. In order to do this, Creative Commons has licences that describe intermediate rights positions between 'all rights reserved' and 'no rights reserved' (Boyle 2008).

The Creative Commons movement was begun by Lawrence Lessig and James Boyle in 2001 with the aim of expanding the collection of creative work available for others to build upon and share (Flew 2005; UKOLN 2008). Its first licence was released in 2002, and although initially developed for use in the United States, it has since been expanding to take account of the legal systems in more than 50 countries.

Creative Commons licences consist of three separate layers (O'Sullivan 2008). The first is the 'human-readable' description of the licence, which explains the rights granted in simple language. The second layer is the licence itself, intended principally for lawyers. Finally there is a machine-readable version of the licence, which enables computers to automatically 'understand' how the content can be shared.

O'Reilly mentions the Creative Commons licences, which were just starting to appear in 2005 when he wrote his seminal article, as they were popularizing a new approach to IPR. They have been a boon for the creation and sharing of user-generated content, as they provide content authors with a mechanism for being clear about the conditions under which their content can be copied, reused or repurposed (Zittrain 2008).

6.3.4 Open Data

Open Data is a term used to describe data that anyone is free to use, reuse and redistribute without restriction (except, perhaps, the requirement to attribute the originators) (Murray-Rust 2008; Rodriguez 2009; Miller et al. 2008). Its most freely available form is data that are fully in the public domain where all rights are waived. There is a particularly strong movement towards open data in the sciences, where the ability to publish experimental data and allow others to re-use it is seen as enormously beneficial, an approach that is closely linked to open access scholarship (Jacobs 2006). There have also been moves towards opening up public sector and Government data sources (Shadbolt 2010).

Open Data is rapidly becoming a very important area that will have profound consequences for the evolution of the Web and we will look at this in more detail in the final chapter.

6.4 APPLYING IDEAS OF OPENNESS TO WEB 2.0

After all these different examples and detailed discussion we should be starting to see that openness is a highly nuanced concept. With this in mind, what does it mean to say that a Web 2.0 service is open? Do we mean that it has been built using open standards? Possibly. Do we mean that its software contains some sort of open source code? Maybe. However, as we should now know, even services that are built using open protocols and open source software can still be 'closed' and proprietary. In fact, when we inspect Web 2.0 services, the most we can say with any kind of reliability is that, from the users' perspective, they are free of charge at the point of use.

If we apply the six big ideas as an analytical tool we will see something quite different. The architecture of participation for example: services that have been designed to facilitate mass user participation in order to accumulate data that will allow the systems to improve themselves as a consequence. Or perhaps data on an epic scale: the huge, proprietary data-sets that are being accumulated by Web 2.0 companies as a consequence of the architecture of participation.

In order to gain insight into some of the implications of this we will look at one more piece of the Web 2.0 jigsaw: so-called *open APIs*, the main tool for the collection and pro-cessing of the phenomenal amounts of data we learned about in Chapter 4. This is impor-tant because, as we know, Web 2.0 was originally coined as a term to describe new business models, and the collection, maintenance and reuse of enormous datasets has become a crucial component of the Web 2.0 business model (O'Reilly and Battelle 2009).

6.4.1 Open APIs

An *Application Programming Interface* (API) provides a mechanism for programmers to use the functionality of a piece of software, and to develop new innovations and services on top of it, without having access to the source code. It is widely used in Web 2.0, for example YouTube, eBay and Twitter all provide APIs that allow other Web services a certain degree of access to their data.

An API that doesn't require the user or programmer to licence or pay royalties is often described as 'open'. However, as we should now be able to see, this is a rather limited use of a highly nuanced term. In fact, although these APIs are free of charge at the point of use, most of them are fully proprietary.* In general, any data that is transferred into the API becomes the property of the company that provides that service.†

This is an important point since, whilst many developers and industry commentators talk about openness in terms of the API, there are those who argue that for a service it is the data rather than the software that need to be open and, further, that to be truly open a user should be able to move or take back their data at will. Tim Bray, an inventor of Extensible Markup Language (XML), argues that a service claiming to be open must agree that: "Any data that you give us, we'll let you take away again, without withholding anything, or

---

* To help improve clarity in these matters, the *Open Knowledge Foundation* publishes the Open Software Service Definition (OSSD), a formal (and strict) definition of what it means to be open when providing an online service.
† Although to different degrees. Compare for example Facebook's API terms and conditions with OpenSocial.

encoding it in a proprietary format, or claiming any intellectual property rights whatsoever" (Bray 2006, webpage).

However, the Web 2.0 business model depends on companies creating and exploiting *unique* datasets (O'Reilly and Battelle 2009), and by definition, datasets cannot be unique if their data are freely available and others are allowed unrestricted access to them. Current logic dictates that in order to extract the maximum economic value from your dataset you need to have exclusive rights to it. Furthermore, to complete the Web 2.0 cycle of creating a blueprint for emerging business models there has to be a way of monetizing the datasets that these companies are creating.

In the past, the value of Web-based businesses has been calculated by ascribing economic value to the rate of growth of the Web as a network. However, the nature of the Web was misunderstood and the methods used to calculate economic value were flawed, and these were contributing factors to the dot-com boom and bust of the early 2000s. In fact, before an accurate system for valuing the datasets of Web 2.0 companies can be developed, there are three remaining questions that need to be answered: how big is the Web, how fast is it growing, and how can these factors be turned into a formula for calculating economic value? This leads us into the last of the six big ideas: the network effect and Web topology.

EXERCISES AND POINTS TO PONDER

1. Compare the terms and conditions of the Facebook API with the OpenSocial API using the criteria discussed in this chapter. What differences do you notice?

2. The W3C's 2010 report on the Social Web stated that "many social networking sites considered privacy and portability to be contradictory" (W3C Incubator Group 2010, webpage). Discuss in class what they might mean by this and undertake some research into what others have written about this.

3. Read the Open Knowledge Foundation (OKF)'s Open Software Service Definition. Compare the requirements with the API of one of the well-known Web 2.0 services, (not Facebook or OpenSocial). Create a table that demonstrates how the service performs in relation to the OKF's criteria.

FURTHER READING

For much detail on the history of the Internet and the origins of the Web see Jafner and Lyon (2003) and Naughton (1999).

For more on hacker culture and the rise of open and free source software, see *First Monday* journal's special edition in 2003: http://firstmo nday.org/htbin/cgi wrap/bin/ojs/index.php/ fm/issue/view/212

For more discussion on net neutrality, see the talk Tim Wu (who coined the term) did for the RSA in 2011: http://www.t hersa.org/event s/audio-and-past-events/2011/the-rise-and-fall-of-in formation-empires

For a much more detailed explanation of the need for Web 2.0 to be open and for online social networks in particular to share data, see the W3C Incubator Group's 2010 report (W3C Incubator Group 2010).

## CHAPTER 7

The Network Effect and Web Topology

What Size and Shape Is the Web and Why Does It Matter?

Advantage came to Google for seeing more deeply into the nature of the network, and building tools to harvest and apply data that was hidden in the network graph.

TIM O'REILLY
(*2008, Blog*)

What we are discovering with Web 2.0 is that companies have learned to capitalize or to monetize this network effect and its exponential value in different ways.

PROF. AMY SHUEN
In Interview (Shuen 2008, 01:10)

In a few years the exact design patterns for triggering a new MySpace, Facebook, or similar social juggernaut will become common … for now the secret balance of Web 2.0 techniques that powers growth through efficient access to network effects is still an art.

DION HINCHCLIFFE
(*2006, Blog*)

The Web is staggeringly enormous: at the time of this writing, it is a network of over 19 billion webpages (nodes), created by over a billion people, and connected by a vast array of hypertext links.* It can be modelled using a mathematical graph and at the heart of Tim O'Reilly's comment (above) is the belief that a truly deep understanding of the sheer scale of the Web and the shapes formed in its graph structure will help define how much money can

---

* Estimates vary, but see: http://www.worldwidewebsize.com/ for an example. Google announced in 2008 that they had found one trillion unique URIs, but this is not quite the same as unique webpages.

be made out of a new Web 2.0 service. In essence, those who understand and 'work with the grain' of the Web are more likely to triumph in the battle for a user's attention and loyalty.

There are two key concepts that have a bearing on a discussion of what it means to work with the grain of the Web in this way. We'll discuss both in detail in this chapter. The first is to do with the size of the Web as a network, or, more precisely, the economic and social implications of adding new users to a Web-based service. This is known as the *network effect* and it draws in historical experiences from earlier forms of network including telecommunications and broadcast TV in order to ascertain the value of a network based on its size and growth rate. In recent years there has been intense debate as to how to do this and some of the ideas about valuation helped to whip up the froth of the dot-com boom and bust in the early 2000s.

The network effect considers macroscopic questions about the Web and it was while investigating how the Web works at this level that a team at Notre Dame University, Indiana, led by Albert-László Barabási discovered something truly startling about the *microscopic* structure of the Web. This led to the development of much theoretical work around the second of our concepts: the detailed topology (shape) of the Web. In particular, the discovery of two structural phenomena, the power law and the small world effect, not only provided new insight into the way the Web works, but also lit the touch-paper on an entirely new interdisciplinary research agenda, now known as *complex networks*.

This chapter will show how researchers, while attempting to calculate the value of the Web based on its size, went from the macroscopic models of the network effect to unexpected findings about the shape of the Web at the microscopic level of the distribution of hypertext links (the power law and small world effect). What they discovered led them to try to model the shape of the Web at the macroscopic level in an attempt to find a unifying model for working at the Internet scale.

7.1 THE NETWORK EFFECT

The network effect is a general economic term used to describe the increase in value to the existing users of a service (in which there is some form of interaction with others), as more and more people start to use it (Klemperer 2006; Liebowitz and Margolis 1994; Easley and Kleinberg 2010). In other words the product or service becomes more valuable or useful the greater the number of people who use it.* It was first remarked upon by David 'The General' Sarnoff (1891–1971), the founder of the TV network NBC, who claimed that the value of the broadcast media he was pioneering (TV and radio) was proportional to the number of viewers or listeners it attracted (Benjamin 1993; Paterson and Smith 1998; Dohler et al. 2008). In effect he was saying that the value of a network is proportional to the number of users. Value in this sense is a nebulous term, but economists talk about the utility or satisfaction gained from a service.

The telephone network provides a helpful analogy in this respect. When a new telephone user joins the network, not only do they as an individual benefit, but the existing users also benefit indirectly since they can now ring a new number and speak to someone

---

* It is often also referred to by economists as network externalities.

they couldn't speak to before. This idea is not confined to telecoms and is widely referred to, for example, in relation to technology products and their markets.

In fact, one of the implications, for technology products, is that it is widely believed that the power of the network effect is so great that it can create a situation where an inferior product can sometimes be widely, or even universally, adopted. The manner in which the VHS video tape format triumphed in the market over Betamax is an oft-cited example (Cusumano et al. 1992). Betamax was introduced in 1975 by Sony and VHS by JVC in 1976. Both provided home users with an easy-to-use video recording mechanism. Despite being first to market, and with a reputation of being slightly superior in terms of playback quality, Betamax fell behind VHS in the late 1970s and was abandoned altogether by the end of the 1980s.

Although economists provide much nuanced argument as to the details of this, it remains a powerful metaphor within technology marketing as it is believed that a new product is more likely to be successful in the long-term if it gains traction and momentum through early adoption, rather than being a superior product. This is relevant to our discussion as there are still echoes of these arguments in operation today as a new generation of Web service companies attempts to make the most of Web 2.0. This race to be first, and build up a powerful network of users for a new idea or service, has been boosted by a rule of thumb that has become known as *Metcalfe's Law*.

7.1.1 Metcalfe's Law and Its Critics

If we accept, for now, that there is a network effect that describes the increase in value to existing users of a network when new users join, the obvious corollary is, by how much? How big is the network effect? Sarnoff ascribed a linear relationship, thus giving the world *Sarnoff's Law*:

$$\text{For } N \text{ users the value } V \text{ of the network is: } V(N) \sim N \qquad (7.1)$$

However, Sarnoff was referring to a broadcast network, one in which there is a single, central node that broadcasts to many viewers (i.e. a one-to-many relationship). There is no return loop. However, telecoms networks act as many-to-many networks in that anyone on the system can pick up the phone and dial another person on the same system. This many-to-many relationship means that for several decades it had been accepted that the value of a telecoms network rises faster than the General's linear relationship (Odlyzko and Tilly 2005). Although quantitative work was undertaken within the telecoms industry into ways to measure this relationship, it was the thoughts of Bob Metcalfe, the inventor of Ethernet,* which crystallized a new proportion to rival Sarnoff. In 1980 Metcalfe produced a series of slides at a trade conference that aimed to demonstrate that there is a cross-over point in the growth of a new Ethernet network, after which the costs of the networking equipment are outstripped by the value that can be ascribed to the network (Li 2008). His slides

---

* Ethernet is one of the foundations of the basic networking technology that underpins the Internet.

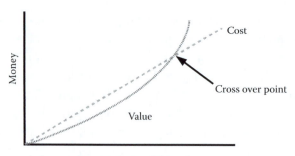

FIGURE 7.1 Bob Metcalfe's rough formula for cost/value crossover point when the value rises faster than the costs of installing equipment. Metcalfe argued that the value approximated to the square of the number of devices, whereas the cost of installing them approximated to a linear line. (Illustration © 2011 by Intelligent Content Ltd Licensed under a Creative Commons Attribution-NonCommercial-NoDerivs 3.0 Unported license [CC BY-NR-ND 3.0]).

included a diagram similar to that of Figure 7.1, which identified the critical mass needed to achieve this.

The cost of the network rises linearly, but the value follows an n^2 relationship. Why n^2? Consider an Ethernet network with two members, A and B (Figure 7.2). There is only one connection. If a third member (C) joins, then there are three possible connections. If the number of users becomes four, then the number of potential connections becomes six. With five, we have ten connections. Above this number it becomes hard to draw, but the formula is:

$$\frac{n(n-1)}{2} \tag{7.2}$$

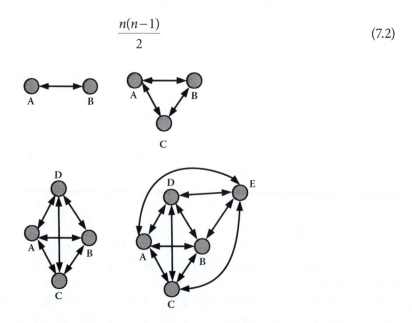

FIGURE 7.2 How the number of possible links grows as new nodes are added to a network. (Illustration © 2011 by Intelligent Content Ltd Licensed under a Creative Commons Attribution-NonCommercial-NoDerivs 3.0 Unported license [CC BY-NR-ND 3.0])

Each user can connect to $(n - 1)$ other users (they do not talk to themselves—or maybe they do but we do not count that kind of errant behaviour). Since each link is two-way (at least, in an Ethernet or telecoms network) then we divide the whole by two. As the number of users, N, becomes large, then the result of the formula approaches $N^2/2$ or as mathematicians say, it is of order N^2 which is written as $O(N^2)$. This therefore gives us Metcalfe's Law: For N users the value V of the network is: $V(N) \sim N^2$.

Although Metcalfe's thoughts were originally intended as a rough empirical formulation rather than a hard physical law, it was subsequently described as such in 1993 by George Gilder, a technology journalist who was influential during the dot-com boom of the 1990s. The problem with this was the way in which Metcalfe's formula was applied, uncritically, to the burgeoning Web in order to calculate its financial value. It was, for example, often used to help justify share issue valuations during the dot-com boom, and in 1996 the US Federal Communications Commission even referred to it as a founding principle for understanding the Internet (Odlyzko and Tilly 2005).

7.1.1.1 Metcalfe's Law and the Dot-com Boom and Bust
When you see reference to a new paradigm, you should always, under all circumstances, take cover.

J. K. GALBRAITH
Author of The Great Crash (Quoted in Keegan 1998, 32).

Prior to 1993 the Web had been a fairly niche Internet application, the preserve of academics and hobbyists. However, following the launch of the Mosaic Web browser in February of that year, ordinary people, using home computers, were able to install a browser and get on to the Web easily for the very first time (Berners-Lee 1999). Mosaic was the Web's first *killer app* (a term used to describe any application that is so compelling it drives adoption rates at breakneck speed, along with the uptake of any technologies associated with it) and all of a sudden, hundreds of thousands of new people started to arrive on the Web, ready to browse webpages, create their own and, increasingly, to search. The success of Mosaic gave the Web mass-market appeal and with the influx of large numbers of new visitors, big companies started to become interested in how to make money out of it.

Based on the perceived power of the network effect, business models in the late 1990s and early 2000s focused on developing the technology infrastructure that would deliver market share, rather than building the bottom line. In their minds, a new paradigm had been uncovered and a number of terms such as 'winner takes all', 'first mover advantage', and 'build it and they will come' were used to justify the large sums of money that were invested in a vast array of start-up Web companies, and Metcalfe's formulation was regarded as an article of faith by many financial consultants working on stock market flotations (Cassidy 1999, 2002). Most of these companies did not initially return a profit and many never did, but the theory was that for those companies that built up a large client base by utilizing the network effect, the rewards further down the line would outstrip the large initial investments in infrastructure. The 'get big fast' motto reflected the dot-com plan to operate at a sustained net loss in order to establish a brand, dominate a market and see off competitors so that they could charge profitable rates for their services later on.

It was a persuasive argument and such was the scale of its power that it drove stock markets around the world to unrealistically high valuations (Kettell 2002). However, even now, long after the dot-com boom and bust, the idea that there are special effects at work on the Internet driven by the scale and topology* of the network remains powerful, and indeed Metcalfe's 'law' is considered by sociologists to be one of the defining characteristics of the so-called information technology revolution (Castells 2000).

7.1.2 Metcalfe on Steroids: Reed's Law

In the late 1990s, the computer scientist David P. Reed began to have doubts about Metcalfe's valuation (Weinberger 2003). In an interview in 2001 he recalled explaining it to a sceptical engineer who immediately grasped that the number of people someone could potentially call on a telephone network grows in proportion to the square of the size of the network. However, the engineer immediately pointed out that: "if you assume that N people make one call each day, the number of calls … will only be proportional to N, and if you charge so much per minute, you can make money each day that is only proportional to the size of the network, not the square" (Weinberger 2001, webpage).

The implication of this is that Metcalfe's 'law' describes accurately the size and growth of a physical telecoms network infrastructure but not its value, and this led Reed into thinking about the concept of value implied by Metcalfe. He realized that the Internet was different from a telecoms network and he concluded that because Metcalfe had been measuring value between points on a telecoms network he had not considered the additional value within the network. On this basis, Reed argued that Metcalfe was actually undervaluing the Internet considerably.

In 1999, Reed published a paper arguing that the key to understanding value within the Internet network was to realize that it enables group-forming, a process which he called *group forming networks* (GFN) (Reed 1999). Thus a person can use e-mail or social networking software not simply to send a message to another node on the network, but to join a group of people with a shared interest. Reed argued that because the Internet (and later the Web) enabled such group forming it was therefore a different form of technology to both the telecoms and Ethernet networks that Metcalfe was discussing and Sarnoff's broadcast media (Reed 2001).

This means that eBay is far more than a traditional e-commerce platform (or *transaction site*): it is a GFN that self-organises around shared obsessions, for example, collectors of vinyl records of 1970s British progressive rock bands. On this basis, the service automatically gets better as more and more people use it (as it is not much fun sharing an obsession with yourself), and Reed used this formulation to predict the huge success of the then just publicly listed eBay.

---

* The topology is the 'shape' and 'connectedness' of the network.

For GFNs the growth in value is actually exponential—proportional to 2^n. If there are n people, they can form $2^n - n - 1$ groups. To demonstrate this, consider three people A, B, and C. They can form three different groups of two people—AB, BC, AC and one group of three. This gives four as predicted by the formula: $(2^3 - 3 - 1)$. As n becomes large this approaches 2^n and therefore we can say that value is of order 2^n, i.e. $O(2^n)$. This gives us Reed's Law,[*] i.e. for N users the value V of the network is $V(N) \sim 2^n$.

Such a formulation implies that for online social networking–type applications in which users form and join a myriad of sub-groups, the rate of growth of the 'value' is dramatic as members join.

7.1.3 A Refutation of Metcalfe and Reed

In 2006, Briscoe, Odlyzko and Tilly published what they described as a refutation of Metcalfe's Law and along the way they also took a shot at Reed's law (Briscoe et al. 2006). In their paper they argued that these formulations are incorrect and that: "the value of a network of size n grows in proportion to $n \log(n)$" (p. 36). A growth of this scale, whilst large, is much more modest than that attributed to Metcalfe. The authors argued that where Metcalfe (and Reed) fell down was in the assignment of value.

What exactly was meant by value had never really been spelled out by Metcalfe's disciples during the dot-com boom. Briscoe et al. argued that whatever it was exactly, the crucial thing to grasp was that it was a mistake to allocate *equal* value to every possible connection between nodes or, in Reed's case, between sub-groups in a network. Such a point of view was not especially new: the authors pointed out that Henry Thoreau (1854, 307), writing over a century ago, had noted the arrival of the telegraph and said: "We are in great haste to construct a magnetic telegraph from Maine to Texas; but Maine and Texas, it may be, have nothing important to communicate."

Whilst it is clear that the people of Maine do have something to say to Texas, they almost certainly have more to say to somewhere much closer such as New York. This is known in telecoms circles as the *gravity law*—an acceptance that distance plays a part in telecoms traffic patterns because of the way people are geographically distributed and socialize. Therefore, although connections exist, they may not always be utilized to an equal intensity and we should not always assign an equal unit of value.

The authors also argued that the logic of Metcalfe's formula dictated that if two existing telecoms companies were to merge then the combined value of the new one would be twice as much as the single networks operating independently: something that, if true, would cause companies to seek to merge in the real world on a regular basis, but which does not actually happen very often. Their alternative formulation, $O(n \log(n))$, they argued, fits the observed behaviour of networks. The gravity law effect means that for two cities that have populations of A and B, the traffic between them is usually proportional to $AB/d\alpha$, where d is the distance, and α is a constant, usually between 1 and 2. This is not a new formulation: it goes back to the nineteenth century and has been observed in postal mail

---

[*] The mathematics to prove this are somewhat complicated, based as they are on set theory, but interested readers can find out more at: http://www.reed.com/gfn.

and telegraph systems as well as modern telecoms (Odlyzko 2000). It is often attributed to George Zipf, a man who we will meet in detail in a moment. Using some calculus and a certain amount of averaging (see the original paper for details) they conclude that these localizing effects give a value of the order of $(n \log(n))$.

Finally, the authors also noted that when we start to consider the Internet and Web (rather than a telecoms network), power laws come into play. We shall discuss these in detail in the next section, but for now we will note that the authors argue that the implications of one in particular, *Zipf's power law*, would support their proposal for value.

Briscoe et al. (2006) also refuted Reed's law, pointing out that again it was based on allocating equal value to all connections formed between all possible sub-groups in the GFN. Commonsense thinking, they argued, showed that Reed's Law could not hold in the real world as it implied that every new person on a GFN doubles the network's value. Adding ten people therefore, by this reasoning, increases its value by a thousandfold (2^{10}). This does not even remotely fit our general experience of the Internet—a network with 50,010 people is simply not possibly worth a thousand times more than the same network with 50,000 people.

In conclusion Briscoe et al. argued that this critique of Reed's Law is quantitatively justified by thinking about the role of value in the network: adding a new person to the network does not provide each and every other person on the network with a single unit of additional value. The additional value varies, depending on what use an existing individual might make of the new one (as an example, some of your e-mail contacts are many times more useful to you than the rest). As this 'relative value' is dictated by a power law distribution, it can be shown mathematically that the network effect is proportional to $n \log(n)$ rather than n^2 or 2^n. The different network laws can be seen in comparison in Figure 7.3.

7.1.4 The Debate Continues

Discussions over the true valuation of the network effect continue and remain an area of active research interest. For example, in 2007 Joe Weinman published an article arguing that there were some fairly obvious real-world limits to the endless growth proposed by Metcalfe's formulation and Reed's Law (Weinman 2007). He argued that the user of a telephone network needs to have full knowledge of all the people on the system, and to want to communicate with all of them, in order to make use of n^2 network growth. He pointed out that although there are billions of people on the worldwide telephone network, we are not likely to speak to more than a few thousand of them in a lifetime and nor, given human socialization behaviour, would we want to.[*] As real behaviour tends to be localized, Weinman argued that such limitations drive the value of the network effect back towards

---

[*] We have a direct interest in talking to family, a few close friends, and a larger number of acquaintances, with only an occasional interest in talking to staff from our bank or insurance company etc.

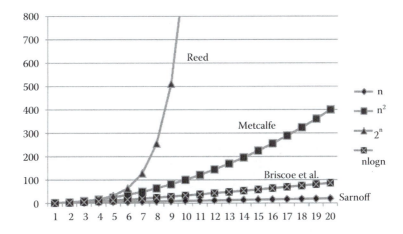

FIGURE 7.3 The respective growth rates of the different network effect formulas. (Illustration © 2011 by Intelligent Content Ltd Licensed under a Creative Commons Attribution-NonCommercial-NoDerivs 3.0 Unported license [CC BY-NR-ND 3.0]).

the linear relationship first mooted by Sarnoff. He concluded by saying that there may well be networks that grow in proportion to n^2 or even 2^n, but at some critical point, real-life limitations will mean that the ability to continue to extract value from each additional node returns growth to linear.

Li (2008) has argued that such limits may well exist for Web 2.0 services. Noting that Metcalfe's original formulation was primarily about establishing a point of critical mass, he has argued that there may well be a second critical mass point at which value starts to go down. For example, an alumni social network site hits a barrier, for an individual user, when all his or her old university friends have joined the network. There is little or no value in millions more joining. Li also pointed out that other critical masses might occur in other online social networks and Web 2.0 applications when the size of the network is so large that individual users find it difficult to use. This critical mass will vary depending on what the user gets out of the service. Let us take the example of Flickr. If you use it exclusively to share photos with your family and close friends, then once all of them have joined and can access and share your pictures, then you have finished: you do not care how many millions more people join. However, if you use Flickr to find and re-use photos in general, then the more who join and contribute, the better (provided the search algorithm can keep up).

Despite the unreliability of using the network effect to place a monetary value on the Web, it is clear that many people still do, although their arguments have moved on. Constantinides et al. (2008) have argued that, commercially, Web 2.0 services "present users with a new value proposition based on network effects" (p. 234). They pointed out that in the past, vendor lock-in to a particular software product has often been a problem, with vendors making it difficult or costly for customers to switch to a competitor's products, but that with Web 2.0 there are no such barriers. Switching is easy and what loyalty there is relates to the network effect. Thus, participants in the social network site MySpace or the online photo-exchange service Flickr will keep using the service if more and more of their contacts and peers do the same, even if there are other, better options available. Indeed, social network sites regularly use the network effect argument ('use us—all your friends are already here') in their promotional material (Bonneau and Preibusch 2010a).

Hendler and Golbeck (2008) noted that whether we are discussing the Web, Web 2.0, or indeed the emerging Semantic Web, the network effect is one of the more important aspects of the Web's power. Despite the debates over the exact valuation (with Briscoe et al. on the low end and Reed at the high end), they point out that: "While none of these effects have been validated in practice, it is clear that the network effect is quite real, and even the most pessimistic view still provides for significant value as the number of connections in the network grows" (p. 2).

They argue that network effect value is created in Web 2.0 through the creation of what they call the *link space*—connections between online content and people. Indeed, they take this further and propose that although one way to measure the value of Web 2.0 is to look at the effort that users put in to creating their own content (blogs, wikis etc.), the true value of the network effect arises from the links between people interacting, thus creating large and valuable social networks. They conclude that the success of Web 2.0 comes "from the rapidly growing social network and the value growth driven by Metcalfe's law operating over the social links" (p. 5).

Reed himself wrote that he believes his law to be an important cultural and economic shift. Crucially he believes GFNs (and therefore by implication Web 2.0) represent a shift in the history of the Internet where the central role is no longer one-to-one transactions but "jointly constructed value" (Rheingold 2002, 61).

Ultimately, there is no universal law, and one should treat such 'laws' with caution. However, the *Framework for Web Science* (Berners-Lee et al. 2006) points out that these discussions form part of a wider debate about the analysis of the Web as an area for research, where an inter-disciplinary approach may be fruitful.

7.2 WEB TOPOLOGY

While some debated how to correctly ascribe value to a rapidly growing network, others were focused on an equally interesting question: just how big is the Web exactly? This was clearly relevant to questions of economic valuation (whatever the final, agreed formula for such a valuation might turn out to be) but it was also profoundly important to the emerging search engine companies of the time (the late 1990s). It was believed that even the largest and most powerful engines had indexed as little as 15% of the Web's full size, but no one was completely sure. Work in the late 1990s, particularly by Steve Lawrence and Lee Giles at the NEC Research Institute, was beginning to come up with answers. However, it was a team from Notre Dame University who finally came up with something so startling that it eventually led to a complete reappraisal of the way science considers how networks form and grow. A whole new way of looking at the Web as a topological structure emerged and

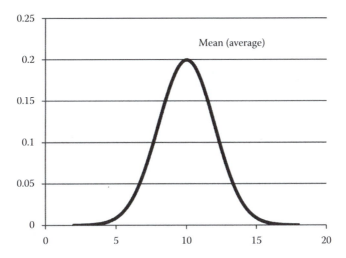

FIGURE 7.4 The distinctive bell-shaped curve of a Gaussian distribution. The mean value is at the peak of the curve. (Illustration © 2011 by Intelligent Content Ltd Licensed under a Creative Commons Attribution-NonCommercial-NoDerivs 3.0 Unported license [CC BY-NR-ND 3.0]).

this had profound implications, not only for the Web 2.0 services that were to emerge later, but also as a way to analyse and measure human society.

7.2.1 Power Laws

As the number of websites and pages began to explode in the 1990s there was an unspoken assumption that the way webpages were linked together via hypertext would follow a Gaussian distribution* (or 'bell curve'), implying that most documents would be roughly equally linked to and therefore in a sense equally popular (see Figure 7.4). The reason this was expected was because it was assumed that the Web would pretty much resemble something called a *random network*. These networks were first described by Ray Solomonoff and Anatol Rapoport† in 1951, but were more famously discussed in a series of mathematical papers by Paul Erdős and Alfréd Rényi in the late 1950s (Newman et al. 2006).

In order to understand this line of thinking we need to look at networks in more detail. In general, networks consist of *nodes* (or 'vertices') connected by *links* (or 'edges'). This applies to any network, even human social networks, and in terms of the Web, webpages are the nodes and hypertext links are the links. These networks can be modelled using *graph theory*, and a random network would be shown on a graph as one in which the links between the nodes are placed completely randomly, i.e. by chance some will have more than others.

---

* A distribution shows how often instances of a certain value or quantity, for example height, appear in a system being studied.

† According to Newman, Rapoport was an interesting character who was ahead of his time. He was Russian and had wanted to become a concert pianist, but he turned to mathematics when he realized he would need a rich patron to support his music career, something that was not available to him. He combined mathematics with biology and is therefore a pioneer of the kind of multi-disciplinary work that much of this book is about.

INTRODUCTION TO RANDOM NETWORKS

The basic mechanism for creating a random network can be described as a kind of game involving a number of unconnected nodes and a die. Decide in advance what your criterion is for connecting a pair of nodes—let's say it is rolling a six with the die. If you roll a six then the nodes can be connected. If you get anything other than a six, then you move on to a different pair of nodes. The important point is that at each decision point we take a random choice (by rolling a die), but that the level of the randomness is equal (i.e. we roll the same die and stick to the same rule of only connecting if we get a six). It doesn't actually matter what the criterion for connecting the nodes is (we can say, for example, we connect if we roll a three) as long as the same probability is used each time (i.e. is equiprobable).

However, despite this randomness, Erdős and Rényi showed that if a network is large enough, almost all the nodes will have approximately the same number of links. Later work in 1982 by Béla Bollobás refined this by proving that the distribution would follow a Poisson distribution (Newman et al. 2006; Barabási 2009), which can be approximated to the Gaussian for large samples (Campbell and Duarte 2008).

Since the great German mathematician Carl Friedrich Gauss (1777–1855) first described and analysed this statistical distribution in 1807 it has been found to be present time and time again in natural and scientific phenomena. Indeed, it is so common that it could be argued that humans seem to have a predisposition to see the world through the lens of this kind of distribution. It is something we learn from an early age and many of you will be able to recall plotting the heights of your classmates on a histogram at school. The plot will typically demonstrate the bell curve shape of the *Gaussian distribution* (also commonly called the 'normal distribution') in which a central peak is accompanied by a slope on either side. Thus we say that human height is 'normally distributed'—most adults are between 1.52 and 1.82 metres tall.

Translating this to the Web, the assumption was that the Web is a random network, and since the distribution of hypertext links is bell-shaped, no website would stray too far from the central peak (i.e. the mean). Although there would be some webpages with a relatively high number of hypertext links, overall they would exhibit a bell-shaped curve with respect to the distribution of links to other pages.

This was certainly what Albert-László Barabási, Réka Albert and Hawoong Jeong, all working in the physics department at the University of Notre Dame, expected to find when they set out to measure the Web in 1998 (Barabási 2002). They developed a Web spider, a piece of software that automatically traverses the Web in order to follow one hypertext link after another and send back information about each one (a technique also used by search engines). They processed the data gathered using statistical analysis and mapped the size of the Web, the pattern of the links and the degree of separation (i.e. how many links it takes to get from one node to another, or the 'node-to-node distance'). What they found surprised them. The spider brought back details of a network of links where many of the websites had a few links only, but a few had an "extraordinarily large number of links" (p. 67). When they plotted the data on a graph they found not the

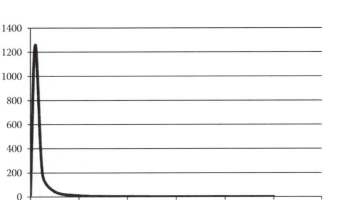

FIGURE 7.5   A plot of a typical power law curve. Note the way the graph is positively skewed, with a long tail of very small values stretching out to the right. (Illustration © 2011 by Intelligent Content Ltd Licensed under a Creative Commons Attribution-NonCommercial-NoDerivs 3.0 Unported license [CC BY-NR-ND 3.0]).

expected Gaussian or Poisson, bell-shaped curve, but something altogether different: a power law distribution.

Despite the apparent ubiquity of the bell curve, scientists had known for some time that not all natural, social or scientific phenomena exhibited the normal distribution. Some displayed a kind of skew, in which the distribution has changed, exhibiting a high peak and then a continuously decreasing curve—a long tail that stretches out along the axis (see Figure 7.5). This skewing can take many forms and can exhibit a rightward long tail (a positive skew) or a leftwards one (negative skew). Positive skewing takes two, closely related forms of particular interest to our discussion: the *log-normal distribution* and the *power law*. It was the latter that was to prove so interesting to computer scientists.

7.2.1.1 Power Law

A power law is one in which y relates to x by the formula:

$$y = kx^a \tag{7.3}$$

where a is the exponent.

In a power law distribution, the probability of an entity having value n is proportional to $1/n^\beta$ or:

$$p(n) = cn^{-\beta} \quad \text{for } (\beta > 0 \text{ and } c > 0) \tag{7.4}$$

The power law decay (the rate of fall-off in the slope) is slower than for a bell curve (see Figure 7.5). Roughly speaking, it decays according to the power (or degree) exponent, β. The power law distribution implies there are a few nodes with high values co-existing with huge numbers of nodes with small values, whereas the exponential tail of the Gaussian distribution makes values that are much larger than the mean to be extremely unlikely

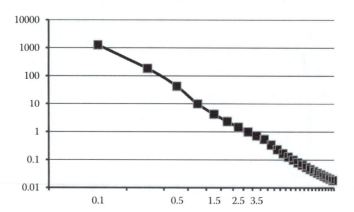

FIGURE 7.6 A plot of a power law curve with both axes as logarithms. This results in the characteristic straight line of a power law. (Illustration © 2011 by Intelligent Content Ltd Licensed under a Creative Commons Attribution-NonCommercial-NoDerivs 3.0 Unported license [CC BY-NR-ND 3.0])

(Adamic and Huberman 2002). If this is plotted on a log–log scale graph, then the exponent defines the slope and the power law demonstrates a straight line (see Figure 7.6).* Such a plot is also referred to sometimes as a complementary cumulative distribution function (CCDF).

The Web can also be modelled as a *directed graph*, that is, each node (page) may have zero or more links (hypertext links) to other nodes and these links are in one direction only. This has become known in the literature as the *Webgraph* (Donato et al. 2007). Each node has two different *degrees*: the *in-degree*, which is a measure of the number of other nodes that link to it, and the *out-degree*, which is a measure of the number of nodes it links to. The team at Notre Dame found that the distribution of incoming links on the Web exhibited a power law with a unique and well-defined degree exponent of close to 2 (Barabási 2002). The out-going links exhibited the same effect with an exponent of 2.5. In other words, confounding their expectations, the team had found that the Web was not a random graph in the style of Erdős and Rényi. As Barabási puts it: "web-page creators work together in some magic way to generate a complex Web that defies the random universe" (p. 68).

The other important characteristic of power laws, and one which has been made much of in discussions about the impact of Web 2.0, is the presence of a *long tail*. As we have previously noted, the power law decay (the rate of fall-off in the slope) is slower than for a Gaussian curve and this results in a long tail of rarely occurring values. The concept of the long tail was popularized by Chris Anderson, editor of *Wired* magazine, in a business book of the same name (Anderson 2006). Essentially his argument was that, in the digital age, the long tail has changed the economics of many businesses since online retailers can

---

* Since a power law is defined as $y = kx^a$, then this can also be written as:

 log y = a log x + log k and thus when plotted in a log–log graph appears as a straight line. Further details in Halpin et al. (2007).

offer niche products from the tail that a physical store would never have sufficient shelf space to provide.

7.2.1.2 Power Laws by Other Names: Zipf and Pareto

Distributions that show a skew from the Gaussian had been known to occur, if only rarely, for some time. As far back as 1897, Vilfredo Pareto (1848–1923) argued that wealth distribution did not follow a Gaussian distribution and in fact was skewed towards the very wealthy.[*] George Zipf (1902–1950) was another scientist who investigated the prevalence of such skews (Ball 2005). He believed that the social sciences differ from the natural sciences in that they are dominated by phenomena that exhibit a different distribution to that of the Gaussian. He collected a lot of empirical data from a variety of human endeavours and demonstrated power laws in areas as diverse as music, the development of language, the distribution of industries and travel statistics. He is best-known for what has become known as *Zipf's law*[†]:

The frequency of occurrence of some event (*P*), as a function of the rank (*i*) when the rank is determined by the frequency of occurrence, is a power-law function:

$$P(i) \sim \frac{1}{i^a} \tag{7.5}$$

with the exponent, *a*, being close to 1.

In short, Zipf's law relates to the ranking of the popularity of an item rather than plotting the actual values themselves. This means that, strictly speaking, Zipf is a *variant* of the power law (Dill et al. 2002).[‡] Zipf plotted rank against frequency which shows the cumulative distribution of an entity, and similar graphs are sometimes referred to in the literature as rank/frequency plots (Newman 2005).

Despite Zipf's hopes, it turned out that power law (and closely related log-normal) distributions are not just a feature of human activity—they are also common in science and the natural world (Limpert et al. 2001; Newman 2005). Many occurrences have been noted in recent years including: concentration of elements in the Earth's crust; the timings of first infection to appearance of symptoms in medicine; and species abundance.

It is because of this history that power laws are, confusingly, sometimes referred to as Pareto or Zipfian distributions or indeed, simply 'heavy tail' or 'long tail' distributions.[§] For students who want to study this further, it is important to remember that it is often difficult to tell whether a skewed distribution is a power law, a log-normal or, indeed, another

---

[*] Pareto was a railway engineer, who in later life devoted himself to the study of economics and in particular to trying to find and describe laws in economics that were of comparable gravitas and accuracy as those used in Newtonian physics. His work on wealth led to the coining of the oft-quoted '80/20' rule (although he never actually used this term in his writings), which states that, for example, 80% of the profits of a company are generated by 20% of the staff.

[†] http://www.nslij-genetics.org/wli/zipf/

[‡] Adamic and Huberman (2002) show the mathematics for yielding a Zipf-ranked distribution from any power law probability distribution.

[§] Indeed, strictly speaking Pareto and Zipf laws differ in the way the data is plotted. Zipf made plots with *x* on the horizontal and *P(x)* on the vertical. Pareto did it the other way around. The data is the same (Newman 2005).

skewed distribution form (Clauset et al. 2009). There are often debates within scientific disciplines as to which is the best fit for a particular set of data and Mitzenmacher (2001) for example, notes the difficulty of deciding whether income distribution is a log-normal or a power law. As Newman (2005, 8) writes: "the scientist confronted with a new set of data having a broad dynamic range and a highly skewed distribution should certainly bear in mind that a power-law model is only one of several possibilities for fitting it".

7.2.2 Scale-Free Networks

Let us return to the work of Barabási and his team's experiments to measure the size of the Web. When they started to look at the size of the Web, they discovered something unexpected about its shape (the *topology*). Instead of finding a randomly connected network, which should have modelled to a Poisson or Gaussian distribution in the style of Erdős and Rényi, when they modelled the Web they found a power law distribution. This discovery meant that the Web could not be a randomly connected network, so the Notre Dame team came up with a new name. They called it a *scale-free network*, to reflect what they found: i.e. Gaussian or Poisson distributions have a 'scale' (in the sense that most values are close to that of the peak), whereas the power law distribution did not—there was no single, characteristic node (webpage) demonstrating what might be called typical values (Barabási and Albert 1999; Barabási and Bonabeau 2003).

In order to understand scale-free networks better, we need to look more closely at some of the characteristics of skewed distributions. Usually in statistics we are interested in what might be considered a *typical value** for a set of data because it gives us a sense of the proportion of what we are talking about (which Barabási conceptualizes as a scale). In a Gaussian distribution this is usually fairly obvious because the model is symmetrical, so it is easy to see that the typical value (in this case it happens to be the mean, or average, value) is at the peak. Skewed distributions are not symmetrical: the peak might be at the left-hand side of the graph, preceded by a short tail but followed by a long tail to the right (as in a power law), or the peak might be at the right-hand side of the graph, preceded by the long tail. The implication of this is that for a skewed distribution, the mean cannot be used as the typical value. Thus we can say that a random network, which, as we have seen, exhibits a Gaussian distribution of its links, is dominated by its mean value, i.e. the value at the peak in the centre of the symmetrical graph. Skewed distributions, however, exhibit non-typical behaviour with regard to averages. Thus, for skewed distributions, it is not always obvious what the meaningful measure of the typical value should be, and therefore it is difficult to determine the scale.

With this in mind, there is another characteristic of scale-free networks that we should be aware of: *self-similarity*. Levene (2006) notes that if a system obeys a power law then it looks the same at all scales. So, if we looked at the distribution of an arbitrary range, say websites with between 10,000 and 100,000 pages, it would look similar to the range of websites with between 10 and 100 pages. As Huberman (2001, 25) writes: "In other

---

* For more information on typical values, see: http://www.itl.nist.gov/div898/handbook/eda/section3/eda351.htm

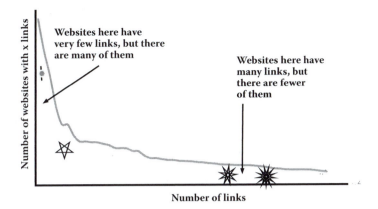

FIGURE 7.7   The long tail of webpage links. Sites on the far right of the diagram have a large number of out-going hypertext links to other webpages, but there are fewer of them. On the left hand side sites have few out-going links, but there are far more of them. The same result is achieved if we plot the in-coming links.

words, zooming in or out in the scale at which one studies the Web, one keeps obtaining the same result".

The logical conclusion to discovering that the Web is a scale-free network was that there must be many, many websites with a small handful of incoming and outgoing hypertext links and only a few highly connected nodes that dominate the network. These consist of *hubs* (sites with large numbers of in-coming links), or *stars* (sites with large numbers of out-going links)*(see Figure 7.7). According to Barabási (2002, 62): "If the Web were a random network, the probability of there being a page with 500 incoming links would be 10^{-99}—that is practically zero, indicating that hubs are forbidden in a randomly linked Web". Yet his team found several hundred of that size on the Web.

We'll see what the implications of this are for Web 2.0 in a moment, but for the time being it is worth reflecting on the point that this was not what was expected. Anybody who sets up a webpage is free to add as many links to other sites as they want; there are no rules. Things should therefore have turned out to be pretty much random. And yet, despite this apparent freedom, somehow the system self-organised to such an extent that a power law distribution was apparent.

The distribution of in-coming and out-going links was not the only feature of the Web that seemed to follow a power law. For example, Lada Adamic and Bernardo Huberman, at the Xerox research centre, found a similar result for the number of pages per website (Huberman and Adamic 1999). They also later found that the way users surf between websites follows a power law. Elsewhere, three Greek brothers (the Faloutsos brothers), all computer scientists and unaware of Barabási's work, discovered that the connectivity of Internet router equipment follows a power law (Faloutsos et al. 1999).

---

* Although it should be noted that the literature is not consistent in its use of these terms and often the two terms are used interchangeably to refer simply to sites with large numbers of links.

The discovery in the late 1990s and early 2000s of scale-free networks on the Web and Internet, along with other networks as diverse as the metabolic systems of biological cells and sexual partners in Sweden, kick-started a highly fruitful period of intense interest in the science of networks (Newman et al. 2006). It was clear that real networks demonstrated properties that had not been anticipated by the idealized models of mathematical graph theory. In recent years a multi-disciplinary research effort, involving mathematicians, physicists, biologists, computer scientists and academics from various branches of the humanities, has been undertaken to explore the implications of what has come to be known as *complex networks*.

However, before we leave the power law behind, we should note research work which suggests that it does not apply to certain sub-sets of the Web where the pages have a shared, common theme, e.g. university homepages[*] (Chakrabarti et al. 2002; Pennock et al. 2002; Benkler 2006). When such clusters of topically related pages are small (in the hundreds or low thousands) the power law distribution seems not to be present. Instead they follow a distribution that still has a very long tail, with a few stars, but the tail is more moderated and looks more like a Gaussian distribution than a power law drop-off. The implications of this are still being explored and we will return to this in Chapter 8. However, despite this potential anomaly emerging, the power law remains a fundamental property of the Web. Indeed, the science writer, Philip Ball, notes that "power laws seem to be a recurring leitmotif" of the Web (Ball 2005, 483) and we will see far more of them when we explore the various Web 2.0 services in later chapters.

7.2.3 Small Worlds

And so the game went on. Our friend was absolutely correct: nobody from the group needed more than five links in the chain to reach, just by using the method of acquaintance, any inhabitant of our Planet.

FRIGYES KARINTHY
Chain Links (short story published in 1929)

In 1967, Stanley Milgram conducted an experiment to investigate relationship chains between humans. His experiment involved finding out how many steps it would take to get a message to a target person in Massachusetts, if, rather than posting a letter directly to them, the letter was sent to a random group of 160 starting people in a few cities many miles away (Wichita, Kansas, and Omaha, Nebraska) (Travers and Milgram 1969). The rules of the psychological 'game' were that:

- You could not mail the letter directly to the target person unless you knew them personally.

- If you did not know them personally, then the letter could only be passed on to another acquaintance (who you were on first-name terms with) and who you thought was more likely to know the target person.

---

[*] This is not the only case of non-power laws within technology. See the Further Reading section.

TABLE 7.1   The Clustering Coefficients and Degrees of Separation of Various Types of Network

Type of Network	Clustering Coefficient	Small Degree of Separation
Random network	Tends to 0	Present
Ordered (regular lattice)	High – tends to 1	Not present
Small World Networks	High	Present

Milgram expected that if the letters reached the target addresses at all, then they would have been through the hands of a hundred people or more, and this was accepted wisdom at the time. Milgram, along with the rest of the psychology world, was stunned when letters began to reach the targets within a few days and even more surprised when they found that the median number of people required to get letters to the targets was 5.2. When rounded down to five intermediaries, this meant that there were six steps between point A and point B. This became the famous 'six degrees of separation', although Milgram never actually used that phrase (it was coined by the playwright John Guare in a play of that title). This is problematic because the experiment was only conducted in the USA and yet it has become an enduring modern myth that everyone on the planet is linked to everyone else by at most six steps. However, it is true that real-world social networks exhibit much smaller small degrees of separation than previously thought, something which has become known as the *small world effect*.

The experiment stimulated an interest in the structure of networks because Milgram's work seemed to indicate that social networks had properties that were different from both random networks and ordered networks (also known as regular lattices), and yet shared some of the properties of both. This meant that Milgram's experiment highlighted a kind of 'grey area' between what were, at the time, the two key network models used by physicists and mathematicians.

In 1998 two mathematicians, Duncan J. Watts and Steven H. Strogatz, published an important paper in *Nature*. They argued that neither random networks nor regular lattices seemed to provide an adequate framework for studying real-world, complex networks[*] and proposed an alternative, which they called *small world networks*, where networks in a wide variety of natural and social phenomena exhibit a small degree of separation in a manner similar to Milgram's experiment (Watts and Strogatz 1998; Newman et al. 2006). They showed how this applied to a range of networks, from the collaborative links between film actors and the neural structure of a worm, and looked at two factors: the *degree of separation* (which they called the *characteristic path length*) and the *clustering coefficient*, a measure of how close-knit, or cliquish, a network was (Barabási 2002; Newman et al. 2006) (see Table 7.1).

---

[*] Amaral et al. (2000) give more detail on a wide range of natural phenomena that this applied to, including chemical reactions, neuronal networks and food chains.

CALCULATING THE DEGREE OF SEPARATION

The *degree of separation* is calculated by finding the distance between all pairs of nodes in the network and then averaging them. The *clustering coefficient* is derived by dividing the number of links between a group of neighbours in a network, by the possible number of links. For example, say I have three friends. If they are also all friends with each other then we can draw a network graph with six friendship links (see Figure 7.8). This network is very close-knit—there are six possible links and all six are in place, so the node 'Me' has a cluster coefficient of 1. However, if two of my friends are not friends with each other, then we remove one of the links and the coefficient for node 'Me' goes down to 0.833 (5/6). The clustering coefficient of an entire network is arrived at by calculating the average of these coefficients across all the nodes present in the network. A high degree of clustering means that there is a heightened probability of two nodes being connected if they have one or more acquaintance in common (Newman 2001; Newman 2003). Or in social terms, 'the friend of my friend is also my friend'.

The formula for the clustering coefficient for the whole network over n nodes is given in Equation 7.5 (Newman et al. 2006, 287):

$$C_{ws} = \frac{1}{n}\sum_{i=1}^{n} C_i = \frac{1}{n}\sum_{i=1}^{n} \frac{(\text{number of connected neighbour pairs})}{\frac{1}{2}k_i(k_i - 1)} \tag{7.6}$$

where C_i is the clustering coefficient for a single node i, and k_i is the degree of node i.

7.2.3.1 Small Worlds and the Web

What has all this got to do with the Web? Barabási's team found that the separation, d, was proportional to the log of the number of nodes, N, by the formula: $d = 0.35 + 2\log N$. In 1998 the Web consisted of approximately 800 million nodes and so degree of separation d was calculated to be 18.59. In other words, webpages are typically around 19 clicks away from each other. This represented a kind of factor for the difficulty of getting from one document to another.

They also found that the degree increased much more slowly than any increase in the number of webpages. The implication of this was that it did not matter so much that the size of the Web was expanding rapidly because the difficulty of travelling across it was not increasing at the same rate.[*] In other words the Web demonstrated the small world effect of Milgram and this has been confirmed by others (Adamic et al. 1999). In addition it was found that the clustering coefficient for the Web was 0.11, high enough for the Web to qualify as a small world network as identified by Watts and Strogatz (Newman et al. 2006).

Broder et al. (2000) confirmed the degree of separation result on a larger dataset, although they found that 75% of the time, for any given randomly selected node, there is no directed path at all to another random node; however when there is a path it is of

---

[*] For a network of N nodes, in which nodes have on average k links, then it can be shown that the average separation follows $d = \log N/\log k$ (Barabási 2002). The presence in the formula of a log shrinks the size of d dramatically.

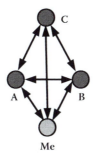 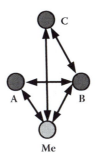

FIGURE 7.8 Measuring the clustering coefficient in a small network. If I have three friends, A, B and C and they are all also friends with each other, then the group is close-knit and my node, *Me*, has a clustering coefficient of 1. If, however, A is not friends with C, then the coefficient is 0.833. (Illustration © 2011 by Intelligent Content Ltd Licensed under a Creative Commons Attribution-NonCommercial-NoDerivs 3.0 Unported license [CC BY-NR-ND 3.0])

mean distance 16.[*] It is important to be clear that the fact that the Web is a small world network does not necessarily make it easy to find what one is looking for (Barabási 2002). The fact that any desired webpage is, on average, only between 16 and 19 clicks away does not make the process of selecting the correct order of clicks easy. Bear in mind that each of those clicks takes you to a webpage full of more links. Thus, we have to make choices and judgements based on information contained within the page, the names of the links etc. By interpreting the links, we avoid having to check all the pages within nineteen degrees (a mammoth task). Search engines have been a huge help in this respect, providing shortcuts to content we want to find.[†]

RANDOM NETWORKS AND SMALL WORLDS

Why do random networks demonstrate small world effects? Consider a randomly linked network with N nodes in which each node has on average k links (Barabási 2002). This means that for the typical node we can reach k other nodes in one step. But in two steps we can reach k^2 nodes, since each of the k nodes we first reach also link to k other nodes. There are roughly k^d nodes that are distance d links away. If k is large, then even for small values of d, the number of steps required, we can reach very large numbers of nodes. As there is a total of N nodes the value of k^d must never exceed N. Therefore we can calculate that $d = \log N / \log k$ as a rough approximation.

The next logical question for the Notre Dame team was how the Web came to be formed in this way and if there is a model that can describe that formation. This was a different kind of question than those that had been asked so far. It was not concerned with building

---

[*] There is a slight difference in the figures that researchers find for mean distance because of issues with sample size. No one has been able to traverse the entire Web in one go in order to ascertain the absolute figure for mean distance—researchers take samples of the full Web. Albert et al. (1999) predicted a figure of 19 for the entire Web, based on sampling a small sub-section of the overall network. They predicted a mean distance of 17.9 for the size of sample that Broder et al. used and so there is less discrepancy than it first appears. Full details are in Chapter 3 of Newman et al. (2006).

[†] For further discussion of search engines and their role in small world networks see Levene (2006).

a model of the Web itself, but rather, building a model of how it was formed. These sorts of models are called *generative models*.

Watts and Strogatz had already tried to develop generative models for their small world networks and had demonstrated that small world effects could be added to an ordered network by 'rewiring' links to incorporate a surprisingly small number of shortcuts between nodes. It is therefore possible that some dynamic action that changes an ordered network little by little, over time, might result in a small world network, without requiring that the overall network size and shape should change.

We can get a feel for what this means by considering our own human social network. In our social network most of us have tightly-knit groups of friends, many of whom are also friends with each other, but we also know a friend or two, or family member, who has moved to another town or country. It is these long-distance links that provide the short cuts necessary to turn our highly clustered social network into a small world that demonstrates the small world effect. This became known as the *Watts/Strogatz* model and the work led to further investigations into small world phenomena and to various refinements to the model although these need not detain us here. It is a highly complex mathematical area and the interested reader is directed to Newman et al. (2006) and Duncan Watts' book (1999) for further details.

However, the enormous fly in the ointment was that, as we have seen, the Web exhibits power law distributions. When Watts and Strogatz published in 1998, scientists thought that their new model could be used to explain the Web and its small world effects but, shortly afterwards, Barabási's team demonstrated that the Web exhibited power laws—not a property found in the small world network outlined in the Watts/Strogatz model (Baldi et al. 2003) Thus, the Web is a small world network, but it cannot actually be explained by the associated theoretical model. Of course, we already know that the Web is neither a random network nor an ordered network, so it became clear that some kind of generative model was required that could deliver a network theory that matched what was being seen on the Web.

7.2.3.1.1 The Web's Generative Model: Preferences   Another generative model was required and once again Barabási and his team had an answer. They argued that there was a mechanism operating which they called *preferential attachment*. When choosing which page to direct a link to there is a tendency, or bias, to link to one that already has a high number of incoming links, a process by which the rich (or the popular) get richer. As individuals we do not necessarily do this consciously, but overall, when evened out across the whole of the Web, this preferencing has led to the creation of hubs and the other topological features we have discussed (Barabási 2002).

Barabási's initial idea is still being built on by other researchers, who argue that people are influenced by factors such as the age of the website (Dorogovtsev and Mendes 2000), quality of the content, specialist nature or salience of the content etc. Also, on social network sites there may be a role for *triad formation*, the idea that a link is more likely to be added to a network to connect a friend-of-a-friend to form a triangular relationship, an important concept in sociology (Zhang et al. 2010). This is a fascinating and evolving area of research in a number of disciplines and there are more resources listed in the Further Reading list at the end of the chapter.

Finally, we should also note that work has been undertaken to try to combine the Watts/Strogatz small world model with that of the scale-free model through the idea of a hierarchy of modules of nodes throughout the network (Ravasz and Barabási 2002).

PREFERENTIAL ATTACHMENT AND SEARCH ENGINES

A real-world metaphor for preferential attachment can be seen in the way that Yahoo! worked in its early years. We have already seen how Jerry Yang and David Filo created the Yahoo! search engine by using the intelligence of human editors to group websites into categories and sub-categories and leveraging the value of the clickstream (see Chapter 4).

The idea of prioritizing search engine results based on popularity is now commonplace but understanding how it works in practice can help us to see Barabási's point. If I want to create a blog item and need to link to some information on, say, English progressive rock bands, then I will usually use a search engine to give me some options. The one I choose will probably be near the top of the list, as I understand that the list is ordered to present me with the best matches first. By creating a link to this website I am essentially making it a bigger hub, increasing the likelihood of it occurring in the top few items of future search results conducted by other people, and therefore increasing the likelihood that others will link to it, which in turn creates a bigger hub.

What would be interesting to know, therefore, is to what extent the preferential attachment mechanism is a consequence of more recent human activity on the Web (e.g. search, blogging). If we were able to model the Web in its early days, before Mosaic brought a large and diverse audience to the Web and before user-generated content really started to take off, would we still see a network that demonstrated a power law distribution?

7.2.4 The Bow-Tie Model

The scale-free nature of the Web was not quite the end of the story however. Broder et al. (2000) published a paper that analysed further the graph structure of a large sample of the Web. The authors looked not only at the distribution of the degree of links at each node but also examined the Web's macroscopic structure by looking at which nodes linked to which other nodes (i.e. not only the number of links, but also where they were going). What they found was surprising: the Web is scale-free, dominated by powerful hubs with large numbers of links, but this widespread topology co-exists with a large-scale structure that resembles a bow-tie (see Figure 7.9).

At its heart is a giant, *strongly connected core* (or *component*) (SCC). Inside the core each node can be reached from every other node in the core, i.e. there is path, a series of nodes and links, between each and every node (Easley and Kleinberg 2010). On either side of the core are two large areas, IN and OUT. The former consists of pages that can reach the inner core, but cannot be reached from it; the latter is the opposite. The authors give the example of a corporate website that can be reached from the core, but the site itself only has links to internal documents. Finally, there are pages known as *tendrils* which cannot reach the SCC nor be reached from it. Each of these four areas later became known collectively as *continents*.

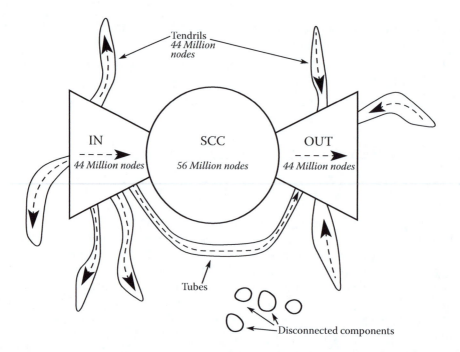

FIGURE 7.9 The topology of the Web resembles a bow-tie. The numbers are long out of date, but the structure has persisted. (Reprinted with permission from Andrei Broder et al. (2000), *Graph structure in the Web.* 9th International World Wide Web Conference [WWW9].)

The authors also found that the continents were roughly the same size, meaning that the core was actually surprisingly small. They also, incidentally, confirmed the results of Barabási's work on the power law and found that it worked on the much larger sample they experimented with, concluding it is a "basic web property" (Broder et al. 2000, 2). Thus they warned:

> In a sense the web is much like a complicated organism, in which the local struc-
> ture at a microscopic scale looks very regular like a biological cell, but the global
> structure exhibits interesting morphological structure (body and limbs) that are not
> obviously evident in the local structure (p. 3).

The implication of this is that drawing conclusions about the structure of the Web graph from a local picture of it may be misleading.

Dill et al. (2002) refined this mapping of the structure of the Web further. They found that not only was the bow tie present at the macroscopic level of the Web, but that it was replicated at smaller scales (between the macroscopic and microscopic scales that Barabási was working with). They identified the formation of what they called *thematically unified clusters* (TUCs), effectively communities of shared interest, with the same bow-tie structure and the same power law distribution as the wider Web.* The cores of each of these clusters

---

* A theme was considered to have been created if a group of websites shared specialist keywords.

are integrated, via the navigational backbone, into the macroscopic core that Broder et al. had discovered. Thus Dill et al. argued: "A striking consequence is that the Web exhibits *self-similarity*, i.e. each thematically unified region displays the same characteristics as the Web at large. In other words, the Web is a 'fractal'" (Dill et al. 2002, 207).

In mathematical terms, this means that the Web is fragmented into continents and communities, each of which demonstrates roughly the same structure. Since hypertext links only allow travel in one direction, there is no guarantee of an inverse path between two nodes, which results in a non-homogeneous network. This was not completely surprising to most mathematicians since all directed graphs fragment, whether they are scale-free or not (Barabási 2002).

7.2.4.1 Or Is It a Teapot?

The bow-tie model is not replicated unilaterally across the Web. Donato et al. (2008) found that some national Web domains, for example the UK and Italy, had a different macroscopic structure with a more tightly connected core encircled by a number of IN and OUT structures—like petals on a flower. Chinese researchers, on the other hand, found that the Chinese domain was shaped more like a teapot (Zhu et al. 2008) (see Figure 7.10). Chung et al. (2009) confirmed that national Web domains differ in shape but currently there is no explanation as to why this might be, and it is an area of interest for researchers.

7.2.5 Power Laws, Small Worlds and Web 2.0

All the world is a graph and the people are vertices.

JENNIFER CHAYES

Microsoft (in Fletcher 2010, Blog)

To recap what we have learned so far: the Web is a scale-free, small world network where the distribution of links between pages exhibits a power law. As Web 2.0 services and applications are part of the wider Web they inevitably demonstrate the same characteristics. Indeed, it is worth keeping in mind these basic topological details when reading each of the chapters on individual Web 2.0 services and in particular the associated research. Time

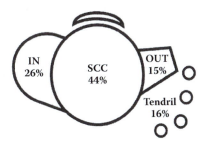

FIGURE 7.10 The teapot graph of the Chinese Web. (Reproduced with the kind permission of the authors from Zhu et al. 2008. *A teapot graph and its hierarchical structure of the Chinese web.* 17th international conference on World Wide Web [WWW2008])

and time again, from blogs to Twitter, the power law is found in various aspects of Web 2.0 life and found again as another new service is introduced.

The Web also displays a network effect, although there is still debate over what this is and the implications it may have. In his original paper on Web 2.0 Tim O'Reilly argued that companies that make the most of the network effect would be successful in the marketplace. It is less clear how services might make use of the topological structure of the Web and in particular the power law. It is likely that in coming years we will hear more about the implications of this feature as companies make more of the long tail. In essence this will be about working with the grain of the Web.

At the same time the Web provides a whole new arena to explore networks at vast scales (Kleinberg 2008). For many decades social science was essentially restricted by the difficulty of obtaining data from large numbers of people, for example concerning their friendship links. Web 2.0 services have provided that data as millions have happily uploaded and shared details of their private lives. It may be taking things a little too far to say, as the philosopher Pierre Lévy told the Royal Society in September 2010, that: "Graph theory will be one of the main bases of the future of the human sciences" (Lévy 2010, 10:33), but it is clear that social media and the exploration of complex networks has opened new and fruitful horizons for the humanities.

EXERCISES AND POINTS TO PONDER

1. Write a computer program to analyse the frequency of the appearance of words in a file of text. Download some sample texts from Project Gutenberg (http://www. gutenberg.org/) and use them to generate word frequency distributions. Does your analysis match the ideas of George Zipf?

2. Write a computer program for a Web spider that can analyse the webpages and links associated with your departmental website (or whole college or similar). Make sure that the code can differentiate between internal links within the website and external links to the rest of the Web. Using the spider, collect the network of internal hypertext links in order to generate a graph of nodes and links. Analyse the graph, either by hand or using analysis software (such as Pajek http://pajek.imfm.si/doku. php?id=pajek). What is the degree of separation of your network? What is the clustering coefficient? What other network parameters can you calculate?

3. Experiments investigating the shape of the Web seem to show that it forms a bow-tie shape (or a teapot shape in China). If we consider the graph formed by the content held within one of the larger social network sites, what might its shape be?

FURTHER READING

Section 7.1: Network Effects

For more discussion of network effects, see Stan Liebowitz's homepage: http://www.utdallas.edu/~liebowit/

For a good introduction to the mathematics and economics involved in network effects see Chapter 17 of Easley and Kleinberg (2010).

Section 7.2.1: Power Laws and Their Relation to Zipf

Zipf, Power-laws, and Pareto—a ranking tutorial by Lada A. Adamic (See: http://www.hpl.hp.com/research/idl/papers/ranking/ranking.html)

A collection of items and links relating to Zipf's law is maintained at: http://www.nslij-genetics.org/wli/zipf/

Section 7.2.1.2: Scale-Free Networks and Complex Networks

For a detailed analysis of the science of networks and a breakdown of the key research papers (which are reproduced), see *The Structure and Dynamics of Networks* (Newman et al. 2006).

For a detailed discussion of the Webgraph and in particular how to develop algorithms to crawl and analyse the Webgraph, see Donato et al. (2007).

See also an online course on the science of networks, given by Barabási: http://barabasilab.neu.edu/courses/phys5116/. In particular note the slides in class 7 (Scale-free networks) which discuss some of the mathematics of the power law and introduce the idea of *ultra* small worlds which are present in some types of scale-free networks.

A course on graph theory and complex networks has been made available online by Maarten van Steen at VU University of Amsterdam. See http://www.distributed-systems.net/gtcn/

For further discussion of non-power laws in other technology areas such as cell/mobile phone call distribution, including the idea of a double Pareto distribution, see Kleinberg and Lawrence (2001); Seshadri et al. (2008); Broder et al. (2000) and Ribeiro et al. (2010).

Detailed discussion of the mathematics of graphs is provided in the *Handbook of Graphs and Networks* (Bornholdt and Schuster 2002).

Section 7.2.5: Power Laws, Small Worlds and Web 2.0

For more on how Web 2.0 companies have exploited network effects, see Chapter 2 of Shuen (2008). For a description of how eBay made the most of the network effect to dominate its market see Parker (2009).

II

Web 2.0 Services

A glance at one of the Web 2.0 news websites such as TechCrunch, ReadWriteWeb or Mashable shows the scale of the explosion in new Web 2.0 services and business start-ups. It would be impossible to cover every type of service, so for Section II I have selected categories of services (blogs, wikis, etc.) that either have some longevity or demonstrate a wide range of ideas.

My aim has been to examine Web 2.0 'in action', so I have attempted to put the services into context by covering their main features, development history, technical development and a summary of the key research areas. In most of the categories there tends to be one or two services that dominate because of their size. I have used these as exemplars as they have usually been the subject of a substantial body of research.

Of the services that did not make it into this part of the book, the most notable are social news aggregation sites such as Digg and Reddit, online communities such as GroupOn and BuyWithMe (who buy in bulk as a group in order to save money), Question and Answer forums such as Quora, virtual world systems such as SecondLife and online social games such as FarmVille, Empire Avenue, World of Warcraft and PetSociety. Social games in particular have attracted enormous interest, and they are often closely integrated with online social networks such as Facebook.

However, services will come and go. Some of them may well grow into the giants of tomorrow's Web, but many more will fade as it becomes clear that their business model does not hold water or that there is little user interest. What is of interest is how a service manifests its 'Web 2.0-ness' and what that might mean for future developments.

## CHAPTER 8

Blogs

Each blog is like a fireplace, and each post is like a log heaved on top to keep the fire burning … As long as a blog puts out heat and light, others who care about the author's subject are drawn to it.

DOC SEARLS AND DAVID SIFRY
(2003, Webpage)

A blog is a frequently updated website that contains fairly short articles, known as *posts*, organised in reverse chronological order (i.e. with the most recent items first). These posts often contain hyperlinks to other websites and blogs, and readers are usually able to respond to posts by making *comments*, usually beneath the original post. Most blogs have a list of other blogs that the author considers to be worth reading regularly, known as a *blogroll*. Whilst the vast majority of blogs are of a personal nature, functioning as a kind of online journal or work record, a few hundred or so have become extremely popular, with audiences measured in the millions.

Blogging is a popular activity for millions of people and creates huge amounts of user-generated content. It is also one of the oldest Web 2.0 services, dating back to the late 1990s and therefore pre-dating the Web 2.0 moniker. In terms of the evolution of the Web, blogs are often seen as a replacement for the individual's personal homepage (Governor et al. 2009; Blood 2004).

8.1 INTRODUCTION TO BLOGS

Of crucial importance to the development of blogging as we now know it has been the introduction of blogging software, a lightweight form of *content management system* (CMS). Content management systems were first introduced to take care of the technical aspects of publishing to the Web so that, for the first time, it became possible to create content without having any technical skills. However, because of the context in which they

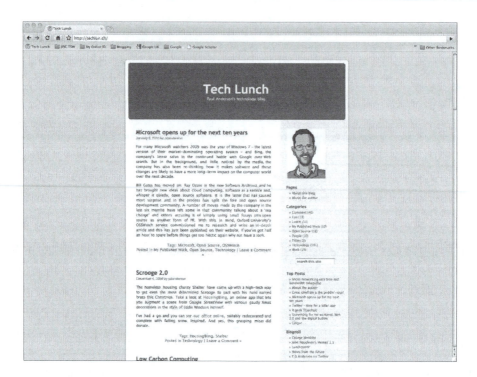

FIGURE 8.1 A typical blog homepage. (Reproduced with kind permission from WordPress, © 2011 WordPress).

were developed,* CMSs tended to be big, expensive pieces of software, out of the reach of most people and usually only installed by large organisations with a lot of content to manage. The developers of blogging software simplified the CMS infrastructure and made it available either for free or at low cost.

Figure 8.1 shows the homepage of my own blog, which uses a fairly typical layout. Clicking on links will take you to pages that are inside the blog's structure, as on a standard website. The name of the blog is in the dark banner or 'masthead' at the top of the homepage and underneath, to the centre and left-hand side is the main text area for the posts, each one with its own title and date/time stamp. On the right-hand side there are links to *pages*, static webpages that tend not to change and are usually used to provide more information about the blog. In addition to this there are standard website features such as search.

8.1.1 Categories and Tags

When a blogger adds a new post they can choose to assign it to one or more *categories*. These essentially function like the folders we are familiar with from word processing

---

* The very first website creators had to know how to write HTML and upload files to a Web server. This was fairly easy when websites only had a few pages and HTML was restricted to fairly basic formatting tags, but as soon as websites started to get bigger and more complicated (for example large corporate websites) they became difficult to manage without considerable technical expertise.

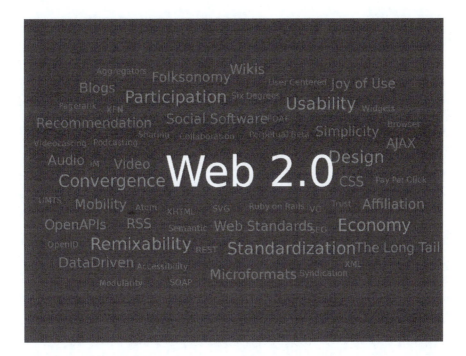

FIGURE 8.2   A tag cloud for Web 2.0. The more popular a word is, the bigger and bolder it appears. (Reprinted from Wikimedia Commons, distributed under CC BY-SA 2.5. Original by Markus Angermeier, vectorized and linked version by Luca Cremonini. See: http://creativecommons.org/licenses/by-sa/2.5/deed.en) File: http://en.wikipedia.org/wiki/File:Web_2.0_Map.svg)

software and are therefore part of the blog's navigational structure, used to help order the posts by topic. Category names can be customized to reflect the content of the blog and when a reader clicks on a category they will be shown all the posts that have been placed under that category heading.

A blogger can also choose to add a *tag* to an individual post. Tags work differently to categories in that they organise content beyond the level of the blog and so are not part of the blog's navigational structure. They are designed to help search engines locate relevant content and, at least in the case of the WordPress blog software, readers can click on the tag-word and be taken to a list of posts from all the other WordPress blogs that have used the same tag. Some blog software applications or hosted services have the functionality to create and display *tag clouds*, images that show the tags at different sizes as a way of visually indicating their popularity (see Figure 8.2).

8.1.2 Comments

A key element of blogging, as most people understand it today, is to allow other people to comment on your posts. Underneath each post there is usually a 'Leave a Comment' link, which links to a comment box, as shown in Figure 8.3. The article being commented on is reproduced so that it is easy to refer back to it. Depending on the blogging software,

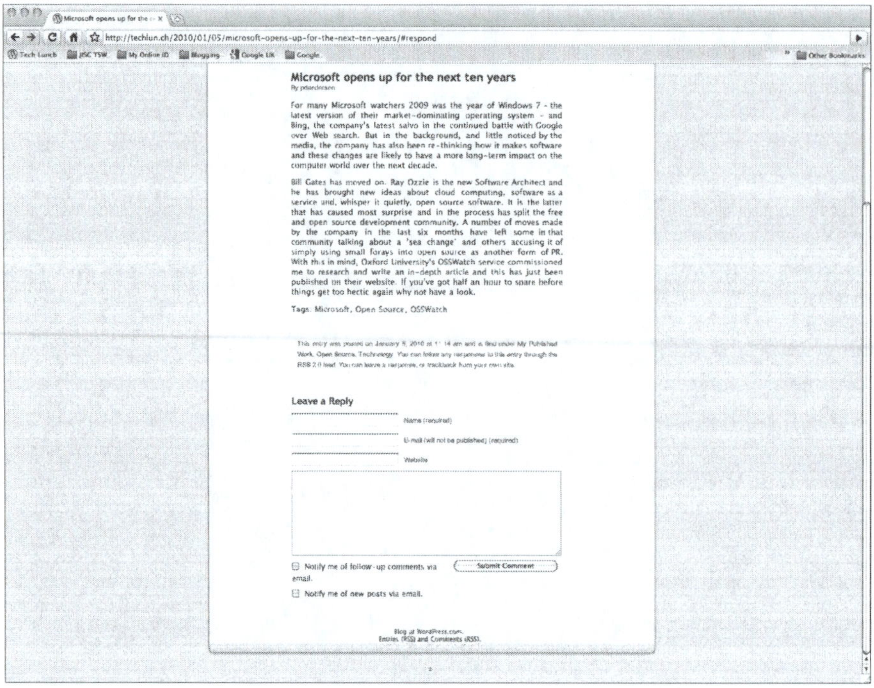

FIGURE 8.3   Adding a comment to a blog post. (Reproduced with kind permission from WordPress, © 2011 WordPress).

comments can be stored so that the blog owner can moderate or edit them before they are published, or perhaps reject them altogether. In this way, blog owners can retain some element of editorial control over their blogs, if they so choose.

For this reason the comment box is often displayed together with other fields for information about the commentator such as a name and e-mail address. These are used to identify the comment poster both to the blog owner, who may be operating a policy of moderation (and therefore might need to e-mail a query to a comment author) and potentially to the readers of the blog. The comment author usually has the choice as to whether their e-mail address is made public or not.

These fields raise questions about anonymity, since it is perfectly possible to enter a pseudonym and choose to hide an e-mail address, and indeed this is common practice. Anonymity is allowed and, it could even be argued, celebrated in blogging culture, and regular readers of blogs will be aware of the interesting variety of pseudonyms on offer. This practice has been the subject of much debate within the blogging world and amongst lawyers and academics who study blog output.[*]

---

[*] Malloy (2006) and Solove (2007) provide introductions to some of the legal issues around, for example, defamation.

8.1.3 Archive

Typically, only the most recent posts are shown on the blog's homepage. The remaining entries are kept in the blog's *archive*. The reader can access these either by date, by clicking on the calendar at the side of the homepage, or from the list of categories.

8.2 A SHORT HISTORY OF BLOGS

The term 'blog' is a shortened version of the original term *weblog*, which seems to have been coined by Jorn Barger. An early user of a previous generation of Internet technologies such as Usenet, Barger set-up his Robot Wisdom personal homepage website in early 1995. By the end of 1997 the site had been converted to the Robot Wisdom Weblog with the intention of being a kind of day-to-day log, or hotlist, of links to interesting material that Barger came across as he circumnavigated the Web. He later told an interviewer that the Web: "had grown into a vast impenetrable treasure cave, generally in pitch blackness. I desperately wanted someone to 'turn on the lights' so I could see what was where, what treasures were there for my enjoyment … So I determined to take on that task" (Rhodes 1999, webpage).

Barger's original concept was very much focused on collecting and publishing (logging), on a day-to-day basis, a series of interesting links. If there was any accompanying text at all it would be a very short, pithy commentary or tag (Blood 2000, 2004). This is a form of what has been called *pre-surfing*: providing a form of 'filter' on the Web's contents for others to use (Herring, Scheidt et al. 2004). Ammann (2009) has pointed out that this is somewhat different to the eventual form that blogging took as primarily a writing space in which users provide comment, opinion and views. Blood (2000) concurs, noting that the introduction of Blogger software can be seen as the point when bloggers began to become less interested in the wider Web and more focused on "short-form journals". She notes how the forms of content management software that were used to support the early blogs presented the user with a box containing the Uniform Resource Identifier (URI) they were interested in commenting on, thus focusing the blogger's mind on the link in question, rather than an empty, free-form box as Blogger did.

The question of who exactly invented blogging (as an activity rather than the term) therefore remains a moot point. By 1997 a number of people had turned their website homepages into various forms of online diary in a manner that resembled what we would now think of as a blog.[*] However, the term 'weblog' was being used to describe the kind of logging that Barger's Robot Wisdom was undertaking. To complicate matters further, even though Barger is widely credited as having invented the term, many bloggers cite Dave Winer, the editor of *Scripting News*, which launched on 1st April 1997, as a key early inspiration. A review of the archived version of the site[†] seems to support the idea that what Winer was doing was indeed a day-to-day log of interesting and newsworthy links to content across the Web and that this happened a few months before Barger. On blogging's tenth anniversary in 2007, technology news site CNet

---

[*] See, for example, Steve Jackson's website in November 1994: http://www.sjgames.com/ill/1994/ill-nov94.html
[†] See: http://www.scripting.com/1997/04.html

argued that a fair amount of the credit should go to Winer (McCullagh and Broache 2007) although in fact Winer himself, an early pioneer of the Web, argues that Tim Berners-Lee's original site at CERN (info.cern.ch) was in fact an early form of weblog (Searls and Sifry 2003).

In 1999 the term began to be shortened to 'blog' and started to be used both as a noun (e.g. my blog) and as a verb (e.g. I blog, I am blogging). In a short essay on the history of blogging Blood (2000) noted that Peter Merholz[*] was responsible for shortening the term and that it may have been something of a joke.

PRE-BLOGGING

BBS AND THE WELL

It should be noted in passing that the idea of posting short texts consisting of personal updates has been around since at least the early days of the Unix operating system.[*] In addition, throughout the 1980s and before the invention of the Web, the Internet hosted what were called *bulletin board systems* (BBSs). These were essentially messaging services where users could also leave responses or make comments, creating a kind of open discussion divided into subjects or threads (Barlow 2007). An important, and similar, pre-cursor was the Unix-based Usenet Internet discussion system (Hauben and Hauben 1998). At least some of the ideas and functionality behind blogging are based loosely on the ideas of Usenet and BBSs.

The WELL was started in 1985 as the *Whole Earth 'Lectronic Link* by Stewart Brand and Larry Brilliant and grew into a small—at most five thousand—but influential community of users. Although overtaken by the introduction of the Web (it was eventually taken over by *Salon* online magazine in 1999 and is still running) many commentators credit it with having had a lot of influence over the development of Web and blogging culture.[†] The WELL explicitly encouraged participation by users with a view to developing a "new public sphere" (Barlow 2007, 147) and a distinguishing feature, which did not transfer across to the blogging community, was the insistence on using one's real name when contributing. The WELL was much influenced by Brand's previous experience founding the *Whole Earth Catalog*[‡] and, according to Barlow, by the idealistic community of US west coasters who had grown up around the rock band the Grateful Dead.

---

[*] Unix is a form of computer operating system developed in the late 1960s by staff at Bell Labs. Early Unix users made use of the .plan file to post personal information. Obviously in these pre-Web days these did not include hypertext links.

[†] See, for example, Kevin Kelly's blog item: http://kk.org/ct2/2008/09/the-whole-earth-blogalog.php

[‡] The *Whole Earth Catalog* was founded in 1968, a product of the ideas swirling around the west coast counter-culture of late-1960s California. Brand created an eclectic catalogue of tools, books and other products that could be used to help the move to a self-sustaining lifestyle. It won the National Book Award in 1972.

8.2.1 Blogging Software

The first rudimentary blogging tool was Pitas, but other notable early examples of software included Blogger, Greymatter and Manila (Du and Wagner 2005; Rettberg 2008). Blogging software is now quite sophisticated and comes in two forms: as a downloadable software

---

[*] See Merholz's blog entry 12th Oct 1999: http://web.archive.org/web/19991013021124/http://peterme.com/index.html

application that is designed to be run on the user's own server or, more popularly, a hosted service where the software is installed and run on the host's servers and which the user interacts with over the Internet. They work on the basis of providing a simple, text entry form that allows a non-technical user to type in the text of their post, add a title, and hit a 'publish' button. The software or hosting service carries out the rest, publishing the post to the blog, organising the content in date order and maintaining an archive. Movable Type is a prominent example of the downloadable software application while Blogger is a well-known hosted service. Many blogging service providers now offer both options, so for example, TypePad is Six Apart's hosted service based on Movable Type software.

A number of blog software companies provide free or low-cost hosting for blogs in exchange either for the right to display advertisements alongside the blog or by charging for additional features over and above the basic blogging service. For example, WordPress makes a small charge for using a domain name that is different from the one they provide (e.g. http://techlun.ch rather than http://tech1unch.wordpress.com).

In 2009 the website Pingdom undertook research into the popularity of blogging software amongst the 100 most-read blogs (as rated by Technorati, the specialist blog search engine).[*] The leaders were WordPress, Movable Type, TypePad and Blogsmith (since bought by AOL[†]). Technorati reports that by far the most common blogging solution is to use a free, third-party hosting service (59% of respondents in its 2009 annual survey) with a further 17% using a paid service.[‡] This leaves a small minority either using an old fashioned HTML-based blog (21%) or who are simply not aware which software they use.

Movable Type was developed by Ben and Mena Trott, a husband and wife team who set up their company, Six Apart, in 2001 (Cadenhead 2005). Six Apart has been one of the prime movers in the blogging world, responsible for driving the development of LiveJournal and also Vox which, like LiveJournal, offers a mixture of blogging and social networking.

LiveJournal was started in 1999 by Brad Fitzpatrick and was later bought by Six Apart. It differs a little from other blog hosting services in that the software also provides some social networking–type facilities. Thus, a blog or 'journal' in LiveJournal has a list of friends. In later years, the software was sold to the Russian company SUP and it remains one of the most visited sites in that country.

Blogger was created in 1999 by a small start-up company called Pyra Labs which was founded by Evan Williams and Meg Hourihan. These two also developed the software and their marketing material declared that it was all about: "Push-button publishing for the people" (Blood 2004, 54). Blogger has an important role in the history of blogging as it was an instant hit when it was launched and is often credited as being the catalyst for an explosion of interest in blogging by millions of Web users in the early 2000s (Shirky 2008), and in 2003 it became part of Google.

Blogsmith was developed in 2003 by Brian Alvey, one of the co-founders of the blog publishing company Weblogs, Inc. which set up some well-known blogs such as Engadget.

---

[*] See: http://royal.pingdom.com/2009/01/15/the-blog-platforms-of-choice-among-the-top-100-blogs/

[†] For some history see: http://www.brianalvey.com/news/2006/11/10/aol-and-blogsmith/

[‡] http://technorati.com/blogging/article/day-3-the-how-of-blogging1/

The software was used by the company for its blogging projects and became part of AOL in November 2006. The software is used in-house by AOL but is no longer available to external bloggers.

WordPress is an open source blogging software application. It was first released in May 2003 and was initially developed by Matt Mullenweg and Mike Little, based on a *fork*[*] of the b2/cafelog blogging code.[†]

8.3 BLOG SOFTWARE DEVELOPMENT

Governor et al. (2009) note that modern blogging software packages and hosting facilities have evolved considerably since they were first introduced and they now provide quite sophisticated publishing software packages for controlling the content of a blog, laying out colours and design, ordering the blogroll, dealing with syndication (see below), archiving and hosting online discussions. Many packages provide a number of additional features (or 'widgets') that pull in additional content, usually displayed at the side of the blog, from the blogger's other Web 2.0 activities such as Twitter and Flickr.

As well as providing useful tools for controlling what the reader sees, blogging software usually provides statistics about how many people have visited the blog and which links they clicked on while they were there.

8.3.1 Permalinks

When a post is published the blogging software creates what is called a permanent link or *permalink* for the item. This is generated automatically and is usually some combination of the blog post's title and the date/time, for example: http://techlun.ch/2009/10/14/mypud/. It is important to be aware that blog software developers have not yet agreed on a standard format.

Permalinks allow other blogs and websites to maintain a permanent hyperlink to a post, long after it has left the blog's homepage and been stored in the archive. Before they were introduced in the spring of 2000, the only way of linking to another blog post was to use the blog's main URI. Unfortunately, items do not stay on the blog's front page for long before being moved off to the archive when new posts are published. This meant that links quickly became invalid which, in turn, held back the conversational nature of blogging that was starting to emerge since it was difficult to keep track of what was under discussion. Permalinks turned the individual post into a discrete unit of blog content, and meant that syndication became possible, since individual posts could be fed (via Really Simple Syndication [RSS]) to aggregators and feed readers.[‡] As Tom Coates, a well-known social software developer puts it: "For the first time it became relatively easy to gesture directly at a highly specific post on someone else's site and talk about it. Discussion emerged. Chat emerged. And as a result, friendships emerged … the permalink was the first—and most successful—attempt to build bridges between weblogs" (Coates 2003, webpage).

---

[*] In open source software development, a 'fork' is a process of branching a collection of code to start a new project.
[†] See: http://weblogtoolscollection.com/archives/2008/07/14/evolution-of-wordpress-b2cafelog-to-wordpress-10/
[‡] Andrew Anker of Six Apart, in a panel discussion at the Web 2.0 conference 2004, stated that RSS turned blogging software from a low-end CMS into something much more powerful (O'Reilly et al. 2004, 05:20).

Permalinks demonstrate an important and desirable feature of a hypertext link: *permanent validity* (Vossen and Hagemann 2007) and Tim Berners-Lee provided a discussion of this issue in his 1998 essay, "Cool URIs Don't Change".[*] However, it is important to note that although the URI might remain unchanged there is no guarantee that the blog post itself has not been changed since its original publication—something that creates difficulties for information scientists. This in turn poses the question of 'versions' of a blog post. Millard and Ross (2006) point out that, traditionally, hypertext systems have supported versioning and that wiki software continues this tradition, whereas blogging does not. This is an important distinction between the facilities provided by wiki and blog software and, consequently, the nature of the two media.

8.3.2 Trackbacks and Pingbacks

Trackbacks are a form of inter-blog communication or notification that facilitates reciprocal (two-way) linking (Blood 2004). The idea was pioneered by Six Apart in their work on Movable Type and they have published a formal definition of the feature.[†]

If blogger A reads something interesting on blog B that she wants to tell her readers about, then she has a choice. She can either include a permalink URI in the text of her post, or she can add a trackback. Adding a URI means that whoever reads her post will be able to click through to the original post on blog B, but no one reading blog B will know that blogger A's post exists because standard hyperlinks are one-way links. However, if blogger A publishes her link as a trackback, a snippet from the text of her post will appear as a comment below the original post on B's blog. By using the trackback and publishing her post as a comment on blog B, blogger A ensures that readers of blog B will become aware of her post and be able to click through to it, if they so choose.

In order to include a trackback, blogger A needs to find the special trackback URI. This is usually displayed beneath the original post on blog B (see Figure 8.4). By selecting and copying the trackback link, blogger A can add the trackback URI to her new post—in the example shown in Figure 8.4 it is via a box labelled 'Send Trackbacks to'. As soon as blogger A publishes her post, the software will notify blogger B's software that someone wishes to create a trackback. Once approved (if comments are being moderated) then blog B's software will publish a comment that says something like "Blog A says" followed by some of the text from blogger A's post. Understanding this can be tricky, and details vary, so it is usually best to experiment to see what happens. It should also be noted that because trackbacks are often abused by spammers in order to distribute their spoof URIs on legitimate sites, many bloggers disable the trackback functionality.

Pingbacks are related to trackbacks in that they also set up reciprocal links between blogs, but whereas trackbacks have to be set up manually by the blogger, pingbacks complete the process automatically. However, pingbacks will normally only work if blogger A includes the permalink to blogger B's post and both blogs are running on software that allows pingbacks.

---

[*] See: http://www.w3.org/Provider/Style/URI
[†] http://www.lifewiki.net/attachments/view/101/2.2

FIGURE 8.4   Adding a new post to a blog. Note the post's text box trackback link (bottom of picture). (Reproduced with kind permission from WordPress, © 2011 WordPress).

Another difference is that pingbacks and trackbacks use different communication technologies (Extensible Markup Language-Remote Procedure Call [XML-RPC] ping and Hypertext Transfer Protocol [HTTP] POST, respectively). Thus, a pingback makes use of a ping signal. In technical terms this is an XML-RPC-based push mechanism that a blog uses to notify a server that its contents have changed.[*] The ping signal is sent to the server that is handling the blogging software for blogger B's blog. The signal contains the permalink of A's post and details of the particular entry on B's blog that she was referring to. B's software undertakes various checks to try and confirm that the ping is valid before regenerating B's post with the new pingback present in the comments section. Further technical details are available.[†]

8.3.3 Syndication

Blogs use *syndication* technologies in order to push out information about new content to the wider Web. By subscribing to a blog's syndication feed a reader can subscribe to a number of blogs (by using specialist feed reader software) and be alerted when new content is published rather than making several return visits on the off-chance that something new has been added. These feeds can also be embedded in other webpages so that a clickable list of titles of blog items appears within the page or within another blog. Blogging software often comes with built-in technology to automatically facilitate this process using either RSS or Atom (see Chapters 11 and 14). When the blog author adds a new post or otherwise changes the content, subscribers to the blog's feed will be informed.

---

[*] See: http://www.xmlrpc.com/weblogsCom
[†] See: http://www.hixie.ch/specs/pingback/pingback

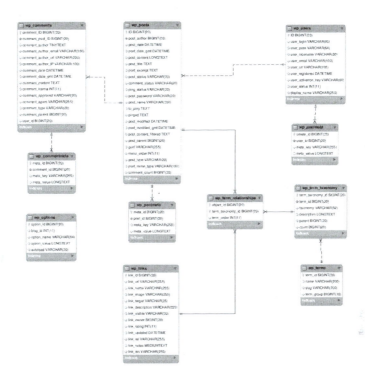

FIGURE 8.5   WordPress 3.0 internal database structure. (Reproduced with kind permission from WordPress, © 2011 WordPress).

8.3.4 Example System: WordPress

It is worth taking a moment to look at the technical infrastructure of blog software. We will use WordPress as an example, since the software is open source and therefore can be reviewed quite easily by an interested reader. Although less open, other systems follow broadly the same pattern.

Technically, WordPress is written in PHP[*] with a MySQL database in support. Like most CMS systems, WordPress is centred around the database and all the blog posts, comments, tags etc. are stored in it (either on the user's own server or at the hosted service). The database consists of ten tables as can be seen in the diagram in Figure 8.5, provided by the WordPress development team.[†]

Readers who are familiar with database structure diagrams will be able to follow the detail of WordPress's internal layout.[‡] If, for example, we look at the table wp_posts (at the top centre of the figure), we see fields for such obvious items as post_title and post_author. Wp_posts is used for posts, pages and for file attachments. Comments are kept in a separate table, wp_comments.

---

[*] PHP is a Web scripting language developed by Rasmus Lerdorf in 1995. The code is embedded in a webpage and then interpreted by a PHP processor on the server side.

[†] See: http://codex.wordpress.org/images/8/83/WP_27_dbsERD.png

[‡] Further technical details are provided at: http://codex.wordpress.org/Database_Description and: http://wpbits.wordpress.com/2007/08/08/a-look-inside-the-wordpress-database/

8.4 BLOGGING TAKES OFF

I still can't contain my amazement about these developments. Never before in history have ordinary people been able to reach out and communicate to so many around the globe.

DANIEL J. SOLOVE
(2007, 20)

For the first few years of the 2000s the number of blogs rose exponentially (Herring, Scheidt et al. 2004). In November 2002, blog search specialists Technorati had indexed 13,000 blogs, but by November 2005 it was 20 million (Weil 2006). As traffic to the blogs also grew, professional journalists and traditional media owners began to take hold of the new media format and the amateur, free-and-easy nature of blogging began to change. By early 2003 there was talk of the emergence of an 'A' list of bloggers and blog sites that seemed increasingly to resemble traditional mass media rather than the link-based blogging espoused by Barger and Winer (Benkler 2006; Shirky 2005). Such blogs attracted a large audience and could be funded by displaying adverts around or at the sides of posts. Well-known examples include the political blog the Daily Kos, news site The Huffington Post, Glenn Reynolds' InstaPundit, Nick Denton's Gawker, the German blog Basic Thinking, gossip blogs such as TMZ and the Drudge Report, and technology sites Engadget, Mashable and TechCrunch. Increasingly, the most popular blogs require teams of people rather than being the work of a lone individual.

Political and show-biz blogs have become particularly popular. Many of these focus on providing commented links to stories from the world's traditional media and press wires, but many also attempt (with varying degrees of success) to break new stories or provide a forum for information leaks. Some sites have become influential because they were able to break news stories and offer readers a scoop that more traditional media either did not get or were slower to pick up on. The Drudge Report is a primary example and is best known for breaking the story of President Bill Clinton's relationship with Monica Lewinsky.

Blogging's sense of immediacy has been taken up by traditional news media (Levene 2006) and the websites of magazines and newspapers have begun to absorb the blogging concept by providing space for their columnists and higher-profile journalists to publish their own blogs. In addition, it is now common for high-profile technology conferences to have attendant blogging reporters who provide an almost minute-by-minute account of proceedings. Technorati's annual reports of 2008 and 2009 noted the "rising class" of the professional blogger[*] and in 2009 they noted a slight decline in the "hobbyist" blogger.[†]

Inevitably, blogging has become a standard corporate communication tool with many companies now hosting blogs on their websites, along with blogs produced by a range of professional communicators on behalf of prominent people and those in the public eye. Sang Lee et al. (2006) note a number of different types of corporate blog including

---

[*] See: http://technorati.com/blogging/article/state-of-the-blogosphere-2009-introduction/page-2/
[†] See: http://technorati.com/blogging/article/day-2-the-what-and-why2/

executive blogs, group blogs* focused on a particular organisational or product support theme, promotional blogs used essentially as marketing and PR for products or services, and individual employee blogs. The latter are sometimes collected together to form a list of company bloggers.[†]

Blogging software is also being used as a lightweight information management technology that can be used to good effect within companies, supported by a number of books and conferences on how work groups can make use of it. Many of these discussions focus on the potential to generate a more personal, two-way conversational style of interaction between companies and their customers and, internally, between work teams and colleagues.[‡]

However, despite the high profile of a blogging 'elite', it should be remembered that the vast majority of blogs remain written by individuals about largely personal interests.

8.4.1 Video Blogging: The Rise of the Vlog

More recently, blogs have moved away from being purely text-based and are now starting to incorporate images, video and audio files (Gao et al. 2010). Early attempts at vlogging involved adding a link to an externally hosted video file within the text of the blog post. Parker and Pfeiffer (2005) cite Peter Jackson's video blog made during the filming of *King Kong* as a primary example of this form of working.[§]

The introduction of YouTube in 2005 made this process of linking to an external video source much easier and as vlogging became more popular, the developers of blogging software started to include video upload and distribution as a feature. For example, WordPress offers VideoPress (for a fee) which handles video upload, distribution and playback. This means that the video can be embedded in the blog post itself, rather than as a link to an external service.

As the different formats of blogging and vlogging (passing on information about interesting content, personal journal writing etc.) have become more familiar and users have become more confident with the technologies, a new format, *lifecasting*, has emerged through experimentation. Lifecasters obsessively document their everyday lives through social media technology.

8.4.2 Blogging Spam

As blogging has become more popular it has attracted the attention of spammers. In 2007, BlogScope reported that half of the blog material they had analysed was spam. Spammer-created blogs are known as *splogs* (Thomason 2007; Mann 2006) and have rapidly risen in number following the widespread availability of free blogging software. Splogs are used to promote unsavoury or illegal products such as pornography, illicit pharmaceuticals and counterfeit software products or are used to fool blog readers into clicking on click-pay advertisements (where the spammer gets paid when a reader clicks on the ad). A mass

---

* Within the corporate world, group blogs (also known as collaborative or distributed blogs) can become quite large company endeavours; for example OracleAppsBlog has hundreds of contributors (Bar-Ilan 2004; Sang Lee 2006).
† See, for example, http://blogs.oracle.com/ and http://www.microsoft.com/communities/blogs/portalhome.mspx
‡ See, for example, Robert Scoble and Shel Israel's *Naked Conversations* (2006).
§ See: http://www.kongisking.net/index.shtml

of interlinked splogs is known as a *link farm,* and they are created in order to 'game' or improve search engine listings for the website of the splogger's client (Kolari, Java, and Finin 2006).

Spammers also generate comments and trackbacks that include spoof or corrupt URIs or links to splogs and a false pinging technique known as *spings* (used to confuse ping servers into thinking new content is available on a splog).

A number of proposals have been made to deal with blog spam and *splog filtering* is an active research area (Agarwal and Liu 2009; Wei et al. 2008). There are various approaches, based on either understanding the structural nature of blogs (i.e. the topology—see Section 8.6.3), or on content analysis, or some mixture of the two. Although this is an ongoing research area, a number of technical solutions have already been implemented. As just one example, Akismet is a leading, free blog spam protection system, provided by the makers of WordPress. When a new comment or trackback comes in to a blog it can be automatically submitted to the service, where pattern matching techniques are used to determine whether it is spam or not. The Akismet system also includes an Application Programming Interface (API) in order that other software developers can also use these spam detection facilities within their own applications (see Chapter 6).

In August 2011 Akismet reported processing over 21 million spam blog comments a day[*] compared to around 1.4 million legitimate posts (what it refers to as *ham*).

8.4.3 Search: Keeping Track of the Blogs

Blog searching is different to Web searching, and a number of special-purpose search engines have been developed to take account of this. For example, every blog post has a date/time stamp, which means there is a temporal element that can be used to organise search results. In addition, content tagged with keywords means that information discovery and analysis based on the popularity and topicality of those keywords is possible (Bansal and Koudas 2007b). However, there are also a number of technical difficulties in reusing traditional information retrieval algorithms for the blogosphere.[†]

Much of the underlying technology associated with blog searching is similar to that of basic Web search in that it uses automatic spiders to retrieve information from the Web. Levene (2006) provides a thorough introduction for the interested reader. However, there is one particular technical feature of blog engines that is worth noting: the ping process. The first example was the Weblogs.com ping server run by MoreOver technologies. It was originally created by UserLand Software and was maintained in its early days by our old friend Dave Winer. It handles about four million pings a day and acts as a hub—a kind of centralized information collection point. Blog search engines then use it to find out about new blog content by polling (checking) for new content at the ping service. Ping-O-Matic is another prominent example of this type of service and is run by the WordPress Foundation.

---

[*] See their live stats: http://akismet.com/stats/
[†] For example, in Section 8.6.4.1 we discuss the sparsity of the blogosphere graph, a topological feature which can hinder search ranking techniques (Agarwal and Liu 2009).

FIGURE 8.6   The IceRocket blog search engine. (Reproduced with kind permission of Blake Rhodes of IceRocket, © 2011 IceRocket).

Specialist blog search engines have tended to come and go, in much the same way as early Web search engines did. Levene (2006), in his detailed study of search engines, noted that the prominent examples were BlogDex, DayPop and Technorati, but today only the latter remains in active service as a blog search engine. Statistics concerning blog search engines are difficult to obtain since they are often conflated with those of general search engines. Notable examples, in my opinion, include Technorati, IceRocket, Techmeme, Google Blog Search, Blogtrackers and BlogScope.

Technorati was founded by Dave Sifry in November 2002 as a blog search engine and analysis tool. It uses the tags that blog authors add to their posts and assigns an authority value which is based on the number of unique incoming links to the blog in question (Searls and Sifry 2003). The site uses this authority value to determine the top 100 blogs (although it is worth noting that since 2009 it has concentrated on English-language sites only).

Icerocket was launched in 2004 by Mark Cuban an Internet entrepreneur and owner of the Dallas Mavericks (see Figure 8.6). It also searches Facebook and Twitter in addition to blogs.

BlogScope is a project that has branched out from the University of Toronto (Bansal and Koudas 2007a). The service reports that it currently has around 53 million sites in its index. It is based on the idea of a 'text stream': a temporally ordered collection of text documents (in this case blog posts). The system fetches tens of thousands of new documents

FIGURE 8.7   The Techmeme technology news aggregation service. (Reproduced with kind permission from Gabe Rivera, Techmeme, © 2011 Techmeme).

per hour, by collating items from RSS feeds, and employs various data mining techniques. The BlogScope homepage provides a display of the 'Hot Keywords' and provides plots of these keywords over time, thus marking bursts of activity. It also displays related words for each keyword.

Techmeme was developed by Gabe Rivera, a former researcher at Intel, and launched in September 2005.* It is slightly different from other engines in that it aggregates content from technology-related blogs and news websites. Stories are detected by an automated process which 'scrapes' for content and then attempts to spot similarities and predict emerging news trends. A seeding list of likely blogs and news sites is used to filter content and help the system build a more reliable list (Strange 2007). This second list details the blogs and news sites that are publishing content related to a story the system considers to be emerging, into a single place on its page (see Figure 8.7). Thus the original source of a story is shown together with any follow-ups, related posts and lists of blogs that have passed comment on the story.

Blog searching is a developing area and is one of the challenges that Web 2.0 poses to existing search engine technology. Hearst et al. (2008) argue that blog search needs to develop the capability to achieve three tasks: find out what people think about a certain topic over time; suggest blogs that are good to read for their style and other quality criteria; find useful information in older blog posts along the lines of standard engines. This is an area of future research potential, likely to make use of developments in machine learning algorithms and data mining techniques (Savage 2010).

---

* See: http://latimesblogs.latimes.com/technology/2008/05/search-and-you.html

8.5 THE BLOGOSPHERE

Goodbye, cyberspace! Hello, blogiverse! Blogosphere? Blogmos?

BRAD L. GRAHAM
(1999, Webpage)

As blogging became more popular, some researchers and writers began to use the term blog-space to describe the collective output. However, this has almost completely died out as a term and *blogosphere* has gained general acceptance (Rosenbloom 2004; Kumar et al. 2004), despite the fact that it is widely accepted that the term was originally coined as a joke by the blogger and St. Louis theatre publicist Brad L. Graham in September 1999. Exact definitions vary and include: "the global network of blog postings" (Scoble and Israel 2006, 2); "the universe of all these blogging sites" (Agarwal and Liu 2008, 18); "a social network between the blogs' authors, which arises from the links between their blogs" (Levene 2006, 278). Despite this variety, the general idea is clear and Scoble and Israel (2006) argue that all bloggers, no matter how many visitors their site receives, are part of this global network.

8.5.1 How Big Is the Blogosphere?

A completely accurate picture of the size of the blogosphere is difficult given its constantly changing nature. BlogPulse (owned by media information specialists, Nielson) reports regularly on the state of the blogosphere. On 10th August 2011 it identified over 167 million blogs, with 89,000 having been added in the previous 24 hours. The number of posts indexed at that time stood at just over one million.

Despite these numbers, blogging regularly is a minority interest for most Internet users. The Pew Internet and American Life project reported in 2010 (the last year for which figures are available) that 14% of all American adults who were online said that they blog (Zickuhr 2010). Figures from other Western countries, Australia for example, confirm a similar level of blogging interest and indeed, blogging may actually be in decline (ARC 2010). In 2007, the Oxford Internet Institute reported that blogging in the UK had declined by 5% since 2005 (Dutton and Helsper 2007). Also in 2007, Gartner reported that the number of new blogs peaked in October of that year and that as many as 200 million blogs were not being used.* In Poland, researchers at Warsaw University found that 65% of the blogs they surveyed were extinct (no signs of recent activity) and a further 23% had never had any content in the first place (Zając et al. 2009). Pew also noted a particular decline in blogging activity amongst the young as they migrate to newer technologies such as Twitter and online social networks: half as many teenagers reported working on their own blog in the 2010 survey compared to 2006 (Zickuhr 2010). This was matched by a corresponding decline in commenting on other people's blogs, something that may result in a 'Catch-22' situation since it seems likely that one of the reasons a blogger might lose interest in blogging is due to a lack of response in the form of comments and trackbacks. Indeed, it could be argued that the logic of the power law, as discussed in Chapter 7, means that many bloggers find themselves at the less active end of the long tail of blog popularity.

---

* See: http://www.guardian.co.uk/technology/2007/mar/27/news.blogging

However, this decline after an initial flurry of excitement may only be applicable to the West. According to the China Internet Network Information Center (CNNIC), which publishes a survey of Internet use in China, the number of Chinese Internet users with personal blogs rose from 73 million in December 2007 to 231 million by the end of July 2010.[*] There are many other studies of the blogosphere covering a wide variety of countries and regions, for example Etling et al. (2009) map the Arabic blogosphere, and Obradovič and Baumann (2008) look at Germany, and these should be taken into account before making generalized statements about the popularity or otherwise of blogging. The World Internet Project also conducts research on Internet use in at least 20 different countries and is likely to be an important source of material for researchers looking to investigate the size of the blogosphere further.[†]

8.6 RESEARCHING THE BLOGOSPHERE

Analysing the blogosphere is not simply a case of counting the overall number of blogs. The levels of activity on those blogs and the nature of the content that is being created are also of interest; blogging has proven to be fertile ground for exploring research questions from a variety of fields. The rise of the blogosphere has provided a rich seam for the development of interdisciplinary research work between computer scientists, librarians, sociologists, physicists, mathematicians, ethnographers, political scientists and legal scholars. Debate about the blogosphere and its wider cultural impact has also drawn in marketing professionals, newspaper editors and even judges. A number of authors have pointed out that studying how the blogosphere operates has implications for the wider study of how information diffusion works in a modern, digital society (Leskovec et al. 2007; Kumar et al. 2004). As Shi et al. (2007) have pointed out: "Tracking information diffusion in the blogosphere is not just an intriguing research problem, but is of interest to those tracking trends and sentiments" (p.1).

Kumar et al. (2005) have confirmed this, arguing that, broadly speaking, analysis of the blogosphere is undertaken for either sociological or technical reasons. Sociological analysis provides interesting insights into various aspects of human behaviour and communication patterns and there are a number of approaches to this. Some, for example, argue that the blogosphere is essentially an online social network of bloggers and can therefore be analysed with techniques used in real-world social network research (Tseng et al. 2005). Technical analysis builds on existing work undertaken into how networks, and in particular the Web, operate at enormous scales and, as already noted, may also have major implications for some of the cultural and sociological interpretations of aspects of blogging.

8.6.1 Tools for Analysing the Blogosphere

A number of specialist tools have been developed to help with the analysis of the blogosphere. Agarwal et al. (2009) list a number of such tools including BlogPulse, BlogScope, the various blog-specific search engines and BlogTrackers.[‡] The latter is typical of the genre

---

[*] See CNNIC's 26th survey report at: http://www.cnnic.cn/en/index/0O/02/index.htm
[†] See: http://www.worldinternetproject.net/
[‡] See: http://blogtrackers.fulton.asu.edu/

and allows the user to crawl blog data and analyse and observe interesting events and trends. It features amongst other things a method for individually analysing blog posts within a set time period and a tool called the Term Frequency Analyzer, which shows the tag cloud for all the blog posts in a given time period. BlogPulse uses a spider to crawl thousands of blogs in order to create a daily corpus from the collection of posts it finds, which it then uses for indexing, phrase finding, analysis and data mining (Glance et al. 2004).

Another specialist tool, which has been developed by researchers at the Japanese company NEC and the University of California, allows the user to search for communities of bloggers and then explore those communities by examining a number of extracted, representative blogs. The researchers refer to Mountain View, a software tool which finds and visualizes the top blogs (based on rankings of inter-connections and mutual linking) in a given community of interest (Tseng et al. 2005). There has also been a body of research work investigating how blogs can be automatically mined and analysed in order to extract information about the views and sentiments being expressed (Pang and Lee 2008; Melville et al. 2009). This has led to the development of a group of sentiment analysis tools, such as HP's LivePulse (Castellanos et al. 2011), which are used by academics and by the marketing and corporate branding industries.

In addition to special-purpose toolsets, Agarwal and Liu (2008) suggest a number of tools that have previously been used for real-world social network analysis including Pajek[*] (Slovenian for "spider"), NetMiner, and the network package in the R statistics software application.

8.6.2 Sociological Analysis

Sociological analysis of blogs has provided insight into various aspects of human behaviour and communication. In general, the main areas of research interest are in how much blogging takes place, categorizing content, and temporal analysis.

8.6.2.1 Levels of Activity

The Pew Research Center reported in 2008 that 5% of Internet users say they usually blog every day (Smith 2008) and blog search engine Technorati reported in its 2010 survey (*State of the Blogosphere* reports[†]) that one in five bloggers claimed to update on a daily basis with a hard core of around 13% (of its survey data) spending more than ten hours a week blogging. The most common rate of updating was two to three times per week.[‡]

Technorati rates bloggers with an authority score which is based on the level of interest that others show in a blog, and notes in its survey findings that those with higher levels of authority post nearly 300 times more content than lower-ranked bloggers. This should not surprise us. As noted earlier, one of the developments in blogging culture has been the emergence of a hard-core of 'A' list bloggers. The Technorati report noted that: "Professional

---

[*] See: http://pajek.imfm.si/doku.php?id=pajek

[†] These reports are based on evidence gathered from Technorati's own work, plus an extensive survey of the blogging activities of 2,800 bloggers from 50 countries. See: http://technorati.com/state-of-the-blogosphere/

[‡] See: http://technorati.com/blogging/article/who-bloggers-brands-and-consumers-day/

bloggers grow more prolific, and influential, every year" and "The blogosphere is also further insinuating itself into the traditional media's historic turf" (McLean 2009, webpage).

8.6.2.2 Categorising Blog Content

Anyone interested in seeing what people are blogging about can watch it in real-time on BlogPulse Live, where blog activity is categorised into key subject areas. This kind of real-time blog tracking can be fun but information scientists have analysed blogs more formally, as a form of human communication (Herring, Scheidt et al. 2004). Much of this work builds on an existing body of knowledge concerning earlier forms of Web-based communication such as the personal homepage, and in some cases traces its roots to the analysis of even earlier forms of communication such as the handwritten diary. In a related piece of research, Herring et al. (2006) noted that a variety of types of analysis have been undertaken including content analysis, rhetorical analysis and ethnographic interviews with bloggers to explore blogging behaviours and motivations, all with a view to: "characterise the forms, functions, and audiences of blogs, as well as people's motivations for blogging" (p. 1).

Grieve et al. (2010) focused on linguistic content and based on this they argue that blogging splits into two camps: personal blogs and thematic blogs (in which the blogger discusses a topic other than themselves). Herring et al. (2004) noted the work of Krishnamurthy who has proposed a classification of blogging into four basic types structured along two axes: personal vs. topical and individual vs. community. This provides four quadrants as shown in the diagram reproduced from their paper (Figure 8.8).

Quadrant one is self-explanatory. Quadrant two is the class of shared, collaborative blogs centred around the development of a community of interest which is focused on personal matters, e.g. an evening class forum. Four is the same kind of forum activity

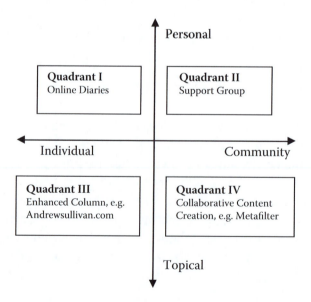

FIGURE 8.8 Blogging can be classified into four different content types. (Reprinted with permission from Herring et al. (2004), page 3, [*Bridging the Gap: A genre analysis of Weblogs*] © 2004 IEEE).

but with a focus on external, topical issues like news, politics or an open source software project. Quadrant three is the area set aside for newspaper-like columnists who write personal opinions about newsworthy or topical issues. Hence there is an important split in the blogging world, also noted by Schiano et al. (2004) and Williams and Jacobs (2004), between a lone individual's work and that of a group. Various studies seem to confirm the prevalence of Quadrant one—the personal journal (see, for example, Viégas 2005 and Schmidt 2007a, 2007b).

In addition, a number of authors have noted that the content of blogs in some ways reflects the age and gender of the blogger (Schmidt 2007a; Pedersen and Macafee 2007; Herring, Kouper et al. 2004). Technorati reports that two thirds of bloggers are male, have some sort of higher education, and fall within the age range of 18 to 44.* This can affect the nature of blogging content, with younger bloggers more likely, for example, to use blogging as a personal journal. However, in its most recent survey (2010) Technorati reports that a new sub-class of female blogger, 'Mom', is growing in influence. Such bloggers are heavily connected to their personal communities and use blogging to keep up with neighbours, friends and family.

It is also worth noting that the practice of blogging varies from country to country, with ethnographers exploring why people blog and how they behave when blogging, for example looking at approaches to privacy and frequency of posting (Nardi et al. 2004). Schmidt et al. (2007a) say that the level of anonymous blogging approaches 30% in Germany, compared to 19% in a non-representative study of English-speaking bloggers (Viégas 2005).

The interactive nature of blogging has also been the subject of investigation. Williams and Jacobs (2004) note that a blog is more than a page of news or information about a particular subject, but is also a "place for a distinctive style to emerge, in the course of writing entries and responding to feedback, that reflects the personal character of the blog's creator" (webpage). They found that blogging had a deeply social nature, not only through the interaction online via comments and trackbacks, but also in generating off-line conversations. Nardi et al. (2004) found that bloggers often developed the style of their blog over a period of time in response to feedback from their audience and that "blogs create the audience, but the audience also creates the blog" (p. 224). Sometimes blogs would even be initiated in response to requests from other people. Other researchers have looked at the conversations that take place when bloggers comment on each other's posts and have developed models for tracking and analysing how this process works (Efimova and de Moor 2005).

There is one final area that needs to be mentioned and that is *clustering*, finding groups of similar blogs (Agarwal et al. 2010; Feng et al. 2011). Similarity may be measured in a number of ways including analysis of the textual content of individual posts, analysis of the depth of connections between different bloggers, and using tags to group-related content. Many of the blog analysis techniques that have been discussed in this section (and in the next one) can be combined to help find similarity. Clustering is an active research area and promises to play an important role in providing new tools for accurate blog searching, analysing information diffusion and in understanding

---

* See: http://technorati.com/blogging/article/who-bloggers-brands-and-consumers-day/

how content is organised across the blogosphere, particularly in the long tail of less popular blogs.

8.6.2.3 Temporal Analysis of Blogging

The temporality of blog-based content is one of the key differences between the blogosphere and the wider Web (Agarwal and Liu 2009), as blog entries may rapidly become obsolete and might not be linked to much beyond their publication date. As blog posts are time- and date-stamped this can be used in academic study, as well as having a practical application for blog spam (Lin et al. 2008). Kumar et al. (2005) have defined *time graphs* to extend the traditional notion of the Web's directed graph, to record the point in time when links are created. Each edge of the graph is a triple, consisting of the details of the nodes involved in any link as well as a time stamp. The researchers noted that blogging was different to other aspects of the Web, being more "bursty" in nature, saying that: "Within a community of interacting bloggers, a given topic may become the subject of intense debate for a period of time, then fade away. These bursts of activity are typified by heightened hyperlinking amongst the blogs involved—*within a time interval*" (p. 570).

Gruhl et al. (2004) argue that this kind of time-based analysis can be useful for studying the way that information is diffused around the blogosphere. Their work also noted the bursty nature of the blogosphere, with the presence of what they call "spikes" (short-term, highly intense discussions of real-world events) and a rare phenomenon they called "resonance" (a massive blogging response triggered by a seemingly inconsequential real-world event). Bansal et al. (2007) have looked at how posts make use of keywords, by parsing blog text and then noting how keywords cluster when topics of a similar nature are under discussion. They also noted the temporal, fleeting nature of these clusters as subjects enter and then drift out of the mainstream.

8.6.2.3.1 Cascading

Various authors have looked at patterns of blog behaviour by analysing the development of blogs over time, reviewing metrics such as the number of posts and looking at the topology of what they call *cascades* (Leskovec et al. 2007; McGlohon et al. 2007).

In this context, a cascade (also known as a conversation tree) describes the pattern of blog posts and their links to other posts and the wider Web. It has a single starting post called the initiator, with no outgoing links to other posts (see Figure 8.9). Posts then become part of the cascade either by linking to the initiator, or to another post that has already linked to the initiator. In this way cascades represent flows of information through the blogging network, and analysing cascades can provide insight into how information diffuses through the blogosphere. The researchers on these particular studies found that cascades form two main shapes: stars and chains.

In this context, a *star* occurs when a single post has several incoming links but links do not propagate any further outwards. This produces a shallow, but wide tree.* A *chain*

---

* The term star as it is used here is different to the one discussed in the next section, where it is used to talk about the popularity (number of incoming and outgoing links) of the blog as a whole rather than the shape of links to individual blog posts.

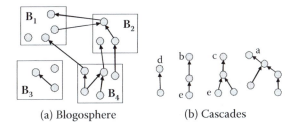

(a) Blogosphere   (b) Cascades

FIGURE 8.9   Cascade model of the blogosphere. (a) The blogs B1, B2 etc. contain posts which link to each other. (b) If we extract these posts and map their links we can see cascades. (Reprinted by kind permission from McGlohon et al. (2007), page 2).

occurs when the root post is linked to by a single post, which in turn is linked to by another post. This creates a deep but narrow tree. McGlohon et al. (2007) found most cascades were somewhere between these two points, with, for example, humour blogs tending to form star shapes, and political blogs tending to have deep, chain-like graphs.

We should also note that Leskovec et al. (2007) found that cascades follow a power law (see Chapter 7). They collected data about all the incoming links to a post and plotted the number of such links occurring each day following the publication of the post. This creates a curve that indicates the rise and fall of "popularity". They found that the popularity of a post drops over time by a power law with an exponent of approximately −1.5, thereby agreeing with Barabási's theory of the heavy tail in Web networks. The authors argue that this is interesting, since intuitively it might be expected that people would lose interest in a post in a way that exhibited a steeper (i.e. exponential) drop off. They note, however, that the power law pattern in this instance is similar to the work by Vázquez et al. (2006) on the frequency of exchange of letters involving famous scientists. Leskovec et al. also found that the size distribution of cascades (i.e. the number of posts involved) follows a "perfect Zipfian distribution" (p. 1) that is, a power law with slope of −2 and that the most popular shape was the star.

Further research work into cascading and the temporal nature of blogging continues. For example, Li et al. (2009) looked at *affinity*—that is, a blog author's inclination to join a particular cascade or not. Decision factors included: the number of their friends involved in the discussion, the number and known popularity of existing participants, the time elapsed since the genesis of the cascade, and the citing factor of the blog author (a measure of how much they like to link from their own posts to other blogs). The researchers have argued that this kind of analysis has bearings on discussions about how information is diffused around the blogosphere and can be of use in marketing. Others have been trying to develop models of how the individual actions of bloggers could lead to the patterns seen in the blogosphere. This is a non-trivial task since it represents an attempt to model human behaviour (Goetz et al. 2009).

8.6.3 Technical Analysis

An alternative way of viewing the development of the blogosphere is to conduct a technical analysis to look at its topology. As a research interest it is part of a wider agenda to understand the underlying structure of the Internet and Web. Recall from Chapter 7 that we can consider the Web to be a gigantic, directed graph of nodes (webpages or sites) with links between them, and it becomes easy to see how analysis could be undertaken on the shape and nature of this graph and its sub-graphs.

As we covered a lot of complex ground in Chapter 7, let's take a moment to consider the main points that are relevant to blogging:

- The Web defies the expected randomness of the distribution of patterns of links between pages and instead follows a power law. It is classed as a scale-free network, which means some sites have far more incoming links than most of the others.

- At the largest scale the Web resembles a 'bow-tie' pattern with a strongly linked core and a number of less well-linked continents. Despite the fact that details of this pattern vary from country to country, it seems that the strongly linked core is a key feature that is replicated at different levels of the Web.

- The Web exhibits self-similarity and therefore when we consider a sub-set of websites, say those that cover a particular theme, a similar pattern appears.

The key point to understand here is that what goes for the Web might also apply to the blogosphere, since it is a sub-set of the wider Web. Recently, network researchers have turned their attention to the blogosphere. They are now considering the similarities and differences between blogs, and both the Web's scale-free network and power law–dominated topology (Agarwal and Liu 2008). Kumar et al. (2005) confirmed that the blogosphere exhibits a power law, with respect to its in- and out-degree links, which they found to have an exponent of −2.1. They also found the presence of a strongly connected core, and although this did not develop until 2001, by 2002 it represented 20% of all blogs. Yardi et al. (2009) confirmed the power law also operates within blogs in a corporate environment. Drezner and Farrell (2004) did not confirm the presence of the power law in incoming links to political blogs, finding a lognormal distribution.[*] However, they point out that this result still implies that there is a skew towards hubs.

Intuitively, we can understand how the power law might work in the blogosphere. Google's blog for example, publishes the major announcements from a company whose activities are watched by large numbers of people. Thousands of smaller blogs will link to particular news items on the Google blog as they appear, perhaps adding a comment of their own, and this creates a large number of incoming links to the Google blog. Each of these smaller blogs will have fewer readers and most likely fewer incoming links of their own. Importantly for this discussion Google does not reciprocate, which means its blog becomes a kind of focus and one of the 'hubs' of the power law mechanism.

Clay Shirky (2005) also noted the presence of the power law in the blogosphere and the emergence of what he called 'stars' which have a very high number of in-coming

---

[*] A random variable x has a lognormal distribution if the random variable $y = \ln x$ has a normal (i.e. Gaussian) distribution. Such a distribution is very similar to a power law. See Mitzenmacher (2001) for more details of the differences.

links. He speculates how the mechanism may work through a process by which people individually choose which blogs to link to and that "the very act of choosing, spread widely enough and freely enough, creates a power law distribution" (p. 46). He made two other important points. Firstly, that the power law distribution does not say anything as to *why* one blog might be preferred over another. Secondly, he argued that the blogosphere exhibits a form of inequality, since some blogs are clearly read a lot more than others, but that the real question is whether the power law's inequality is 'fair'.

This latter question is one that a number of scholars have considered and it brings us to considering the implications of blogging, where we will consider why all this discussion of topology matters.

8.6.4 Implications of the Blogosphere

The blogosphere might be seen as a kind of giant town meeting, or series of such meetings.

CASS SUNSTEIN
(*2006, 185*)

A number of writers and academics have commented on the potential for blogging to act as a new form of mass communication that facilitates cultural and political opinion-forming. Herring et al. (2005) noted that a number of academics have argued that blogging offers a new form of social interaction, a massively distributed but connected conversation, and that the widespread adoption of blogging software has lowered the technical barrier for getting a personal presence on the Internet and joining the debate (Governor et al. 2009). Whether or not this is true is still very much open to debate, but early pioneers of blogging certainly saw it as a new form.

Indeed, there is a developing body of work about how blogging has changed journalism with Blood (2004), for example, arguing that: "Weblogs could become an important new form of alternate media, bringing together information from many sources, revealing media bias, and perhaps influencing opinion on a wide scale—a vision I called 'participatory media'" (p. 54). Benkler (2006) has argued that blogging changed the nature of websites in the late 1990s in two key ways. Firstly, the regularity with which blogs can be updated means that they operate in 'journalism time' (i.e. they can be updated on a daily or even hourly basis) as opposed to the slower-moving, standard Web publishing model. Secondly, blogs allow readers to add comments beneath posts, and also to comment on those comments, thus enabling what he describes as a "weighted conversation".*

So, whilst the study and analysis of the blogosphere's technical structure is an interesting research question in itself, and can have implications for the development of specialized search engines and anti-spam mechanisms, there is a deeper purpose. The blogosphere can be seen as a gigantic, global conversation, a kind of real-time crucible in which opinion and views are weighed, measured and sorted, and many protagonists have argued that it

---

* Benkler argues that it is weighted in that blog owners have the most power or authority because they can moderate the comments or simply delete them.

has profound implications for questions about free speech, democracy and the formation of public opinions. The analysis of the structure and technical nature of the blogosphere has an important bearing on these discussions and a key figure in these debates is Yale University law professor, Yochai Benkler, who discusses them at length in his book, *The Wealth of Networks* (Benkler 2006).

What is important here from the point of view of discussions about free speech and political/cultural discourse is that, at least initially, Benkler felt that the power law was "dismal" news for democracy on the Web. The topology that was emerging from experiments to measure the shape and size of the blogosphere seemed to argue against ideas about equal voice and egalitarianism. He argued that what we might be seeing in the blogosphere is the creation of a new hierarchy and based this claim on the growing body of literature about how webpages and blogs are linked together. Benkler warned that this structure could offer a "serious theoretical and empirical challenge to the claim that Internet communications of the sort we have seen here meaningfully decentralise democratic discourse" (Benkler 2006, 241).

The implication of what Benkler found was that the way the blogosphere operates is forcing us to abandon an assumption that is inherent in truly random networks: their 'democratic' nature (Barabási 2002). The presence of highly connected stars and hubs and the pre-eminence of 'A' list bloggers surely points to some having more of a voice than others. These kinds of debates hark back to a time when the Web first emerged and when there was much talk of its 'levelling' power, providing everyone with a voice and allowing a form of purer democracy to emerge. This was often given the label 'Everyone a pamphleteer' (Kochan 2006; Moe 2010; Rettberg 2008) and harks back to the seventeenth century when pamphlets were a radical new form of communication which became popular thanks to the development of the printing press, higher literacy levels and the lifting of censorship laws. Polemic publications were popular, with published claim provoking counter-claim, a process that seems remarkably similar to today's blog conversations. Surely the uneven distribution of the readership of blogs, as represented by the power law, means that the utopian dream of the early Internet has gone sour.

Not according to Benkler, who has argued that if you accept that a true comparison should not be made with some entirely 'pure' form of egalitarianism, but rather with traditional media such as newspapers and broadcast TV, then what he calls the Networked Public Sphere (the Web and blogosphere) stands up well in comparison. Moreover, it is the topology of the blogosphere that tells us this. The topological features that computer science has unearthed indicate the presence of a "meaningfully participatory form" (p. 247).

The reason for Benkler's claim is that there are a number of key topological features that impact on this debate. It is important to realize for this discussion that the Web (and blogosphere) can be viewed at different scales (i.e. a large, or macro, scale, when we might consider thousands or even millions of blogs or websites, in comparison with a fine-grain, micro scale). The features that Benkler argues are particularly important are:

- Sites form clusters: at the micro level, sites cluster around topic- and interest-related issues and they are tightly linked

- The power law and the presence of hubs and stars mean that a kind of content filtration process operates within the power law's long tail distribution of blog popularity

- The bow-tie model: at the macro level, the blogosphere has a giant, strongly connected core, i.e. areas where 20% to 30% of all sites are highly and redundantly interlinked and this is repeated within smaller grained clusters

- The small world effect, where there are short paths that link most sites

Benkler describes the basic processes at work as follows. At the fine-grain scale, a substantial number of the topical or interest-related sites are moderately connected and therefore act as an intake to the rest of the cluster. Within each cluster the stars or hubs—those with a high degree of visibility—act as 'connectors', or links to other clusters. Even when we look at clusters at the small scale, there are a few high-visibility hubs and then a long tail of less-linked-to blogs. These hubs serve as "points of transfer" to larger clusters providing an "attention backbone" to transmit information around the blogosphere (p. 254).

Drezner and Farrell (2004) describe how this process works in relation to political blogging (a key area for those interested in questions of democracy in the blogosphere):

> When less prominent bloggers have an interesting piece of information or point of view that is relevant to a political controversy, they will usually post this on their own blogs. However, they will also often have an incentive to contact one of the large "focal point" blogs, to publicize their post. The latter may post on the issue with a hyperlink back to the original blog, if the story or point of view is interesting enough, so that the originator of the piece of information receives more readers. In this manner, bloggers with fewer links function as "fire alarms" for focal point blogs, providing new information and links. (Quote reproduced with kind permission from the authors and publisher, Springer Science+Business Media, from Drezner and Farrell (2004), page 13. © Springer Science+Business Media, BV 2007.)

Thus, the networked structure of the blogosphere allows interesting arguments to make their way to the top of the blogosphere.

The small world effect means that a user within a small cluster can nevertheless traverse the blogosphere quite quickly to find diverse sites. Of particular importance is that there is significant redundancy of paths through the various hubs such that no single hub or collection of hubs controls the flow of information in the connected core. According to Benkler the topological research says this is true both within clusters of bloggers with a shared interest, and at the scale of the entire blogosphere. Within a larger interest cluster, say political blogging, it is true that there may be distinct sub-clusters, for example, liberal (or left-wing) and conservative, and these distinct areas are not as densely linked to each other as they are within the sub-clusters. However, there is enough interlinking, especially via the hubs, to allow opinion and views to circulate.

Such effects are further enhanced by the emergence of group blogging, since each node in these topological discussions might also be a blog or website where more than one writer can interact to produce content. This means that each node is potentially a cluster of writers, readers and commentators.

Finally, Benkler points out that the long tail of less popular and therefore less well-connected blogs acts as what he calls a "peer-produced filter and transmission medium" (p. 255) and he argues that this has been shown empirically to have emerged on the blogosphere. A filter process operates in which statements, opinions etc. are synthesized "locally" in the long tail and then "regionally" before reaching the wider Web. Or, as Drezner and Farrell (2004) put it (quoting Scott Rosenberg in *Salon* magazine): "The editorial process of the blogs takes place *between and among* bloggers, in public, in real time" (p. 25).

Benkler concludes that the network topology shows that:

- The networked public sphere (Web and blogosphere) allows hundreds of millions of people to publish easily—whenever and whatever.

- It does not descend into the kind of "cacophony" that some critics had predicted at the beginning of the Web (i.e. when everyone speaks no one can be heard—what he calls the Babel objection).

- The effect of the blogosphere is to filter and focus attention without recreating the highly concentrated model of the mass media.

- The network at all levels demonstrates and follows a form of loose order different to that of mainstream media.

8.6.4.1 Counter-Arguments and Methodological Refinements

Understandably, concerns have been raised about the validity of using Web topology findings as a basis for analysing the blogosphere. Agarwal and Liu (2008) write: "First, models developed for the web assume a dense graph structure due to a large number of interconnecting hyperlinks within webpages. This assumption does not hold true in the blogosphere, since the hyperlink structure in the blogosphere is very sparse" (p. 20). Sparsity[*] can be a rather vague concept, but what the authors mean is that when we analyse the structure of linking between blogs, we find that the number of links is comparatively small when compared to the wider Web (where the majority of the topological work has been done). Shi et al. (2007) found that from a dataset of over a million blogs, only 10% had links within their posts to other blogs in the dataset. Herring et al. (2005) report that nearly 50% of blogs contain no links at all to another blog and that: "it seems likely that the much-touted textual conversation that all of the blogosphere is supposed to be engaged in involves a minority of blogs as well, and sporadic activity even among those blogs" (p. 10). This may seem surprising given talk of the blogosphere and its 'conversation' but it may reflect the growing preponderance of personal, journal blogging. And it perhaps fits

---

[*] A sparse graph is one in which the number of links is much lower than the possible number of links. http://xlinux.nist.gov/dads/HTML/sparsegraph.html

Shirky's claim that a lot of blogging, like much user-generated content is not intended for an audience (see Chapter 2). It should be noted however that these analyses did not include any links that might be present within the comments that had been added to any posts, nor in trackback data.

That having been said, this line of enquiry leads to research interest in whether there is more to the graph of the blogosphere than merely the network of hyperlinks. Indeed, researchers worry that focusing on the hyperlink graph gives undue prominence to the 'A' list when any kind of ranking or other analysis is undertaken. Simply looking at links fails to take into consideration implicit connections between blogs based on either the similarity of the topic under discussion or the fact that one person may write or contribute to many blogs and indeed comment on posts in many others.

Others have taken issue with the idea that there is blanket coverage by the power law across the blogosphere, with, for example Drezner and Farrell (2004) finding that in the clustering of political blogs, the tail is lognormal in nature. This means that although there are still a few stars and hubs, the fall-off in the tail is not so dramatic: there are more moderately connected blogs than a power law would decree. In a similar vein Pennock et al. (2002) discovered that the power law breaks down when considering websites from the same category (e.g. all newspaper sites).

Yet another complicating factor is the dynamic nature of the blogosphere, where temporal aspects are more important than they are when analysing the Web. This has led researchers to look at more specific models of the blogosphere as we discussed in Section 8.6.2.3.

These are important debates about the impact of Web 2.0 on our society. For the time being, the weight of Benkler's evidence seems in his favour, but as this is an active area of research it is wise to keep an eye on developments.

EXERCISES AND POINTS TO PONDER

1. Think about the nature of blog spam and how it might differ, in terms of its content and the way it links with other content, from ham. For example, how might the graph of blog spam differ in structure from the wider blogosphere? How might a spam filter be constructed to take advantage of these features?

2. Consider how blogging has changed the way people find out about news or current affairs. For example, you might consider how we learn about new developments in computer science or the introduction of new technology. Has blogging been of benefit in this respect? Consider issues of trust and the role and influence of the 'star' bloggers. You might also like to discuss this in tandem with the issues explored in Chapter 13.

3. Review Figure 8.10, which shows three blogs, a series of blog posts and the links between them. For each blog post (P1 to P10) calculate the in-degree and out-degree for the node. Calculate the clustering coefficient for the whole network (you may need to refer to Chapter 7).

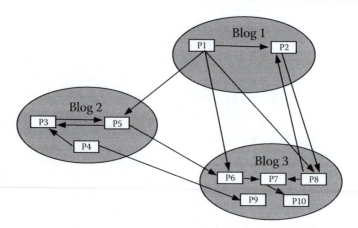

FIGURE 8.10   Exercise 3 (Illustration © 2011 by Intelligent Content Ltd Licensed under a Creative Commons Attribution-NonCommercial-NoDerivs 3.0 Unported license (CC BY-NR-ND 3.0)).

FURTHER READING

For more detail on methods for analysing blog cascades and other social media, see Jure Leskovec's tutorial at WWW 2011 (Leskovec 2011).

For more on the motivations behind blogging, and how they differ between countries see Kobayashi (forthcoming).

The role of blogging in current affairs and the rise of citizen's journalism is covered in Reynolds (2006), Barlow (2007), Gilmour (2004) and Sunstein (2007).

The role of blogging as both a personal journal and a form of interpersonal communication, as well as its function with respect to (real-world) social network ties, are all elaborated on in Stefanone and Jang (2007).

For a detailed discussion of the rise of vlogging see Gao et al. (2010).

For much more discussion on the modelling of the blogosphere, the mining of blogs for data and research into how influence and opinion work across blogs, read the e-book from Agarwal and Liu (2009).

For a detailed discussion of the issues surrounding blog spam see Kolari et al. (2006).

## CHAPTER 9

Wikis

A WIKI IS A WEBSITE THAT CAN BE EDITED by its readers without the need to access the back-end content management system. The basic concept is that a webpage is served with a clearly marked 'edit this page' button that gives the reader access to a simple text editing facility. This idea, of a collection of webpages that can be edited by many different people, has meant that wikis have become very popular as online publishing tools to facilitate collaboration. There are two main uses of a wiki: those that are used in closed workgroups (say within the confines of a company's intranet*) and 'open' wikis, which anyone on the Web can edit.

Most people come across wikis through the popular and well-known Wikipedia.† Andrew Lih (2009) claims that few people understand that Wikipedia is actually a wiki, produced by thousands of unpaid people collaborating online to write and edit articles. In fact, Ebersbach et al. (2006), Sunstein (2006) and Lamb (2004) all report that people who hear about wikis for the first time often experience a form of culture shock. They are likely to worry about vandalism and respond with statements such as: you mean "anyone can come along and change my text?" (Ebersbach et al. 2006, 9). There is a fear that allowing anyone to edit a page also implies a risk of them ruining the content.

There are indeed problems with vandalism, but the perception of how severe this is will vary from person to person. Spinellis and Louridas (2008) found that 11% of Wikipedia's articles had been vandalised at least once, but how significant this appears to be will depend on the value that individual users place on the overall usefulness of the product when compared to the exact level of accuracy.

Over time a wiki philosophy known as the *wiki way* has emerged as different groups of collaborators have explored the social and publishing issues that surround group work over the Internet. A form of what Lamb (2004) calls "soft security" operates, in which the

---

* While groupware systems that provide similar facilities have been in existence for a number of years, wiki software is usually cheaper and easier to use.
† In fact there are now thousands of wikis, and prominent examples include: Wiktionary, Wikitravel, Wikinews, Hudong (the largest Chinese language encyclopaedia site) and LyricWiki (song lyrics). Within the scientific community, notable examples include Scholarpedia and OpenWetware.

collective will of the community tends to keep order where the technology does not enforce it (although the technology can be configured to enforce certain rules).

9.1 INTRODUCTION TO WIKIS

In essence, wiki systems are another interpretation of the functionality provided by a content management system (CMS), discussed in Chapter 8. As we have already seen in Chapter 2, the early Web was designed to be readable and writable, but during a series of ports to different computers the ability to edit through the Web client was not included. Content management systems were a stop-gap solution in that they provided a means to publish to the Web without needing any technical skills, although they tended to be expensive and were generally only available in corporate environments. Blog and wiki software provide lightweight tools based on different aspects of a CMS: blogs are principally designed to publish one person's work while wikis are designed to publish work that has been created by large numbers of people who are collaborating on the same content.

In a large CMS, where there are likely to be many authors and editors working together, there needs to be a system for keeping track of what goes on in order to establish accountability. As a minimum this will usually include recording who creates a new piece of content, who checks it (usually not the person who created it) and who publishes it. It will also probably include tracking changes made to text, such as who made the change, when, and why. It is also quite usual for the CMS to be configured to prevent people from undertaking tasks they are not authorized to carry out; for example, by setting up a rule that prevents an author from publishing something before it has been checked by an editor or proofreader.

However, some people believe that there are significant differences between CMSs and wikis. For example, Shirky (2008) argues that creating a wiki is a hybrid of tool and community rather than merely a content management process: that the power of the wiki concept comes from the active engagement of a collaborative community of editors rather than the sophistication or otherwise of the wiki software itself.

It is important to understand the distinction between a wiki—the content that has been developed collaboratively—and the underlying wiki software or *engine* which provides the functionality. There are two ways of running wiki software: third-party hosted services and systems that run on a local server. In the early days of the Web a wiki software engine *had* to be installed on a user organisation's own server and connected to the wider Internet (Evans and Coyle 2010), a process that required considerable computer system administration skill. In recent years the hosted alternative has gained in popularity. A group of connected servers that provides a wiki hosting service is often called a *wiki farm*, and there are a number of farms that offer free services (usually in exchange for permission to display advertising). Hosted examples include: OpenWiki, SocialText, Wikispaces, Wikia, Wikidot and PBWorks.* Such services use either their own custom-made wiki engine or make use of the best-known engine, MediaWiki, to provide the service.

---

* There are many more. Further information from http://www.wikimatrix.org/ and http://www.dmoz.org/Computers/Software/Groupware/Wiki/Wiki_farms/

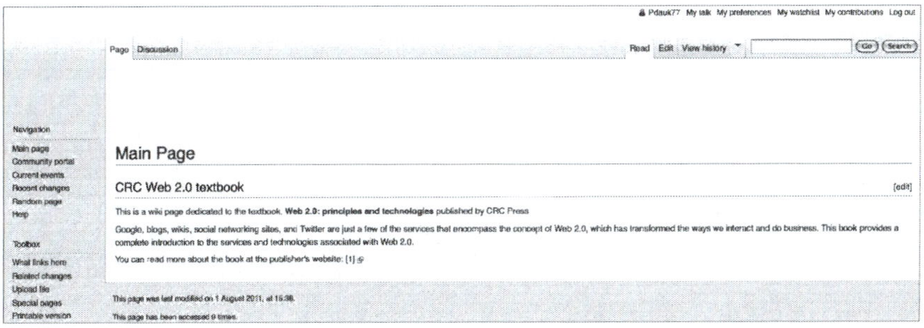

FIGURE 9.1 An example of a MediaWiki page. Note the action tabs on the right hand side for accessing a deeper level of functionality. Further actions are available via the drop-down menu next to the 'view history' button. (Screenshot courtesy of WikiNet.org).

In order to illustrate some of the important technical and functional aspects of wiki software engines we will look at MediaWiki* as an example.

9.1.1 Overview

Each wikipage has a title and a body of text (see Figure 9.1). The page may function as a stand-alone article or be nested so that it appears as one of several sub-pages (designated by a forward slash in the Uniform Resource Identifier [URI]). New pages are created by doing an initial search for the page's name. If the page does not exist, the search will fail and then the user is given the option of creating the page.

The sidebar on the left-hand side contains various navigation links, help facilities and the toolbox (a list of wiki-related activities that varies depending on the page being viewed but includes functionality such as displaying a printable version of the page). Above the title are the *top tabs*—functionality for working with the page. If a reader wants to alter a page they only have to click on the 'edit' tab and the text will appear in a text edit box, ready to be changed.

MediaWiki also allows users to register with a username and password. Registration provides a number of additional features, including a degree of personalization (e.g. tailoring the behaviour of the wiki to your own preferences and keeping track of changes you have made over time). While changes can be made by anyone, there is a sense in wiki culture that registering and being open about who has made an edit to a page is part of the community spirit. Each registered user can create a personal wiki article to describe themselves and their interests, and this is allocated to the User namespace (see next section).

MediaWiki also provides functionality for administrators, who have the authority to oversee and control the maintenance of the site in a similar way to what are more usually called system administrators. It should be noted that within the Wikipedia community, administrators are significantly different from system administrators, and this is discussed later in this chapter.

---

* This is a brief summary. Considerably more information is provided in Barrett (2009).

9.1.2 Namespaces and Categories

In general, categories are created by users as they add new pages and edit existing ones, and they can be changed easily. Namespaces are more permanent features of the site that divide it into sections with a particular purpose, e.g. all material to do with help is designated as part of the Help namespace. In MediaWiki, namespaces can only be created by administrators.

A wikipage title will contain a prefix that shows which namespace the article belongs to, e.g. Help:Some Help Stuff is the full title of a wikipage called 'Some Help Stuff' that is held within the 'Help' namespace. MediaWiki supplies sixteen default namespaces including:

User: Optional pages about individual, registered users of the wiki

Image: Uploaded image files

Talk: Discussion of articles

9.1.3 Top Tabs

The Top Tabs (as shown in Figure 9.1) contain a list of 'actions' that can be performed on a page. Some of these will be available to everyone while others, such as those that provide a level of personalization, will require registration. The number of tabs available varies between each MediaWiki implementation but they usually include 'Edit', 'Discussion' and 'History'.

9.1.3.1 Action: Edit

The fundamental core of the wiki process is the edit action, which usually allows anyone to change the text of a page, although some configurations of the software restrict editing to those who have registered with the site. The edit action also provides a comment box to record, for example, information on why the changes were made. These comments appear in the article's history and it is good practice to make brief, but explanatory comments to help other editors.

9.1.3.2 Action: Discussion

Every wikipage has an associated Discussion (or Talk) page. This is the place to air different viewpoints over the page's content and put forward comments and corrections for debate. Discussion pages are fundamental to the collaborative nature of the wiki concept.

9.1.3.3 Action: History

MediaWiki keeps a record of every modification to the text of articles along with who made the change and when. Various functions based on this action are provided, e.g. to compare different versions of the page and to undo the last revision.

9.1.3.4 Action: Watch

Registered users can elect to 'watch' a particular wikipage that they are particularly interested in by adding it to their *watchlist*, which displays recent changes to the selected page. To make things easier a user can opt to be e-mailed when a page on the watchlist is modified.

9.1.4 Links

As with standard webpages, wikipages can link to internal and external content. They may also contain special links such as interwiki (links between wikis), interlanguage, graphical and file links.

9.1.5 Wikitext

MediaWiki pages are not written in HTML but in *wikitext* or *wikicode*, another type of markup language. Wikicode consists of plain text but includes a number of easy-to-use markups that its proponents argue are much simpler than HTML, both to learn and to use (Lamb 2004). However, it is worth noting that there is no standard for marking up wikicode. This may obviously present problems when transferring content between wiki systems.

As with HTML, special symbols and tags are used to mark how the text is to appear and show links to other wikipages or websites. Indeed, readers familiar with HTML will notice many similarities: lists can be created, tables displayed, headings defined etc. There is not the space here to describe the full set of wikitext symbols but a few important ones include:

Bold: 3 single quotes e.g. '''this is bold'''

Italics: 2 single quotes e.g. ''this is italic''

Underline: <u></u>   e.g. <u>this is underlined</u>

To make life even easier, MediaWiki provides text edit functionality with a number of buttons that provide a quick way of inserting the various markup symbols. Selecting text and pressing a button labelled 'B' on the MediaWiki interface for example will insert the 'bold' wikicode around the selected text.

In wikitext, internal links are created by surrounding the title of the target article to be linked to with double square brackets e.g. [[Van der Graaf Generator]]. External links are created by simply using either the URI by itself or contained within single brackets.

9.2 A SHORT HISTORY OF WIKIS

The system that became the prototype for the wiki was developed by Ward Cunningham, a software designer from Portland, Oregon, and launched in March 1995.[*] For many years he had been working at a computer company called Tektronix where he had responsibility for developing a repository of software engineering design patterns that others within his company could contribute to. At first he experimented with an early piece of Apple computer software called HyperCard,[†] but with the wider use of the Internet in the early 1990s

---

[*] The site can still be seen at: http://c2.com/cgi/wiki

[†] Launched in 1987, HyperCard allowed a user to create stacks of virtual, hyperlinked index cards that could be read, edited and indexed on the screen. Conceptually, it anticipated the Web and its inventor, Bill Atkinson, has since expressed regret that he didn't spot the potential of linking stacks of cards over the emerging Internet. See: http://www.wired.com/gadgets/mac/commentary/cultofmac/2002/08/54370

FIGURE 9.2   The Wiki-Wiki bus at Honolulu International Airport. (Reprinted from Wikimedia Commons, distributed under under Creative Commons CC BY-SA 2.0. Original picture by Andrew Laing. Source: http://en.wikipedia.org/wiki/File:HNL_Wiki_Wiki_Bus.jpg).

Cunningham began to wonder about how to take the HyperCard concept and transfer it to the Web.

By then he had left Tektronix and was working for himself, but he was still looking for ways to keep track of developments and projects in software engineering. His solution was the Portland Pattern Repository, based on a database and a Perl[*] script-based collaboration system that he called 'WikiWikiWeb'. It was named after the 'wiki-wiki' (meaning 'super quick' in Hawaiian) airport shuttle bus that he had used on his honeymoon (Lih 2009), in order to express the idea that the system was designed to be a fast way of publishing to the Web (see Figure 9.2). Ward Cunningham's concept was taken up by others, most notably by Clifford Adams, who developed UseModWiki, the system that underpinned the launch of Wikipedia.

9.3 EXAMPLE SYSTEM: MEDIAWIKI

The MediaWiki engine operates under the classic client-server model. It is stored, and runs, on a server connected to the Internet (Ebersbach et al. 2006). It runs under Linux, Microsoft Windows and Apple Macintosh operating systems, usually uses the Apache Hypertext Transfer Protocol (HTTP) server software, and is supported by a database held in either MySQL or PostgreSQL database systems. MediaWiki also requires PHP, a programming

---

[*] Perl is a Web scripting language (http://www.perl.org/)

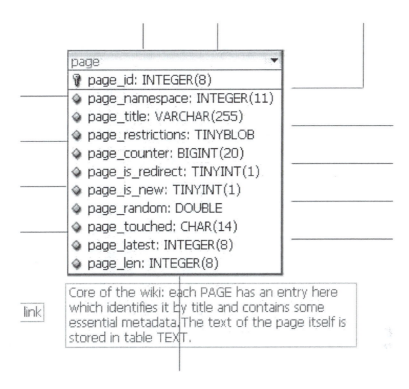

FIGURE 9.3 A section of the MediaWiki database table illustrating the way that wikipages are stored within the database. (Adapted from MediaWiki.org, distributed under Creative Commons CC BY-SA 3.0. Authored by Krinkle. Source: http://www.mediawiki.org/wiki/File:MediaWiki_database_schema_1-17_%28r82044%29.png).

language interpreter. User authentication (log-in etc.) is handled by MediaWiki's own internal system but it can also be configured to use authentication systems that are popular in corporate environments such as Kerberos, Lightweight Directory Access protocol (LDAP) and Active Directory.

The core of the wiki engine is the database, which stores details of individual pages, site users, revisions, discussions etc. (see Figure 9.3).[*]

One particularly notable technical aspect of MediaWiki is the provision for third-party extensions, which add functionality to the wiki engine without the need to disturb the core code. There are hundreds of extensions already available—a prominent example is the HotCat JavaScript module that helps editors with categorization tasks—but a user can also create their own using PHP. A familiarity with the way that PHP uses classes is required, as is a working knowledge of how MediaWiki classes work.[†]

---

[*] The full database table layout is shown in a diagram: http://upload.wikimedia.org/wikipedia/commons/4/41/Mediawiki-database-schema.png. Further details: http://www.mediawiki.org/wiki/Manual:Database_layout

[†] Further technical details: http://www.mediawiki.org/wiki/Extension:Contents and http://www.mediawiki.org/wiki/Hooks

9.4 WIKIPEDIA

Imagine a world in which every single person on the planet is given free access to the sum of all human knowledge. That is what we're doing.

JIMMY WALES
Wikipedia Founder, quoted in Lih (2009, 1)

More young people will learn about IBM from Wikipedia in coming years than from IBM itself.

THOMAS FRIEDMAN
The World Is Flat, quoted in Lih (2009, 11)

In 1403 the Ming dynasty emperor Yongle commissioned the Yongle Encyclopaedia, a vast work of Chinese scholarship that ran to more than 11,000 volumes and involved 2,000 compilers. It remained the world's largest encyclopaedia for six centuries until overtaken in the late 2000s by Wikipedia. The site is by far the biggest and best-known wiki on the Web and editions exist in more than 250 languages with a combined total of more than 17 million articles. It is firmly established in the top ten of most visited websites (Lih 2009) and in some countries, Germany and Netherlands for example, it has been ranked higher than any domestic news service. Tens of thousands of unpaid volunteers have worked together since its launch in 2001 to develop the content, supported by a paid team of only around a dozen people at the WikiMedia Foundation Inc., a nonprofit organisation.[*] Volunteers operate at all levels: basic fact checking, writing and modifying articles, proofreading and editing. It is grounded in an ethos which argues that articles that are collectively edited and refined over time by many people are likely to emerge as good, if not better, representations of human knowledge than articles written by lone experts supported by the traditional publishing process.

9.4.1 Wikipedia's History

Wikipedia was created by Jimmy Wales and Larry Sanger in 2001. Lih (2009) traces the genesis of the site to Jimmy Wales' early life and a fascination with encyclopaedias, in particular, a frustration with the printed book's inability to keep up with the information about the space race of the early 1960s that he was so interested in. A new edition of a book might only come out every few years but space age technology was moving much faster. As a way around this, in the 1960s and 1970s, encyclopaedia publishing companies sent out stickers with amended text, to be stuck onto existing pages in order to update them. Even so, the printed book was always behind the latest news from the space race.

---

[*] The Wikimedia Foundation is the body that oversees the long-term development of the Wikipedia project. It is a charitable corporation organised under the laws of Florida, USA. The Foundation has a number of projects that run in parallel to Wikipedia, including: Wiktionary (a multilingual dictionary); Wikinews (news articles and original material); Wikisource (historical source material); Wikiquote and Wikiversity. Wikimedia Commons provides a central repository for free photographs, maps, videos, music and other free media.

After his education in his native Alabama, Wales entered the finance industry of 1990s Chicago and during this time became interested in the early Internet. In 1996 he founded Bomis, Inc. with Tim Shell, in order to explore potential dot-com business ideas. They tried a variety of projects including a directory service providing lists of links for the Chicago area.

In parallel, DMOZ was being created by two engineers from Sun Microsystems. It was the first large-scale online content project with an ethos of open collaboration, borrowed from the open source software community. Their idea was to set up a common directory listing that anyone could edit and add to, in the hope that volunteers would help generate the content. The idea took off and the project was renamed as the Open Directory Project.*

According to Lin (2009), Wales was inspired by the Open Directory Project to start an online encyclopaedia. Wales was not alone in having this idea but he had the advantage of financial backing through his work with Bomis. In addition, Wales had long held an interest in philosophy and in particular Ayn Rand's objectivist philosophy (the idea of gaining objective knowledge from perception by measurement), which Lin argues underpins Wales' belief in a collective reference work created by the masses. Sanger was a philosophy student who was just finishing his PhD studies in epistemology (the study of knowledge) and the two met through a philosophy e-mail discussion list (Sanger 2006). Wales wanted a philosopher to lead his new project and in early 2000 he asked Sanger to join him to work on a new project—Nupedia. According to Lin they both saw Nupedia as a way of turning objectivist philosophy into practice.

Nupedia was set up to tap into the knowledge of volunteers on the Internet in order to create encyclopaedic content. There was only one snag: the team insisted on a very rigorous editorial system that included seven steps of writing, reviewing and approval. Volunteers were expected to be experts in their chosen subject, ideally holding a PhD. Even the originators now admit that the process was cumbersome and took "forever" to get articles through the system (Lih 2009). By the end of the first year only twelve articles had been published.

At this point there are differences over the exact details of the story. It seems that at some point in January 2001, Sanger met Ben Kovitz, a programmer he knew online from the philosophy e-mail lists. Kovitz told him about Ward Cunningham's WikiWikiWeb. Sanger thought it was the solution to Nupedia's problems: use the wiki software to open the whole project up to anyone and let them get on with editing. According to Lin, Wales has claimed that in fact he was also told about wiki software by a different person, at the same time. Whatever the truth may be, it was Sanger who named the new concept—Wikipedia—and on 15th January 2001, Wikipedia.com was officially launched.

Within a few weeks there were large numbers of visitors to the new site and by the end of the first month, 600 articles had been contributed. By the middle of the following month there were 1,000 articles and by the beginning of 2002 it had 20,000 articles. This was the start of a long period of rapid growth.

---

* http://www.dmoz.org/

9.4.2 Five Pillars: The Wikipedia Ethos

Wikipedia has five 'pillars' which act as the cornerstones that summarize its published aims and objectives:

1. Wikipedia is an encyclopaedia.

2. Wikipedia has a neutral point of view.

3. Wikipedia is free content.*

4. Wikipedia has a code of conduct.

5. Wikipedia does not have firm rules.

In order to help maintain this position, Wikipedia has a number of policies that, within the limits of common sense, all users should normally follow, as well as guidelines that are meant to contain best practices for doing so. Broughton (2008) has argued that there are three core policies for content that are particularly important in defining the nature of the site:

- No original research

- Verifiability

- Neutral point of view

It is important to understand that Wikipedia references other published material—it is not a first place to be published, a place to announce new research or a source of any new knowledge. Everything that appears must, wherever possible, cite other published works. Where possible, such sources should be those with an existing reputation for fact checking and accuracy (for example, national or local newspapers, science journals, government reports etc.). Any statement that might be considered controversial or contentious absolutely must have a cited source.[†]

Neutral point of view (NPOV) is a cornerstone of the Wikipedia way of working[‡] and Wales argues that it is the only non-negotiable policy (Lih 2009), although he accepts that true neutrality is always a goal to strive for rather than a final destination. In terms of Wikipedia he argues that this means: "an article is neutral when people have stopped changing it" (Weinberger 2007, 136). In this way, neutrality is a function of social interaction and not simply concerned with the quality of writing or expertise of a single author. This is achieved by requiring editors to: present different, significant viewpoints in proportion to the existing (external) published materials and sources; represent fairly any differing views of a topic; write without bias—covering facts rather than opinions (Broughton 2008).[§]

---

* 'Free content' means text is available under the GNU free documentation licence or Creative Commons.
† Further details can be found by typing 'WP:RS' into the Wikipedia search box.
‡ Further details are available by typing 'WP:NPOV' into the Wikipedia search box.
§ This last point is particularly subjective as the creation and selection of 'facts' can be extremely controversial—consider the debate around the facts surrounding global warming, for example.

Much of this policy is enforced through the social norms of the Wikipedia community working together, rather than being formally policed. There is an etiquette to carrying out the work known as *wikiquette* (Sunstein 2006) as well as an assessment scale against which articles can be judged.*

One other issue worth discussing with respect to editorial policy is what to include. This is a perennial debate within the Wikipedia community. Unlike a paper encyclopaedia there are no physical limits to the eventual size of the system. There are differing opinions, which Lih (2009) and Lam and Riedl (2009) argue form roughly two factions: the *inclusionists* and the *exclusionists* (or *deletionists*). Generally speaking, the former can be characterised as wanting to include everything that is verifiable and factual, without any limit. The latter argue that only items that are factual, verifiable and, importantly, *notable* should find their way into the system. After much discussion, there has been some convergence and debates now centre on defining what precisely is meant by notable.†

9.4.2.1 Vandals, Trolls, Sock Puppets and Spam

As we noted earlier, many people's first response to the news that anyone can edit a wikipage is one of incredulity. Surely someone will come along and simply mess up the text or write an untruth or edit the article in favour of a particular point of view. In wiki communities such individuals are known as *vandals* and *trolls*, although it should be noted that these terms have a much longer history, having emerged from the pre-Web culture of bulletin board systems and e-mail lists.

Trolls are individuals who delight in tying the Wikipedia community up in knots by sowing discord, for example by creating spurious debates about policy or what to include in a particular article (Shachaf and Hara 2010). Vandals specialize in the destruction of content or the addition of malicious, obscene or useless content (Broughton 2008; Geiger and Ribes 2010; Mola-Velasco 2011). Spammers, too, insert links to external content that promotes a point of view or a particular product. Finally, sock puppets are false user registrations, created to hide the identity of a vandal or spammer. Since there is no limit on the potential number of registrations, spammers (for example) can easily create thousands of false accounts.

Despite these threats the Wikipedia community has evolved a response process to keep vandalism to a minimum. Broughton (2008) documents four key lines of defence:

- *Bots:* This is automated software that spots patterns of vandalism and spam.

- *Recent changes patrol:* These are human editors who work together to monitor all changes across the site with a view to spotting bad behaviour.

- *Watchlists:* The most likely person to spot damage to an article is a person who is particularly interested in the topic and has registered it in their watchlist.

---

* See: http://en.wikipedia.org/wiki/Wikipedia:WikiProject_Council/Assessment_FAQ
† See: http://en.wikipedia.org/wiki/Notability_in_Wikipedia

- *Readers:* If they spot an error or some damage they can fix it themselves or at least notify someone who is involved in the editing of that article.

The key response to a vandalism or spam incident is to revert to an older, pre-vandal version. There is also a system for reporting attacks, issuing warnings and blocking access to pages that particularly attract vandals (e.g. famously, George W. Bush's page had to be blocked).

It is worth noting that, generally, Wikipedia operates a policy of assuming good faith in others (the AGF policy) when reviewing user contributions, and all contributors are expected to adhere to basic forms of civility and not indulge in personal attacks (the civility and no personal attacks (NPA) policies). It is expected that the entire community works together to enforce these policies and to root out those who do not. Wikipedia also has administrators who, rather than acting as system administrators for the software, are editors who have earned a level of special authority. This means that they can deal with breaches of policy and block persistent offenders from the site.

9.4.3 Technology

The site was originally powered by UseModWiki, an open source software project derived from Ward Cunningham's original wiki system. Later in the project, this code was replaced by a new system written by a German programmer, Magnus Manske, based on a MySQL database, and this became the underlying MediaWiki engine still in use today (Sanger 2006).[*] The MediaWiki engine runs under the standard Linux stack (LAMP[†]) and makes use of PowerDNS which distributes wiki content requests geographically, among the three different worldwide server locations currently in use.

As the project experienced rapid growth in the number of site visitors there was a steady process of increasing the number of servers that were used to hold the engine and the associated database. Soto (2009) has documented some of the developments in server capacity required to support the growth of Wikipedia over the last decade. He notes the need for increased capacity in the United States with the addition of new facilities in California and Florida, and the donation of capacity in Europe by Dutch agency Kennisnet, while in Asia, Yahoo! has lent support at its South Korea server centre.

By 2004 more than thirty servers were attempting to cope with Wikipedia's exponential growth rates (Lih 2009). At this point the project team installed *squid servers*, a form of caching system to help with the load. Squid server[‡] is an open source project to develop a server system that can deliver content quickly by storing frequently accessed webpages in a server's (faster) cache memory rather than in the backend database. Content that is currently being accessed a lot (say a wikipage about a prominent news-related topic) is held in the cache memory and can thus be delivered faster than a fetch from the SQL database. Lih (2009) reports that the project team found that the squid system ran at a hit rate of 75%, effectively quadrupling the server capacity.

---

[*] There were a number of iterations of the project involving various people. Further details at: http://www.mediawiki.org/wiki/MediaWiki_history

[†] Linux (operating system), Apache HTTP Server, MySQL (database software), and PHP.

[‡] See: http://www.squid-cache.org/

By 2010, Wikipedia was running on about 350 servers, mainly distributed across two centres in Amsterdam and Florida (Miller 2010d) and the Foundation had announced plans to expand in 2010/2011 by adding a new centre in the United States. Further technical details are provided in Bergsma (2007), the Data Center Knowledge website[*] and in the Wikimedia Foundation's annual reports.[†]

9.4.4 Growth

By any standards, Wikipedia has experienced phenomenal growth in terms of its content and its popularity since its launch. In January 2002, there were 20,000 articles. By spring of the following year there were 100,000 articles. In the autumn of 2006 it broke into the top ten websites (measured by visitor traffic) and has remained there ever since. Today there are over three million articles on the main English language site and ten million visitors an hour.[‡] Further details about growth are provided in Section 9.6.1.1 on Wikipedia research.

One aspect of growth has been the way that Wikipedia has coped with language and internationalization. At first it was an all-English language project, although editors were attempting to submit articles in other languages within a month of the launch in early 2001. By March of that year Jimmy Wales had registered new domains for French, German and Spanish versions of Wikipedia. German Wikipedia started on 16th March and French followed a week or so later. These versions were allowed to develop as the community wished—cultural differences, for example, on how to interpret NPOV, were observed—and articles were not always simple translations of existing content. The introduction of non-Latin-based languages such as Japanese and Korean initially presented the Foundation with problems with the way the wiki engine encoded letter characters. Although the details of what was undertaken are complex, in summary the solution was the adoption of the Unicode Transformation Format (UTF)-8 standard for encoding.

9.5 THE WIKISPHERE

Despite its massive popularity, Wikipedia is not the only wiki project. There are many thousands of others demonstrating varying degrees of success. Camille Roth (2007) for example, shows that 95% of the wikis in his sample had fewer than 900 users.

Collectively they form what is referred to as the *wikisphere*. Research has shown that the wikisphere demonstrates a power law distribution in both numbers of users and the amount of content, i.e. most wikis have only a handful of pages and/or users but a small number exhibit very large values (Stuckman and Purtilo 2009).

9.6 RESEARCHING THE WIKISPHERE

Despite the existence of a wider wikisphere, researchers have tended to focus on Wikipedia. There are two principle reasons for this. Firstly, on a purely practical level Wikipedia is easier to study. This is because the Foundation makes its database dumps available to researchers for analysis. These provide a detailed breakdown of all the edits, editor interactions,

---

[*] See: http://www.datacenterknowledge.com/archives/2008/06/24/a-look-inside-wikipedias-infrastructure/

[†] See: http://wikimediafoundation.org/wiki/Financial_reports#2010-2011_fiscal_year

[‡] For the most up-to-date statistics see: http://stats.wikimedia.org/EN/TablesArticlesTotal.htm

reversions etc. that have ever taken place. Secondly, the site provides a profoundly important representation of the scale and reach of the Web. Suh et al. (2009) argue that Wikipedia has attracted considerable interest from researchers because of the speed of its growth, its apparent aggregation of vast amounts of human knowledge and as an example of peer production. It has become, in their words, a "living laboratory" for the study of user-generated content production and online community.

This laboratory has attracted a wide range of researchers. Voss (2005) and Soto (2009) note that Wikipedia research is undertaken in many different disciplines including computer science, media studies, psychology, sociology and library studies. Research into Wikipedia can also be considered to be part of a wider agenda looking at the economics of open innovation and peer-produced goods such as open source software (Anthony et al. 2005).

However, Kittur and Kraut (2010) warn that although the focus on Wikipedia is understandable it is not clear that findings from research on Wikipedia can be used to generalize about the use of wikis in other contexts. The authors have begun to explore similarities and differences between what is known about Wikipedia and the wider wikisphere. Their work suggests that there may be 'common laws' that apply to how co-ordination works in order to harness the power of the crowd, but it is early days in this emerging line of enquiry.

9.6.1 Researching Wikipedia

Soto (2009) has argued that studies of Wikipedia can be broken down into a number of key classes including: quantitative analysis; quality of the contents produced; Web graphs and linking patterns. These categories provide a useful framework for the discussion of current research issues related to Wikipedia.

9.6.1.1 Quantitative Analysis

This type of research focuses on the empirical measurement and statistical analysis of various features of Wikipedia. In general, quantitative analysis has been undertaken to measure growth (in terms of the number of articles or total number of words and how that changes over time), and the number and activity of editors.

Firstly, we will consider the size of Wikipedia and the analysis of its growth since its launch in 2001.[*] Research by Jakob Voss (2005) looked at a number of measures of the site's growth between its launch and 2005 including: the number of articles,[†] the total number of words, the number of active editors and the total size of the associated SQL database. In all cases he found that after a short, start-up phase of linear growth, Wikipedia developed exponentially. Almeida et al. (2007) differ slightly in their opinion, finding that Wikipedia grew more than exponentially between 2001 and 2003, and then settled into an

---

[*] Wikipedia itself has information on its growth: http://en.wikipedia.org/wiki/Wikipedia:Modelling_Wikipedia%27s_growth

[†] It is worth noting in passing that researchers do not always make it clear what they are measuring when counting articles. Wikipedia contains a large number of stubs (articles that are in embryonic form and contain only a few sentences) and also redirect pages (for disambiguation).

exponential growth rate. They found that the rate of growth of the number of articles fitted the exponential curve:

$$A(t) = Ce^{at} \tag{9.1}$$

where $A(t)$ is the cumulative number of articles at time t, and C is a constant. They calculated that $a = 2.31 \times 10^{-8.}$

However, more recently, Suh et al. (2009) have shown that the rate of growth is starting to slow. For example, they found that the number of monthly edits is starting to shrink and that the number of active editors has also stopped growing, peaking at 820,532 in March 2007 and fluctuating since between 650,000 and 810,000 (last results from late 2009).

Suh et al. have suggested that the slowdown they detected might indicate that Wikipedia is reaching a point where it represents the total encyclopaedic knowledge available to humankind. However, they quickly counter this by pointing out that there is a general sense that the stock of knowledge in the world is rising, e.g. continual growth in scientific knowledge, which leaves the question of why there has been a slowdown. They considered editorial reverts and found that their number has been growing, particularly with respect to edits made by low-frequency or occasional editors. Finally, they found evidence that the survival rate of entirely new pages was falling. On average, in January 2005 the survival rate was 75% but by the end of 2007 this had deteriorated to 72%. The authors' conclusion was that Wikipedia had stopped growing and they speculated that factors associated with this may include:

- Growing resistance to new content especially when contributed by occasional editors (this may be an indication of the growing strength of 'deletionists' over 'inclusionists')

- Greater overheads imposed by increased co-ordination

- A fall in the availability of easy topics to write about (Wikipedia has covered what the authors call 'low hanging fruit' and new material increasingly requires deep specialism and more time and effort)

- Constraints imposed by the wiki software and interface as it struggles to cope with the scale of growth

Whatever the reasons, it is possible that there has been a further marked decline in interest since this research, with Jimmy Wales telling the Associated Press in August 2011 that there were only 90,000 active contributors and the foundation was actively considering ways to "replenish the ranks" (Estrin 2011, webpage). Wales himself argues that it is a sign of the original, and mainly young, Wikipedia contributors moving onto other ventures, growing up and getting married. Others, he feels, have lost interest since there are fewer new articles to be added.

Lam and Riedl (2009) found that Wikipedia exhibits a power law (see Chapter 7). Noting that the Encyclopaedia Britannica Online has around 65,000 entries, they found that Wikipedia's top 65,000 articles (ranked by popularity) received less than 60% of the total visits to the site. The remaining 40% of the visitors read one or more of the several million less-popular articles demonstrating the attractiveness of material in the long tail.

A major area of quantitative study revolves around the question of who does the work on Wikipedia. There has been much debate about whether the site is mainly edited by a small number of what might be called 'elite' users or whether it is a genuine expression of the power of the crowd. Kittur et al. (2007) point out that Wikipedia editors themselves have argued that a small number of elite editors have in fact been responsible for the bulk of the material. Their research examined the work of the administrators, a class of Wikipedia editors who are peer-selected for their abilities and long-term contribution to the site and are rewarded with extra responsibilities. The authors calculated the percentage of edits by this class compared to the total and found that this peaked in late 2002 at 59% and was roughly maintained until around 2004, after which there has been a steady decline (to around 10% of edits by late 2006).

This decline in the proportion of edits was not matched by any evidence that administrators were undertaking less overall work, rather that despite an increase in the amount of work to be done the administrators were doing a similar amount of work and Kittur et al. concluded that there is a "growing influence of the masses" (p. 3). To be sure, they also looked at categorizing every editor into one of five categories, depending on the total number of edits they had ever made on the site (i.e. ignoring the status of being an administrator and simply looking at actual workload). They found the same pattern—a decline in the elite (the *wiki warriors* with more than 10,000 edits under their belts) and a rise in the percentage of edits by users with fewer than 100 edits—the rise of what the authors term the 'bourgeoisies'. They conclude:

> In the beginning, elite users contributed the majority of the work in Wikipedia. However, beginning in 2004 there was a dramatic shift in the distribution of work to the common users, with a corresponding decline in the influence of the elite. (Kittur et al. 2007, 8)

Almeida et al. (2007) took a different approach and segmented contributors to Wikipedia into groups based on when they joined the site in order to analyse their behaviour over time. The authors write: "interestingly we can observe that as our old users get tired of creating new articles and lose their enthusiasm, users that recently joined Wikipedia are getting more passionate about creating new articles" (p. 5). Perhaps more interestingly they found that contributors/editors could be split into two camps: a small number of contributors (totalling roughly 5,000) who produce a large number of articles (more than 1,000 each) and the vast majority of contributors who, for the most part, produce well below the 1,000 article mark. They measured contributions by different editors and then ranked them in terms of the updates they had made. Similar methods used to measure website content have shown the presence of Zipf's law.

In this case the authors found two Zipf curves that fitted the data. You may recall that a Zipf's distribution is a ranking of the power law in which the number of updates made by the contributor in position r of the rank, $P(r)$ is as follows:

$$P(r) \propto \frac{1}{r^k} \tag{9.2}$$

In this case the authors found Zipf curves with parameters of k at 0.65 and 1.63, representing the two different types of contributor.

The presence of two types of contributor to Wikipedia has also been commented on by Bryant et al. (2005) and Panciera et al. (2009). The former note the presence of editorial 'novices' and 'experts' (or *Wikipedians*). Whereas initially, novices tend to focus on correcting individual articles, once users become Wikipedians, their goals expand. Bryant et al. (2005, 9) conclude:

> They identify the site, not as a random collection of articles, but as a community of co-authors … They move from a local focus on individual articles to a concern for the quality of the Wikipedia content as a whole and the health of the community.

However, later research from Panciera et al. (2009) seems to suggest that novices do not gradually turn into Wikipedians, but that they demonstrate a different attitude from day one (for example, by making an average of 15.1 edits on their first day, compared with those who remain as novices making a mere 3.5 edits).

A number of other researchers have also considered the role of frequent editors versus occasional contributors, and note the potential for the Gini coefficient[*] to describe how the number of revisions work out as a proportion of the number of editors (Kittur et al. 2007; Soto 2009; Stuckman and Purtilo 2009). Soto (2009), for example, found that 90% of the editorial revisions on the site were made by 10% of the users in the English-language Wikipedia. The Gini coefficient was 0.9360 (i.e. highly unequal). Stuckman and Purtilo (2009) found that the coefficient was 0.87 for their sample of the wider wikisphere. This is slightly less inequitable, but they excluded users who had made no edits, which Soto did not, and this is likely to account for the slight difference in the two sets of results. The authors argue that this inequality might cast doubt on the 'wisdom of crowds' theory of wiki content production.

Another metric that has attracted attention is the distribution of the number of edits per article. Wilkinson and Huberman (2007a) found that: "The lognormal distribution of edits per article in Wikipedia means that a small but significant population of articles experience a disproportionally high number of edits and editors, while the vast majority of articles undergo far less activity" (p.158). Since the logarithm is normal this shows the presence of a heavy tail of highly edited articles.

Finally, we should note the work of IBM researchers who have developed what they call the History Flow technique (Figure 9.4).[†] This is a visualization technique that shows the interaction of editors working on the same article over a period of time. Each editor is allocated a different colour, and the ebb and flow of the interactions is shown in the coloured patterns that emerge.

---

[*] The Gini coefficient is a measure of inequality, used widely in economics, which shows how equitably a variable is distributed across a population. The formula generates a number lying between 0 (perfect equality) and 1 (total inequality).

[†] See http://www.research.ibm.com/visual/projects/history_flow/explanation.htm

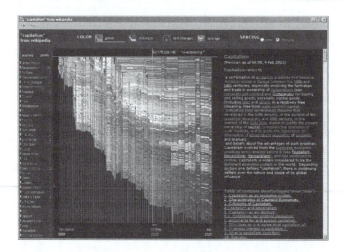

FIGURE 9.4 The History Flow visualization technique being undertaken on data from a discussion on the Wikipedia entry for capitalism. (Courtesy of International Business Machines Corporation, © 2003 International Business Machines Corporation).

9.6.1.2 Qualitative Analysis

Wikipedia's embrace of miscellaneous, anonymous authorship engenders resistance so strong that it sometimes gets in the way of understanding.

DAVID WEINBERGER

(*2007, 134*)

Criticism directed at the quality and reliability of Wikipedia content has dogged the site since its launch. Suh et al. (2009) list the main ones as: lack of authority, unreliability, lack of neutrality on some topics, evidence of conflicts of interest and vandalism. However, a study by *Nature* magazine in December 2005 (Giles 2005) found that Wikipedia was not far short of the Encyclopaedia Britannica Online in terms of quality. Specifically, it found that each wiki article surveyed had an average of four errors, compared to an average of three errors for articles in the Britannica Online (Tapscott and Williams 2007). These claims were not uncontentious, and perhaps understandably Britannica contested the methodology of the survey and there was considerable publicity and public debate.[*]

Other researchers have also considered the quality question. Stvilia et al. (2005; 2008) were the first to present detailed theoretical studies as to what should be considered when investigating quality. The authors built on existing knowledge concerning suitable metrics for evaluating the quality of both paper-based encyclopaedic content and library metadata[†] to develop a number of metrics for Wikipedia. They created an IQ (information quality) assessment framework consisting of seven metrics: authority, completeness, complexity, informativeness, consistency, currency and volatility. Each one was calculated using a combination of various statistical measurements taken from a dump of Wikipedia data

---

[*] See: http://www.nature.com/nature/britannica/index.html
[†] For example Dublin Core.

that included: number of unique editors who have worked on a page; time between edits; number of reverts for an article etc. This IQ framework was then used to explore the way in which Wikipedia's own internal quality systems worked and to better understand how what at first might seem quite "anarchic" (their term) resolves itself into a system that ensures article quality. The framework was later expanded to 22 dimensions divided into three categories: intrinsic, relational and reputational.

Wilkinson and Huberman (2007a; 2007b) studied all 50 million edits that had been undertaken on the English-language Wikipedia between 2001 and November 2006, excluding edits made by the automated bots. The authors demonstrate that there is a strong correlation between the number of edits, the number of distinct editors and subsequent article quality. They also found evidence of greater co-operation in the development of higher-quality articles. This evidence includes a strong correlation between discussion (talkpage) activity and article quality and more edits per editor on high-quality pages.

Wikipedia itself has information quality assessment criteria: the *Featured Article Criteria*. Featured articles are selected, by an editor review process, as representing the best of Wikipedia in terms of quality, accuracy, style etc. and Viégas et al. (2007) describe the process in detail. Wilkinson and Huberman (2007a) demonstrated a correlation between editing and article quality by comparing edit counts and distinct editors on featured articles with other parts of Wikipedia. They showed that featured articles had received more edits by more editors than other articles, by a statistically significant margin.

They also measured levels of co-operation for articles by analysing the corresponding discussion pages. This showed a strong correlation between the number of comments posted on the discussion page and the quality of the corresponding article, i.e. featured articles generated significantly more discussion. Indeed, interestingly, the authors noted that the margin was even higher than that found for number of edits or editors, suggesting that "co-operation could be a more important indicator of quality than raw edit counts" (Wilkinson and Huberman 2007a, 161). In conclusion they note: "article growth follows a very simple overall pattern on average. This pattern implies that a small number of articles, corresponding to topics of high relevance or visibility, accrete a disproportionately large number of edits, while the vast majority of articles experience far less activity" (p. 162).

Anthony et al. (2005) have argued that quality of contribution can be measured by calculating what percentage of a contributor's editing is retained as the article ages—known as *survivability*. Their work identified two different sets of editors who provided high-quality contributions to Wikipedia: Zealots, who are registered users with a high level of commitment and provide frequent, high-quality contributions, and Good Samaritans, who also do high-quality work but only contribute occasionally.

In a similar vein, Adler et al. (2008) proposed a metric called *edit longevity*, which combines the amount of change performed by an editor with how long it lasted (a measure of its decay). They argue that this can be used as a metric for assessing user contribution to Wikipedia or any other wiki, and can be used as part of a reward system. For example, in wikis that generate revenue, measures of contribution can be used as a basis for deciding how revenue should be shared. Such metrics might also be used to guide the level of trust for particular content based on the 'reputation' of the contributors (Adler and Alfaro 2006;

Alfaro et al. 2011). The authors propose an idea for colouring the text of Wikipedia based on such trust metrics, giving readers some guidance as to the likely quality of the text. This has been implemented as an extension to the Firefox Web browser.* On installation, an extra button will appear in Wikipedia labelled *wikitrust* which will re-display the article page in the coloured, trust version.

Chesney (2006) has also reviewed article quality but using a different approach. He asked experts to read Wikipedia articles both from their field and on subjects that were chosen at random. They were then asked to complete an online questionnaire that attempted to capture their views on the various articles' credibility, the writers' credibility, Wikipedia's credibility in general and a measure of how 'cynical' the respondent is of information taken from the Internet. A number of characteristics were used for assessing the credibility of the article and how it was authored including: believability, accuracy, trustworthiness, bias and completeness (a wider set of measures were used for Wikipedia as a whole). This work suggested that the accuracy of Wikipedia was high and, interestingly, that experts found the information in their field of expertise more credible than did the non-experts. The authors however indicated that this could not be considered conclusive due to the small sample size.

Debates about the quality of Wikipedia continue.† For some, it is counter-intuitive to have an encyclopaedia—a primary source of knowledge—to which anyone can contribute and in which there may be inaccuracies in many of the articles. Others argue that the site provides a good place to start an exploration of a topic or subject area, with most entries at least being "serviceable" (Sunstein 2006, 154).

These debates are important since, increasingly, Wikipedia is becoming a source of record, cited by mainstream media and in academic circles (Anthony et al. 2005). Jimmy Wales has himself gone on record as saying that while he thinks Wikipedia is useful for many things, he does not recommend it for serious research. Within education, teaching staff often worry that it has become the first port of call for students rather than set texts or academic papers and there has been a deal of head scratching as to how to respond to this, even to the point of debating whether or not to discourage its use for citations (JISC 2009; Head and Eisenberg 2010; Tapscott and Williams 2007). All we can usefully say right now is that this remains a rich seam for further academic research.

9.6.1.3 Web Graphs and Linking Patterns

The final class of analysis carried out on Wikipedia builds on work already undertaken into the topology and linking patterns of the wider Web, which we discussed in Chapter 7. To recap, the Web exhibits a number of topological features that can be measured. In particular the Webgraph, the pattern of hypertext links between webpages, can be examined using software tools to crawl across the links. Recall that we also discussed the concept of preferential attachment to explain the way in which links between webpages evolve—that is, 'the rich get richer'.

---

* Further details at: http://wikitrust.soe.ucsc.edu/
† For further discussion of quality metrics in Wikipedia see Wöhner and Peters (2009).

Spinellis and Louridas (2008) have noted that Wikipedia presents an important opportunity to examine these processes. In the past it has never been possible to examine the emergence of scaling in big, real-world networks like the Web as there is no full record of their evolution. Wikipedia now allows us to witness, and either validate or refute, preferential attachment at work on its graph, and provides an *in vivo* test of Barabási's scale-free network development theory. The authors put forward an adapted form of the preferential attachment for Wikipedia and note evidence of a growth mechanism, whereby a reference in an existing article to a non-existent article (a precursor to a 'stub') appears to be positively correlated with the creation of the non-existent page, usually within a month. There is also evidence of collaboration, since only 3% of non-existent articles are added to by the person who created the reference to the non-existent article in the first place. Thus there is a strong argument that articles are added to Wikipedia in response to a form of need, expressed by a link to a stub or to a non-existent article.

Capocci et al. (2006) have undertaken a similar analysis of Wikipedia, following links between and within articles. They concluded that the Wikipedia graph exhibits a topological bow-tie structure (see Chapter 7), that Wikipedia exhibits preferential attachment in the same manner as has been proposed for the wider Web, and that the frequency distribution for the number of incoming and outgoing links (links or edges on the graph) decays as a power law. However, they also found that the strongly connected core (SCC)—the central core—was relatively large (82.41% in the English Wikipedia version), which is different from the wider Web. Kamps and Koolen (2009) and Buriol et al. (2006) also confirmed results along similar lines.

Capocci et al. (2006) express some surprise at these similarities, in particular at what appears to be the preferential attachment mechanism in operation. They argue that preferential attachment is a sign of information dissemination inefficiency in a network. It is present in the wider Web because individual authors of webpages lack the knowledge to be able to link to the most relevant sources of information for their purpose (since the Web is so vast), and so tend to link to popular (richer) webpages. The authors: "expect the coordination of the collaborative effort to be more effective in the Wikipedia environment since any authoritative agent can use his expertise to tune the linkage from and toward any page in order to optimize information mining" (p. 4). This does not appear to be happening, at least according to the topological evidence and they conclude:

> [E]mpirical evidences show that the statistical properties of Wikipedia do not differ substantially from those of the WWW. This suggests two possible scenarios: preferential attachment may be the consequence of the intrinsic organisation of the underlying knowledge; alternatively, the preferential attachment mechanism emerges because the Wiki technical capabilities are not fully exploited by Wikipedia contributors: if this is the case, their focus on each specific subject puts much more effort in building a single Wiki entry, with little attention toward the global efficiency of the organisation of information across the whole encyclopaedia. (p. 4, quote reproduced with kind permission from the American Physical Society. Copyright © 2006 American Physical Society)

If the former is true, then there is material here for epistemologists to reflect on. If the latter is true, then there is food for thought for Wikipedians.

Zlatic et al. (2006) report that the linking structure of Wikipedia follows a power law for a number of different languages. The power law had an average γ for the different languages of $\gamma in = 2.15$, $\gamma out = 2.57$ and $\gamma undirected = 2.35$.* These figures, the authors argue, agree with those found for the wider Web. They also looked at path length and found Wikipedia exhibits small world effects (see Chapter 7). The average path length in the English-language Wikipedia was 4.90 (directed path) and 3.28 (undirected), the latter matching the average path length of a random network. They conclude that there are many similarities across different language versions of Wikipedia in all the measured characteristics and suggest the presence of the same kind of complex network in different stages of development.

Understanding the difference between Wikipedia and the wider Web may have longer-term implications for understanding information retrieval. Kamps et al. (2009) argue that linking in Wikipedia may be different from the wider Web in that links between wikipages tend to be contextual rather than purely navigational. The encyclopaedic nature of the content, the collaborative nature of editing and Wikipedia's social norm of only adding links when necessary and relevant to the context mean that studying the link structure of Wikipedia may also help to research the Semantic Web (see Chapter 15).

EXERCISES AND POINTS TO PONDER

1. Working as a group, identify a topic or niche area of interest (for example the page for your local university, college, or sports team) that either has no Wikipedia entry or whose entry could be improved. Explore the process of adding/editing the text and **engaging** with others through the discussion feature. How does your relationship **develop** both with other contributors outside your core group and with elite users who are responsible for overseeing the site?

2. Read the *Nature* report which found that "the difference in accuracy [between *Encyclopaedia Britannica* and *Wikipedia*] was not particularly great" and *Encyclopaedia Britannica's* response (Giles 2005). What do you notice about the different perspectives/assumptions of each set of authors? How might these have affected both the research carried out by *Nature* and *Britannica's* rebuttal?

3. Using a free, hosted wiki service, such as Wikispaces, Wikkii, Wetpaint or Wikidot, set up a wiki for a small group within your class to use. Pick a topic, or focus on notes about the Web 2.0 course you are currently undertaking and, over the course of a number of weeks, develop the wiki content on the hosted site. Add pages of content, images and links both between wikipages and with external Web content. What issues emerge, especially when working with a number of different people?

---

* Recall that an undirected link is a reciprocal link, i.e. both ways.

4. Read the *Guardian* article[*] about the role of academics and researchers in contributing to Wikipedia. What might prevent academics from engaging fully with the site? How might researchers make more use of the wiki way of working?

5. The average path length (degree of separation) for Wikipedia is 4.9 (see Section 9.6.1.3). The same figure for the Web is between 16 and 19 (see Chapter 7). Why do you think such a difference might exist?

FURTHER READING

For further, detailed exploration of the impact that wikis have had on business and government see the books by Don Tapscott and Anthony Williams (2007) and Cass Sunstein (2006).

To learn more about how wikis are used in educational settings and to explore setting up your own wiki for a classroom project or local community activity see the Wetpaint Wiki Educational Community (http://wikisineducation.wetpaint.com/).

For a step-by-step guide to setting up a wiki using PBwiki see Chapter 4 of Evans and Coyle (2010).

For further discussion about the pros and cons of Wikipedia see Silverthorne (2007).

There is much discussion of different methods for deciding the reputation of contributors to wikis and how trustworthy they might be in Alfaro et al. (2011).

For much more information on the ongoing research into wikis and their impact see the Wikimedia Research Index (http://meta.wikimedia.org/wiki/Research) and the Wikibibliographie ENCYCLEN maintained by the Veille Scientique et Technologique, Institut National de Recherche Pedagogique in Lyon, France (http://wikindx.inrp.fr/biblio_encyclen/index.php).

For further discussion of issues concerning content quality in social media, in particular the role that data mining and analysis techniques can play, see Agichtein et al. (2008) and Figueiredo et al. (2009).

---

[*] http://www.guardian.co.uk/education/2011/mar/29/wikipedia-survey-academic-contributions

## CHAPTER 10

Online Social Networks

Suddenly, socializing online was no longer about hiding from the real world, because the two were becoming indistinguishable.

SARAH LACEY
(2008, 96)

If you're not on MySpace, you don't exist.

SKYLER SIERRA
Interviewed at age 18 (boyd 2008a, 170)

Online social networks allow members to formally articulate and maintain connections between themselves and others, commonly referred to as 'friendships'. The software lets users create a profile describing themselves and their social relationships, and share various types of personal information such as snippets of news about what they are doing and where they have been, music preferences, photos, video clips etc.

In the space of a few short years the giants of online social networking, Facebook, MySpace, Cyworld (South Korea) and QZone (China) have amassed more users than the populations of entire countries, even continents. In June 2011, Facebook was well on its way to chalking up its 750 millionth user and is reported to be handling more than 30 billion items of user content a month (Miller 2010e; Su 2011). In South Korea, over 30% of the country's entire population, and over 90% of its young people, are active members of Cyworld (Solove 2007). In the UK, research shows that at least half of all children under the age of seventeen have set up a profile on at least one online social network (Ofcom 2008). As an online activity it has effectively become even more popular than e-mail, the original 'killer app' of the Internet. It is no wonder then that online social networks are one of the most talked about, and researched, aspects of Web 2.0.

More than any of the other Web 2.0 developments, online social networks have drawn people and the links between people—relationships—into the Web. What sets them apart from other forms of Web-based media is the primary emphasis on social interaction as opposed to generating and sharing content (Fogg and Iizawa 2008; Kim et al. 2010).

Their potential significance, therefore, stems in large part from the importance of networks to human society. As the leading sociologist of the information and communications technology (ICT) revolution, Manual Castells has written: "Networks are very old forms of human practice, but they have taken on a new life in our time by becoming information networks, powered by the Internet" (Castells 2001, 1).

A Note on Terminology: In the press and in everyday conversation, sites such as Facebook, MySpace and Orkut are commonly referred to as *social networks* and using them is described as *social networking*. However, this is problematic in the more formal world of academic research since real-world human networks have a long history of being referred to as social networks. The first academics to consider in detail what were then newly emerging online networks, argued that they should be referred to as *social network sites* (SNS) (boyd and Ellison 2007). Their line of thinking was that 'networking' implies relationship initiation, i.e. to search out and make new friends or contacts. Whilst this is possible it is not, they argued, the primary purpose of these sites, which is to "enable users to articulate and make visible their social networks" (p. 1). Obviously this is not a hard and fast rule and, as we shall see, SNSs vary widely as to their purpose and intended audience (LinkedIn, for example, helps business people to make contacts through their networks—i.e. networking). Others prefer the term *online social network* (OSN). For the purpose of this book we will use either the term social network site (SNS) or online social network (OSN), and reserve the term 'social network' for a real-world human network.

10.1 INTRODUCTION TO SOCIAL NETWORK SITES

In line with blogs and wikis, the software that drives SNSs can also be seen, in a more abstract way, as another form of content management system. However, rather than managing an overt, intentional content creation process, content production is more of a by-product of communication and social interaction. In the course of using the service more and more content is generated, which keeps the site fresh and means that users come back for more.

In general, the SNS facilitates two main types of communication: incoming and outgoing. Incoming communication is usually found on the homepage, which presents information that has been derived from the activity streams of a user's friends and collated from across the network (see Figure 10.1). These activity streams may include news 'feeds' (news

FIGURE 10.1   A Facebook homepage screenshot showing the stream of news coming in from friends and the 'What's on your mind?' status update box. (Reproduced with kind permission of Facebook Inc. © 2011 Facebook Inc. and Raza Rizvi.)

of friends' activities, perhaps apps they've downloaded or comments they've posted), alerts (messages that something of interest has happened elsewhere on the site, e.g. a friend has been invited to join a new group), new photographs that have been added and various sorts of status updates. Outgoing communication, from a user to his or her friends, can consist of blog posts, messages (a kind of internal e-mail system) and status updates. This outgoing content is usually generated from the user's profile page.

Terminology for the different types of communication varies. Cyworld provides 'ilchon pyung' for friends to leave a 'testimonial' on a user's homepage (Ahn et al. 2007), whereas Orkut provides each user with a 'scrapbook'—a place where all public text messages are displayed (Benevenuto et al. 2009). Facebook has a mechanism known as 'poking' (Koutrika et al. 2009), which sends a simple alert (with no accompanying message) to a friend, a friend-of-a-friend or someone in a shared group on the system.*

This is one of the key distinguishing factors between SNSs and earlier forms of group communication such as chat rooms and blogging: SNSs are predominantly based on social relationships rather than creating a connection through a shared interest. In their report into users' attitudes and behaviour when using SNSs, the UK's telecommunications regulator, Ofcom, makes the point that through the rise of SNSs: "Online communication has changed from being merely task-based or for sharing information and is increasingly an end in itself" (Ofcom 2008, 12). Many academics emphasize the notion of articulating friendship links as fundamental to the concept of SNSs and a more formal definition is provided by boyd and Ellison (2007) who describe SNSs as Web-based services that allow users to:

- Construct a public or semi-public profile within a bounded system

- Articulate a list of other users with whom they share a connection

- View and traverse their list of connections and those made by others within the system

Although there are many different SNSs in existence there are a number of general features that most SNSs display. These include a homepage, a profile page and a process for articulating friendships and the formation of groups.

10.1.1 Homepage

When a user logs in to the service they are usually taken to the homepage, where various streams of information have been collated from activities elsewhere in the network. For example, the bulk of a Facebook homepage is taken up by what is called the 'News Feed', a stream of updates and comments from a user's friends (Veer 2010) (see Figure 10.1).

---

* This is not without controversy. Fogg and Iizawa (2008) argue that it has a slightly provocative nature, although Veer (2010) maintains it is more like simply tapping someone on the shoulder.

10.1.2 Profile Page

In contrast to the homepage, the profile functions as a user's personal webpage and although the exact format varies from site to site, it usually includes information such as date of birth, gender, religion, political views, home town and college or university attended, together with various lists of favourite films, music and hobbies. The profile is completed by filling in an online form, and in addition to the profile information, the user can often design how the information will be displayed to other people and add content such as photos and video clips. It is interesting to note that boyd (2008b) argues that these SNS profiles still retain echoes of their dating service roots.

10.1.3 Friendship

Clearly the articulation of friendships is the defining characteristic of SNSs, and a key day-to-day activity for any user is to find and make connections with friends, colleagues, former classmates etc. There are various mechanisms for this. Many sites allow you to add a friend's e-mail address so that they can be sent an automatic invitation to join the site. Another method is to peruse other users' profiles and add people of interest to your list of friends, usually by clicking some kind of 'Add as a Friend' button displayed on the profile page, or to accept automatic recommendations based on what the site software knows about you (for example, attendance at the same school in the same decade or similar hobbies). It is usually possible to import contacts from instant messaging services such as AOL and Skype and some services will also make recommendations based on mutual acquaintances ('friend-of-a-friend'). In most networks friendship is a process of mutual approval, so that an offer of friendship has to be agreed by the other party before the system will accept it.

10.1.4 Groups

Groups or communities allow people with a shared interest, hobby, political bugbear, locality etc. to join together within the confines of the site. Groups may be closed or open and most SNSs have thousands of such groups (see Figure 10.2).

10.2 A SHORT HISTORY OF SOCIAL NETWORK SITES

As ever with Web developments, SNSs did not appear, ready formed, out of thin air. The concept of an online social network stretches back to at least the mainframe computer environment of the 1960s.[*] The problem, in trying to put together a short history, is that, as we have already discussed, there are hundreds of SNSs. Therefore, in this section I will discuss a representative sample, taking into account key developments in the SNS story and a site's current popularity.

---

[*] Gross and Acquisti (2005) argue, for example, that the University of Illinois's Plato—a computer-based education tool—is a very early example.

FIGURE 10.2   A screenshot of the list of communities that are available on Orkut. (Image courtesy of Google. © 2011 Google Inc.)

10.2.1 The Early SNS Pioneers

Two early pioneers in the formal study of SNSs argue that the first recognizable site, in the context of Web 2.0, was SixDegrees.com, launched in 1997 (boyd and Ellison 2007). This site, now defunct*, allowed users to create profiles, list their friends and surf their friends' lists to make new connections. Although some of the site's features were based on early online dating websites, the process of listing friends was a new development. The service attracted a large number of users but failed to become a sustainable business, and closed in 2000. Many commentators believed that all the pieces were in place but it was simply too far ahead of its time. Cheng et al. (2009) note a similar situation in China with an early site called Zhanzuo. com, which successfully attracted considerable investment initially, but subsequently faced strong competition from a newer site, Xiaonei (since renamed Renren.com).

Between 1997 and 2001, a number of other sites appeared that incorporated elements of the model that SixDegrees had attempted to pursue. boyd and Ellison (2007) cite BlackPlanet, LiveJournal, LunarStorm and Cyworld. One site that is particularly worth

---

* The site closed in 2000, although recently it appears to have been restarted.

mentioning is Friends Reunited, which was founded in the UK in July 2000 by Steve and Julie Parkhurst to help people find and get back in touch with old school friends. Despite being largely unknown outside the UK, it was the first site to really bring the online social network concept to the British public and at one point the site had nearly half the UK's Internet population registered as users. Friends Reunited was one of the first SNSs to charge for access to its facilities and its key contribution to the story of online social networks is to demonstrate the difficulty of attempting this.*

The next wave of SNSs really arrived with the launch of Friendster in 2002, a site that many academics and commentators credit with lighting the touch paper on the online social network explosion. Developed by Jonathan Abrams, a former Netscape programmer, Friendster was designed to compete with online dating services—in particular Match.com. The key differentiator was that where online dating services attempted to match complete strangers together, Friendster would try to get friends of friends together. It quickly popularized the key characteristics of SNSs: profiles, public comments and publically articulated and traversable lists of friends and contacts (boyd 2008b; Fraser and Dutta 2009), and by May 2003 it had 300,000 users through word of mouth alone.

However, the site's success was brief. Friendster restricted people from viewing profiles of individuals who were more than four degrees away (i.e. friends-of-friends-of-friends-of friends). This restriction simply encouraged users to find work-arounds by creating fake profiles in order to extend the reach of their profile. The company responded by attempting to police the site and banning these 'fakesters'. This perceived authoritarianism, together with some technical difficulties, led to its decline in the USA in the late 2000s, although it remained active, and popular, in the Far East (Lacey 2008).† There remains much sympathy in the Web 2.0 community for Abrams and his Friendster project. As Lacey writes: "Abrams got a lot of social networking right, with features that dozens of companies have emulated" (p. 108).

Following in the footsteps of Friendster, many other sites were launched in the mid-2000s. Due to the large number of SNSs that are currently operating, the rest of this section is devoted to the four main English-language sites, although a more representative list is provided in Table 10.1.

10.2.1.1 MySpace

MySpace was the first of the current giants of online social networks. Founded in Santa Monica, California, in 2003 by Tom Anderson (sadly, no relation to me) and Chris DeWolfe, MySpace was able to grow rapidly because of the prevailing difficulties with Friendster—in particular, a number of popular indie bands were expelled from Friendster for failing to comply with rules about profiles and took themselves and their fans to MySpace. boyd (2008a) notes that music is a kind of cultural glue among young people and the 'bands and

---

* See, for example: http://www.independent.co.uk/news/business/analysis-and-features/the-rise-and-fall-of-friends-reunited-1628278.html
† This is probably at least part of the reason the site was sold to the Malaysian company MOL Global at the end of 2009. In April 2011, the firm announced that the site would be focusing on becoming a social entertainment site (games and music) and would be integrating with Facebook. See: http://techcrunch.com/2011/04/26/social-network-pioneer-friendster-to-erase-all-user-photos-blogs-and-more-on-may-31/

TABLE 10.1   A Top 25 of SNSs as Measured by Registered Users

Name	URI	Registered Users (millions)	Launch Date	Notes
Facebook	http://www.facebook.com/	750	2004	World's largest
Qzone	http://qzone.qq.com	480	2005	Huge Chinese site
Bebo	http://www.bebo.com/	117	2005	Popular amongst teens in UK; part of AOL, but declining
Friendster	http://www.friendster.com/	115	2002	Early pioneer
LinkedIn	http://www.linkedin.com	100	2003	More professional, job-hunting oriented site
VKontakte	http://vkontakte.ru/	85	2006	Aimed at Russia, Ukraine etc.
Hi5	http://www.hi5.com/	80	2003	Aimed at younger users and heavy investment in social games
Orkut	http://www.orkut.com/	67	2004	Huge in India and Brazil; part of Google
Netlog	http://en.netlog.com/	64	2003	Belgium-based, but acts Europe wide
MySpace	http://uk.myspace.com/	63	2003	One of the early giants of social networks; reinventing as music site
Xanga	http://www.xanga.com/	40	1999	Started as music review sharing site; expanded into social networking
Sonico	http://www.sonico.com/	40	2007	Popular in Latin America
Viadeo	http://www.viadeo.com	30	2009	European professional/ networking site
Nasza Klasa	http://nk.pl/	27	2006	Polish; users register as attending schools or colleges
Skyrock	http://skyrock.com/	21	2002	Based in France; popular in a number of EU countries
Cyworld	http://us.cyworld.com/	18	1999	Very popular in S. Korea; US version ceased in early 2010
BlackPlanet	http://www.blackplanet.com/	16	1999	Black American community
Mixi	http://mixi.jp/	15	2004	Japanese; strong emphasis on blogging & anonymity of users
meinVZ	http://www.meinvz.net/	12	2008	German site
Hyves	http://hyves.nl/	10	2004	Dutch site

(Continued)

TABLE 10.1   A Top 25 of SNSs as Measured by Registered Users (Continued)

Name	URI	Registered Users (millions)	Launch Date	Notes
Xing	http://www.xing.com/	9	2003	More professional, job-hunting oriented
Yonja	http://www.yonja.com/	6	2003	Turkish
Wer-Kennt-wen	http://www.wer-kennt-wen.de/	5	2006	German site
Tuenti	http://www.tuenti.com	5	2006	Spanish site
BigAdda	http://www.bigadda.com/	5	2007	Popular amongst the young in India

Note: A number of caveats apply to this table: a variety of sources for the numbers of users have been used, many from companies' own press releases, which are potentially less reliable. The data on users is changing all the time making this more of a snapshot in time.

fans' dynamic became an important early growth hormone for MySpace. This also illustrates an important point about online social networks: fashions and loyalties change and users can rapidly move *en masse* to rival services.

MySpace experienced exponential growth in its user population during the first four years or so and at one point in 2008 it was the leading SNS in terms of users and their activity (Caverlee and Webb 2008; Torkjazi et al. 2009). However, its importance in the online social network story rests not only on its sheer size, but also on the way in which it used a shared interest—music—in order to rapidly grow a large, young audience.

Weaver and Morrison (2008) showed that "the concept of sharing media is at the core of MySpace, and the idea of sharing music naturally expanded to sharing video" (p. 98), noting that users can create profiles that are more like miniature website homepages and are allowed to embed music and video. They also note that MySpace emphasizes that its members retain intellectual property rights on the material they upload and that this has been an important incentive for independent musicians who do not have a recording contract.

Another important feature in MySpace's growth and development was to allow profiles to be highly personalized by inserting Hypertext Markup Language (HTML) and Cascading Style Sheet (CSS) code into the profile form (boyd and Ellison 2007). This is a key differentiator between MySpace and Facebook (which does not allow such modification), turning MySpace profiles into: "an explosion of animated chaos that resembles a stereotypical teenager's bedroom" (boyd 2008b, 123).

In July 2005, News Corporation purchased MySpace for US$580million but recently it has struggled to compete with Facebook and in October 2010, in response to falling audience numbers, a complete re-design of the site was undertaken with a renewed focus on music and film.[*] The site was subsequently sold to Specific Media in January 2011 with the pop star and actor Justin Timberlake taking a stake in the new business.[†]

---

[*] See: http://www.bloomberg.com/news/2010-10-27/myspace-recast-as-entertainment-hub-in-news-corp-quest-to-recapture-young.html

[†] See: http://www.bbc.co.uk/news/business-13969338

10.2.1.2 Bebo

British-born Bebo's principal contribution to our discussion of SNSs is that it is a primary example of the fickle nature of audience engagement. Bebo was founded in January 2005 by the physics graduate and IT contractor, Michael Birch and his wife Xochi. They were inspired by Friendster (as were many early SNS pioneers) and Birch admits that he studied the site before spending thirteen days coding his own version. This initial effort was launched as Ringo, which they sold six months later. Based on the lessons learned from that project they launched Bebo in 2005.

AOL bought Bebo in March 2008 with a view to expanding its operation beyond its home base of Britain and Ireland. At the time, the *Times* newspaper printed an interview with the founding couple and noted that in 2005, Bebo was ranked as the third most popular SNS in the world, after MySpace and Facebook.* However, this turned out to be the site's peak year and in April 2010, AOL announced that it was either shutting down or selling the service following a dramatic decline in its user figures. Bebo had drawn in only 12.8 million unique visitors in February 2010, down 45% from the same period the previous year, whilst other social networks, particularly Facebook, had boomed. It was eventually sold to Criterion Capital Partners and Birch, who had left after the AOL buy-out, has returned to the company with a mission to "re-invent Bebo".†

10.2.1.3 Facebook

Currently, Facebook is the second most visited website (next to Google) according to site analysts Alexa, and announced its 750 millionth member in June 2011.‡ *New Yorker* magazine reported in September 2010 that at least one in every fourteen people in the world now has an account (Vargas 2010) and, although the precise figures vary from country to country, Livingstone et al. (2011) present figures showing the almost total dominance of Facebook amongst young people in Europe (most popular in 17 out of 25 countries).

The site was started in February 2004, as TheFacebook.com, by Harvard University undergraduate Mark Zuckerberg and was based on a Harvard tradition of producing paper-based 'facebooks'—collections of photographs of new undergraduates. Each Harvard 'house' (or 'college' in collegiate UK universities) maintained its own facebook, held on the house's internal computer network. Once a year, the university as a whole produced a printed facebook called the *Freshman Register* using data from the individual houses. Zuckerberg noticed that copies of this *Register* were extensively annotated by students during the course of the year and his idea was to put the facebook on the Web in order to allow students to create their own annotated profiles and link to other students. Zuckerberg enlisted the support of a number of friends from Harvard including Eduardo Saverin, Dustin Moskovitz, Andrew McCollum and Chris Hughes. Within a month of its launch, half the campus had accounts and it was soon extended to other universities down

---

* See: http://business.timesonline.co.uk/tol/business/article3559414.ece
† See: http://eu.techcrunch.com/2010/12/09/birch-returns-to-help-re-invent-bebo-puts-his-money-where-his-mouth-is/
‡ Readers interested in other statistics produced by the company are referred to their page: http://www.facebook.com/press/info.php?statistics

the eastern seaboard of America. In August 2005, it became facebook.com and the site was opened up to users based at American high schools.

According to Kirkpatrick (2010a) this was not a new idea, and had even been suggested by Harvard's own student newspaper, *The Crimson*. In fact, the Winklevoss twins, who were at Harvard at the same time as Zuckerberg, have claimed prior ownership of the idea and pointed out that Zuckerberg worked for them as a programmer on a social network site called ConnectU during part of 2003 (Bull 2010). A legal case was settled out of court in 2008, although there remains some dispute concerning the valuation of the company that was used to set the rate of compensation.

These roots in the undergraduate community are important for understanding the way in which Facebook has developed (boyd and Ellison 2007). The site was initially designed to support distinct, pre-existing, real-world networks of social connections in a campus environment. Indeed, at least initially, a prospective user had to have a college e-mail address to even register with the site, and everything was structured around separate college communities. Critics of the site argue that these beginnings as a 'closed' environment still echo today, as it has created what is sometimes called a *walled garden* (see Chapter 6), with few opportunities to connect a person's profile through to other sites or sources of content (Fraser and Dutta 2009). As one example, Stross (2010) argues that Facebook can access Google's data, but not vice versa.

10.2.1.4 Google+

In the summer of 2011 Google introduced a new SNS, Google+. The name reflects the tight integration of the new system with Google's existing products such as search, YouTube, Google Reader and its online document systems. It is too early to say what impact this new arrival on the social networking scene will have, but it is worth noting that the company claims to have made particular efforts to analyse what users really want from an SNS. In particular they have introduced mechanisms, such as Circles, which allow more control over which friends see what news and content (see Figure 10.3).

10.3 EXAMPLE SYSTEM: FACEBOOK

As the largest and best-known of the SNSs it is worth taking a little time to discuss some of Facebook's features in detail. This will also give us the opportunity to discuss some of the ideas around the social graph (the network of connections between users) and the site's use of applications, as well as to explore the way its technical infrastructure has coped with rapid growth.

10.3.1 The Social Graph

Facebook staff use the term *social graph* to describe the network of interconnections between users on the site. Graph is a mathematical term for diagrams that show nodes and the links between them. In Facebook, each person (node) creates a profile containing their personal details, and then creates links to profiles of other people that they know.

FIGURE 10.3:   Screenshot of the Google+ online social network. The figure shows the Circles feature which allows a user to allocate their friends and acquaintances into different social circles. (Image courtesy of Google. © 2011 Google Inc.)

Although Zuckerberg is widely credited with inventing this term, Fraser and Dutta (2009) point out that the term has been used by sociologists for decades.

In the real world, the social graph is the map of the social connections that people have. A distinguishing feature of Facebook as opposed to some other SNSs, is that its founders were not trying to create a social graph, but rather to mirror what existed already (Lacey 2008): to show who knew who on campus.

However, increasingly, the Facebook graph has also begun to include the connections between people and other information artefacts within the site, e.g. events, photographs etc. (Zeichick 2008a). Technically, every object (person, event, photograph etc.) in the Facebook social graph has a unique identifier and the data associated with the object is fetched using a Uniform Resource Identifier (URI) that is based on that identifier, e.g. https://graph.facebook.com/ID. All such objects are connected to other objects via relationships and these can be obtained in a similar manner, e.g. to find friends of the node *ID* type in: https://graph.facebook.com/ID/friends. By electronically tracking every interaction a user has with either another user or another information artefact, Facebook is able to map connections that would be invisible to the cartographers of (real-world) social networks. The Facebook social graph is thus a complete representation of all the connections that make up the Facebook social network (Goldman 2009).

10.3.2 Facebook and the Open Graph

At Facebook's annual developer conference in 2010, Zuckerberg announced what he referred to as the *Open Graph*. Noting that different SNS companies are each building their own graphs, Zuckerberg told the conference: "If we can take these separate maps of the graph and pull them all together, then we can create a Web that's smarter, more social, more personalized, and more semantically aware" (McCarthy 2010, webpage). The practical manifestation of this is the Open Graph protocol—a set of markup tags that other websites can use to describe their content objects so that they can be incorporated within Facebook's social graph. So, for example, the Internet Movie Database (IMDb) is using the

Open Graph protocol to mark up pages for individual movies. Hitting the 'Like' button on an IMDb movie page will automatically add that movie to the 'Favorite Movies' section of a Facebook user's profile. Note that the Open Graph protocol is only one-way—sites are providing data to Facebook. This is in contrast to OpenSocial, Google's alternative system, which exchanges data between SNSs.

10.3.3 Facebook Technical Architecture

A Facebook webpage is assembled from data drawn from a variety of software systems spread across a number of data centres and third-party information suppliers (Cass 2011). So, for example, news of friends, photographs, 'Like button' data and third-party games information is all pulled in from different servers and collated, in HTML, on the webpage that the user sees. Facebook uses a LAMP stack (Linux, Apache, MySQL and PHP) with Memcached, a distributed memory caching system that helps speed up the operation of databases. This runs on a network of at least 60,000 servers and handles 25 terabytes of user data a day (June 2010 figures).* The main code runs under this architecture with a number of additional services, such as the advertisement server and the blog system, written in a wide range of software languages including C++ and Erlang, with Thrift used to help programs compiled from different languages work together (Zeichick 2008a; Goldman 2009). The server system is split into three tiers with a top tier of Web servers running Apache, a bottom tier of MySQL servers and a middle tier of cache servers running Memcached. This caching technology is the key component that allows Facebook to scale and handle the hundreds of millions of users. As part of this layer the development team has built a custom caching system that can handle the peculiarities of the social graph. For example, there is a special cache handling system that keeps track of what is happening in a user's network of friends and is able to return the core set of results very quickly without a visit back to the underlying database (Naone 2009).

In addition to this, there are two key aspects of Facebook's technical architecture that need further explanation: platform and apps, and FBML.

10.3.3.1 Platform and Apps

The Facebook Platform was launched on 24th May 2007 by Zuckerberg, at the Facebook f8 event in San Francisco (Goldman 2009). It is the set of Application Programming Interfaces (APIs) and tools which enables developers to gain access to the social graph—allowing them to develop applications (apps) which integrate with Facebook either directly through Facebook. com or via external websites and mobile devices (Nazir et al. 2008; Nazir et al. 2009).† Goldman (2009) argues that this makes Platform akin to an operating system for SNSs.

Facebook apps run within what is known as the *canvas page*, a display area within the Facebook navigation frame, as it is displayed within the browser window. When a user

---

* The company's data centre acreage is constantly expanding in response to the site's growth and, as with all Web 2.0 companies, Facebook is tight-lipped about the exact details. Latest updates can be found at: http://www.datacenter-knowledge.com/the-facebook-data-center-faq-page-2/
† Details of the Facebook API are here: http://developers.facebook.com/docs/reference/api/

wants a particular app, a request is sent to the Facebook server. The server then analyses the request and, if valid, passes the request on to the server that runs the application (which often belongs to a third party, i.e. the company or individual that makes and distributes the app). The app's server then processes the request and may make any number of calls back to the Facebook server to obtain further data from the social graph. When the app has finished it will produce results in Facebook Markup Language (FBML) which are transferred back to the Facebook server. The server will then parse this document to turn the FBML into HTML in order to display it in the user's browser.

Initially, apps could only run within the Facebook site, but in late 2007 the company worked with Bebo to develop apps that would run in both networks. Shortly afterwards Facebook announced that it was opening up Platform's architecture to make it available to other SNSs to licence and to allow ordinary websites to integrate Facebook content within their pages. The end result was initially branded separately as Facebook Connect, but has subsequently been subsumed into the overall Platform concept.[*]

10.3.3.2 Facebook Markup Language (FBML)

FBML is an extension of HTML that is used within Facebook Canvas pages to render content within a browser window. Anyone who is familiar with the concepts behind HTML will quickly understand FBML. A series of markup tags have been introduced, each beginning with the prefix *fb*, e.g. *fb:name*, which in the case of 'name' renders the specified user and a link to details from their profile. The Social Graph identifier that we discussed previously is important for using these tags. For example: <fb:name uid="12345"></fb:name> will return the name of the node with the given identifier.

FBML operates in tandem with a number of other technologies that Facebook has built into their platform. These include Facebook Query Language (FQL), Facebook Javascript (FBJS) and various client libraries. Although the technology is still supported and widely used, the company announced plans in March 2011 to move away from FBML in order to make more use of open Web standards (Gannes 2011). FBML is therefore in flux.[†]

10.4 SNSs TAKE OFF

In the late 2000s online social networks captured the public's imagination and sites such as Facebook, MySpace, Orkut, QZone and RenRen attracted tens of millions of users. The rapid uptake of SNSs could be described as one of the most significant cultural developments in the last decade as it has precipitated a dramatic shift in the way people communicate and organise their social and working lives (Harkin 2009; Denham 2009). This amount of growth has a number of implications with regard to user privacy, information overload and the portability of data between sites.

---

[*] Full details at: http://developers.facebook.com/

[†] For this reason it is worth reviewing the documentation: http://developers.facebook.com/docs/reference/fbml/

10.4.1 SNS Aggregators

As the number of online social networks and indeed other forms of social media rises, users have begun to complain of information overload and the difficulty of keeping various profiles up-to-date. Developers have responded to this concern with a number of tools—aggregators—that allow access to multiple sites and collate feeds and content from those sites (King 2007; Benevenuto et al. 2009). Online social network aggregators typically communicate with SNSs using open APIs, which the sites provide, in a two-stage process. First of all, the user interacts with the aggregator and then the aggregator interacts with the SNS (technically this forms a two-tiered, real-time Hypertext Transfer Protocol [HTTP] connection). Examples of this include FriendFeed, Plocky, Profilactic, MyZazu, and NutShellMail. The exact nature of the service they provide varies and as this is a rapidly developing area there is little value in documenting details.

10.4.2 SNSs and Privacy

Privacy is a recurring theme in discussions on the impact of SNSs (Chen and Shi 2009; Bonneau and Preibusch 2010a). As online social networks expand there is an increasing propensity for users, especially the young, to divulge large amounts of personal information through their profiles, shared photos and by making public their real-world social connections (Gross and Acquisti 2005). As teenagers mature into adults a steady stream of online content accumulates to build a record of an individual's life. The end result is that SNSs are creating centralized repositories of personal information which are persistent, cumulative and reflect real-world life (Barnes 2006; Maximilien and Grandison 2008). As Daniel Solove notes in his excellent book on privacy and the Internet, many of us are, in effect: "invading our own privacy by exposures of information we later come to regret" (Solove 2007, vii).

10.4.3 Data Portability

Related to privacy is the issue of data portability—to be able to transfer data easily between services, and even remove it altogether (Bojars et al. 2008; Razmerita et al. 2009). As a plethora of SNSs emerge and become established, users question why each works in a slightly different way and why the same data must be entered each time they join a new service. Others, who wish to leave a service or move to a different one, would like an easy way of doing so and, incidentally, a guarantee that their original data has been destroyed.

However, the companies that provide SNSs are unwilling to share their data with other services (Recordon 2009; McCown and Nelson 2009; W3C 2010) and the architecture of participation requires that they keep hold of as much data as possible. This means that users find their data is held in what amounts to a *data silo*, a self-contained store within a particular service (W3C 2010). Many are concerned that the average Web user has a fragmented identity spread across several different SNSs (Rowe 2009).

Closely related to this, as part of their wider response to the emergence of Web 2.0, librarians and archivists also worry that there is not an easy way to access and archive the data held by SNSs, which poses problems with regard to recording, for posterity, what is happening now (McCown and Nelson 2009).

In response to growing concerns about this situation, in March 2007 Google unveiled plans to standardize some aspects of SNSs through a development community they call OpenSocial (Weaver and Morrison 2008; Mitchell-Wong et al. 2007). Formally launched on 1st November 2007, OpenSocial allows SNS user profiles and data, across different networks and contexts, to be shared through the adoption of a common API.[*] The OpenSocial API provides methods for accessing information about people, their friends and their data, within the context of what it calls a container (an application or a website). OpenSocial allows online social network data to be transferred between SNSs, and other sorts of websites to access SNS profiles and data. The basic process for the latter is described in OpenSocial network documentation.[†]

An additional benefit of adopting the OpenSocial way of working is that developers who want to design a social networking application can build one app and with relatively little tweaking have it working under a number of SNSs. Contrast this with the Facebook markup language (FBML) which allows development of Facebook-only apps. Any SNS which complies with the OpenSocial framework should be able to run an app built to the specification. Prominent SNSs who work this way include: LinkedIn, Orkut, MySpace, Ning, Xing, Cyworld, Friendster and Hi5.[‡]

Although initiated by Google, OpenSocial is a community of developers and online social network companies working together to develop the standard. There is a potential fault line opening up between the OpenSocial approach and that of more proprietary solutions. Fraser and Dutta (2009) argue that those sites that support open systems are gaining momentum, but this is a rapidly developing area. Indeed, a project has begun to develop an open source SNS.[§] Diaspora aims to create a distributed system where each person manages their own data rather than trusting it to a central hub run by a private company.

There is also the Data Portability project[¶] which launched in 2007 and brings together members from various organisations to discuss portability issues from a technical and legal standpoint. This all forms part of much wider debates about the future of data: ownership and the rights of users versus the companies who provide services. Recognizing the potential for problems to arise Joseph Smarr, Marc Canter, Robert Scoble, and Michael Arrington issued a draft Bill of Rights for Users of the Social Web (4th September, 2007).[**] It is one of the most important debates concerning the future of the Internet and students of Web 2.0 are urged to keep an eye on developments.

10.5 THE SNS ECOSYSTEM

A glance at Table 10.1 gives some idea of the large number of SNSs that operate on the Web. Indeed, this table only shows what, in my opinion, are the more important and representative

---

[*] See: http://opensocial-resources.googlecode.com/svn/spec/1.0/OpenSocial-Specification.xml

[†] See http://docs.opensocial.org/display/OSD/Share+and+access+data+on+the+web

[‡] A regularly updated list is at: http://wiki.opensocial.org/index.php?title=Containers

[§] See: http://osswatch.jiscinvolve.org/wp/2010/05/13/build-a-better-facebook-through-open-innovation/

[¶] See: http://dataportability.org/

[**] See: http://opensocialweb.org/2007/09/05/bill-of-rights/

sites: there are hundreds if not thousands more. In the spirit of Web 2.0, Wikipedia provides a fuller (200+) list which, presumably, is undergoing regular maintenance.*

It is important to recognize that despite Western media attention on a handful of big US names such as MySpace and Facebook, which seemingly dominate the SNS market, this is far from the whole story. Not only are there very large SNSs in other parts of the world, for example QZone in China,† but there are a large number of niche players serving differing demographics and interests. Indeed, there is evidence of SNSs tending to follow cultural and linguistic lines, and few sites successfully support groups from different nation states, although exceptions include Orkut (popular in India and Brazil) and Cyworld (S. Korea and China) (boyd 2008b). Bonneau and Preibusch (2010a) note that almost all SNSs are in competition for users in the countries they operate in and often there is a national 'home-grown' service competing with one or more of the super-large networks. This is particularly the case in mainland Europe, where, to pick one example, Hyves is in competition with Facebook for the Dutch market.

In addition, there is a large number of SNSs serving niche interests. These range from ResearchGate and NatureNetwork (which provide online networking for scientists), through Dogster (a social network for pet dogs), to Netmums (in the UK). This variety presents the scholar with a categorization problem. Fraser and Dutta (2009) suggest organising them into five categories as follows:

- **Egocentric**—the massively popular profile-based sites such as Facebook, MySpace, Orkut

- **Community**—sites that aggregate members based on a strong, real-world identity e.g. BlackPlanet for US-based African Americans

- **Opportunistic**—sites that people join for professional or other rational reasons, e.g. LinkedIn, Sermo, Yammer

- **Passion-centric**—shared interest communities, e.g. Dogster, CarDomain

- **Media-sharing**‡—communities built around content, e.g. YouTube, Ping, Flickr

The authors point out that the motivations for joining a social network can very broadly be characterised as *rational* or *non-rational*. Professionals who join LinkedIn are primarily motivated by rational calculations related to their career development. Teenagers who join MySpace to collect 'friends' are motivated by non-rational social needs to develop community bonds.§

However, according to Veer (2010) one of the differences between online social networks is their attitude to the notion of friendship. Facebook, he argues, values truthfulness and

---

* See: http://en.wikipedia.org/wiki/List_of_social_networking_websites
† For a discussion of the situation in China see Jackson (2010) and http://techrice.com/2011/03/08/chinas-top-15-social-networks/
‡ In this book we consider media-sharing sites as a separate type of service—see Chapter 11.
§ The classic description of these two impulses comes from the nineteenth-century German sociologist Ferdinand Tonnies who wrote about *gemeinschaft* ('community') versus *gesellschaft* ('self-interest').

the maintenance of an accurate reflection of real-life networks, whereas within MySpace there is more emphasis on making a large number of new contacts online.

The degree to which an SNS can be said to be open is also an important differentiator. As one example, the aSmallWorld SNS was originally intended as a highly exclusive network much like a country club. Potential new members had to be put forward by five existing members, all of whom must be linked by three degrees of separation at the most. Despite these restrictions its membership climbed to 300,000, prompting those who had sought true exclusivity to move on to even more tightly controlled networks for the rich. The authors cite a number of other successful, closed networks including Pingsta (IT professionals) and Sermo (US-based physicians).

Discussions over open versus closed often end up in debate about how social networks make money from their members. Most of the super-large SNSs are free to join, open to all and still seeking an appropriate business model, or, in the jargon, 'seeking ways to monetize the users'. Placing paid-for advertising alongside the SNS content is the prevailing business model. Closed networks however provide opportunities to market and advertise to a more defined and exclusive set of people, particularly if they are supposed to be rich like those of aSmallWorld. This is increasingly pertinent since a number of the larger SNSs are being floated on stock markets (e.g. both LinkedIn and China's Renren undertook IPOs in May 2011).

SOCIAL ADVERTISEMENTS

Unfortunately for the owners of online social networks, users do not always like being monetized. Although most people seem to accept banner advertisements as a fair exchange for free access, they are more wary of other methods of marketing. In late 2007, in a well-known case, Facebook attempted to increase what they referred to as *social ads* through a system called Beacon (Fraser and Dutta 2009). This alerted a user's friends when he or she made a purchase from a website participating in the scheme. So, for example, if a user bought a song on iTunes then an alert would be sent to their friends.

One can see the logic. There is little more powerful in the world of marketing than a word-of-mouth recommendation. However, perhaps unsurprisingly, large numbers of Facebook users rebelled and protested at this new development. Many were particularly incensed that the system was an opt-out rather than opt-in arrangement. Four weeks later Facebook resiled and made the system opt-in.

Finally, we should mention Ning, which is an unusual SNS. This service provides the infrastructure for others to create and host their own customized online social networks. More than 300,000 small businesses, community groups, sports clubs, educational establishments and so forth have created their own online social networks using the software. Initially the service was provided free-of-charge, but this was changed in April 2010, a reflection perhaps of the pressure SNSs are under to develop viable business models.[*]

---

[*] See: http://techcrunch.com/2010/04/15/nings-bubble-bursts-no-more-free-networks-cuts-40-of-staff/

10.6 SNS RESEARCH

Before we embark on an introduction to some of the research work that is taking place into online social networks it is worth reflecting on why such research should be carried out at all. Krishnamurthy (2009) argues that the sheer number of people involved begs attention from the research community: perhaps a tenth of the world's population uses SNSs. This represents a major change in the way in which society communicates and is likely to increase dramatically with widespread access via mobile phones.

Such large numbers afford a unique opportunity according to Yong-Yeol Anh et al. (2007) and Kleinberg (2008). Both sets of authors point out that social scientists have considered networks of people for decades, but that this work has necessarily focused on relatively small groups due to the difficulty of obtaining large datasets. Backstrom et al. (2006) note that the formation of groups and communities constitutes a major part of this branch of social science research and that this kind of network analysis is made far easier by the availability of data from SNSs. The way that users interact with each other and behave online is also of interest to marketing, business studies and economics (Benevenuto et al. 2009; Domingos 2005). For these reasons researchers from an increasingly diverse set of academic domains are becoming involved and this provides an opportunity to bring social, economic and computer sciences closer together (Mislove et al. 2007).

A second reason to undertake studies in SNSs is that this kind of research can form part of a wider investigation into complex networks (Leskovec et al. 2008). Such work has emerged in recent years within a number of disciplines including physics, biology and computer science. In particular, research into SNSs forms part of a larger body of work investigating the topology and dynamic structure of the Web (see Chapter 7).

Finally, there are inherently pragmatic reasons to study online social networks in that they form an increasingly large proportion of the Internet's traffic. Understanding their dynamics and the way that users interact with these systems may help engineers design better communication networks and server infrastructure (Benevenuto et al. 2009; Krishnamurthy 2009; Mislove et al. 2007).

However, despite the opportunities for study provided by the enormous scale of SNSs, it is worth noting that gathering data is not as straightforward as it may at first appear (Krishnamurthy 2009). Crawling software must access the SNS and search, parse and extract a wide variety of information including links between friends, links between users and groups, links to content such as video, individual profile pages and navigational links. A typical network will have many millions of items of data and all this takes place in a highly dynamic environment in which data is changing on a minute-by-minute basis as users change their status and link to new friends (Willinger et al. 2009).

Such difficulties are compounded by the restrictions imposed by many of the major SNSs. In part, this is because the researchers want to get access to the social graph—the commercial heart of an SNS operation. Many SNSs place restrictions on the number of times, for example, that a call can be made to the API to extract data within a specific time period. There is therefore a risk of relying on too small a subset of data or what may turn out to be a non-representative sample.

10.6.1 User Demographics, Behaviour and Friendships

An important area of interest to various types of researcher is investigating who exactly is using SNSs. This kind of work looks at the demographics of users and considers various social and personal characteristics. These types of analyses are made easier by the fact that large numbers of users provide quite detailed profiles. In the United States, the Pew Research Center's Internet and American Life project is a notable source of information on what users are doing online and Lenhart et al. (2010b) note that research undertaken there has found that: 73% of American teenagers who have access to the Internet make use of SNSs and 47% of American adults use SNSs. Among adult users, 73% have a profile on Facebook, 48% have a profile on MySpace and 14% have a LinkedIn profile. Younger users are more likely to make use of MySpace, which, as we have noted previously, focuses on music and bands.

Caverlee and Webb (2008) undertook analysis of MySpace and found, perhaps unsurprisingly, that teenagers and people in their twenties form the largest group of users, with usage peaking at the age of 17. There were two anomalies: a peak at age 69, which may be a joke or a contrivance to allow users interested in sex to find each other via a fake, age-related search. Again at age 100 there is a spike—probably an example of false reporting rather than a surge of activity from those who have received a telegram from the Queen.[*]

Evidence is also beginning to emerge of a possible demographic split between the American giants of online social networks, Facebook and MySpace. The *New York Times*[†] reported a speech by danah boyd (*sic*) in which she gave an early indication of research results showing a trend for white, college-bound teenagers to migrate to Facebook, with less educated and non-white teenagers remaining on MySpace. According to boyd, this may be an early indication that SNSs reflect or even magnify existing demographic divisions within society.

10.6.1.1 User Profiles and Language

Other researchers have considered the differences between social groupings based on user profiles and the language used to create them (Caverlee and Webb 2008; Arjan et al. 2008; Liu 2007; Lampe et al. 2007; Thelwall et al. 2010). The details of how models of language and semiotics are used in this kind of research are somewhat complex and need not detain us here, other than to note three things. Firstly, the presence of so much online material rich with personal data opens up new avenues for this kind of work. Secondly, that these researchers are particularly interested in the way in which users describe themselves, and thirdly, to note that gender and age differences have been found to be stark.

There were also considerable differences when looking at high-ranking terms across different age groups. In the 80-year-old and above category the top three terms were: 'scudda'

---

[*] In the UK the Queen sends a telegram to anyone who reaches the age of 100. http://news.bbc.co.uk/1/hi/uk/366998.stm

[†] See: http://gadgetwise.blogs.nytimes.com/2009/07/09/does-social-networking-breed-social-division/

(presumably a reference to the 1948 film *Scudda Hoo*), 'ClarkGable' and 'DiMaggio'. In the over 30-year-old category it was: 'parent', 'married', 'art' and 'travel'. Perhaps these findings are rather unsurprising, but of more value to psychology or social studies are the more general results published by Arjan et al. (2008) who found that teens tended to use more terms that referred to themselves and articulated more negativity. They also found that teens have much larger networks of friends compared to older users, but older users have friends from a more diverse age range.

Lampe et al. (2007) found high levels of profile completion amongst the Facebook users they surveyed (figures included 92% giving a valid e-mail address, 83% their real date of birth etc.) and that the act of completing profile fields is strongly associated with social degree (the number of friends a user manages to secure). A number of elements were particularly important in helping to increase social degree (i.e. number of friends), including filling in the name of their high school, favourite music, birthday and instant messaging address. The authors argue that some of these fields might be important because they help to maintain pre-existing, off-line networks.

Building on these findings the authors considered the place of the SNS profile in the wider, pre-existing literature regarding social signalling and the use of cues to facilitate communication. Individuals form impressions of others when deciding whether to pursue a relationship with them and they do so through various social signals, linguistic cues and self-presentation behaviours. With SNSs there is obviously almost total reliance on verbal and linguistic cues rather than non-verbal communication (body language etc.) and the authors put forward the, admittedly uncontroversial, view that the user profile is a vitally important part of this process. There is a rich history of work in psychology and sociology in this area, for example the work of Erving Goffman on self-presentation, and it will be interesting to see how new data obtained from the growing SNS dataset informs these discussions.

10.6.1.2 Ethnography

A primary, and much cited, example from the field of ethnography is the work of danah boyd (boyd 2008a, 2008b) who studied teenagers and their use of social media as part of her doctoral work at the University of California. She makes use of Mizuko Ito's concept of networked publics[*]—virtual spaces created through the use of social media technologies, which at the same time are imagined communities that emerge through the interaction of people, technology and practice. She compares these to traditional unmediated publics, say a public park, and points out that the new publics have unique characteristics as follows:

- Persistence: online material is automatically recorded and archived

- Searchability: online search is becoming increasingly powerful

- Replicability: online material is copyable

- Scalability: vast potential visibility of online material due to huge audiences

---

[*] See: http://networkedpublics.org/

boyd writes:

> In unmediated social situations, people tend to know who is present to witness a social act. This is not often the case in networked publics where audiences are invisible and access is asynchronous. Physical limitations help control the boundaries of unmediated environments—walls define the space and expressions can be witnessed only in hearing or visual range. Online, boundaries are porous—search collapses contexts, replicability allows traces of social acts to be copied to other spaces, and the persistence of data means that acts performed are not bounded by ephemerality. (Quote reproduced with the kind permission of danah boyd from *Taken Out of Context: American Teen Sociality in Networked Publics*. PhD thesis, 2008, University of California– Berkeley, Berkeley, CA; p. 159.)

She argues that teenagers in particular have made use of the new technology, and as they learned to navigate the new social networks they also developed strategies for coping with what in effect was a new world. Her research explores the reality for teenagers learning to work their way around this new technology and incorporate such a networked public into their lives. Others have also taken this path, for example, Clarke (2009) and Subrahmanyam (2008), have explored how psycho-social influences on teenagers' lives are altered by their use of SNSs.

10.6.1.3 User Behaviour in Online Social Networks

Clearly, by any measure, social network sites are changing the way we form and maintain our relationships with others, with demonstrable benefits.

ELLISON ET AL.
(2009, 9)

Another area of interest for researchers from a wider variety of backgrounds is to analyse what users actually do when logged on to an SNS. Ofcom (2008) undertook qualitative research into what motivates users and found that, in the UK at least, they tend to fall into five distinct groups based on their behaviours and attitudes:

- Alpha Socializers—(a minority) people who use sites in intense, short bursts to flirt, meet new people and be entertained.

- Attention Seekers—(some) people who crave attention and comments from others, often by posting photos and customizing their profiles.

- Followers—(many) people who join sites to keep up with what their peers are doing.

- Faithfuls—(many) people who typically use SNSs to rekindle old friendships, often from school or university.

- Functionals—(a minority) people who tend to be single-minded in using sites for a particular purpose.

Golder et al. (2007) studied millions of Facebook messages over a period of 26 months (a time when it was mainly being used by university students) and found that the site exhibited consistent temporal rhythms. For example, among other insights, the data strongly suggested that college students followed two patterns, a 'weekend' pattern between midday Friday and midday Sunday, and a 'weekday' pattern at all other times. They also made the claim that their detailed work in time patterns supports the view that Facebook, and by implication other SNSs, is something that is done in parallel with computer-based college work during the week rather than a leisure activity. Indeed, this work might support the *displacement* model of Internet use proposed by Nie and Hillygus,* which argues that using the Internet over the weekend can lead to a *decrease* in sociability.

Golder et al. (2007) found that in comparison with e-mail, Facebook messaging was infrequent (an average of 0.97 messages per user per week). The distribution of message frequency had the familiar long tail pattern, implying that a small number of users were prolific in their message sending. Sending a message or a 'poke' can be considered to be a proxy for indicating some kind of meaningful social gesture between users and so tracking these is a useful measure of the strength and structure of the social network. The strength of a tie between two users can be measured by looking at the volume and pattern of such messaging. The researchers found that 90.6% of messages and 87.5% of pokes were exchanged between people who had listed one another as friends. However, not all friends exchange messages. Of the friend links surveyed from 4.2 million users, only 15% of these pairs ever exchanged messages.

Benevenuto et al. (2009) based their analysis on detailed clickstream records (see Chapter 4) showing every browser action that users undertake (e.g. clicking on a link, viewing a video etc.) These can be obtained by accessing records of the HTTP message exchanges between the client browser and the server, although it is important to note that researchers anonymize this kind of data. The sites involved included MySpace, LinkedIn, Hi5 and Orkut, and the researchers found that:

- There was a significant variation in usage patterns with session duration demonstrating a long-tailed distribution.

- There was evidence of significant exposure to friends of friends (or '2-hops') i.e. users actively visited friends and *their* friends' pages.

- Individuals varied widely in the frequency with which they accessed social networks and the amount of time they spent there.

- Users spent far more time browsing (92%) than undertaking activity. The average user interacted with 3.2 friends over a 12-day period but only with 0.2 friends in a visible, active manner, e.g. sending a message.

- The amount of interaction does not increase significantly with an increase in the user's social degree. Thus having a lot of friends does not lead to more interaction.

---

* See Nie and Hillygus (2002).

- 80% of media content on the sites was found through a 1-hop friend, emphasizing the word-of-mouth spread of information around networks (sometimes known as the *social cascade*).

Wilson et al. (2009) have proposed the *interaction graph*—similar to the social graph, but different in the sense that it relies on information about interactions in order to demonstrate a link between users. Importantly, they found that the properties of the interaction graphs differ from the standard social graph. The authors looked at Facebook and found that users tend to interact with a small subset of their friends, often having no interaction with as many as half of their displayed social links. They also found that the bulk of Facebook interactions are generated by a small subset of users. They found that for the vast majority of users (approximately 90%), 20% of their friends accounted for 70% of all their interactions. Looking at the distribution of total interactions they found that the top 1% of most active Wall posters accounted for 20% of all Wall posts and the top 1% of those who commented on uploaded photos accounted for nearly 40% of all comments.

Further analysis of these and other statistics lead the authors to conclude that the interaction graph demonstrates a distribution based on the power law. Viswanath et al. (2009) demonstrated similar results, finding interaction activity was far smaller than the potential offered by the wider social graph and that users only really interact with a sub-set of their social graph links and that this tends to be bounded at around 100 friends.

Group formation, within the wider online social network, is another important area of study (Backstrom et al. 2006). Of particular importance is the role that friendship and other social connections play in group-joining processes. It is a fundamental premise in studies of how behaviour diffuses through a community that an individual's probability of adopting a new behaviour increases with the number of friends already engaged in that behaviour. Backstrom et al. looked at this question in the context of two SNSs and they found that the propensity of individuals to join communities, and for communities to grow rapidly, depends in subtle ways on the underlying network structure. The results included the finding that one is significantly more likely to join a community if it contains friends of yours who also 'know' each other (i.e. are linked in some way within the community).

This kind of result, obtained from newly emerging datasets, illustrates the potential importance of SNS research. Sociological principles support two views of group formation: *weak ties* and *strong ties*. The weak ties argument supports the notion that it is an advantage to have friends in a community who do not know each other since it provides a number of potentially unconnected ways to find out about and join a group. On the other hand there is a strong argument based on notions of what is called *social capital*, that people are more likely to join a group in which they can feel some trust due to the presence of friends who already know each other. The authors argue that the results from the online data might indicate that social capital has a stronger effect on group formation than that of weak ties.

Considering the question of social capital in relation to SNSs has been another area of activity (Ellison et al. 2007; Ellison et al. 2009). Although exact definitions vary, social capital broadly refers to the resources accumulated through the relationships between people.

Interestingly, the authors' work seems to show that, after controlling for demographic factors, psychological well-being measures, and general Internet use, the extent to which students used Facebook intensively contributed to heightened self-reporting of increased social capital among students. Interestingly, general Internet use was not a significant predictor of social capital, suggesting that only certain kinds of Internet use support the generation and maintenance of social capital.* They report that students who showed low satisfaction and low self-esteem appeared to gain in social capital if they used Facebook more intensely, and suggest that SNSs allow users to manage a wider network of weak ties and thus increase social capital.

Finally, it is worth pointing out that user behaviour online is rarely restricted to one particular online service, or indeed a single SNS (Zafarani and Liu 2009). Researchers have struggled with the need to make sense of user behaviours, such as the formation of communities, when they are carried out across a disconnected series of sites; this remains an active agenda.

10.6.1.4 Friendship

Adams (2010) and Veer (2010) both argue that one of the differences between online social networks and the real world is their attitude to the notion of friendship. As Ofcom notes in its report into SNSs: "social networking sites stretch the traditional meaning of 'friends' to mean anyone with whom a user has an online connection. Therefore the term can include people who the user has never actually met or spoken to" (Ofcom 2008, 7). It is relatively easy to acquire 'friends' in cyberspace as the social cost of maintaining the friendship is small (e.g. one simple update to an SNS newsfeed and all your friends know what you are doing). Indeed, Fraser and Dutta (2009) argue that the word friend has effectively become a verb, with people spending hours 'friending' on sites in a competitive process.

This contrasts with the way we behave in the real world. Strahilevitz (2005) points out that although the sociology studies vary, it appears that in the real world the median adult has met or otherwise interacted with approximately 1,700 people. This does not mean that the average person has 1,700 active ties, but rather that he or she has 'known' this many, in some manner. Most of us can, and do, differentiate in our daily lives between close friends, family, work colleagues and someone we met at a conference three years ago. Research by Google seems to show that on average people have between four and six groups of connections to people that they would like to keep separate from each other (Adams 2010). Sociologists talk of the difference between 'strong' and 'weak' social ties—nuances—and recognize the importance of this difference in the way social relationships are structured in different societies (Gross and Acquisti 2005; Donath and boyd 2004). What SNSs offer, however, are friendships that are mutual, public, un-nuanced, and decontextualized. By this we mean that friendship is usually two-way, always in public (to varying degrees depending on the site) and tends to lack any social context (for example, you cannot elect

---

* The research actually distinguishes between *bridging* social capital (that is, loose connections between people that offer avenues for learning new information or seeing new perspectives) and *bonding* social capital (which is more about emotional support). The former is what network researchers have also referred to as 'weak' ties. Readers interested in the details here are referred to the paper and to Putnam (2000) .

to show only part of your personal information to just a selection of your connections such as work stuff with work colleagues etc.). However, it is worth noting that Google+ takes account of some of these social realities (see Section 10.2.1.4).

These issues are starting to come to the fore, with Xiang et al. (2010), for example, considering how a number of statistical methods can be used to process inter-user interactions in order to infer the strength of relationships. They note, incidentally, that Facebook has introduced a third-party app, Top Friends, which allows users to demarcate their most important relationships.

This is directly related to the number of relationships a person can effectively manage. The number of friends that a person has is known as the social degree in social network theory and a number of researchers have looked at this measure for a range of SNSs. Golder et al. (2007) found that in Facebook the median degree was 144 and the mean was 179.53. Viswanath et al. (2009) gave similar mean numbers in Orkut (100) and Facebook (120) although in their sample of over four million users they found 11 who had more than 10,000 friends. The existence of users with very large numbers of friends (sometimes known colloquially as *whales*) is an indication of the problematic nature of the concept of friendship within SNSs.

Golder et al. (2007) also found that the pattern of online friendships changed dramatically at around the 250 mark—relatively few people had more than 250 online friends—and Caverlee and Webb (2008) reported similar results for MySpace. This is interesting because it bears some proximity to 'Dunbar's number', a measure of the number of meaningful social relationships a human can maintain at any one time, based on research work into the capacity of the brain's neocortex and named after Robin Dunbar, a British anthropologist.* Whatever the exact number that the average neocortex can handle it seems common sense to say that no one can really have 10,000 friends in the sense of how the term is used in the real world.

Related to how many online friends one can meaningfully have is the question of how much of that friendship is reciprocated by mutual linking. Kumar et al. (2006) found that in Yahoo! 360° (now defunct), the reciprocity rate was over 80%, implying that friendships are highly mutual and Leskovec et al. (2008) found similarly high numbers for a number of networks. Kumar et al. (2006) also found that this happened rapidly, with the vast majority of mutual linking occurring within a day. The authors argue that, for technical reasons, this is important, since it allows for the working assumption that the social graph is pretty much undirected (i.e. all links are two-way) and removing the relatively few uni-directed links will not affect the results.

Wilson et al. (2009), Viswanath et al. (2009) and Gilbert and Karahalios (2009), amongst many others, consider what the observable interactions between users on SNSs can tell us about the *strength* or otherwise of online friendships. Relationship strength and differentiation between different types of connection (e.g. a close friend, colleague or old acquaintance) has long been an area of interest to social scientists. It is now an important area of academic cross-over between computing and the social sciences (in particular work that

---

* The number is thought to range between 100 and 230, but a commonly detected value is 150 (Hernando et al. 2009).

builds on the ideas of Mark Granovetter[*]) and one in which the analysis of SNSs can play a major role (Xiang et al. 2010).

Social psychologists have long observed the existence of social relations that involve little interaction. One primary example is Stanley Milgram's 1972 essay on the *familiar stranger*—individuals that we regularly observe but do not interact with.[†] The presence of this kind of relationship is confirmed by Donath and boyd (2005) who have observed that online social network users often display large numbers of connections as a form of self-identity and status.

This research is not only of theoretical use: Wilson et al. (2009) note that there is a class of application that uses the relationships in social networks to improve protection against spam and other forms of abuse. Such systems make use of the implicit trust implied by the presence of social links between users, but as the authors note, such links do not always constitute a functioning relationship.

There is one other area of friendship that we should mention in passing and that is *closing the triangle*, or *triadic closure*, a well-known feature of real-world studies into human social networks (Easley and Kleinberg 2010). In a triangle there are three people: A, B, and C, where A is linked by friendship to both B and C. Closing the triangle involves the formation of a relationship between B and C, allowing all three to be classed as friends.[‡] Leskovec et al. (2008) found that as many as 60% of new links in the SNSs they studied could be classed as closing a triangle, demonstrating the prevailing power of the mutual connection i.e. any friend of yours is a possible friend of mine. It seems this process operates online in the same manner as it does in the real world.

10.6.2 Privacy

As we have already mentioned, users of SNS are divulging large amounts of personal information through their profiles, shared photos and by making public their real-world social connections. Felt and Evans (2008) report that a demographic study of Facebook-using students from Carnegie-Mellon University found that 89% disclosed their birth date and gender to their campus network, and 46% also posted their current address. Krishnamurthy et al. (2008) found that 80% of Bebo users and 76% of MySpace users allowed their profile and friends to be viewable by *anyone* on the network (i.e. they did not bother to change the default settings). It should be noted however that this does not mean that users do not care about privacy per se, and research with users seems to confirm this (boyd and Hargittai 2010; Bonneau and Preibusch 2010a).

Part of the problem is that users misunderstand the nature of the audience who may gain access to private information, and Gross and Acquisti (2005) have argued that the SNS software may use private information in ways that the user is not aware of, and could

---

[*] A Stanford University sociologist, Granovetter, proposed important ideas about strong and weak relational ties in real-world social networks in the 1970s (Scott 1991; Easley and Kleinberg 2010).

[†] See: http://www.paulos.net/research/intel/familiarstranger/index.htm

[‡] It is worth noting that the clustering coefficient that we discuss in Chapter 7 (when debating small world networks) reflects how strongly the process of triadic closure has taken place within a particular node's neighbourhood in the network.

not anticipate at the time they uploaded it. A primary example of this is Facebook's News Feed service which, when it was introduced in 2006, caused a stir as users were surprised to find that their personal information was being automatically passed on to other people within their network through a system of news alerts (Solove 2007, 169). Although this was pre-existing information that had already been provided in public profiles, users expressed dismay in large numbers (several thousand people joined a protest group on the site) at the way it was being freely re-distributed.

Related to this is what Oqvist (2009) describes as the blurring of the lines between work-related networking and more personal or social activities and warns that it is common for employers, for example, to investigate the online identity of prospective employees. Interestingly, this is also reflected in an early, internal debate within Facebook: whether or not a user should be allowed to have two identities, one for work and one for leisure. Kirkpatrick (2010a) quotes Zuckerberg as saying that the "days of you having a different image for your work friends or coworkers and for other people you know are probably coming to an end pretty quickly" (p. 50). Zuckerberg argues that even if Facebook had allowed more than one identity, such a system would not be sustainable. Bearing in mind what we said earlier about employers researching the online identity of prospective employees, this decision may represent one of the most important social consequences of the rise of SNSs: in the past it has been far easier for people to present different images in different social situations.

In terms of who sees what, the way SNSs are structured can be misleading: the manner in which the focus is on a network of 'friends' can make it seem like the network is merely a "semi-public stage on which one can act in the privacy of one's social circle" (Chew et al. 2008, 1). Bonneau and Preibusch (2010a) provide a detailed, comparative analysis of privacy practices and policies in online social networks. Privacy settings can often be opaque and default configurations err on the side of maximum public exposure. Configuration controls for privacy settings are also varied on a regular basis by the site's operator, and this often leads to confusion. The Electronic Freedom Frontier singled out Facebook in this regard in a talk in May 2010 (Opsahl 2010) and Matt McKeon's series of diagrams shows how Facebook's privacy settings have changed over time.[*] In a review of fifteen SNSs and user-generated content sites, the Organisation for Economic Co-operation and Development (OECD, 2007)[†] noted the following:

- Sites collect personal information relevant to the service.

- Some sites provide such information to third-party advertisers in such a way that individuals are identifiable. This is sometimes used to provide targeted advertising.

- Most sites reserve the right to transfer personal data when a site is bought by another company.

---

[*] See: http://mattmckeon.com/facebook-privacy/ and click on the years listed on the right-hand side to see a kind of animated view of how the privacy settings have changed.

[†] The Organisation for Economic Co-operation and Development: http://www.oecd.org

There is further danger as SNSs develop in sophistication (Gao et al. 2011). Felt and Evans (2008) make the point that the growing use of third-party apps by SNS users presents new privacy challenges. Application development environments such as Facebook's Platform and OpenSocial give developers access to varying degrees of data that would not be available to them through the standard user interface. So, for example, sites that use the OpenSocial standard allow third-party app developers to access information about the users who have opted to install and use their application. Facebook goes further and allows app developers what is known as *second-degree access*, i.e. when a user installs an application, the third party can also request information about that user's friends. There is also an increased risk of a user's data being shared and reused as constituent parts of data mash-ups (see Chapter 14) and through aggregation of data from more than one SNS (Maximilien and Grandison 2008). There is also some evidence of what is known as 'leakage', whereby a user's personal information is obtained by third parties who are providing a service to the SNS, for example, by serving the adverts that appear on most sites (Krishnamurthy and Wills 2010).

Bonneau and Preibusch (2010a) note the difficulties that arise from attempts to anonymize the social graphs of these websites before the information is passed on to third parties. Their research shows that this is very difficult in practice given the detailed personal information often held within these graphs—i.e. simply removing the person's name is not enough.

To conclude, personal information that was once localized and scattered amongst a person's disparate social groups and unconnected friends and colleagues, and which was, most importantly, *forgettable*, has become permanent and searchable by vast audiences of strangers. Of course privacy is not the only social issue with regard to the rise of SNSs and others include: rapid circulation of misinformation and malicious rumour; changing social norms as to what is acceptable behaviour in what are effectively public places; identity theft and faking; stalking; the need for the law to keep up with what this new technology brings with it. Readers who wish to explore these issues further are directed to Daniel Solove's detailed work on these matters.

10.6.3 Implications for Software Designers and Developers

It is important that software designers are aware of this kind of research and that of its close cousin, social capital, as it explores the lived reality of the systems they have developed (Hochheiser and Shneiderman 2010). Designers of SNSs should strive to understand the social implications of their work and to work towards better designs that can adapt to increasingly diverse populations (no longer just undergraduates and teens) and new goals (for example in helping civic engagement through online groups/communities) (Ellison et al. 2009). As danah boyd notes in her paper (boyd 2008b), these services are creating a public space that is as new to adults as to teenagers, who are in effect the first generation to be born into the Web. Nobody yet knows the long-term implications of being socialized into a culture rooted in networked publics. As she concludes: "They are learning to navigate networked publics; it is in our better interest to figure out how to help them" (p. 138).

10.6.4 Topology and Structure

As we have already seen in Chapter 7, the structure of the Web has been widely studied. Such studies form part of a wider investigation into the nature of large, real-world, complex networks and have considered a number of topological features such as the size and structure of the graph formed by links, clustering effects, and the degree distribution of nodes.

Similar investigations have been undertaken into the underlying structure of the networks formed by SNSs, in effect investigating particular sub-domains of the wider Web. Much of this work involves considering the SNS being studied as a *directed time graph* consisting of a number of nodes and links, each of which has an associated time stamp that records when they were created. For much of this research a node is made up of a user and their associated profile data, but might also include content such as a picture or a video. It is important to realize that given the dynamic nature of SNSs, time plays a more important role than it does in research into the wider Web.

10.6.4.1 Degree Distribution

Measuring the degree distribution (the in-degree and out-degree) means counting the links between nodes in the SNS graph. This usually means analysing who is friends with whom, but might also mean looking at the links between non-social content in the network, e.g. uploaded photos. Kumar et al. (2006) found the degree distribution of Yahoo! 360° (now defunct), to follow a power law (an expected result, since this had already been shown for the Web in general). Ahn et al. (2007) undertook similar measurements for three SNSs: Cyworld, MySpace and Orkut. For the latter two they found clear evidence of a degree distribution that followed the power law with an exponential approximating to 3.1 and 3.7, respectively.

However, the plot of the Cyworld distribution seemed to show two distinct regions: one in which the exponential approximates to 5 (and is therefore rapidly decaying) and a second where the exponent approximates to 2 (and therefore has a long tail). The distribution is therefore multi-scale and the split occurs somewhere between 100 and 1,000 links. This was unexpected, since the Web in general demonstrates power law decay and, perhaps more importantly, real-world human networks appear to demonstrate power law distribution with an exponent between 2 and 3. This means there are hubs (people with large numbers of links), but the vast majority of people only have a small number of links. According to the authors, this suggests that Cyworld consists of two distinct types of user which they speculate may be due to the way the system encourages the creation of 'clubs', whose organisers tend to attract larger numbers of friends. Gjoka et al. (2010) found that Facebook also exhibits a non-power-law degree distribution. They found two regions of degree distribution ($1 \leq$ node degree < 300 and $300 \leq$ node degree ≤ 5000) each of which exhibited a power law with differing exponents (1.32 and 3.38, respectively).

Mislove et al. (2007) studied Orkut and LiveJournal and confirmed power law distributions for both in-degree and out-degree. They found that Orkut exhibited a degree of 1.5 for both and LiveJournal exhibited 1.59 and 1.65, respectively. Thus, in both cases, the out- and in-degree are the same or very similar. This is notably different from the wider Web where the in-degree is 2.09 and the out-degree is 2.67. This is explained by the Web's propensity to have popular pages that are linked to by many other pages: high in-degree stars, and hubs, reference pages with many links to other sources of information (high out-degree). By way of contrast, nodes in SNSs tend to have symmetrical linking (or *link symmetry*) and the authors see this as evidence of reciprocity between users. So, for example, the authors found that the top 1% of in-degree nodes overlapped by 65% with the top 1% of out-degree nodes.

10.6.4.2 Clustering Coefficient and the Small World Effect

A number of researchers have considered whether SNSs are small world networks, as originally outlined by Watts and Strogatz (Wilson et al. 2009; Mislove et al. 2007; Ahn et al. 2007; Kleinberg 2008; Zhang and Tu 2009). Recall that a Watts-Strogatz small world network demonstrates both the small world effect (that is, it takes on average relatively few links to travel from one node to another in the network) and has a high degree of clustering within local neighbourhoods. The former is especially pertinent for SNSs since the small world effect owes much to the work of Stanley Milgram whose work in social psychology led to the popular, although potentially inaccurate, idea that human social networks demonstrate 'six degrees of separation' between individuals.

Determining whether a network adheres to the Watts-Strogatz model or not involves calculating two sets of figures: the clustering coefficient and the average path length (the formulas for these are in Chapter 7). Wilson et al. (2009) found that Facebook has an average clustering coefficient of between 0.133 and 0.211 and this compares favourably with Mislove et al. (2007) who found that Orkut has a coefficient of 0.171. This means the SNSs exhibit higher levels of local clustering than either a random graph or one dominated by a power law.

Wilson et al. (2009) calculated the average path length[*] and found it to be 6 or lower, "lending credence to the six-degrees of separation hypothesis for social networks" (p. 209). These numbers, together with some other figures concerning the relative clustering of users with different social degrees, led the authors to conclude that Facebook is a small world network. Mislove et al. (2007) found similar path lengths of 5.10 and 5.88 for Orkut and LiveJournal respectively and also concluded in favour of small world networks.

10.6.4.3 Overall Structure of the Network

Kumar et al (2006) investigated the overall structure of Yahoo! 360° and found that users could be placed into one of three major 'regions' within the SNS as follows:

- **Singletons:** zero-degree nodes—a member who has joined but not made a connection with another user.

- **Giant component:** the main component of the network—a large group of people who are well connected to one another through paths in the social network.

- **Middle region:** the remainder—consists of various isolated communities/small groups that interact with each other but not the network at large.

---

[*] Note that this is computationally infeasible due to the size of the graph in question. The authors used a statistical sample that averaged 22 regional Facebook networks. In fact the table in their paper lists the ten largest regional networks and shows a range of path lengths of between 4.71 and 5.13.

The authors found that the middle region consisted of about 10% of users and discovered the presence of 'stars'—single, charismatic individuals around whom isolated communities developed. They found that these stars quickly attracted friends before either merging with the giant component (a tightly interconnected core of very active members who form the 'heart' of the social network) or ceasing altogether when the individual lost interest.

Mislove et al. (2007) found a similar structure for Orkut and LiveJournal with a densely connected core of nodes that demonstrate a high degree of inter-connectivity with each other. At the fringes of the network they found strongly clustered, but low-degree nodes. Golbeck (2007) showed a similar pattern in two older SNSs—Dogster and Friendster.[*] What is interesting about both sets of findings is that although SNSs have a giant component in the way that the Web has a single, large, strongly connected core, the relative size of the component is much larger than that found on the wider Web.

What are the implications of these findings? Mislove et al. (2007) note that the existence of a well-connected core implies that information which begins in a core node will spread rapidly through the entire network. This may be of benefit for information diffusion, but has the drawback of providing a convenient mechanism for rapid distribution of spam and viruses. Golbeck (2007) makes an alternative point. Observing that *centrality* is a key concept in the study of human social networks (i.e. how close a particular node/person is to the central core of the network) she posits that this is an important measure of influence in human social networks.

10.6.4.4 Models of How SNSs Grow

Finally we should mention the work of a number of researchers who are exploring how to build a theoretical model that describes how an SNS grows over time. This work builds on the ideas of how complex networks grow, which we discussed at some length in Chapter 7, although Bonato et al. (2010) point out that to date there have been relatively few models developed for SNSs. Recall that a key proposal for complex networks was the idea of *preferential attachment*, a sort of 'the rich-get-richer' argument, in which a new node in the network is more likely to link to an existing node that has many links. SNSs provide another opportunity to revisit these models, armed with a large amount of data.

Leskovec et al. (2008) argue that their work showed that the inherently non-local nature of preferential attachment was fundamentally unable to capture important characteristics in these SNSs. By this they mean that they found that most links spanned very short distances and acted in a way that closed triangles, something that a 'pure' preferential model cannot reproduce. They propose an alternative that builds on preferential attachment by adding features which model the lifetime of a node and the time gap between instances of adding links to nodes. Their work showed that the resulting (what they call *evolutionary*)

---

[*] Jennifer Golbeck has an excellent diagram of this at: http://firstmonday.org/htbin/cgiwrap/bin/ojs/index.php/fm/article/view/2023/1889

model produced the required power law distributions in networks such as LinkedIn, Delicious and Flickr (their work assumed Delicious and Flickr are SNSs).

Others take what might be referred to as a more deeply mathematical approach. Bonato et al. (2010) for example, made use of m-dimensional hypercubes in their Geometric Protean (GEO-P) model. Many readers may be pleased to learn that a detailed discussion of this and other such theoretical models is beyond the scope of this book.

EXERCISES AND POINTS TO PONDER

1. Review the work of Gross and Acquisti (2005; Acquisti and Gross 2006) which explored the information that college students revealed on their SNS profiles. Repeat the experiment within your own peer group, looking for similar types of information. How have Facebook's privacy controls changed since the authors undertook their original work?

2. Group programming task: Lattanzi et al. (2011) undertook an experiment to try and replicate the famous Milgram experiment online by analysing connections between authors of computer science papers on the online bibliography database DBLP. Write a computer program to download and analyse the data in DBLP in order to build a social graph of the connections between authors. Can you replicate their results? Note to teachers: This task may need to use a subsection of the database depending on resources available.

3. Review the papers discussed in Section 10.4.3 (Data Portability) and read the information and blog items at the Data Portability project.* Write a short summary of the issues with regard to portability, some of the proposed solutions and the current state of play. Is the technology website, TechCrunch, right to argue that there is a "war between Google and Facebook" over data and its ownership?†

4. Group programming exercise: Review the papers by Kumar et al. (2006), Ahn et al. (2007), Gjoka (2010) and Katzir et al. (2011) which investigate the degree distribution of various SNSs. Using a service's API, can you write a computer program to replicate their findings with respect to the degree distribution of an SNS? For example, use Facebook Query Language to retrieve information about who is a friend with whom. You may find that some services have applied restrictions on how much of this type of information you can extract. For this reason, consider carefully the discussions in Gjoka and Katzir et al. concerning different types of crawling routines and sampling rates.

5. An important principle in social science is that of homophily, the principle that contact between people with similar views, interests and backgrounds occurs at a higher rate than among dissimilar people (McPherson et al. 2001). Reflect on how this

---

* http://dataportability.org/
† http://techcrunch.com/2010/11/04/facebook-google-contacts/

principle can be explored in the new terrain of online social networks. What kind of experiment could be constructed to investigate its presence in an SNS? Having reflected on this, undertake a literature review to see what others have actually done.

FURTHER READING

For a detailed discussion of methods, tools and approaches to building SNSs see Gavin Bell's book (Bell 2009), and Hartl and Prochazka (2007). For more on the technology behind SNSs see Kim et al. (2010). A detailed discussion of the realities of technical development at Facebook is provided by a Facebook Front End Tech Talk video (5th August 2010), available at: http://www.facebook.com/video/video.php?v=596368660334&ref=mf

For more analysis of types of SNSs, a taxonomy and breakdown of popular social networks by country see Kim et al. (2010) and Pallis et al. (2011). The latter work also provides more information on the technical infrastructure of a number of leading services.

For further discussion on the nature of friendship both off- and online and the separation of online acquaintances into groups see Adams (2010). It is also worth reflecting that there are sometimes cultural aspects to friendship and group formation and these can be reflected in SNSs: Yu and King (2010) offer some insights from China.

For more on Stanley Milgram and the role of six degrees of separation in models of SNSs see Lattanzi et al. (2011).

For far more on the early history of Facebook see David Kirkpatrick's 2010 book, the *Facebook Effect* (Kirkpatrick 2010b). For a description of how Facebook overtook MySpace in the race to control the market for SNSs see Sean Parker's presentation to the Web 2.0 Summit, 2009 (Parker 2009).

For further discussion of data silos, walled gardens and the need for open standards in SNSs see the W3C's report (W3C 2010).

For a detailed discussion on the issues surrounding the permanence of data in online social networks and other Web 2.0 services see Mayer-Schonberger's (2009) book, *Delete*.

For detailed discussion of the technical issues surrounding the process of crawling an SNS in order to obtain data for research studies (such as measuring the degree of the graph) see Shaozhi et al. (2010).

Many of the research issues surrounding the study of the structure of online social networks are covered in a slide presentation from Alan Mislove, given to the International School and Conference on Network Science (NetSci'10). Available online at: http://www.ccs.neu.edu/home/amislove/slides/SocialMedia-NetSci-slides.pdf

## CHAPTER 11

Media Sharing

M EDIA SHARING SITES HAVE REMOVED MANY of the technical barriers to publishing on the Web by providing simple interfaces for users to upload and share various types of media. As we have already seen, this kind of user-generated content is a major component of the modern Web and millions of users make use of these services every day.

In this chapter we will consider three of the most important forms of media-sharing service: podcasting (audio), photo sharing and video. However, these are just some of the Web 2.0 media sharing services and other popular forms include document sharing (most notably through the Scribd service), slide sharing (e.g. SlideShare) and music playlist sharing (examples include Spotify and Ping).

We begin with podcasting. This is partly because it was the first of the media sharing services to be developed (and indeed, like blogging, slightly pre-dates the introduction of the Web 2.0 moniker), but also because the ideas that were fundamental to podcasting re-emerge in other services.

11.1 PODCASTING

Welcome to podcasting, the medium that promises a future where anyone can make radio, instead of just listen to it.

ANNALEE NEWITZ
Writing in Wired Magazine (*Newitz 2005, Webpage*)

Podcasts are audio recordings, usually in MP3 format, that can be distributed over the Web and played on a desktop PC, a handheld media player or a smartphone. The term derives from the conflation of the words 'iPod' and 'broadcast', although it is important to realize that there is no need for an Apple iPod per se to be used. Podcasting as we now know it materialized in 2003 and became particularly popular in the mid-2000s. At the end of 2005, the *New Oxford American Dictionary* selected 'podcast' as its word of the year. In recent years podcasting has become very popular in education, and universities and colleagues have invested considerable resources in it, seeing it as a key component of e-learning (Walls et al. 2010).

The roots of podcasting are in audio blogging, the process of adding audio files to blogs. It is often likened to a kind of time-shifted radio broadcasting and the audio files are sometimes known as episodes, referring to the idea that this is a form of Internet radio (Gunawardena et al. 2009; Crofts et al. 2005). However, Tsagkias et al. (2008) note three important differences between podcasting and radio broadcasting. Firstly, the targeted and specialist nature of much podcast material makes it more akin to a form of 'narrow-casting' (broadcasting to a niche audience). Secondly, podcasts, because they are hosted on the Web, are designed to be available for a considerable period of time and so have more longevity than radio. Finally, the ease with which podcasts can be made and distributed means there is a distinct flavour of user-generated content (UGC) to podcasting. However, the subtlety of this distinction is often lost in the academic literature, and the terms audio blogging, Internet radio and podcasting tend to be used interchangeably.

11.1.1 A Short History of Podcasting

By the time the different components that constitute podcasting came together in 2003, Internet radio had been around for approximately ten years and a number of people had just begun to experiment with audio blogging.* One of these was Dave Winer, author of the Scripting News and a leading light in the world of blogging. In 2001 he was experimenting with audio blogging and Really Simple Syndication (RSS) syndication technology, an Extensible Markup Language (XML)-based data format.

The key to understanding what RSS does is to look at the two ways that the acronym is usually expanded: Rich Site Summary and Really Simple Syndication. RSS publishes a summary of what content is available and the details of the server it is available from, and syndicates it around the Internet by means of a Web 'feed'. Users register an interest in a particular source of information by subscribing to this feed of data, which 'pushes' new information about forthcoming content to the subscriber (there is more on this in Chapter 14).

RSS had been around since 1995 when its embryonic form was developed by Ramanathan Guha at Apple (Hammersley 2003; Sterne et al. 2008). Winer proposed an extension to RSS to allow non-text items to be described by adding what became known as *enclosures*. In particular, MP3 audio and music files could be referred to by these enclosures through the simple process of recording the Uniform Resource Identifier (URI) where the file in question was located. To demonstrate the technology, Winer successfully enclosed a Grateful Dead song in a post to his blog on 11th January 2001.†

Winer had developed the new RSS format (it would become RSS 0.92) in response to discussions he had been having with Adam Curry, an MTV video DJ who is credited with some of the early ideas that led to podcasting (Jardin 2005; Crofts et al. 2005). In fact,

---

* According to Geoghegan and Klass (2005) a Canadian blogger named 'jish' is claimed to have been the first person to do audio blogging, in 2001.
† See: http://scripting.com/2001/01/11.html

Curry was initially more interested in video and, in particular, how to deliver high-quality video given that the Internet's bandwidth was, at that time, relatively limited (many users were still making use of 56K modems) (Winer 2001). Curry's idea was that, as Winer tells it, they should develop Internet technology that could be used: "in the middle of the night, while I'm not using my computer … downloads huge video and audio stuff to my local hard drive" (Winer 2001, blog).

This meant that by the time users wanted to play the video it would already be available from their hard drive. However, while this solved the bandwidth problem it raised another issue: the user would need to know, a day in advance, what video they might want to watch the following day. Curry's idea was that users would subscribe to favourite sources of video and audio that had been curated by trusted individuals such as MTV DJs.

This early impetus to podcasting's development had a major consequence. According to Sterne et al. (2008, webpage): "The RSS dimension creates an expectation of seriality which shapes both production and consumption practice: podcasts are supposed to repeat over time, so listeners subscribe to 'shows' and podcasters make 'shows'."

At this point in the story Christopher Lydon, a Boston-based media professional who had once worked for the *New York Times* and had also fronted various local radio shows, becomes an important figure (Sterne et al. 2008). By the summer of 2003, Lydon's career was undergoing difficulties and Dave Winer encouraged him to restart things by publishing a blog, in particular drawing on Lydon's experience of covering presidential campaigns (since there was an election due in 2004). Lydon demurred, arguing that he believed his true forte was radio. Winer responded by suggesting he work with Bob Doyle of the New Media Lab, Cambridge (Massachusetts) to pull together various technologies in order to create an audio blog. In particular, Winer suggested they make use of the RSS enclosure that he had been experimenting with.

The resulting experiments in technology were documented on the BlogAudio website and Lydon launched a series of audio interviews on his blog. This began in July 2003 with an interview with Dave Winer,[*] an event that was later described by Winer, arguably inaccurately, as the first podcast in history. Both men were also heavily involved in BloggerCon I, the first blogging conference which took place in October 2003 and which featured a number of discussions and demonstrations of audio blogging technology.[†]

Adam Curry was to play one more role in the development of podcasting (Sterne et al. 2008). Impressed by Lydon's audio blogging and enjoying the recently released Apple iPod he began to wonder how easy it would be to get the audio files across the Web and onto the MP3 player. Curry, following discussions with Dave Winer, produced a small AppleScript[‡]

---

[*] http://blogs.law.harvard.edu/lydondev/2003/07/09/spoken-word-a-few-good-bloggers/

[†] See: http://www.bloggercon.org/day1/grid

[‡] A scripting language developed for the Apple Mac operating system. See: http://developer.apple.com/library/mac/#documentation/AppleScript/Conceptual/AppleScriptX/AppleScriptX.html

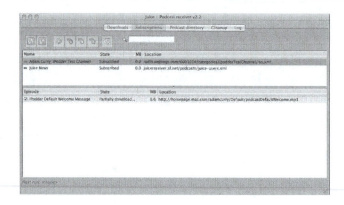

FIGURE 11.1 Screenshot of the Juice podcasting software. (Reproduced with kind permission from Juice and Active8 [Netherlands]).

demonstration program in July 2004 that allowed audio clips to be automatically down-loaded onto MP3 devices by using RSS and the enclosure tag.*

Curry's initial effort was built upon by a software development team from the Dutch company Active8 and became iPodder (the software would later be renamed Juice). To test his software Curry launched the *Daily Source Code*, in August 2004, the first podcast show with a regular production schedule. It was just the right time—inexpensive MP3 players were beginning to flood the market, including the Apple iPod.

The term itself was coined by Ben Hammersley in a *Guardian* newspaper article[†] in February 2004 describing the work of the audio bloggers. It was picked up that summer by 'Doc' Searls, a well-known technology evangelist, in a widely read blog article. Searls discussed the new term in the context of comparing it with traditional radio, noting that podcasting was 'Net-native': "That is, it's archived in a way that can be listened to at the convenience of the listener, and (this is key) that it can be linked to by others, and enclosed in an RSS feed" (Searls 2004, webpage).

11.1.2 Using Podcast Client Software

The basic requirement is some form of podcast feed aggregator and player, with well-known examples including Juice (see Figure 11.1), iTunes, Doppler, Podget and RSSRadio. These days various e-mail clients and Web browsers also support subscription to podcast feeds. Once subscribed to, the software will update itself automatically with the latest audio files.

There are directories that list podcasts, for example Odeo, PodCast Alley, Podcast Pickle and BBC Podcasts. In addition, iTunes maintains its own directory as well as being an aggregator. Some of these directories allow users to leave comments about a podcast and

---

* There is some dispute as to where the idea for a script might have come from, with CNet reporting in 2005 that Kevin Marks, an engineer at Technorati demonstrated such a Python script at BloggerCon I, an event that Curry attended. See: http://news.cnet.com/8301-10784_3-5980758-7.html and Marks' own view of events at: http://www.epeus.blogspot.com/2005_12_01_epeus_archive.html#113346118625477822. Dave Winer himself also lays claim to developing a form of the iPodder software with his Radio Weblog software (http://images.scripting.com/archiveScriptingCom/2004/10/30/enclosurePrefs.gif) and http://scripting.com/2005/05/14.html#When:8:02:28AM

† http://www.guardian.co.uk/media/2004/feb/12/broadcasting.digitalmedia

also rate them. Podcast readers are often integrated with services such as Facebook and Twitter, which means that details of the podcasts are disseminated widely across various Web 2.0 services.

11.1.3 Technology

Podcasting depends on using RSS to syndicate information about audio files. Within the RSS text file is some XML code that defines the details of the audio file in question including the title, a description, the date and the all-important location of the file.

A typical example of RSS code might look like this:

```
<?xml version="1.0"?>
<rss version="2.0">
<channel>
<title> Paul's English Prog Rock Podcast</title>
<link>http://yeoldehostingservice.com/pdanderson/audio.rss </link>
<description> A really strange podcast about prog rock from
Britain </description>
<item>
<title> This Morning's Music News from Britain </title>
<description> Some news this morning </description>
<pubdate>Thur, 1 July 2010 09:00 </pubdate>
<enclosure url ="http://yeoldehostingservice.com/pdanderson/pod_
cast_morning.mp3"
length="140000" type="audio/mpeg"/>
</item>
</channel>
</rss>
```

The majority of this is self-explanatory. Within each podcast there are one or more items, each of which includes the key piece of information—the enclosure. Within the enclosure are the details of where the audio file is being hosted, its size and its type. This means that rather than including the file in the RSS code, only a reference to the file is enclosed.*

11.1.4 Research into Podcasting

In comparison with other media-sharing services there has been little formal research undertaken into podcasting. There is however quite an extensive literature focused on the educational uses of podcasting and, although this is outside our scope here, Harris and Park (2008), McGarr (2009), Edirisingha and Salmon (2007, 2008), and Campbell (2005) provide useful overviews.

Gunawardena (2009) investigated podcasting services by exploring who was creating podcasts, the popularity of different podcasts and the processes for dissemination of information about what is available. Perhaps unsurprisingly they found that the

---

* See: http://www.rssboard.org/rss-specification#ltenclosuregtSubelementOfLtitemgt for more details.

publishers were a mixture of professional and amateur producers. Most content was regularly updated either weekly (30%) or daily (10%) and the median file size was 15 megabytes (MB). They noted that people subscribed to around six podcasts on average but got around to playing fewer than four a week, indicating that although subscription could be interpreted as an expression of interest it did not necessarily translate into consumption. They also found that 80% of the plays were for the 20% of podcasts that had the most subscribers (an example of a form of Pareto's distribution). In addition, they argue that "podcasts currently constitute a delay-tolerant service" (p. 210), since the median delay between when podcast episodes are released and when they are played is about 10 days, and that this delay falls to one day (or less) for only 1% of podcasts. They note the contrast with (the then-emerging) real-time Web 2.0 services such as Twitter, which are not delay-tolerant.

Tsagkias et al. (2008) undertook research into what they termed the *podosphere*, the collection of podcasts available across the Web. They also note the wide range of content—from professionally produced, radio-quality material, to unedited and unscripted user-generated content, usually of poor quality. In particular they looked into the credibility of podcasts based on four types of indictor: content, the podcaster, context and technical execution. Their analysis formed the basis of later work which looked at developing an automatic classification system for podcasts that could be used to recommend material to users (Tsagkias et al. 2010).

Madden and Jones (2008) undertook research for the Pew Internet and American Life Project and found that the podosphere was growing rapidly (one service alone—Podcast Alley—had doubled in size in just under two years), with 19% of Internet users in the United States reporting that they had downloaded a podcast, although only 3% downloaded a podcast on a typical day. This compares with figures quoted by McLaughin (2006) of 6% of American users in 2006. More recent figures from the UK seem to show an increase in interest in podcasting. The Radio Joint Audience Research (RAJA) report, published in 2010, found that 60% of UK adults who had access to the Internet had downloaded a podcast at some time, and nearly half (44%) of those who did use podcasts said that they did so once or more a week (RAJAR 2010). The typical UK user subscribes to around five podcasts and spends under an hour a week listening to them.

Besser et al. (2008) analysed a small sample of university-based podcast listeners to explore the ways in which they located content that matched their interests. They found that 50% of the users found content by browsing, 40% from a friend's recommendation and 24% from a specialist podcasting search engine (such as iTunes or Podcast.net). The most popular topics were technology and music and the favourite podcasts were professionally produced.

Banerjee et al. (2008) undertook detailed profiling of various characteristics of podcasting and also measured Internet traffic associated with podcasts in order to generate data about the potential effect on network bandwidth. They found that the average podcast file is 17 MB, three orders of magnitude greater than the average Hypertext Transfer Protocol (HTTP) file and that the distribution of file sizes follows a skewed bimodal Gaussian distribution.

11.2 PHOTO-SHARING SITES

Photo hosting and sharing services allow users to upload digital photographs to a website and to use the site to organise and share them with others. Files are typically uploaded in the more common photography formats such as JPEG, PNG and GIF. Although the functionality varies from site to site, an important component is the development of a user community, based on the notion that viewing and sharing photos is a fundamentally social activity. It is this aspect that sets the Web 2.0 photo-sharing services apart from pre-existing Web photo storage websites. The first and best-known photo hosting and sharing service is Flickr, which is now part of the Yahoo! family of products and hosts over six billion photos with 2,500 images uploaded per minute.[*] Other mainstream examples include: PhotoBucket, Fotki, Fotolog, Kodak Gallery, Shutterfly, SnapFish, ImageShack, and Zoomr.

Some online social networks also provide photo-sharing facilities and indeed there is strong competition in this area with Facebook in particular, rapidly overtaking other services in terms of numbers of users and photos uploaded.[†] We should also note the recent rise in dedicated services for users of smartphones, with companies like Instagram, Path and Picplz growing rapidly.[‡]

There are a number of features that most of these sites have in common, including the following:

- Remote storage and back-up of photos

- Ways of tagging photos with descriptions and metadata

- Browsing and searching

- Methods for categorizing and organising photos into collections or sets

- Methods for commenting on other users' photos

- Methods for befriending and communicating with other users (in a similar manner to SNSs)

- Rating tools that highlight personal favourites

- Integration with other Web 2.0 services such as publishing a photo on a blog

Most services are free, at least for the basic level of access to the site. Some services offer photo printing as an additional feature, at a cost.

Flickr is the market leader in photo-sharing services and, as it has been the subject of the vast majority of the research work that has been undertaken in this area, we will use it as our example system.

---

[*] August 2011 figures; see: http://blog.flickr.net/en/2011/08/04/6000000000/

[†] It was estimated in February 2011 by Photo Weekly magazine that Facebook would reach 100 billion photos by the summer of that year (Eger 2011). See also: http://techcrunch.com/2009/02/22/facebook-photos-pulls-away-from-the-pack/

[‡] http://techcrunch.com/2010/11/18/photo-sharing-is-the-next-evolution-of-social-tctv/

11.2.1 A Short History of Flickr

Flickr was born out of serendipity. The site was first developed by Ludicorp, a games developer in Vancouver, Canada and launched in February 2004. The idea of sharing photos came out of discussions about extra features that could be added to an online game called NeverEnding that they were developing. The husband and wife team who ran the company, Caterina Fake and Stewart Butterfield, quickly realized that the photo-sharing feature had more potential than the proposed game. As Fake later told the *USA Today* newspaper: "Had we sat down and said, 'Let's start a photo application,' we would have failed …We would have done all this research and done all the wrong things" (Graham 2006, webpage). These roots in game play are important according to Flickr's general manager, Kakul Srivastava, who told the UK's *Daily Telegraph*: "It began as a game, and as you go through Flickr having all these little interactions, leaving comments, inviting people to look at photos or join a group, it's that game play that leads to the unique culture and creativity that exists on the site" (Harrod 2009, webpage).

Cox (2008) reports that the early development process involved intense interaction with the user base and that the site, in common with many Web 2.0 services, displayed a *beta* logo until May 2006. The site then became *gamma* (an unusual step in Web 2.0 development) before stabilizing a year later—an achievement that was acknowledged by displaying "Flickr: loves you" on its homepage. Early traffic growth was rapid and increased even further after the site was purchased by Yahoo! (for US$30 million) in March 2005. In the following 12 months the site went from 250,000 registered users to more than 2 million. In April 2008, Flickr also started to allow videos to be uploaded to the site.

In early 2008 Flickr undertook work with the Library of Congress to make available a number of famous and important photographic images in a project called *The Commons*. A number of other institutions are now participating including the UK's National Archive and the Swedish National Heritage Board. Users are free to add their own tags to these images.*

11.2.2 Using Flickr

There are three key aspects to Flickr: uploading photos and organising them, social interaction, and tagging.

11.2.2.1 Photos

The basic unit of Flickr is of course the individual photo, and a user's collection of uploaded photos is known as the *photostream*. Other users can view photos that have been designated as 'public'. When another user sees a photo they also see the metadata associated with it including the title, the tags, a description and additional (varying) information such as the rights associated with the photo, the number of times it has been viewed and the date uploaded (see Figure 11.2).

Flickr's Organizr application allows the user to create *sets* and *collections* from the photostream. Sets provide a way of organising photos into topics, events or related subject

---

* See: http://www.flickr.com/commons

FIGURE 11.2 Viewing a photo on Flickr. Note the comment box below the photo and the facilities to add tags on the right hand side. (Reproduced with kind permission of Yahoo! Inc., © 2011 Yahoo! Inc. Flickr and the Flickr logo are registered trademarks of Yahoo! Inc.)

areas. Each set has, like individual photos, its own privacy settings and a photo can be in more than one set at a time. Sets can also be grouped together into collections.

At the centre of the Organizr is the *workspace*, where photos are dropped so that they can be allocated to sets and collections. At the bottom of the workspace is the Findr, where the user's photostream is displayed and where there is a second search box which only searches the user's photostream. Figure 11.3 shows a user in the process of creating a new set called 'German Trains' and dragging a photo into the set's workspace.

FIGURE 11.3 Using Flickr's Organizr application to create a set of photos called German Trains. (Reproduced with permission of Yahoo! Inc., © 2011 Yahoo! Inc. Flickr and the Flickr logo are registered trademarks of Yahoo! Inc.)

11.2.2.2 Social Interaction

The social aspects of Flickr are also a key part of the site's *raison d'être* and Flickr provides its own in-house e-mail system to help users keep in touch with each other. There are two principal ways in which social interaction is facilitated:

- **Contacts:** Other registered users you wish to be kept in contact with, but are not automatically reciprocal. In practice this means that you will be updated with information about changes to their photostreams. Designating a contact as a 'friend' or 'family' implies a closer relationship and gives them access to photos with a higher privacy level. In this way the user can control who gets to view which parts of their photostream. Access to information about all of a user's contacts, including family and friends, is through the 'Contacts' menu item on the user's homepage.

- **Groups:** Self-organising communities with declared, common interests. The main purpose of a group is to facilitate photo- and metadata-sharing in what are called group pools. Negoescu and Gatica-Perez (2008) identify a number of types including: geographical or event-oriented groups; visual style groups; quality-focused groups (membership is often by invitation only). Groups have various privacy settings and also facilitate discussions between members.

11.2.2.3 Tags and Commenting

Tags and the process of tagging are important components of the Flickr service as they are key to navigating the enormous database of stored photographs (Cox 2008). Tags provide useful information about the content of a photo and may also record other data such as the quality of the picture, the time of year and the location. We discuss tagging more generally in the chapter on social bookmarking but it is important to note that in Flickr, for the most part, owners of photographs tag the photos themselves. Although it is possible for others to tag a photo (if they are a friend and the owner has set permissions to allow this), this does not tend to be widely used (Cox 2008). For this reason, tagging on Flickr usually comes under the category of folksonomy rather than collaborative tagging (see Chapter 5).

Viewing permissions (privacy settings) and metadata (such as a name, description and tags) are added to the photo when it is uploaded. By default, any images uploaded will be marked '© All rights reserved' and will not therefore be licensed for use by others. Users who would like others to be able to use their images can change the rights to a Creative Commons licence.[*]

11.2.3 Technology

As is typical for Web 2.0 services, Flickr provides access to its data and functionality via an Application Programming Interface (API). Developers who wish to use the API must obtain an API key before they are allowed to access and modify the photographic store.

---

[*] Details of these are at: http://www.flickr.com/creativecommons/

In addition, a number of client libraries exist for different programming languages (e.g. PHP, Ruby), making life a little easier for the developer.[*]

Flickr officially supports JPEGs, non-animated GIFs, and PNGs. Users can also upload TIFFs and some other file types, but they will automatically be converted to and stored in JPEG format. Each photo has a sequentially allocated ID which is added during the upload process. The lowest ID is 74—the first photo ever uploaded to the service.[†]

11.2.4 Research

In this section we will discuss some of the research that is being undertaken into photo-sharing services, and tease out some of the live research issues. Note that the bulk of the work has focused on Flickr unless otherwise stated.

11.2.4.1 Content Analysis

Although there has been some general work on analysing the content of online photography services,[‡] the majority of research has concentrated on how to organise and search these repositories. As a panel at the International Workshop on Multimedia Information Retrieval in 2007 made clear,[§] this is an active research area thanks to the significant growth rate in online photo and video repositories and because of the increasing reliance the general public places on these services to record their important social and family life-events (Li et al. 2007).

A number of researchers have looked at tags and how they might be used to help to categorise and order photographic content (Kennedy et al. 2007; Joshi et al. 2012; Li et al. 2008; Rattenbury et al. 2007; Maala et al. 2007). Of particular interest has been how tags can help determine what the photo is about and, importantly, where it was taken. This information is sometimes combined with the global positioning system (GPS) location of the photograph (as newer digital camera technology can automatically associate this with the photo). Serdyukov et al. (2009) note the extensive body of literature on the use of geo-tagging with photographs and Crandall et al. (2009, 761) write: "Photos are inherently spatial—they are taken at specific places—and so it is natural that geospatial information should provide useful organising principles for photo collections."

Others, such as Cox (2008), Burgess (2007), and Prieur et al. (2008) have analysed Flickr from the point of view of what the photographs tell us about the changing nature of photography, placing it in the context of developments in the social use of the camera since mass ownership began. Cox reports that Flickr is used for a far wider range of activity than traditional domestic photography. Burgess notes the changing nature of what it means to undertake amateur photography and, echoing the discussion about the rise of the amateur in Chapter 2, writes: "If amateur photography in the twentieth century was defined by Kodak's slogan, 'You push the button, we do the rest', then the

---

[*] Further details are at: http://www.flickr.com/services/api/

[†] See: http://www.flickr.com/photos/bees/74

[‡] Herring (2010), for example, places photo-sharing websites into the wider context of Web-based content and discusses whether traditional methods of content analysis can be applied to these new forms.

[§] See: http://mmc36.informatik.uni-augsburg.de/acmmm2007/

slogan of Web 2.0 models of amateur creativity such as Flickr's might be, 'Here are the buttons, you do the rest'" (p. 3). Prieur et al. (2008, 8) conclude: "the main originality of Flickr is the way it facilitates conversations between amateurs of photography, who don't know each other in real-life and who both play and gain reputation *with* photography" (their italics).

11.2.4.2 User Behaviour and Popularity

A number of researchers have considered how people use Flickr, for example how they search for photographs and patterns of behaviour in uploading new material. Lerman and Jones (2007) have looked at how people find images to view. They argue that although Flickr provides many ways of finding images—tags, sets, groups etc.—a process of *social browsing*, i.e. reviewing the photostreams of friends and contacts, is responsible for the bulk of user activity. They found that the number of views an image gets correlates most strongly with the number of *reverse contacts* that the photographer has, i.e. the number of other users who list them as a contact. This was backed up by analysis of the commenting that took place on photographers' photos. The authors concluded that this shows the developing power of social browsing as opposed to traditional search box techniques (a topic I return to in the concluding chapter).

Van Zwol (2007) investigated the viewing habits of users, plotting the distribution of the number of views per photo on a log–log scale in order to demonstrate that a power law was in operation. He found that the probability of having x visits to a particular photo is proportional to $x^{-0.7}$. In other words, in a pattern familiar in much of Web 2.0, it is very skewed and a few photos generate most of the viewings. He found that the top 7% of the most frequently viewed photos are responsible for almost 50% of total views and less than 10% of the photos had more than eight views.

Van Zwol also looked at the temporal aspects of viewing and found that photos tend to have a high number of views per photo on the first day, which grows even further on the second day and then steadily declines. The decline matches an exponential decay so that the number of views on day x after upload is proportional to $e^{-1.1x}$. He also found that for the top 10% most popular photos, 65% of new ones had been discovered and viewed within 3 hours and this grows to over 90% within two days. He also considered the comments that photos received. The most popular 10% of photos received almost twice as many comments as the next popular 10%. Popular photos also tended to be uploaded by individuals who had a larger number of contacts on the site and who were also associated with more groups. He concludes: "In other words, the social affiliation of users within Flickr is important: people that are highly interconnected will have their photos viewed many times" (p. 190).

Negoescu and Gatica-Perez (2008) agree with this conclusion, arguing that Flickr should be understood not as a simple photo repository but as a complex social system. In particular they point out the importance of groups on the site and have undertaken various statistical analyses of this feature. Amongst their findings was that the mean number of members per group was 317.9 and the median was 85. The mean number of photos per group was 3,191 and the median was 492. The distribution of both these features, when plotted, approximated to a lognormal distribution. Based on their sampling the authors say that just over 50% of all Flickr users share at least one photo with at least one group; 26% share more than 50 photos, and 9% share more than 200 photos. Of those who do share, the mean percentage of their photostream that they share with groups is 29%. In the 50% who share, behaviour can be characterised as moderate sharers (members of fewer than five groups), average sharers and extreme sharers (hundreds of groups). In a more recent paper the same authors also compare how sharing works on both Flickr and Kodak's Gallery (a site which they argue has more of a focus on obtaining physical copies of digital photos) (Negoescu et al. 2010).

Prieur et al. (2008) found very different results with respect to groups, with their data showing that only 8% of Flickr users were members of a group.* The authors also calculated that private photos formed around a third of the repository. They found that 20% of users owned more than 82% of the photos—a striking similarity to the 'eighty-twenty' rule that has been derived from Pareto's work (see Chapter 7). They also looked at user activity, finding that 39% did not seem to do anything on the site and have not uploaded a public photo (although it is possible they have done so in private, of course). A further 23% had not uploaded a public photo but had used the social networking facilities. The remaining 38% are the more active users and the authors argue this represents a split within Flickr between those who simply use it to store and those who use it to communicate.

Cha et al. (2009) took a different tack, analysing the way information diffuses around the site. As we have noted previously, photo-sharing sites can be considered to be a form of online social network, since they allow users to exchange messages, post comments etc. As one of the distinguishing features of social networking sites is the potential for information dissemination along the social links, the authors argue that Flickr's topology could indicate a potential for wide-spread dissemination of information. They found, for example, that over 50% of users found their favourite pictures from their friends.

They also considered popularity. They examined photos based on three metrics: number of views, number of fans (i.e. those who make a photo a favourite) and comments. All three showed heavy-tail distribution patterns, so for example whilst millions of photos have fewer than 10 fans, more than 200,000 photos have more than 1,000 fans. They also looked at the temporal aspects of picture popularity and found that many popular photos (those with more than 100 fans) show an active rise in popularity in the first few days after upload. After around 10 to 20 days the popularity of these photos enters a period of steady linear growth, which is often maintained for a year or more. Photos with fewer than 100 fans also become popular early on but they then become dormant after the first few months. The authors claim their results show: "that only a small fraction of pictures achieve high popularity and thus have the potential to spread widely through the social network" (p. 723).

---

* Their data sample was taken a year earlier than Negoescu et al., but this seems unlikely to explain such a large disparity.

11.2.4.3 Topology

A number of researchers have considered the topology of some of the network graphs that are formed from data generated by Flickr, often using (real-world) social network analysis techniques (Tojo et al. 2008; Cha et al. 2009; Mislove et al. 2008; Lee et al. 2010; Valafar et al. 2009). Cha et al. (2009) constructed a directed social graph from the 2.5 million users they located from an automated crawl of the system, such that each node represented a Flickr user and each link represented a friendship connection. They found that 68% of links were reciprocal and the majority of users were connected to only a few others (55% of the nodes had just one outgoing link and 90% had an out-degree smaller than 10), with an average out-degree of 14. However, as ever with Web 2.0, a few nodes had a very large number of outgoing links numbering tens of thousands. They found that the maximum path length between any two nodes was 27, while the average length was 5.67. The clustering coefficient for the better-connected nodes varied between 0.05 and 0.1, whilst for less well connected it was between 0.2 and 0.4. These kinds of characteristics indicate a small world network, as discussed in Chapter 7.

Mislove et al. (2008) considered similar aspects and found strong evidence of reciprocity that occurred rapidly (over 80% of reciprocal friend links were created within 48 hours of the initial link being created). The authors also considered the structure of the in-degree and out-degree graphs and examined whether the preferential attachment model could be applied to Flickr. However, they found that the model could not quite account for the structures and the way they developed over time, arguing that there may be factors concerning the way the site works that could explain this (e.g. there are few site-wide signposts for finding other users such as "most popular user"). These results obviously form part of the on-going debate about the dynamics of Web 2.0 social network formation.

11.3 VIDEO-SHARING SERVICES

Video-sharing services allow users to upload and share short digital films (usually up to a maximum of 10 minutes). In keeping with the spirit of Web 2.0, much of this content is produced by amateurs although increasingly there is the opportunity to view professionally produced content and to catch up with TV shows and events broadcasting from the mainstream media.

Video sharing is different from video-on-demand (VoD) in that the latter describes online conduits (such as Hulu, Seesaw and Blinkbox) for streaming films and professionally produced material made for broadcast, and as such are of less interest to us here. Unfortunately some of the literature on Web 2.0–style video-sharing sites uses the term video-on-demand indiscriminately, causing confusion.

Video-sharing services are growing in popularity in all demographic groups and are outpacing the adoption rates of other Internet activities (Madden 2009; Moore 2011). More than 70% of adults who use the Internet have watched at least one video on these sites and online video viewing is near universal amongst young adults and teens. Indeed, Pew reports that in 2011 watching videos online still slightly out-ranks all other forms of online

Web 2.0 activity in terms of popularity amongst adults, although online social network site usage is likely to catch up rapidly.[*]

Although YouTube is widely seen as by far the market leader there are, in fact, a number of other services. Notable examples include: Yahoo! Video, Vimeo, MetaCafe, Blip.TV, Veoh, Revver, Daum (Korea), Youku (China), Tudou (China), and DailyMotion (France). In addition, some social network sites also support video. This list is in no way exhaustive and it is the nature of this relatively new market that the situation is constantly changing. Indeed, the technology website TechCrunch lists at least thirty competitors on its YouTube profile page.[†]

The following section will outline the way in which YouTube works, as an exemplar video-sharing site. YouTube is suited to this because of its market-leading status and because it has been the subject of analysis in the vast majority of the research that has been undertaken in this area.

11.3.1 A Short History of YouTube

The two kings have gotten together, the king of search and the king of video. We're going to have it our way.

CHAD HURLEY
Speaking on the day Google bought YouTube (Lacey 2008, 1)

They say that necessity is the mother of invention and three PayPal employees came up with the idea of an online video-sharing website in 2005 when they could not find a service that did what they wanted (Sahlin and Botello 2007; Lidsky 2010). The three—Chad Hurley, Steve Chen and Jawed Karim—were at a party and a number of guests were shooting video and taking digital photos. Afterwards the group tried to get the results distributed amongst friends via e-mail but they were presented with a number of technical difficulties to do with file formats and video codecs. They resolved to make the process much simpler and development started on 14th February 2005 with the team assembling, like so many Silicon Valley pioneers before them, in a garage. Development was rapid and the first video, "Me at the Zoo" showing founder Karim in front of the elephants at the San Diego Zoo, was uploaded in April. The first public beta of the software was available by May and the official launch took place in December, with the now famous strapline, "Broadcast Yourself".[‡] Google bought the company in October 2006 for US$1.65 billion and this was arguably the moment when Silicon Valley realized that there was the potential of another dot-com boom—albeit this time built on the ideas of Web 2.0 (Lacey 2008).

This was followed by a period of rapid growth and by the summer of 2011 the company was handling over 400 million users worldwide who were streaming 3 billion videos a day

---

[*] Pew reports that in summer 2011, 71% of American adults use video-sharing sites, compared to 65% using online social network sites. The latter, however, is growing rapidly. For further details and regular updates see: http://www.pewinternet.org/Home/Static%20Pages/Trend%20Data.aspx

[†] See: http://www.crunchbase.com/company/youtube

[‡] To see how the site developed in the early days, see the Internet Wayback archive: http://wayback.archive.org/web/20051001000000*/http://www.youtube.com

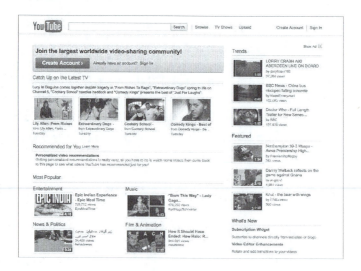

FIGURE 11.4   YouTube homepage 2011. (Image courtesy of Google, © 2011 Google Inc.)

and uploading 48 hours of material every minute.* Although some of the content is uploaded by professionals and traditional media companies, the vast majority is the result of the creative endeavours of amateurs, either making their own or uploading material from other sources (Kruitbosch and Nack 2008). This makes for an eclectic mix and as Kruitbosch and Nack put it: "YouTube is an environment full of mash-ups, parodies, malapropisms or simple copies" (p. 7). A well-known example of what might be called more uplifting content, and a good example of how 'broadcast yourself' can apply in new and interesting ways, is provided by Professor Martyn Poliakoff of the University of Nottingham. His channel—Periodic Videos—contains over a hundred videos about the periodic table plus regular updates on other aspects of chemistry.†

11.3.2 Using YouTube

The main homepage presents a kind of snapshot of what the site 'thinks' is likely to be of most interest at a particular time (see Figure 11.4). This includes a selection of the latest TV shows that are available, the most popular videos organised by category, and trending videos (related to the topical issues of the day). A user simply clicks on a video thumbnail image to see that video's homepage and access the control buttons and feedback functionality.

Although it is perfectly possible to view videos without registering, users who want to upload video need to become a registered user. YouTube also has a class of accounts for specialist users through its Partner Program and these accounts operate according to special privileges and rules.

When watching the video, the user has a number of options, displayed as small buttons below the video. These include play/pause buttons, sound adjustment, and full screen.

---

* The latest statistics are regularly updated on YouTube's press pages, see: http://www.youtube.com/t/press_statistics
† http://www.youtube.com/user/periodicvideos

Below these are a number of sharing options, such as saving the video as a favourite or to a playlist.

YouTube content is organised around two key ideas: finding content, either by searching or browsing, and social interaction.

11.3.2.1 Search

Searching for content is through the search box, as one would expect. The results prioritize 'promoted' videos, followed by 'channels' that match the search term, then users' playlists (a personal selection of videos) that match, and finally individual videos. There are of course a number of advanced search options and ways to configure the results.

11.3.2.2 Channels

The channel is the basic way of giving access to a particular user's uploaded videos, playlists and other material. Each user has a channel created for them when they register (although organisations, such as media companies, can also set up channels) and other users subscribe to channels in a similar way to RSS and podcasts. Once a user has subscribed an icon appears in their list of subscribed channels. As new content is added to the channel, the list of subscriptions is updated. One of the key ways to find content on YouTube is to subscribe to other people's channels.

The diagram in Figure 11.5 shows a channel that has been set up for this textbook.

FIGURE 11.5 YouTube channel for *Web 2.0 and beyond* (textbook). In the playlist 'Videos about Web 2.0' there is a newly added video called 'The Machine is Us/ing Us'. This is a very famous YouTube video, created by Dr Michael Wesch at Kansas State University, which describes Web 2.0 in simple terms. (Image courtesy of Google, © 2011 Google Inc.)

FIGURE 11.6   Finding a video using YouTube's browse feature. Here, the user is browsing the News & Politics category. (Image courtesy of Google, © 2011 Google Inc.)

11.3.2.3 Browse

Clicking 'Browse' takes the user to a screen that provides a way to locate videos by genre (i.e. videos, TV shows, movies and music). Each genre has its own set of categories, which a user allocates to their content when they upload it to the site.

Within categories there are ways to refine browsing even further. Figure 11.6 shows the News & Politics category in the Videos genre. See how, by using a drop-down menu (labelled 'more'), the user can add another layer of content filtration such as 'most recently added', 'most discussed' etc. It is worth noting that the list of videos presented to the user defaults to 'most viewed', although the 'popular' menu is positioned next to it and so it is easy to switch (all other choices appear under the 'more' menu). Although YouTube has not said precisely what the difference is between 'most viewed' and 'popular', they have indicated that the latter is based on an algorithm that takes in a number of signals (e.g. how long other viewers have watched a particular video) whereas the former is simply a count of viewing frequency.* Presenting content to the viewer based on popularity and viewing figures "results in a positive feedback mechanism leading to rich-get-richer vote accrual for the very popular items" (Szabo and Huberman 2010, 80). Clearly there are cultural implications in guiding viewers in this manner.

11.3.2.4 Social Interaction

It is important to understand that YouTube is more than a well-executed way to upload and share video. It is also a community of users and in many respects operates in a similar manner to online social networks in that members can become friends with each other, tag videos with descriptions, post comments on each other's videos and channels, and exchange messages (Biel and Gatica-Perez 2009). Indeed, Gill et al. (2007) argue that the combination of abundant content *together* with social networking and tagging functions makes YouTube "the quintessential Web 2.0 site" (p. 16).

---

* For more detail on this see a report in the *LA Times* in 2009: http://latimesblogs.latimes.com/technology/2009/02/you-tube-popular.html

11.3.2.4.1 Sharing When a user has played a video that they would like to share, they can send a link to the video via e-mail or directly by YouTube message. There are also various methods for incorporating a YouTube video into another Web 2.0 service, for example MySpace, a Wordpress blog, or eBay. This is sometimes done by extracting a short piece of HTML code (which YouTube provides) and adding it into the secondary site or by clicking on various buttons beneath the share button which automatically shares the content with services such as Twitter and Facebook. Users can also use the same process to embed video in their own webpages.

11.3.2.4.2 Friends and Contacts As well as being able to subscribe to another user's channel, one can also choose to become their 'friend'. Clicking the 'Add as Friend' button sends a message to the prospective new friend, who needs to agree to the connection before the system sets it up.

Every new friend a user makes becomes listed as a 'contact' and the list of contacts can be split into friends and family. This means that it is possible to alert, say, only relatives to a new video featuring a family get-together.

11.3.2.4.3 User Interactions with Content Other ways in which YouTube facilitates interaction is by collecting data about what users are doing on the site and recycling this as content. To illustrate this we will look at a selection of items from the 'more' filter, which we have mentioned already (see Figure 11.6):

- **Top Favorited:** When a user marks a video as a favourite it is added their profile page so they can easily find it again. Marking a video as a favourite is an important part of the YouTube experience and the website aggregates data on favourites and makes it available through the 'Top Favorited' menu (Sahlin and Botello 2007).

- **Most Discussed:** Filtering according to 'Most Discussed' displays the videos that have had the most comments. In the interest of promoting uplifting content, during June 2010 one of the most discussed videos in the News category was Philip Zimbardo's talk at the Royal Society for the Encouragement of Arts, Manufactures and Commerce on the meaning and perception of time.[*]

- **Most Responded:** Rather than merely commenting on a particular video, YouTube allows registered users to upload a video response. The 'most responded' filter displays these video responses in rank order.

11.3.3 YouTube and Copyright

Since YouTube's launch in 2005 there has been considerable controversy surrounding the issue of copyright infringement. The ease with which digital video can be copied and uploaded has meant that there has been considerable infringement of professional content producers' copyright.

---

[*] See: http://www.youtube.com/watch?v=A3oIiH7BLmg

Over the years the big media businesses have expressed their concern and indeed, during Google's purchase of YouTube, some analysts were worried as to the long-term financial implications of these legal issues (Monica 2006; Breen 2007; Reisinger 2010). Whilst YouTube was a relatively penniless start-up there was little point in mounting serious legal challenges, but when Google took over, things changed. Most media owners were content to simply force YouTube to take down materials that infringed their rights, but in 2007, Viacom sued Google for US$1 billion in copyright fees. However, matters are generally confused by the fact that many media companies now use YouTube as a legitimate service for their own material through what are called 'Brand Channels', which provide revenue through advertising.

The technical details of the legal debates around YouTube's position are beyond the scope of this book, but it is worth noting in passing the concept of *Safe Harbour,* as this is applicable to many other media hosting services (Kim 2007). According to a House Report of the 105th Congress, the Digital Millennium Copyright Act (DMCA) was enacted in the United States "both to preserve copyright enforcement on the Internet and to provide immunity to service providers from copyright infringement liability for 'passive,' 'automatic' actions in which a service provider's system engages through a technological process initiated by another without the knowledge of the service provider" (Breen 2007, 154). This resulted in the creation of a number of Safe Harbours, one of which may be applicable to YouTube: protection from legal action for those who store material at the direction of the user as long as the service removes it at the request of the rights holder (Bangman 2007).

Sahlin and Botello (2007) argue that this has been a benefit to YouTube because although a lot of copyright-infringing material remains on the site, the rights holders have not requested that YouTube remove it. This material often consists of short clips of noteworthy moments, recorded by amateurs, from TV shows or news bulletins. Sometimes such clips go 'viral' and are passed as links around the Internet. In other forms of content, users overdub existing, copyright material with their own sound track. It is in YouTube's interests not to actively remove such material as: "it's exactly this type of content that users love, and it's exactly this type of content that has made YouTube so successful" (Sahlin and Botello 2007, 323). Copyright holders, too, are often well aware of the infringements but refrain from acting as having the video on the site can be viewed as a form of publicity. Cha et al. (2007) quote figures to the effect that as much as 10% of YouTube content is material uploaded without a rights holder's permission, and yet they found that only 5% of videos that are deleted are done so at the request of the rights holders.

The importance of the Viacom case for the wider world of Web 2.0 companies was highlighted in 2010 by the announcement that several other big Web companies including Facebook and Yahoo! had supported YouTube in their case (Valentino-DeVries 2010). It appears that Google (YouTube) have won the case brought against them by Viacom, with the judge deciding that Safe Harbour does protect YouTube and Google (Lefkow 2010), although it is likely that this will go to appeal.

11.3.4 Technology

The video and audio content on YouTube is encoded in Adobe's Flash video format using the H.263 codec (Kruitbosch and Nack 2008; Gill et al. 2007; Miller 2007). Users may upload video material in a variety of formats including WMV, MPEG and AVI, but YouTube converts them all to Flash before making them available on the site. This allows users to view the video without additional browser plug-ins since it is known that the Flash browser plug-in is present on well over 90% of clients.

In contrast to podcasting, where a file is downloaded to an MP3 player, the video is *streamed* using Adobe's Flash progressive download technology,* which allows playback to start before the video has finished loading. In fact, this is known as *pseudo streaming* as it uses standard Web servers (using HTTP/TCP and based on commodity PC technology),† as opposed to traditional media streaming (which requires dedicated, specialist streaming servers).

YouTube assigns each video an 11-digit ID and a series of metadata such as uploader's username, date, category, length, user rating, number of views, rating and comments, list of related videos (content with similar tags or subject area, as chosen by the user) (Cheng et al. 2008).

Originally the uploaded file size was limited to 100 MB but this has been increased recently, most notably to 2 GB in 2009 in order accommodate high-definition video.‡ However, the length of each video is capped at ten minutes, except for specialist users.

11.3.5 Research Issues in Video Sharing

Just as with SNSs, video-sharing sites provide a rich source of primary research data and it is possible to gather large amounts of quantitative data from services such as YouTube (Cairns and Blythe 2010). For this reason, there is a notable body of research work into video sharing, although the vast bulk of this concentrates on YouTube.

11.3.5.1 Content Analysis

Content analysis represents one of the key areas of research interest in video-sharing services generally. Although we might now question the importance of differentiating too strongly between amateur and professional content (see Chapter 2), Kruitbosch and Nack (2008) examined a sample of YouTube content with a view to determining 'user-generated' (i.e. amateur) and 'professional'. They used the following categories:

- User-generated: content observed by and recorded by a user using a webcam, mobile phone or similar (e.g. family gathering)

- User-generated of a professional performance: as above but of a professional performance, e.g. a concert

- Professional recording: content recorded for professional purposes, e.g. TV show

---

* See: http://www.adobe.com/devnet/flash/learning_guide/video/part02.html
† See: http://highscalability.com/youtube-architecture
‡ See: http://techcrunch.com/2009/07/01/youtube-increases-file-size-limit-to-2gb-now-allows-direct-hd-embeds-and-links/

What they found may be interesting with respect to YouTube's 'Broadcast Yourself' slogan: user-generated material consistently received fewer views than professionally created videos and user-generated material is not usually present in the site's list of most viewed videos (although it is clearly present when one considers a random list of uploaded material). The authors posit that their results show that professional content, either unadulterated or mashed up with other material, plays the most important role. They argue that although YouTube can be seen as a means to promote individual creativity, as an outlet for user-generated content it is, in fact, more of a social system.[*]

Cheng et al. (2008) have also looked at content on YouTube, collecting data from three million videos. Users categorise their video when it is uploaded and the authors found that the most popular were music (22%), entertainment (17%) and comedy (12%). They also analysed the length of videos, finding that a plot of the distribution of lengths (between 0 and the allowed maximum of 10 minutes) exhibited three peaks. The first peak at within one minute represents more than 20.6% of videos, thus showing the prevalence of short material. The second peak is at 3–4 minutes (17%) and is caused by the music category. The final peak is at around 10 minutes, since some users try to disguise longer clips from movies by splitting them into segments.

Siersdorfer et al. (2010) took a slightly different tack, focusing instead on the comments that users post. They analysed six million comments on 67,000 YouTube videos. They found that the distribution of comments followed the traditional Zipf pattern: a long tail with a small number of videos attracting comments in the thousands. On YouTube it is also possible for other users to rate a comment that someone else has made about a video. The authors looked at this and found there is a slight tendency to be positive rather than negative. They also looked at the textual content of comments. Unsurprisingly, comments that were more likely to be highly rated included words such as 'best', 'amazing', 'awesome' and 'nice' whereas negative ratings were more likely to be applied to comments that included words like 'worst', 'dumb', 'ugly' and various swear words.

11.3.5.2 User Behaviour and Content Popularity

Cha et al. (2007) argue that the scale and the dynamic, decentralised nature of user-generated sites like YouTube mean that the popularity of content demonstrates very different patterns to that of traditional media such as broadcast TV. There is more change and more unpredictable behaviour. The audience is more fragmented and people are less likely to be watching the same things in the way that they are, in a sense, forced to through traditional broadcast channels.[†] The authors write: "Constant waves of new videos and the convenience of the Web are quickly personalizing the viewing experience, leading to a great variability in user behavior and attention span" (p. 1). Despite this, understanding, or at least attempting to understand, how popularity and demand work in video sharing is important, not only as a research exercise in itself but also to help with more practical matters such as search engine design, network traffic prediction and development of targeted advertising.

---

[*] As do a number of other researchers. See Lange (2008) for further discussion.
[†] Although TV is changing due to the introduction of hard disc recorders like the Tivo or SkyBox.

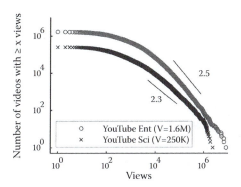

FIGURE: 11.7 Popularity distribution for YouTube videos in the Science and Environment categories both exhibit a power law with a truncated tail at the right hand side. (Reproduced with kind permission from a slide by Meeyoung Cha [Assistant Professor Graduate School of Culture Technology, KAIST] used in a talk to accompany the paper by Cha et al. (2007)).

The authors found that 10% of the most popular videos account for nearly 80% of views and that this was the case both for YouTube and for the Korean video site Daum. The authors wonder aloud as to whether this is symptomatic of the fact that people naturally wish to view what others are viewing or whether there are some technical or informational barriers to finding out about less popular material (i.e. might better search or recommendation systems alter this skew?). When they analysed the popularity of content in detail they found that the distribution exhibited a power law for most categories of content but that for science and environmental-related material there was also a truncated tail[*] (see Figure 11.7)

The authors speculate on the possible reason for this tail truncation. Their argument is complicated, and interested readers are referred to the original paper, but in brief they argue that YouTube viewers only want to see a video once and that this can be likened to the 'fetch-at-most-once' user behaviour observed in peer-to-peer networking which seems to result in a truncated tail similar to the one found in YouTube.

Cha et al. (2007) also looked at some of the temporal aspects of YouTube, finding that after a single day, 90% of newly uploaded videos had been watched at least once, with 40% watched more than 10 times.[†] Generally though, the probability of a given video being requested decreases sharply over time. The authors then go on to speculate as to whether it is possible to predict future popularity based on early viewing and their work seems to suggest that there is a correlation between second-day views and future popularity.

---

[*] They found the distribution followed a power law that sometimes operates with what is called an exponential cut-off, and this depends on the category of video in question. A power law with exponential cut-off has an exponential decay term e^{-yx} that overwhelms the power law behaviour at large values of x. For $x < 1/y$ it is almost identical to a normal power law, but for $x > 1/y$ it reverts to a normal exponential decay. For more on power laws see Chapter 7.

[†] However, as an aside, the authors do not seem to take account of the fact that most uploaders probably visit the site to play the video and check that it works.

These kinds of insights can be useful for predicting the caching technology that might be needed for these kinds of video services.[*]

In a similar vein Gill et al. (2007) conducted detailed analysis of YouTube usage patterns, file properties and popularity metrics. They found that the daily top 100 list of videos varies quite often, but that the monthly and all-time lists change rather slowly. It takes approximately eight times as many views to enter the all-time list from the monthly top list. They also found that long-term popular videos tended to be shorter (52.3% of the videos in the all-time popular category were between three and five minutes long). The authors also considered popularity by category, finding on a daily basis that entertainment and sport were the most popular, followed by news and comedy.

Santos et al. (2009) found that the number of videos a user has watched follows a distribution with a power law. Mitra et al. (2009) observed similar results for a range of services including YouTube, Veoh and Yahpp. Benevenuto et al. (2008) investigated a number of user behaviour features on YouTube, with a particular focus on the manner in which people respond to other users' videos. They also considered the problem of video spam, a growing problem partly because the user starts to play the video before realizing it is spam, which achieves the spammers' objectives. In an attempt to understand and perhaps tackle spam the authors investigated the temporal aspects of video responses (which have been shown to be important in tackling e-mail spam).

Biel and Gatica-Perez (2009) look at how users behave on YouTube and, in particular, how this relates to the roles that they play out and define themselves with. They sampled 270,000 users and found that a high level of interaction and participation is concentrated on a relatively small, but significant group of users and follows recognizable patterns. In particular, they found, perhaps not surprisingly, different patterns of behaviour between standard users and the special types of user that YouTube provides for (such as politicians and directors). For example, Politicians tend to spend more time simply uploading rather than watching others' material (readers may care to reflect on the similarities between this and the real world). They also found evidence that, generally, users who are members of these special classes are more interested in engaging with the wider community across the YouTube site and on obtaining more views and subscriptions to channels and playlists.

11.3.5.3 Topology

A number of researchers have also considered the topology of various network-related features of YouTube and other video-sharing services (Cheng et al. 2008; Paolillo 2008; Halvey and Keane 2007; Pedro et al. 2011). This work considers video-sharing services as (real-world) social networks and considers issues such as the graph formed by the connections between users created by friendship links or commenting on other people's videos. There are many similarities with the research work into online social networks that we looked at in Chapter 10 and many of the results echo those reported there (e.g. the presence of power law distributions and the small world effect).

---

[*] As a general point about popularity on media services the authors note problems with what they term video 'aliasing', i.e. multiple copies of the same video across the system. This has an effect on popularity measures and so could impact on the design of systems.

POINTS TO PONDER AND EXERCISES

1. Apple's iTunes seems to increasingly dominate the market for podcasting aggregation and playback. What do you think the implications of this development might be?

2. Read Cheng et al. (2008) describing their experiments with YouTube and then review the details of the datasets, and their formats, that they have collected (http://netsg. cs.sfu.ca/youtubedata/). Download one of their datasets and develop a small software program to process the dataset to (a) produce a bar chart of the distribution of category of videos (similar to that shown in Cheng et al. 2008, Figure 1) and (b) produce a graph of the distribution of video length. How would you go about creating a network graph based on the list of related videos provided within each set of data about a video?

FURTHER READING

Podcasting

The books *Podcasting for Learning in Universities* (open University Press, 2008) and *How to Create Podcasts for Education* (open University Press, 2008) both by Gilly Salmon and Palitha Edirisingha, are useful introductions to educational uses.

The University of Leeds provides an online introduction to creating a podcast: http://www.sddu. leeds.ac.uk/online_resources/podcasting/creating.html

For an introduction to podcasting and its role in education see Campbell (2005).

Flickr

Flickr Bits is a useful website that lists tools, applications and plug-ins that make use of the API: http://www.flickrbits.com/

For a detailed look at the role of groups and their characterization on Flickr see Cox et al. (2011).

Researchers have also considered some of the privacy implications of Flickr and other photo-sharing sites. See, for example Ahern et al. (2007) and Nov and Wattal (2009).

For more on the role of friends and other contacts within Flickr, and how this helps build an online social network within the site, see Lerman and Jones (2007).

YouTube

YouTube publishes detailed advice on copyright as part of its terms and conditions for using the site. See: http://www.youtube.com/t/howto_copyright

For more on user behaviour when using YouTube, in particular the use of user categories (Director, Musician etc.) see Biel and Gatica-Perez (2011).

For more analysis on user behaviour on YouTube and in particular the motivations for sharing photographs and getting involved in groups see Malinen (2011).

Researchers have also looked at privacy issues with respect to video-sharing sites. See Lange (2008).

For more technical details on how YouTube copes with scaling of its services, see the Google Tech Talks video at: http://video.google.com/videoplay?docid=-6304964351441328559#

## CHAPTER 12

Social Bookmarking Sites

I keep being told that we're the poster child for Web 2.0 … It freaks me out a little bit.

—JOSH SCHACHTER
Founder of Delicious, November 2004 (In: Heilemann 2006, webpage)

Social bookmarking services (SBSs) allow users to store and organise links to interesting websites and, crucially, share them with others (the social aspect). Essentially, they replicate the process of bookmarking webpages, which all browsers offer, but add the functionality not only to share them with other people but also, since they are stored remotely, to access the same set of bookmarks from different computers. During the storage process one can usually organise and categorise the bookmarks in various ways and an important component of social bookmarking is to be able to store and share metadata about a website.

Social bookmarking services attempt to solve a problem long-known to computer science—how to help users navigate and retrieve useful data from large information spaces (of which the Web is by far the largest example). As Joshua Schachter, inventor of the Delicious bookmarking service, told *MIT Technology Review*: "You bookmark for one of two reasons: either you think you're going to need that page again somewhere down the road, or you don't have time to read it now, but you want to read it later … The challenge is, once you've got all these bookmarks, how do you manage them?" (Surowiecki 2006, webpage).

This was the problem that Schacter set out to solve in 2003. Whilst there are now several SBSs to choose from, Delicious is the largest and most popular. It is because of this that most of the research into SBSs has concentrated on Delicious and for this reason we will use it as an exemplar system for discussing some of the features of SBSs in general.

12.1 INTRODUCTION TO DELICIOUS

Delicious provides bookmarking tools that supplement the capabilities of a Web browser. Figure 12.1 shows the three new buttons that have been added to the Firefox browser's toolbar when the Delicious system has been downloaded and installed: Delicious, Bookmarks

FIGURE 12.1 When Delicious tools are installed, three new buttons are added to the browser tool bar, just to the left of the Web address window. These are, from left to right, Delicious, Bookmarks, Tag. (Reproduced with permission from AVOS Systems, Inc. All rights reserved.).

and Tag. Saving a webpage as a new bookmark is as simple as pressing the 'Tag' button. A new interface box then pops up for the user to enter the metadata they want to store alongside the Uniform Resource Identifier (URI) of the bookmarked page (see Figure 12.2). This metadata might consist of a title for the page, free text descriptive notes and, most importantly for the sharing process, a series of space-delimited, single keywords known as *tags*.

An important feature of SBSs is to tag a site using more than one keyword thereby allowing it to belong to more than one conceptual category (a common limitation in browser bookmarking facilities). Using a space to delimit the beginning and end of a keyword means that for two-word tags one has to either join the words together (e.g. 'sanfrancisco') or use another method, such as a hyphen (e.g. 'san-francisco'). As part of the service, Delicious recommends tags that the user might like to associate with a particular website, based on knowledge gained from other users.

Once a user has saved a number of bookmarks, they can look at them by clicking the 'Delicious' button at the top of the page. This produces a screen where the stored bookmarks are listed alongside their metadata (see Figure 12.3). From here, the user can edit the bookmarks, delete them, and control how they are displayed, i.e. in alphabetical order

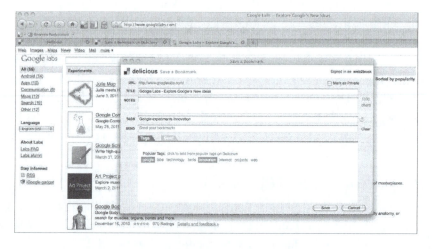

FIGURE 12.2 Entering metadata about a bookmark. (Reproduced with kind permission from AVOS Systems, Inc. All rights reserved.)

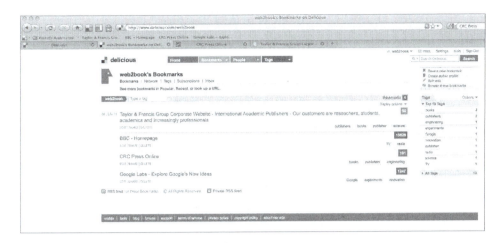

FIGURE 12.3   Bookmarks in Delicious. A list of bookmarks is shown to the left of the screen. To the right there is a list of the user's tags. Access to other people's bookmarks is through the People menu at the top centre of the page. (Reproduced with permission from AVOS Systems, Inc. All rights reserved.)

or by date etc. To the right of this screen there is a list of the user's tags, which can be reordered. Tags can also be viewed as a tag cloud (in a 'cloud' the size of the word reflects its popularity) and be given its own description (which helps when more than one user makes use of the same tag but ascribes different meanings).

As the user collects more and more bookmarks and tags the functionality improves. A user can, for example, use tags to display lists of bookmarks which have all been tagged with the same descriptor, or bundle the tags into groups to create a sort of logic in which a number of tags are conceptually linked. So, for example, a user might organise 'cats', 'dogs' and 'pythons' tags into a bundle called 'pets'.

Although one can use the Delicious system on its own, its real power emerges when bookmarks and tags are shared. It has long been the practice of Web users to share lists of their favourite websites with each other, but until the introduction of social bookmarking tools this could be quite awkward (users might swap e-mail lists of URIs within a work team for example, or export copies of their browser's own bookmark lists).

Sharing bookmarks has a number of consequences. For example, if a user views their own list, they will see a number, on the right-hand side, showing how many other people have bookmarked the same webpages. Clicking on the number shows the details of the other users and the metadata they have added. In this way a user can find others who have similar interests and see their whole bookmark collections. In addition, a user can click on another user's tag and see what else they have tagged with that particular keyword. This creates a kind of tag-based serendipity as a user browses from one tag collection to another, surfing the use of tags.

A third consequence is that users share explicitly by publicizing their Delicious URI. So for example, I have: www.delicious.com/web2book. By adding this to my e-mail signature or by placing a link in my blog I can make my bookmark collection public. Anyone can click on this link and see my list of bookmarks, but only those that have not been marked as private.*

12.1.1 Collective Tagging

Delicious was originally designed to help the process of finding and re-using links. As more and more people used the site however, it became clear that something else was emerging—a form of collective endeavour that tagged and shared website links from across the entire Web. There was no one in charge and individual users made their own decisions freely about what and how to tag: there was no taxonomy nor any control over the process.

One of the most powerful features of Delicious, and other similar systems, is to click on a tag and drill down to see the webpages that other people have tagged with that descriptor. This ability to reorientate the view by clicking on tags is called *pivot browsing*, and it is an alternative to search engines as it provides an intuitive mechanism to navigate the aggregated bookmark collection (Millen et al. 2005).

Delicious also creates a webpage for each tag so the user can see at a glance a list of all the pages that have been bookmarked with that particular tag. Alternatively, there is a page for just the most popular sites for a given tag.†

12.1.2 Messaging

Social bookmarking sites provide messaging facilities to promote interaction between users, as this can be used to share bookmarks. Every user has an in-box, a sort of e-mail system, and bookmarks are sent to other users by adding a tag labelled 'for: auser', where 'auser' is their site username (carried out when adding the bookmark's metadata), and can also be sent to Twitter or to a standard e-mail.

12.1.3 Networks

Delicious users can also create a Network, a group of other site users who they know personally or work with. This is accessed via the 'My Network' link on a user's homepage. After adding people to a network, clicking on 'My Network' will collate and display all the bookmarks that the users in the network have added recently.

12.1.4 Subscriptions

A user can 'watch' a favourite tag or tags by *subscribing* to them. The system will then monitor the entire site for new bookmarks with particular tags and display them in the user's subscription page. In this way a user can keep track of developments in a particular subject.

12.1.5 Search

Delicious provides a sophisticated search mechanism with a timeline, showing when bookmarks were added and allowing the user to refine the search to a particular time or

---

* When a new bookmark is being added to the system the user is given the choice as to whether to make it private or not. Non-private bookmarks (the default) can be seen by, and searched for, by other users.
† So, for example, compare http://delicious.com/tag/web2.0 and http://delicious.com/popular/Web2.0

FIGURE 12.4   A tag cloud of the most popular tags on Delicious. (Reproduced with permission from AVOS Systems, Inc. All rights reserved.).

date. The system also provides suggestions, as the user types in their search terms, as to other ways that the search might be refined. So, for example, as one types in 'Web 2.0', suggestions appear that include 'Web 2.0 conferences', 'Web 2.0 applications' and 'Web 2.0 design'. Requesting only those results that match a particular group of bookmarks refines the search further. Thus, a user can search for all the bookmarks that match the search term 'Web 2.0', added in the last 24 hours, that have been tagged with 'MySpace'. Another alternative is to use the 'Explore' menu from the Delicious homepage, which presents a tag cloud of the most popular tags in the system (see Figure 12.4).

12.1.6 The Bookmarking Zeitgeist

Finally, it is worth noting that by visiting the Delicious homepage (rather than a user's own homepage) one can see a selection of the most popular and recently added bookmarks. This provides a kind of ever-changing snapshot of what users are currently interested in and can be used as a way of keeping up with what's happening on the Web. This page also displays a list of the most popular tags, allowing the user to drill down quickly to the bookmarks associated with those tags.

12.2 A SHORT HISTORY OF DELICIOUS

Delicious was developed by Joshua Schachter, an electronics graduate and equities analyst at Morgan Stanley, in September 2003 (Heilemann 2006; Surowiecki 2006). It was originally known as del.icio.us, a brand name and URI naming 'trick' that it retained until mid-2008. As is often the case with the genesis of new developments on the Web, Schachter was driven by his own personal need. He was the founder, in 1998, of a multi-author blog called Memepool. As an early example of blogging, it was more of a list of interesting links than the kind of online journal or commentary we are familiar with today, and as such it needed to handle large numbers of links to other websites.

Schachter had over 20,000 webpage bookmarks in a file and he wanted a way to organise them, so he wrote a programme, which he called MuxWay, that organised the links based on tags. Interest in his solution grew and following a rewrite of the system he launched it on the Web as del.icio.us. He presented an early version of the system at Foo Camp,* 2003. At the camp his demonstration impressed Web browser pioneer Marc Andreessen, who provided servers to help support the development of the project (Lacey 2008). In 2005, Schachter resigned from his job at Morgan Stanley and devoted himself full-time to developing the site, which was acquired by Yahoo! later that year. In June 2008 he left Yahoo!, just a month or two before the company released a new version and renamed the site with its current brand—Delicious. In December 2010 Yahoo! announced that it was considering plans to seek a new home for the bookmarking site outside the company[†] and the site was sold to AVOS (a start-up led by YouTube's Chad Hurley and Steve Chen) in April 2011.[‡] In September 2011 AVOS announced plans for a revamped site that will organise and share links focused on topical issues and events (Wortham 2011).

12.3 THE SOCIAL BOOKMARKING ECOSYSTEM

Although it is the most widely used, Delicious is not the only social bookmarking system. Indeed, IBM's DogEar, which now forms part of the company's Lotus system, was one of the first to pioneer social bookmarking (Millen et al. 2006) and Redden (2010) cites evidence of a notes system called itList. As with many Web 2.0 ideas there have been a number of similar systems that have ceased functioning as the market has matured, including Furl and BackFlip.

Currently, the WordPress blogging software provides a plug-in that claims to help bloggers post the links they find to more than 200 different SBSs (although this includes a number of non-English language services). Other well-known examples include Yahoo! Bookmarks, Google Toolbar Bookmarks, Diigo, BlinkList, Faves, ZigTag[§] and ShiftSpace.

Some of these systems have additional features often known as *collaborative annotating*. Diigo for example allows a user to highlight text on a webpage and add 'sticky' notes that can be shared just like tagged bookmarks. The open source ShiftSpace offers a similar set of features. When a ShiftSpace user presses the shift and space keys together (when viewing a webpage), other users' metadata (such as highlighted sticky notes) are displayed on top of the Web content.

In addition to these general-purpose solutions, a number of specialist, academic reference systems have also been launched. These have additional features that make them more useful for academic research, e.g. to automatically extract citation metadata from a

---

* An annual technology conference hosted by O'Reilly Media.
† See http://thenextweb.com/media/2010/12/17/official-delicious-is-not-shutting-down/
‡ See: http://www.avos.com/delicious-press-release/
§ ZigTag is interesting as it also provides for what it calls 'defined' tags. The user can choose tags from lists of words with clear, pre-defined meanings rather than use their own words with their own personal meanings.

bookmark's source. Popular examples include CiteULike, Zotero, the University of Kassel's Bibsonomy, and *Nature* magazine's Connotea.

Academic libraries have also become involved in the development of tagging tools to bookmark specialist content. Leading US examples include Pennsylvania State University's PennTags system and Harvard's H20. Related to this is the LibraryThing Web service, which provides users with a way to document their book collections and reading lists, tag them, and share the information.

12.4 RESEARCH

Although there is a body of research dedicated to the study of social bookmarking it is worth noting that a great deal of this material relates to tagging content more generally, and there is a strong cross-over with research into media sharing systems, which also use tags, such as Flickr. Ding et al. (2009) for example compare Delicious, YouTube and Flickr. Related to this is the discussion of tagging in *harnessing the power of the crowd* (Chapter 5). It should also be noted that there has been considerable interest in the applicability of tagging systems to digital libraries, with considerable debate over concepts such as indexing and controlled vocabularies.[*]

Farooq et al. (2007) point out the importance of understanding tagging behaviour in social bookmarking systems and being able to develop metrics for it. This is because such work feeds into improving the systems and informs wider discussions about knowledge diffusion. Ding et al. (2009) argue that as tagging systems are implicated in any discussion of the wisdom of crowds they may help with the continuing problem of finding information on the Web. Understanding bookmarking systems and their processes can also help in the fight against spammers, who target sites like Delicious more and more often (Markines et al. 2009) in order to direct traffic to certain sites or more simply, just to disrupt the system.

As a final point, it should be noted that although we have made a clear distinction between folksonomies and collaborative tagging, this is often lost in academic literature, where the two terms are often used interchangeably. Recall that in Chapter 5 we noted that folksonomy is a process of tagging by oneself for oneself and that although this is sometimes carried out in a social setting (and may result in a collection of tags that are shared), the actual process is not intentionally collaborative. Since my approach has been to retain the terminology used by the original researchers, students will need to refer to the original papers to ascertain exactly how the terms are used.

12.4.1 Social Bookmarking and Tag Metrics

As we should now be able to see, measuring the size and growth of Web 2.0 services is pretty much standard practice and social bookmarking is no exception. Ding et al. (2009) found considerable growth in Delicious over the years since its launch, which was substantiated by Wetzker et al. (2008) who note that nearly 300,000 tags and 50,000 users per month were being added by early 2008. However, the TechCrunch technology

---

[*] McGregor and McCulloch (2006) provide a useful introduction.

website quotes more recent figures that seem to show a slight drop-off in activity in 2010.[*]

Golder and Huberman (2006) reviewed site usage over time, looking at Delicious in the summer of 2005. They found that users vary enormously in how frequently they use the site and the nature of that use. The size of the tag sets that users maintained—the number of unique tags that they allocated to bookmarked sites—also varied widely. There were thousands of users who had fewer than 100 unique tags in use, but a small number made use of between 800 and 900 tags. Interestingly, there was *not* found to be a strong relationship between the number of bookmarks that a user created and the number of unique tags used. For example, some used a lot more unique tags as the number of sites they bookmarked increased, whereas in other cases users tended to retain the same set of tags and constantly re-use them.

These results have been replicated by other researchers, with several finding that the application of tags follows a power law (Halpin et al. 2007; Farooq et al. 2007; Wetzker et al. 2008; Zhang et al. 2006). Wetzker et al. (2008) also showed that the number of bookmarks per URI follows a power law.

Cattuto et al. (2007b) reported similar findings for Bibsonomy as well as Delicious. They found that the characteristic path length of Delicious was about 3.5 and remained fairly constant despite the rapid growth of the site during the test period. The clustering coefficients were quite high at 0.86 for Delicious and even higher, 0.97, for Bibsonomy. These figures indicate the presence of a small world network as discussed in Chapter 7. Short path lengths mean that users may easily find new content serendipitously since it is relatively easy to traverse the entire network of tagged content.

12.4.2 Tag Analysis

Golder and Huberman (2006) have analysed the tags according to seven different functions:

- Identifying what (or who) the bookmarked site is about: this covered the majority of tags

- Identifying what it is: whether it is a blog, journal article, book's site etc.

- Identifying who created the bookmarked content

- Refining tags: adding detail to existing tags

- Identifying qualities or characteristics: adding descriptive words such as 'funny'

- Self-reference tags: tags beginning with 'my', e.g. 'mystuff'

- Task tags: sites that have been collated for a particular task, e.g. 'jobsearch'.

As the authors point out, the tension between tags that are useful only to the individual and those that might be of more interest to the wider Delicious user base is clear. The first three types of tag are clearly likely to be of wider relevance whereas this is less so as we get

---

[*] See: http://www.crunchbase.com/company/delicious

to the end of the list. Ding et al. (2009) provided a similar analysis, but compared the types of tags used and their frequency across Delicious, YouTube and Flickr.

Suchanek et al. (2008) looked at nearly 300,000 tags in Delicious and found that more than half did not appear in a dictionary, i.e. did not have a recognizable meaning.* This, they argue, confirms the widespread use of made-up personal tags (such as 'toberead') and misspellings, personal abbreviations and proper nouns. Unsurprisingly, this was found to be much higher than a similar analysis that was undertaken on the meaningfulness of words used in the titles and content of webpages. They also found that amongst the 'meaningful' tags there is a great deal of polysemy—words that have more than one meaning. However, further analysis showed that the most popular tags for a resource, i.e. the ones used most often by different users for the same bookmark, consisted of more meaningful terms. Furthermore, the larger the number of users who tagged a bookmark, the more meaningful the top tags became, and this improved significantly once 100 users had tagged a resource. Yeung et al. (2009) took the analysis of tags further, considering the social and conceptual context in which the tag word is used and addressing problems of tag ambiguity.

This kind of work is very closely related to discussions about folksonomy and collaborative tagging and often involves the development of models in which users, tags and the resources being tagged are related through graph structures.

12.4.3 Stability

A central question with respect to SBSs is whether or not they can become relatively stable over time. That is, can the users develop a reasonable *consensus* over which tags are best as descriptions of a particular webpage (Halpin et al. 2007). Since there is no centralized expertise involved, nor an overarching controlled vocabulary, it is possible that no such consensus will ever emerge. Questions of stability with respect to the use of tag vocabulary on SBSs have a direct link to debates about so-called collective intelligence, discussed in Chapter 5. A related, and emerging area of study (which assumes that stable vocabularies can and do emerge out of these systems), is *semiotic dynamics*, which investigates how humans establish and share meaning within systems (Cattuto et al. 2007a).

Golder and Huberman (2006) found that an individual URI tends to be tagged in a pattern that stabilizes over time. As a URI is bookmarked by different users, the set of tags used and the frequency with which they are used represents the combined description of many users. The authors found that after a URI had been bookmarked around 100 times, each tag's usage became a nearly fixed proportion of the total frequency of all the tags used. They argue that this shows that after a relatively small amount of activity on the site, a "nascent consensus seems to form, one that is not affected by the addition of further tags" (p. 206). Since this happens at around the one hundred tag mark, a site's URI does not need to be particularly popular for its associated tag collection to be of use to the wider community. The authors speculate as to the cause of this process, arguing that it may be

---

* They used a dictionary consisting of a combination of WordNet and YAGO, two semantic databases.

due to something known as *social proof*,[*] i.e. viewing an action as correct because others are doing it (since the Delicious system makes suggestions based on the tags others have already used). Alternatively, the consensus may in fact represent genuine shared knowledge among the taggers. The research team concludes by arguing that this stability may mean that social bookmarking is of use in the on-going struggle to navigate the Web.

In contrast, Farooq et al. (2007), when looking at CiteULike, found that the tag vocabulary seemed to demonstrate consistent growth. Over the period of their investigation, the number of new tags being applied was around 130–550 per month and stayed within this range throughout the 2.5 years of the data collection period (November 2004 to February 2007). They speculated that CiteULike was still maturing, with consistent growth in new users being reflected in new vocabulary. The authors posit that this may be in contrast to the manner in which Delicious has developed, since CiteULike is a niche product aimed at academics and therefore may take longer to reach tag use maturity.

The authors also looked at data for tag reuse across different bookmarks. They found that this followed a power law with an exponential of −1.67 showing that a large number of tags (over a thousand) were re-used once and around 500 were re-used twice, followed by a rapid drop-off with the familiar long tail. Further analysis showed that most users did not re-use tags from other users, but did re-use tags from their own personal collection of previously used tags. This seems to be in sharp contrast to the analysis of Delicious. The authors speculated that this may be due to the way that the CiteULike interface worked at the time (i.e. it did not prompt users with tags from other users when the tag allocation process was taking place). They also found that there were 1.59 users per tag, which they argue is fairly low compared with other social bookmarking systems.

Halpin et al. (2007) found that the frequency of tag usage on the most heavily tagged webpages[†] on Delicious exhibited a power law with an exponential of −1.278. They argue that SBSs can be thought of as examples of the kind of complex network systems that we discussed at length in Chapter 7. If this were true then SBSs ought to exhibit forms of tag use stability, and in particular would show power law distributions, something that their research confirmed. The authors conclude that what they see in Delicious shows that "over time a stable distribution with a limited number of stable tags and a much larger 'long tail' of more idiosyncratic tags develops" (p. 220).

An alternative analysis of stability has been provided by Ding et al. (2009) who looked at the top twenty tag terms across the years 2005–2007 for Delicious. They found that these sets were relatively stable and, they argued, show that the users have a particular interest in programming and Web development.

12.4.4 Relationships between Tags

If two tags are used more frequently by different users, or are used to bookmark the same websites, can they be considered to be more related to each other? These sorts of questions

---

[*] Social proof in tagging also relates to the idea of literary warrant, which has been used for decades in the library community.

[†] They looked at those awarded a 'popular' status by Delicious.

are at the heart of research into the relationship between tags with, for example, Shen and Wu (2005) arguing that these kinds of connections can be used to model the properties of the 'folksonomies'* that different sites are constructing, and thus have important implications for some of the issues discussed in Chapter 5. The authors created a graph of nodes, each of which consisted of a tag taken from Delicious. The links between nodes represented instances where tags shared a correspondence, that is, both tags were used on a particular bookmark. So, if the tags 'Web 2.0' and 'Internet' were both applied to a particular book-marked URI, then a link would be made between these tags. This was then repeated for all the bookmarks in the system. The resulting tag graph demonstrated properties associated with small world networks, with an average path length of 3.4. The graph also demon-strated the properties of a scale-free network.

In a similar vein, Ding et al. (2009) analysed sets of what they called *co-tags*, different tags that have *co-occurred*, i.e. been applied to the same webpage by different taggers. They examined data from Delicious and found ten primary clusters of such tags. For example, one cluster consisted of the tags: ajax, C, code, development, html, java, library, .net, python and rails—all software development–related words. Yeung et al. (2009) have also undertaken a similar analysis, exploring the differences between co-occurrence in different scenarios.

12.4.5 Tag Recommendation Systems

Tag recommendation systems automate the process of selecting tags to add to websites when they are being bookmarked (Song et al. 2011). Research into suitable methods and the development of systems form part of a wider study into the recommendation problem in general, for example to suggest books on an e-commerce site or make music recommen-dations etc. (Adomavicius and Tuzhilin 2005).

As we have already seen, Delicious recommends suitable tags for a resource based on what other users have done, and Song et al. (2011) argue that there are two main approaches: user-centric and document-centric. The former aims to model user interests based on informa-tion about how they have tagged content in the past, and also on tag data from users who have similar interests or belong to the same groups. Examples of this way of working include Jäschke et al. (2008), Bogers and Bosch (2008), Boratto et al. (2009) and Lipczak (2008).

Document-centric approaches focus on the resource being tagged, and analysing its con-tents. Examples of work using this approach include Chirita et al. (2007) and Adomavicius et al. (2005). There have also been some attempts to develop hybrid techniques and a useful introduction to these is provided by Adomavicius and Tuzhilin (2005).

12.4.6 User Motivation

Strohmaier et al. (2010) and Körner et al. (2010) summarize research work in another important area: motivations for tagging. They note two key areas: categorization and

---

* Note that although the paper discusses the role of tags in creating a folksonomy in two different types of system (book-marking and photo sharing) in fact, based on the observation made earlier, the author uses the terms collaborative tag-ging and folksonomy interchangeably.

description. This distinction may seem slight to some, but to others, particularly those who work in information science, it is very important.

In a nutshell, the two teams of researchers found that users who tag and categorise are focused on constructing and maintaining a navigational aid for browsing, whilst users who tag and describe are creating a resource for searching. However, it is clear that taggers often use the techniques interchangeably. Both sets of research demonstrated that motivation varies between and within different tagging systems and that motivation has an effect on the tag collections that are produced. This may matter for how future social bookmarking systems are developed, since the motivation for tagging can be linked to the usefulness of a set of tags for a particular information retrieval task.

Heckner et al. (2009) also considered motivation, but concluded that how and why people use social bookmarking remains an open research question. They interviewed individuals about their use of tagging systems and compared their data with other systems such as Flickr and YouTube. They argue that users have two clear intentions: personal information management (i.e. for their own retrieval) and resource sharing across a community. They found that personal information management is the more important motivation for Delicious and Connotea users.

Related to this is the *balance* between social bookmarking for one's own personal information storage and retrieval processes, and more co-operative and social bookmarking in order to develop the site as a community tool (Lipczak and Milios 2010; Suchanek et al. 2008; Ding et al. 2009). This type of work is important since it relates directly to the claims made by proponents of the idea of folksonomies.

To aid investigation into the communal nature of SBSs, Capocci et al. (2009) have looked at temporal patterns in tagging by studying Delicious, CiteULike and Bibsonomy. In particular they were interested to see if there was evidence of some form of co-operation between users across the site. They looked at the time interval between different uses of the same tag across a system and found that the tag inter-arrival time followed a power law distribution with an exponent of 1.3. Using a rather complex analysis they concluded that this particular measure does not indicate some kind of interaction between users, since it reflects statistical properties of language.

However, they observed that the inter-arrival times of tags for the same resource are distributed according to a power law with a sharp drop off at large values of time, but extend in a long tail towards infinity. This, they argued, shows that users are not tagging completely independently of each other. This is further backed up by evidence (also found by others) that the vocabulary (i.e. the use of distinct tags by different users for the same resource) grows in a sub-linear manner so that the pace of introduction of new tags decreases over time. In other words, users have a tendency to employ previously used tags when describing the same resource. Incidentally they also speculate that their statistical methods may be of use for spotting tags that are spam.

In contrast Rader and Wash (2008) reported that a user's tag choice is not the result of imitating others, but seems to fit individual, idiosyncratic patterns. This would imply that users are tagging predominately for personal, 'selfish' reasons, i.e. to order their own information. Their work involved analysing the behaviour of 12,000 Delicious users who had tagged thirty, randomly selected URIs in June 2007. They categorised the tags into three groups: imitation (tags that imitate previous users who have tagged the same page); organisation (users that re-use tags they have applied to other pages) and recommendation (tags that are chosen from the Delicious list of recommended suggestions). They found a clear pattern—the strongest influence was users' previous tag choices. Further work using computer models of tag choice strategies seemed to confirm these results and in addition, Lipczak and Milios (2010) back up these conclusions, finding little evidence in their results for collaborative behaviour between users.

EXERCISES AND POINTS TO PONDER

1. Compare the facilities offered by Delicious and one of the academic bookmark systems, for example CiteULike, Bibsonomy or Zotero. Write a short note on what the key differences are. What are the features of the academic systems that make them more suitable for scholarly activity?

2. Over a period of weeks, create and curate a social bookmarking account within Delicious (or another system of your choosing) to use in your studies. What do you notice about the relationships between the tags that you assign? How useful is it to see what others have tagged with the same terms? Compare your tag collection with another student's collection. What features would emerge from a folksonomy based on your two tag collections?

3. The tag cloud is an important concept in social bookmarking and in developing Web-based software that exhibits some of the ideas of collective intelligence discussed in Chapter 5. When you have read these two chapters, develop a software program to display tag clouds. In order to do this, set up an account on the Delicious social bookmarking site and populate it with content and suitable tags. Develop a software program that uses the Delicious Application Programming Interface (API) to extract details of these tags and then display a tag cloud. Details of the Delicious API are provided at: http://www.delicious.com/help/api and you may find this Web Monkey article on the API also of use: http://www.webmonkey.com/2010/02/using_the_delicious_api/. There is also a detailed discussion of different programming approaches in Chapter 3 of Satnam Alag's book (Alag 2009) which you may find helpful.

FURTHER READING

As is the case with other social media, bookmarking systems are also the target of spam, for further information see Kolay and Dasdan (2009).

An emerging research area is the impact of social bookmarking and tagging on existing information retrieval (IR) techniques. A useful introduction is provided in Seki et al. (2010).

In Chapter 15 we discuss the future of the Web including the emerging Semantic Web. There has been an overlap in research work that studies folksonomies, tagging and recommendation systems and investigations into the ontological aspects of the Semantic Web. Useful introductions to this include Specia and Motta (2007), Angeletou et al. (2007) and Gruber (2007).

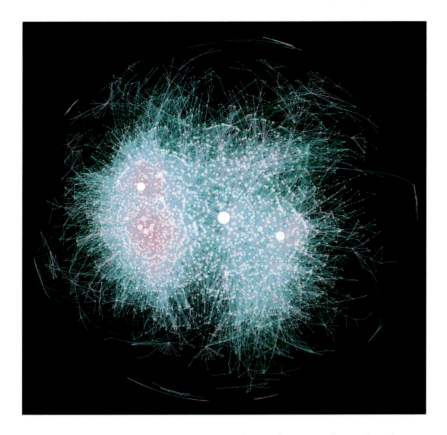

FIGURE 0.1   Internet blog map. Computer generated map showing relationships between Internet weblogs (blogs). (From Matthew Hurst/Science Photo Library. With permission.)

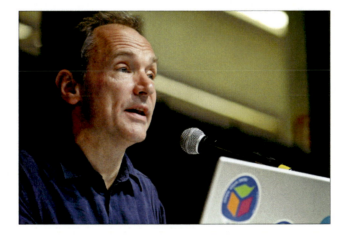

FIGURE 1.1   Sir Tim Berners-Lee (From Flickr, photo by Silvio Tanaka, Creative Commons Attribution 2.0 Generic (CC BY 2.0) See: http://www.flickr.com/photos/tanaka/3212373419/)

FIGURE 1.2 Tim O'Reilly (From Flickr, photo by Robert Scoble, Creative Commons Attribution 2.0 Generic (CC BY 2.0). See: http://www.flickr.com/photos/scobleizer/2228299097/sizes/l/in/photostream/)

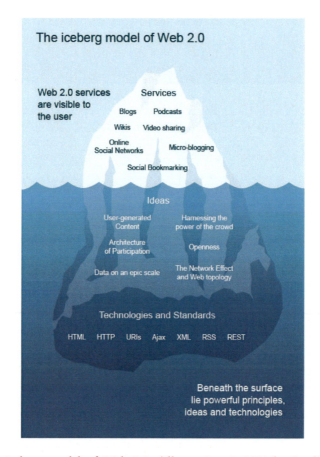

FIGURE 1.3 The iceberg model of Web 2.0. (Illustration © 2011 by Intelligent Content Ltd Licensed under a Creative Commons Attribution-NonCommercial-NoDerivs 3.0 Unported license (CC BY-NR-ND 3.0))

FIGURE 13.3 The Twitterverse. (From Brian Solis, published by Flickr, distributed under Creative Commons CC BY 2.0. See: http://www.flickr.com/photos/briansolis/5317948711/sizes/l/in/photostream/)

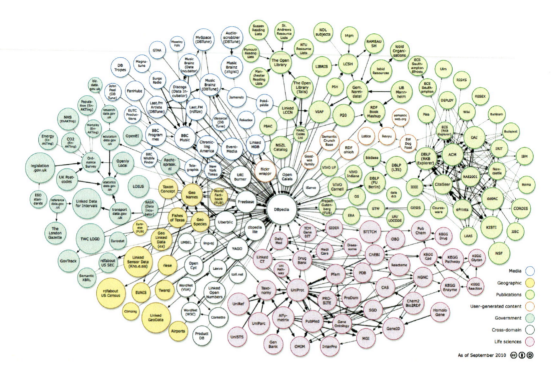

FIGURE 15.3 The Linked Data Cloud showing datasets that are published in Linked Data format and interlinked with other datasets in the cloud. As of September 2010. (From Wikimedia Commons, image by Anjeve and Richard Cyganiak. Attribution-ShareAlike 3.0 Unreported (CC BY-SA 3.0).*)

* See: http://en.wikipedia.org/wiki/File:Lod-datasets_2010-09-22_colored.png

## CHAPTER 13

Microblogging Services

We've been described as a "telegraph for Web 2.0".

ALEX PAYNE
Twitter engineer (Venners 2009, webpage)

Present tense blogging.

JASON GOLDMAN
Product manager for blogger (Stone 2006, webpage)

Microblogging software provides a kind of quick and easy instant messaging service for the Web. It is usually used to publish links to interesting content and post updates on what users are currently doing, where they are, what they are thinking about etc. It forms a key part of an emerging set of real-time information tools that allow the generation and consumption of nearly instantaneous information. Sometimes referred to as the *real-time Web* (Phelan et al. 2011; Bermingham and Smeaton 2010), other examples of these tools include Facebook's newsfeeds, data streams provided by Web apps and new generations of mobile, sensor-based and ubiquitous computer applications.

Java et al. (2007) note two key, related differences between blogging and its micro cousin: thanks to the brevity of posted messages microblogging provides a much faster means of communication which in turn encourages far more frequent updating. The authors note, seemingly without irony, that "By encouraging shorter posts, it lowers users' requirement of time and thought investment for content generation" (p. 57). This speed and brevity has been the catalyst for a change in the way that people communicate. For example, microblogging is increasingly being used by non-journalists to break news stories and pass on time-sensitive information, disintermediating the mainstream media. During various protests across the Middle East in the early spring of 2011, Twitter was used extensively to pass on information about what was happening 'on the ground'. As new media consultant Brian Solis put it in a Bloomberg *Businessweek* debate: "News no longer breaks, *it tweets*".*

---

* http://www.briansolis.com/2011/05/this-just-in-news-no-longer-breaks-it-tweets/

However, Twitter is just one of a number of microblogging services that include: Identi. ca (based on free software called StatusNet), Jaiku, Yammer, Tumblr, Hictu, EdModo, Bloomba, Plurk, Bliin, and Sina Weibo (a leading Chinese service). Indeed, microblogging is particularly popular in China, where they make use of the largest non-Twitter services. In addition, Chinese character writing means that far more information can be conveyed in the small number of words allowed in a microblogging post, altering the nature of this kind of Web 2.0 activity in China (a whole news story can, for example, be contained in a hundred or so characters) (Canaves 2001).

Of course, not all microblogging sites provide the same type of service. For example, Bloomba focuses on providing a user with a way to tell a story about a particular event in their life by adding photos, video and messages related to that event, rather than simply posting a short message. Services like this form a bridge between microblogging and another form of Web 2.0 service known as lifelogging or *lifecasting*, in which users record as much as possible about their daily lives and provide the information, in real-time, to the wider public.[*] However, for the purpose of this chapter we will stay with Twitter as it is by far the most popular and best-known microblogging service, and it has been the subject of the largest body of research.

13.1 INTRODUCTION TO TWITTER

The basic mechanism of the Twitter service is the update or 'Tweet' of 140 characters[†]—a short, pithy response to Twitter's persistent question: 'What's happening?' A user can opt to 'follow' other users, which means that they register to receive all the Tweets posted by those particular people. These are then combined into one big, real-time 'conversation' on the user's private homepage.

WHY 140 CHARACTERS?

People often wonder why there is this limit. When the system was originally built it was designed to use the mobile/cell telephone network's Short Message Service (SMS) text message service which has a limit of 160 characters. Twitter needed to include a username with each message so they compromised on a maximum of 140 characters for the message plus 20 characters for the username. This should have been a handicap, but in fact there has been considerable experimentation, for example in the use of slang, shortened lingo, ASCII (pronounced ask-ee) emoticons and other tokens (Davidov et al. 2010). This enforced brevity has not only made this form of communication attractive to large numbers of people, but also facilitated the development of a kind of pithy but continual global conversation. Or as Twitter co-founder Biz Stone put it to the *San Francisco Chronicle*: "Creativity comes from constraint" (Zinko 2009, webpage).

---

[*] Key examples of this kind of service include Your Truman Show and Ustream.

[†] Technically it is 140 bytes rather than characters. The system uses the UTF-8 character encoding (a standard way of representing written text in computer systems) and since some special characters in that encoding can take up to four bytes, a Twitter message may in fact be shorter than 140 characters but still take up the full number of bytes.

FIGURE 13.1 A Twitter homepage. On the left hand side is the Twitter timeline. On the right hand side is the most recent Tweet, details of the user's followees and followers, plus various suggestions from the site's software of people to consider following. (Reproduced courtesy of Twitter Inc., © 2011 Twitter Inc.)

Figure 13.1 shows a logged-in user's homepage, the main hub from where the Twitter conversation flows. A long list of incoming messages from a variety of sources is displayed down the left-hand column of the page. These messages are arranged in chronological order and this column is known as the *Twitter timeline*, a kind of information junction to which messages flow. This constitutes a user's personal Twitter conversation with others.*

At the top of the right-hand column is the user's most recent Tweet and a running total of the number of sent messages. Perhaps unsurprisingly the *following* link takes the user to a list of all the people they are following,† together with buttons that permit certain actions to be carried out on each one. For example, one can decide to temporarily block someone if their Tweets are becoming unsavoury or boring, stop following them all together, or report them for sending spam. The 'followers' link is equivalent to the 'following' link, but for people who are following the user.

The other important aspect of Twitter is the Profile page, which displays personal information about the user and a list of the Tweets that they have sent recently. It is also the publicly accessible homepage for a particular user and is therefore their public representation on Twitter, but it is also more than this: it is a way of distinguishing the individual from the conversation.

13.1.1 Sending a Tweet

Figure 13.2 shows the process of sending a Tweet. As the user types, a grey number next to the 'Tweet' button changes to red as the number of available characters diminishes. If the user goes over the allotted 140 characters then the number becomes negative and the message cannot be sent. A message posted in this way is public—anyone using Twitter can see it by visiting the user's profile page. However, most Twitter users do not usually view others' messages in this way—they elect to follow them instead.

---

* Note the format of the messages: there is a picture or photograph of the person who sent the Tweet (displayed as a hyperlink through to that user's Twitter homepage), the text of the message (which may contain links to webpages) and, below the message, the time or date the message was sent.

† Early versions of Twitter used the term 'friends' to describe the people you followed. The Twitter Application Programming Interface API still makes reference to this term and some academic research also discusses 'friends' and 'friendship'.

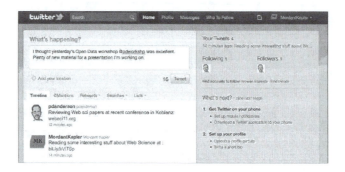

FIGURE 13.2   Adding a Tweet. Note the small grey counter next to the 'Tweet' button that shows how many characters are left. Clicking the button will publish the message. (Reproduced courtesy of Twitter Inc., © 2011 Twitter Inc.)

A useful innovation has been the widespread adoption of what are called *hashtags*.* These are single words preceded by the 'hash' (#) sign and are used in a similar way to tags, to indicate what the Tweet is about. So a user might include #pinkfloyd when writing about the English rock band. Hashtags are usually agreed to amongst the community, although sometimes this is done more formally. For example, if one is attending a conference then the organisers may pre-announce the agreed hashtag so that attendees can make sure they all use the same one. There are no rules however, and any user can make up their own tag and attempt to get wider adoption.

13.1.1.1 Replying, Mentioning, Retweeting and Direct Messaging

Twitter is essentially a real-time conversation and the software provides a number of ways, other than a standard Tweet, to exchange messages with other users. The first, and most important, is known as a reply.

Every Tweet that appears in the timeline includes a *reply* link beneath it. Clicking this link creates a new Tweet in the text entry box, beginning with the @ sign and followed by the username of the person who published the original message.† Beginning a Tweet with the @username format means that the message will appear in both the user's and the originator's timeline. It is used to make a comment or add further information to the originator's Tweet. However, things can get complicated and the first-time user is encouraged to experiment. For example, who exactly sees the reply? The basic rule is that if a person you are following replies to another person you are following, then the reply will also appear in your timeline. Otherwise it does not. This default can, however, be changed by adjusting one's user account settings.

Twitter provides an easy way to see what people are saying in response to your Tweets by filtering all messages to find those that *mention* you, i.e. any Tweet that has included your '@username' identifier. These are presented as a list that is accessed through

---

* To make use of hashtags, a user must follow the @ hashtags service at: http://twitter.com/hashtags. Further details and the search facility are at: http://www.hashtags.org/

† For students of technology history, it is worth noting that the use of the @ symbol to indentify a particular user harks back to an older technology known as Internet Relay Chat (IRC) (boyd et al. 2010). In this context, @ was used to demarcate the IRC channel operator from other users.

the '@mentions' link (see Figure 13.1). This may seem a bit odd, since you can already see any replies in the conversation timeline. However, the timeline only shows Tweets from the people you are following, whereas the @mentions list shows mentions from all parts of the Twitter 'forest'.

Retweeting is essentially a technique for forwarding a Tweet in a similar way to forwarding an e-mail (boyd et al. 2010). Again, as with replying, there is a 'retweet' link beneath the original message. Clicking this link will copy the message to your followers where it will appear with a small retweet icon and the usernames of both the originator and the retweeter.

The fourth way to communicate is to send a *direct message*. This is a bit like an e-mail in that messages are sent directly from one user to another (they can only be sent between people who are following each other) but they are not displayed in public and do not appear on any conversation timeline. Access to direct messages is through the 'Messages' menu, which takes the user to a screen that is similar to an e-mail client. There is also the option to configure your user account so that direct messages are also sent as real e-mail to an e-mail address.

13.1.2 Following the Twitter Conversation

In order to follow another user the first step is to find them. The easiest way is to use their Twitter Uniform Resource Identifier (URI) which links to their profile page. Just beneath their name and photo there is a 'follow' button, which adds that particular user to the list of people you are following.*

Another way to find people to follow is to look at other users' profile pages and see who they follow. Maybe there is someone who is a mutual friend or someone who looks interesting. Clicking on their profile name links to their profile page (as above) where the follow button is. This is similar to the pivot browsing techniques used in social bookmarking systems.

A third way to find people to follow is to use the 'Who to Follow' menu item that is available on the homepage of every user (see top right-hand side of Figure 13.1). This takes you to a search box which can be used to find a particular person's name or Twitter username. Twitter also makes recommendations as to who you might like to follow based on your existing followees and followers. There is also a browse facility that takes you to a list of topics such as science and politics. Once you have chosen a topic, you are presented with a list of suggestions for people to follow, put together by the Twitter system and based on an algorithm that uses popularity as an important factor. Finally, there are also several other ways to find people including inviting, by e-mail, non-Twitter users to join in.

An important debating point within the Twitter community is over whether one should always follow someone who follows you. Krishnamurthy et al. (2008) conducted research into the number of people each user followed and the number of people they are followed by and found three broad groups. Firstly, the *broadcasters*: those who follow a much

---

* This assumes you have registered with Twitter and logged into your account before attempting to follow.

smaller number of people than follow them. Many of these turn out—unsurprisingly—to be organisations such as the BBC or *New York Times* rather than individuals.

The authors call the second group *acquaintances*: users who tend to exhibit reciprocity in their relationships. Thirdly, there are the *evangelists*: a group who follow far more people than they have followers (in the thousands). The authors' interpretation of this was that evangelists contact and follow anyone they can, in the hope that this might be reciprocated. However, some of this third group might also be spammers.

13.1.3 Searching Twitter

There are two main ways to search Twitter: the search box at the top of the page and via a separate search tool at: http://search.twitter.com/. The former provides a 'saved search' facility in order to repeat a particular search via a single click. The latter provides additional ways to filter the search results through an advanced search box (e.g. filter by language or date) and provides a list of trending topics.

Twitter also uses a secret algorithm to analyse the content stream in order to produce a list of the top ten trending topics (Kwak et al. 2010). By default this shows worldwide topics, but it can be configured to show an individual country or even a handful of US cities.

As well as the official Twitter search and filter mechanisms, there is a growing collection of third-party services and search engines that offer similar or related capacity (McFedries 2009). Some of the key services are: Twitterfall, Monitter, TweetBeep, TweetMeme, TwitterMonitor, What the Trend, RowFeeder and TwitAlyzer.

These tools form part of what is starting to be called *real-time search* (Carr 2010; Geer 2010). A number of the leading search engine companies are engaged in research and development to perfect a search tool that can handle the continuous stream of real-time content being generated by Twitter and its ilk. A number of these tools also incorporate information from other Web 2.0 services such as online social networks and news aggregators. There is considerable interest in real-time search, in part because of the potential for what is known as *sentiment mining*—analysing the microblog conversation to gauge changing public opinion etc. (Bollen, Mao, and Zeng 2011; Jansen et al. 2009; Bollen, Mao, and Pepe 2011).

Real-time data presents different challenges from traditional webpage-based search since the information corpus changes rapidly. Google and the other engines track links and analyse various signals (e.g. title of page, keywords in the text etc.) in order to provide a high-quality search result (see Chapter 4). This does not work for real-time search since speed is the overriding priority. A social network site (SNS) or Twitter message may lose its relevance within minutes of being published as the conversation moves on. Early examples of real-time search included OneRiot, CrowdEye and Collecta, but all these services have since closed or are in the process of developing new business models, a sign of how fluid and active this area of technological development is.*

---

* See http://searchengineland.com/what-is-real-time-search-definitions-players-22172

13.1.4 Blogging versus Microblogging

One of the most important uses for Twitter is to pass around useful or interesting weblinks just like the first bloggers. It seems that this urge to spread news about links still remains an important part of the Web's everyday life. Links can be added into the text of a Tweet in their entirety, but since many of them are quite long, most people use a URI shortening service such as TinyURL or Bit.Ly.[*]

However, there are also certain differences between microblogging and blogging and indeed, other forms of social media that are worth highlighting. Unlike blogging, a reader cannot post a comment beneath a Tweet, and conversations are not 'threaded' into subject areas as they might be on an e-mail list or bulletin board. In addition, if a user elects to follow another person this does not have to be reciprocated, unlike other forms of online social networking (Huberman et al. 2008a; Yang and Counts 2010).

13.1.5 Twitter Bots

Not all life on Twitter is human. There are also automated Twitter accounts that are known as *bots*. These can be programmed to respond in certain ways when certain messages are sent to them. A good example is the timer bot (twitter.com/timer). By sending it a message along the lines of 'timer 60 finish chapter', the message 'finish chapter' will be sent after an interval of 60 minutes. There are of course a number of other bots including one for the Internet Movie Database (IMDB), stock updates, a mapping bot, and a weather forecast.[†] In coming years we are also likely to see an increase in the number of Tweets being generated automatically without a prompt message from a user. This is likely to vastly increase the volume of Tweets.[‡]

13.2 A SHORT HISTORY OF TWITTER

oh this is going to be addictive

ONE OF THE FIRST TWITTER MESSAGES SENT DURING TESTING IN 2006

(Sagolla 2006)

In 2005, Evan Williams and Biz Stone left Google to form Odeo, a podcast company. By early 2006, Odeo had shipped a podcast product, but was facing stiff competition from Apple. The spotlight fell on Status, an internal R&D project being developed by Jack Dorsey that pulled together ideas from three technology areas: Internet Relay Chat (IRC), instant messaging (IM) and mobile/cell phone SMS. They were all technologies that had been around for a number of years, and many Internet and mobile/cell phone users had grown up used to this short, punchy way of communicating. However, there was a fourth aspect, which came from Jack Dorsey's experience in the logistics industry writing software for

---

[*] These services turn a full, and usually long, HTTP Web address into a coded URI which is only a few characters long. When a user clicks on the shortened address it gets converted back to the original and takes the user to the correct webpage.

[†] A list is maintained at: http://twitter.pbworks.com/Bots

[‡] See for example Semantic Web entrepreneur Nova Spivack's thoughts on automated Twitter at: http://semanticweb.com/ spivacks-bottleno-se-built-to-match-scale-of-exploding-message-stream_b19023

dispatch riders who communicated using short messages to identify where they were and where they were going (Makice 2009b; Sagolla 2009; Brian et al. 2010).

Status was eventually renamed—the team wanted something more reminiscent of the buzzing of a mobile or cell phone as a new message comes in so they brainstormed and came up with Twitch. It wasn't quite right, so as Dorsey later told the *LA Times*: "So we looked in the dictionary for words around it, and we came across the word "twitter," and it was just perfect. The definition was "a short burst of inconsequential information," and "chirps from birds" (Sarno 2009, website). The software was first released in July 2006 as Twittr, and then taken forward by Twitter Inc., formed in 2007.

Twitter started off slowly, as most technical innovations tend to. In early 2007, it was handling around 20,000 Tweets a day. The first time that the wider Web community took notice of the new product was at the 2007 South by SouthWest (SXSW) conference in Austin, Texas, where the embryonic company had set up large TV screens displaying Tweets about the event as they streamed in. It broke the 60,000 messages a day mark over the weekend of the conference. This led to tremendous interest within the technology development community and within a year it was handling one million messages a day.

In April 2008, the company launched a Japanese version after they noticed a huge surge in traffic from Japan which turned out to be driven by the Tamagotchi craze as each pet was being given its own Twitter account. Growth continued rapidly, approaching 1,400% a year by May 2009 with over six million unique visitors a month. By April 2010, MIT *Technology Review* magazine reported figures of 75 million users (Talbot 2010). A few months later Pew Internet reported that 13% of American adults who were online used Twitter, a significant increase from the previous year (Smith 2011).

13.3 TWITTER TECHNICAL ARCHITECTURE

To a certain extent Twitter has been the victim of its own success and during its first five or so years experienced 'growing pains' (Borland 2008). It was initially developed architecturally as a content management system, written in Ruby on Rails and designed to serve up content in the form of webpages, pulled from a back-end database system. However, the Twitter team learned, as the number of users rose, that a messaging system needs to be more responsive than this structure permits. During the early years, users would sometimes see a picture of a whale (the so-called Fail Whale) displayed on their screens when trying to use the system—this was the company's way of indicating that the amount of traffic had temporarily overwhelmed the company's technical architecture.*

Twitter handles over 1,000 Tweets per second and over one billion search queries a day (Busch 2010). As time has gone by, more of the site's traffic comes via the API than the website, to the extent that, in 2010, this represented 75% of all traffic and changed the requirements for infrastructure (Adams 2010a). To give one example of how such a high rate of growth can affect operations, in 2009 there was an event known as the *twitpocalypse*, when the 32-bit signed integer used for Tweet IDs ran out of available numbers (it is limited

---

* Originally designed by Australian artist Yiying Lu, the Fail Whale has become an iconic symbol of the company (Walker 2009).

to 2^{32}) (Parr 2009). The company's response to this and other issues has been to use intensive and detailed analysis of the traffic metrics to find weak points in their infrastructure and then fix these bottlenecks.*

In 2008, in response to these performance issues, parts of the back-end system were rewritten in a functional programming language called Scala and transferred to Java Virtual Machine (JVM) (Krishnamurthy et al. 2008; Venners 2009). Under the new arrangement, Ruby handles Twitter's user interface and website, but many of the individual tasks required to carry out user actions (such as electing to follow another user) become internal messages between the users and are queued into a messaging system with back-end JVM daemons (processes) to handle them. This change has made Twitter much more scalable.

In a presentation in 2007, company engineers described the hardware architecture they were using to run Twitter. It consisted of eight Sun servers, a single MySQL database running on an eight-processor core server with Memcached caching (Cook 2007). This infrastructure has since been upgraded on a number of occasions and although the company, like many Web 2.0 services, is reluctant to talk about its networks, engineer John Adams told the Velocity 2010 conference that there were "thousands" of machines involved (Adams 2010a, 12:55). A known major change however is the move from the MySQL to the Cassandra database (a Java-based data store, first developed to help Facebook cope with scaling issues, and now being developed as open source under the auspices of the Apache Software Foundation) (Lai 2010). In response to continual growth the company announced in July 2010 that it is to develop its own purpose-built data centre in Salt Lake City, Utah (Boulton 2010).†

13.3.1 Twitter Platforms

Nielsen, the media analysis company, note at least thirty alternatives to the Twitter website including: TweetDeck, TwitPic, Twitstat, Hootsuite, Twhirl, EasyTweets, and Tumblr (Martin 2009). Talbot (2010) presents figures for the breakdown of Twitter traffic from various platforms: Twitter website, 39.9%; UberTwitter, 8.5%; TweetDeck, 6.2%; Twitterfeed, 5.6%; Echofon, 3.7%; twidriod, 2.0%. Other unidentified applications and traffic from smartphones make up the remainder.

These services offer additional features to those provided by the Twitter website including: attractive graphical layout of the Twitter timeline; various ways to organise how Twitter messages from different sources are displayed (e.g. showing all messages from individual followers in discrete columns); and the ability to create groups that filter messages according to various criteria. It is worth pointing out that these applications tend to be developed in one of the emerging Rich Internet Application (RIA) technologies such as Adobe Air, which we will discuss in Chapter 14.

---

* The day-by-day status is reported at: http://status.twitter.com/ and the API status is at: http://dev.twitter.com/status
† These plans may since have been put on hold, at least temporarily, according to the Data Center Knowledge website: http://www.datacenterknowledge.com/archives/2010/12/15/twitter-scouting-sites-in-sacramento/

13.3.2 The Twitter API

Twitter provides an application programming interface (API) for developers looking to access and modify Twitter data from other applications (Makice 2009b). In effect there are two APIs: one that allows developers to access core Twitter data, and a Search API that provides ways for developers to interact with Twitter Search and its trends data.* To help developers in their work, a number of libraries have been introduced for a variety of languages including PHP, C++, Java, Perl and Ruby.

The API adheres to the principles of Representational State Transfer (REST), meaning that access is gained by making Hypertext Transfer Protocol (HTTP) requests using the standard URI system (see Chapter 14). The API permits three kinds of HTTP request: GET, POST and DELETE, with the default being GET. So, for example, to obtain the IDs of a user's followers, the following call is made by submitting the URI to the Twitter server: https://twitter.com/followers/ids.xml.

Many of the API methods also require a number of parameters and these are passed as part of the GET or POST request. A primary example is a user's identification which can be in the form of their ID number or their Twitter username.

Most API requests need authentication with a valid username or password. Twitter has recently moved to OAuth,† a system that allows users to authenticate an application to undertake a task on their behalf and share data without the need to transfer a username/password over potentially insecure Internet connections. OAuth works by handing authentication 'tokens' between sites rather than transferring user/password information. Each token grants access to a specific site for specific resources and for a defined duration.‡

A controversial issue with regard to the API has been the subject of *rate limiting*. As we have discussed previously, Twitter's growth has at times challenged the company's abilities to scale their server infrastructure and this has led to the need to restrict what developers can do with the API (Siegler 2010). During particularly busy periods, users became used to seeing the 'Fail Whale' logo, so a process of 'throttling' or limiting the number of API requests each client could make was introduced in late 2007. The limit varies depending on the type of request being made, up to a maximum of 350 requests an hour. Most developers can live with this level of restriction, but for the specialist applications that need more, Twitter provides what they refer to as a whitelist, whereby special permission can be granted to allow up to 20,000 requests per hour.§ As part of the response to concerns from developers about these limits, in mid-2010 the company announced work had begun on beta testing the Streaming API, which would allow third-party Twitter clients to receive continuous Tweet updates in real time. This is likely to be used by, amongst others, search companies, who use this 'fire hose' of data for their search engines (Carr 2010).

---

* The details change on a fairly regular basis so readers are advised to check the Twitter API wiki (http://apiwiki.twitter. com/) and follow Twitter's own Tweets at: http://twitter.com/twitterapi.
† See https://dev.twitter.com/docs/auth/oauth/faq
‡ Further details from: http://hueniverse.com/oauth/guide/
§ Further details at: http://dev.twitter.com/pages/rate-limiting

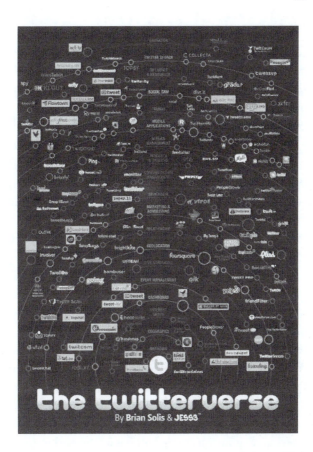

FIGURE 13.3   (See colour insert.) The Twitterverse. (From Brian Solis, published by Flickr, distributed under Creative Commons CC BY 2.0. See: http://www.flickr.com/photos/briansolis/5317948711/sizes/l/in/photostream/)

13.3.3 Archiving Twitter

Twitter's terms of use give the company the right to archive all public Tweets, and in April 2010 Twitter and the Library of Congress announced that a digital archive would be created of all public Tweets sent since the launch of the site (Campbell and Dulabahn 2010). As the vast majority of what a user does on the site is considered to be in public (some private account/profile information and deleted Tweets are not considered public), this initially consisted of a data file of approximately 5 terabytes. In addition, a process for the library to receive incremental updates has also been set up. Whilst this resource will be available within the library for non-commercial private study, scholarship, or research, it will not be made available online for the wider public to use.

Third-party tools have also been developed to allow individuals or organisations to develop their own archives of Tweets (e.g. TwapperKeeper). However, there have been complications due to the terms and conditions of Twitter's API.*

---

* This is a fluid situation, see for example, Brian Kelly's blog at UKOLN: http://ukwebfocus.wordpress.com/2011/03/17/a-few-days-left-to-download-a-structured-archive-of-tweets/

13.4 THE TWITTER ECOSYSTEM

As well as the various third-party services, there are thousands of other applications that provide Twitter-based services (see Figure 13.3). This is sometimes known as the Twitter ecosystem or Twitterverse (Laive 2009; Makice 2009a). Many of these services have sprung into being in order to fill what is known as a service gap, that is, to provide some feature that the main Twitter service does not (Johansmeyer 2010). Not all these services have been purely commercial: for example the TwapperKeeper, Tweet archiving system was extended for use by UK universities. However as Tom Johansmeyer points out, Twitter has been proactive in extending their service to plug gaps as they have become exploited. Makice (2009a) provides a summary of the situation in 2009 and Brian Solis (2011) undertook a survey in early 2011. The latter structures his findings around 19 categories of activity, for example, sites that deal with location-based Tweets, sites that help develop brands on Twitter, sites that provide analysis of Twitter use etc.

13.5 RESEARCH

Microblogging is a relatively new phenomenon and although there is a growing body of academic work, the research is still at a very early stage (Grace et al. 2010). It probably comes as no surprise to learn that the vast majority of research into microblogging concentrates on Twitter thanks to its widespread uptake and rapid growth rate (Shamma et al. 2011). As Kwak et al. (2010, 600) write: "Twitter with its open API to crawl … and the retweet mechanism to relay information offers an unprecedented opportunity for computer scientists, sociologists, linguists, and physicists to study human behavior."

Finally, although there is no longer a concept of friendship embodied in Twitter,[*] several groups of researchers have created their own, different definitions that allow them to conduct specific types of analysis. This means that we can divide the on-going research effort into three key themes (of which friendship is an aspect of more than one theme), namely: size and growth; usage; and topology. We shall consider each of these in turn.

13.5.1 Size and Growth

Since its launch, Twitter has generally experienced a very high growth rate in terms of the number of users and the volume of messages. Although, as with most Web 2.0 services, the companies involved are reluctant to talk too much about site growth, there is some information in the public domain. For example, Twitter operations engineer John Adams told the Velocity'09 conference that the company experienced a growth rate in users of 752% in 2008. Twitter's chief operating officer, Dick Costolo, told a conference in the summer of 2010 that the site was attracting 190 million visitors per month and generating 65 million Tweets a day.[†] In July 2011 the company updated its reported stats, indicating that it had 200 million users who sent 200 million Tweets a day (Olivarez-Giles 2011).

Rejaie et al. (2010) argue that it is difficult to be accurate about the true state of these services. Firstly, because companies are reluctant to share too many operational details,

---

[*] Although the term 'friend' was used in early versions of the site.
[†] See: http://techcrunch.com/2010/06/08/twitter-190-million-users/

particularly negative ones such as a slowing growth rate. Secondly, what statistics there are do not take account of the registered users who are no longer using the service but have not deleted their account, for whatever reason. The authors identify what they call *tourists*—users who try a service for a brief period before losing interest. They argue that these factors mean that the active population of sites like Twitter is an order of magnitude lower than the reported totals.*

In terms of demographics, a survey by Pew Internet in 2011 found that 13% of American adults who were online used Twitter (up from 8% in the previous year), with 3% doing so on any typical day (Smith and Rainie 2010; Smith 2011). The survey also noted that some demographic groups were notable users of the service, particularly African American, Latino, young adults (18–29 years), and those who lived in urban areas.

In a wider context, Krishnamurthy et al. (2008) undertook analysis into the geographic location of twitterers, using clues such as the time zone, set when creating an account. Based on this analysis the most active countries were: the United States, Japan, Germany, the UK, Brazil, Holland, France, Spain, Belgium, Canada, and Italy. These eleven countries accounted for around 50% of users in the datasets.

In China, microblogging (or Weibo) is more common than it is in Australia, Canada, France, India, the UK, or the United States (Goad 2011). The leading site, Sina Weibo, has experienced "explosive" growth since its launch in 2009 and has over 100 million users (Canaves 2001).

13.5.2 Usage

Broadly speaking, there are two main aspects to research on Twitter usage: how often people Tweet and what they use it for. However, by far the biggest body of work has been directed into the latter as a way of exploring not only human behaviour, but also wider issues of information diffusion. There are several methods that have been used: content analysis, for example, has been used to categorise content and draw conclusions based on insights generated from the categorization process. There has also been significant interest in how hashtags and retweets are used, particularly with respect to information diffusion, as these represent measurable actions that confer value or weight to the original Tweet.

13.5.2.1 How Often People Use Twitter

In terms of frequency, Smith and Rainie (2010) found that just over a third (36%) check at least once a day, whilst just over 40% said they only checked every few weeks or even less frequently. A survey by audience analyst company CrowdSciences found that 46% of users checked the site daily and 27% tweeted a message (Crowd Sciences 2009). However, a quarter of users in their sample say they have never tweeted or have stopped doing so.

Huberman et al. (2008b) collected data on just over 300,000 users, together with the date and time of Tweets. They found that only around 200,000 users had posted at least twice and they called this subset the active users. They found that 25% of all posts by the

---

* This may well chime with the kinds of audience figures that independent analysts publish. For example, Compete, the analysis company, has statistics showing that there were 36 million unique visits to Twitter in August 2011 (see: http://siteanalytics.compete.com/twitter.com/)

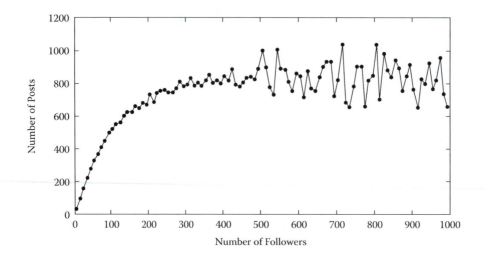

FIGURE 13.4   Sample of Twitter showing the number of posts as a function of the number of followers. After a rapid increase the number of posts stablizes at around 800. (Reprinted with the kind permission of the authors and publishers. Source: Huberman et al. 2008. *Social networks that matter: Twitter under the microscope*. Published originally in First Monday [http://firstmonday.org]).

active group were directed (i.e. aimed at a specific person using the @username symbol), a surprisingly widely used feature.

They went on to create a category of 'friend', which they defined as anyone that a user had sent at least two direct messages to. They found that users who had more friends were more active and posted more Tweets and directed messages, and that some users had posted as many as 3,000 direct messages and had several hundred friends. The number of posts initially increased as the number of followers increased, but this activity eventually stabilized at around the 800-Tweet mark as the number of followers reached around 200 (see Figure 13.4). They also found that a graph of the number of followees against the number of friends rises sharply and then levels out as the number of followers approaches 200.

The authors argue that the number of friends (according to their definition) is a more accurate predictor of likely activity on the site than the number of followers. They defined a measure, d, of number of friends divided by number of followees. Since 98.8% of users have fewer friends than followers, d is almost always less than 1. They found that the average of this value was 0.13 and the median is 0.04. This indicates that the number of friends a user might have is very small compared to the number of people they actually follow. So on Twitter, users tend to follow many people, but keep in touch with a smaller number. Thus, the authors argue, although the network formed by the declared followers and followees appears to be dense, the actual network of friends is sparse.

They conclude that their work shows that Twitter can be considered to be two networks—a very dense one made up of followers and followees and a sparser one consisting of a network of 'friends'. It is the latter—what they call the hidden social network—that matters most when considering how information is diffused on the site. It is those people with many friends who seem to use the site more often and drive Twitter activity.

13.5.2.2 How People Use Twitter

A number of researchers have considered the content of Tweets and direct messages. Honey and Herring (2009), for example, note that what people do on Twitter has changed over time. The site's original tag line was: "what are you doing?" but research has shown that even in the relatively early days of Twitter, more than 50% of messages did not actually address this question. The authors also note the long history of research into the nature of computer-mediated conversation and the inherent difficulties in achieving what is known as *coherence*: sustaining a topic-focused, person-to-person exchange. This is partly because the conversation takes place in multi-participant and public environments and is also partly due to the lack of face-to-face contact (no visual conversational cues).

Their interest is in how Twitter has been appropriated to enable extended conversations. In particular, how the '@' symbol has been used as a form of a marker for 'addressivity', which is particularly useful in maintaining some kind of coherence in exchanges. They also found that the majority of conversations in Twitter, at least in their sample, were dyadic (i.e. two-person) with exchanges of three to five messages sent over a 15- to 30-minute period. They conclude by arguing that, although some people maintain that Twitter was not designed as a collaboration tool, their research shows that users are actively using it for conversation and group interaction.

Naaman et al. (2010) analysed a sample of over 100,000 Tweets. They found there were four dominant types of content: information sharing, opinions and complaints, simple statements (e.g. it is raining in Nottingham today), and what they call 'Me Now' (e.g. I am tired and hungry). The latter was dominant, constituting 40% of the sample. At the level of individual users they found that for an average user, 41% of their Tweets could be categorised as Me Now. They also found that messages posted by women, or from some kind of mobile device were more likely to be Me Now. They suggest the existence of two types of user—the 'Meformers', whose communications are dominated by 'Me Now' type messages, and the 'Informers', who engage in information diffusion.

Others have considered the role of the retweet and how this affects the conversational flow of Twitter (boyd et al. 2010; Kwak et al. 2010; Macskassy and Michelson 2011). boyd et al. argue that whilst retweeting can be seen simply as a process of copying and rebroadcasting, it can also be considered to be a contribution to a conversation. They note that Twitter's structure means that conversations are not constrained within bounded spaces or groups and that many people talk about a particular topic at once. Users can get the sense of being what they call "surrounded by a conversation" (p. 1), and not necessarily driven to participate in it. In addition, their work includes a discussion of why people retweet and the emerging role of the hashtag (#). Their research found that compared to a random sample of standard Tweets, retweets contain more than twice the number of hashtags and URIs.

Huang et al. (2010) focused their analysis of Twitter on the use of hashtags and they noted the difference between hashtag use and other forms of tagging, as used in services such as social bookmarking. In these other services the tag is used *a posteriori*, i.e. as a tool of recall, whereas in Twitter it is used to filter and promote content. The authors posit that Twitter users have developed a technique, which the authors call *micro-meme*, whereby topic hashtags are adopted and used for "massively multi-person conversation by tweeting their thoughts about the topic prompted by the hashtag" (p. 174). They argue that hashtagging is a new form of social tag which they label 'conversational'.

The nature of conversation on Twitter and what it tells us about long-standing questions in media communications research is explored by Wu et al. (2011). They argue that Twitter is one of an increasing number of social media tools that are changing the nature of communication and that Twitter offers a "striking illustration of this erosion of traditional media categories" (p. 706). They note how celebrities and politicians are by-passing traditional media to reach followers numbered in the millions. They also note the rise of what they call "semi-public" individuals such as bloggers, authors and journalists who have gained large followings on Twitter.

Their work presents a number of findings about the nature of communication on Twitter including evidence that might support ideas about the fragmentation of the audience in modern media. However, despite this, they find evidence that 20,000 elite users[*] (who comprise less than 0.05% of users) attract almost 50% of the attention on the site.

Diffusion of information across Twitter was the focus of work undertaken by a team at Yahoo! research. They wanted to know if Twitter had *influencers*: key people in the word-of-mouth, information dissemination process (Bakshy et al. 2011). They argued that studying these processes in real-life social situations has proven difficult in the past and therefore sites like Twitter offer a unique opportunity for empirical study of information diffusion. They note that microblogging is even more useful in this regard than social network sites, since friendships are expressly devoted to participating in, and following, conversations.

In 2009, when they conducted the research, the Yahoo! team found that the maximum number of followers for any one person was 4 million.[†] They noted how highly skewed the follower statistic is in comparison with the out-degree (i.e. the number of people that other users are following) which levels out at about 700,000. This reflects the one-way nature of the follow action on Twitter: reciprocation is not guaranteed. The median numbers for followers and followees were 85 and 82 respectively for their sample. The mean numbers were 557 and 294, reflecting the presence of a high degree of skew.

They also analysed how often and when a URI was retweeted as a measure of information diffusion and they were able to extract what they call cascades (trees of links between users, similar to those found in blogging research). They found that the distribution of cascade sizes followed a power law, i.e. the vast majority of posted URIs were not passed on at all (the average cascade size was 1.14), whilst a small percentage were passed on thousands of times. They also found—somewhat counter-intuitively, at least to marketers—that the most efficient way of diffusing information was by many small cascades from ordinary users rather than by relying on the 'superstars' of the Twittersphere. However, the authors emphasize the tentative nature of their results and the need for further work.

---

[*] The authors used various statistical methods to determine elite users including analysis of Twitter lists. See the paper for details.

[†] Lady Gaga currently has over eight million followers and a dozen or so other international celebrities have between three and six million.

Similar results were found by Cha et al. (2010) who highlight the *million follower fallacy*, a phrase coined by software developer Adi Avnit,[*] to indicate that those users with a high in-degree (i.e. thousands or even millions of followers) are not necessarily influential.

Information diffusion is also the subject of research by a team at Cornell and Carnegie Mellon universities, who analysed how hashtags spread across the network (Romero et al. 2011). They argued that their work may well be the first large-scale validation of a theory in sociology known as *complex contagion*, which posits that an individual needs repeated exposure to a controversial idea, from a variety of people, before adopting it himself. By measuring how and when people adopt a hashtag they were able to spot unusual patterns for certain types of topic or idea, which seemed to correlate with a sense of controversy. They also analysed what they call Twitter *idioms*—concatenations of common words to form a unique hashtag that is briefly diffused around the network. Twitter users will be familiar with this idea, for example #musicmonday, #followfriday.

Finally, Kwak et al. (2010) have developed a technique they call *retweet trees*, a way of representing how the information contained in a Tweet is diffused as a consequence of being retweeted by others. Each link in the graph represents a retweet as it spreads out across the network (see Figure 13.5). Their work found that the distribution of users involved in retweeting follows a power law and that the largest tree consisted of eleven 'hops'. Over 95% of trees were only one hop.

13.5.3 Topology

Other researchers have considered the topological features of Twitter, i.e. the structure of the graphs formed when analysing links and communications between users. Kwak et al. (2010) analysed information on 41 million users and over 100 million Tweets. To gain a sufficient start on the user profile data, they began with Paris Hilton's Twitter page and then tracked her one million followers using a breadth-first search. They also constructed a *complementary cumulative distributed function* (CCDF)[†] graph of the distribution of numbers of followers and followings (see Figure 13.6).

The researchers noted a number of glitches in the followings line. The first of these occurs at $x = 20$. They account for this by explaining that when a new person registers, the Twitter service makes a recommendation of an initial twenty users who might be worth following. This can be done with a single click during sign-up, and therefore many users take up this opportunity and do not bother to add any others. The second glitch is at $x = 2,000$ (before 2009, Twitter had this as its upper limit).

They found that the line for followers fits our old friend the power law in values up to $x = 10^5$ with an exponent of 2.276. The law breaks down at the higher end of the graph as there are users with many more followers than the power law predicts. The authors note that similar tail behaviour has been found in Cyworld but not in other online social

---

[*] See: http://pravdam.com/2009/08/20/the-million-followers-fallacy-guest-post-by-adi-avnit/

[†] A method (a variant of CDF) for studying the heavy tail of power law functions. For more details on the mathematics see Crovella and Bestavros (1997) and Newman (2005).

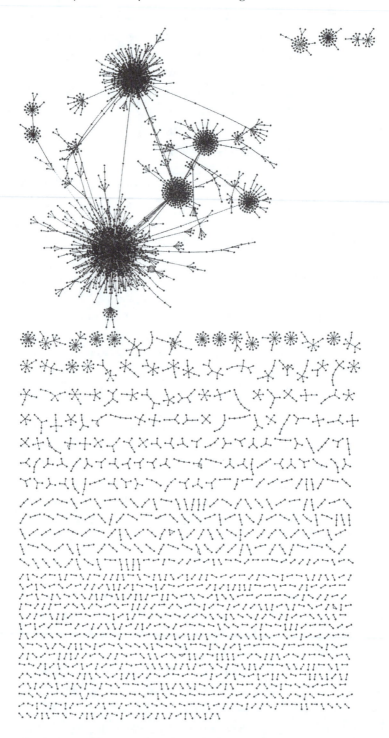

FIGURE 13.5 Retweet trees for the topic 'air france flight'. There are many one- or two-hop chains (bottom) and a smaller number of more esoteric shapes formed by multi-hop tweets (top). (Reprinted with the kind permission of the authors and publisher. From Kwak et al. 2010. *What is Twitter, a social network or a news media?* Published by The International World Wide Web Conference Committee (IW3C2)).

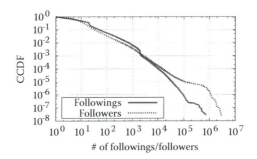

FIGURE 13.6 The long tail in action on Twitter. The graph shows the Complementary Cumulative Distribution (CCDF) of followers/followings. The solid line shows the distribution of followings and the dashed line shows followers. (Source: Kwak et al. 2010. *What is Twitter, a social network or a news media?*).

networks. The shared characteristics between these two services may be accounted for by the presence of celebrities in the tails.

The team also looked at the degrees of separation in order to see if the small world effect was operating within Twitter (see Chapter 7). They note that the main difference between other SNSs and Twitter is that Twitter is directed (there is no obligation for a follower link to be two-way). They found that only 22% of user pairs were reciprocal, so they expected the path lengths to be longer across the network (since hopping from one node to another is more difficult if there is not always a forwards and backwards path between two nodes). However, their experiments showed an average path length of 4.12 (with median and mode of the distribution being 4). For just over 97% of node pairs in Twitter, the path length is 6 or shorter. This, they note, was rather unexpected, being quite short for a network of Twitter's size, especially considering that it is directed. Bakhshandeh et al. (2011) concurred, reporting a degree of separation of 3.43 for Twitter.

Krishnamurthy et al. (2008) also investigated the relationships between users and followers and found a similar CCDF. Kwak et al. (2010) posit that this may demonstrate that Twitter is an information source as much as it is an online social network: the act of following is as much about discovering information as it is about indicating a form of relationship.

Java (2008) and Java et al. (2007) investigated a number of topological features of Twitter and compared them with both the wider Web and the blogging ecosystem. The properties investigated and the results are shown in Table 13.1. The in-degree and out-degree both demonstrate a power law distribution with exponents of approximately −2.4 for each (see Figure 13.7 and Figure 13.8). The authors note the similarity with the value for the wider Web which is −2.1 for in-degree. They also found a high level of reciprocity and a degree correlation[*] that implies that there are a large number of mutual acquaintances. Thus, the authors conclude that in terms of degree distribution, Twitter can be seen as being more like the Web, but in terms of reciprocity and degree correlation, it is more like an online social network.

---

[*] A measure of how similar adjacent nodes are in terms of degree properties. See Chapter 7 for details.

TABLE 13.1   Various Topological Properties of Twitter

Property	Twitter Stats
Total nodes	87,897
Total links	829,247
Average degree	18.86
In-degree slope	−2.4
Out-degree slope	−2.4
Degree correlation	0.59
Diameter	6
Clustering coefficient	0.106
Reciprocity	0.58

Source: Adapted from Akshay Java, Xiaodan Song, Tim Finin, and Belle Tseng. 2007. Why we Twitter: Understanding microblogging usage and communities. 9th WebKDD and 1st SNA-KDD 2007 Workshop on Web Mining and Social Network Analysis, 12th–15th August, at San Jose, California. Proceedings published by the Association for Computing Machinery.

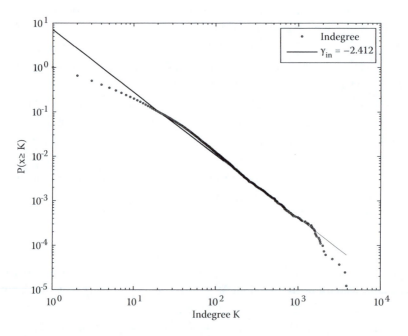

FIGURE 13.7   The in-degree distribution of Twitter. (Reproduced with the kind permission of Akshay Java, © 2008 Akshay Java (2008)).

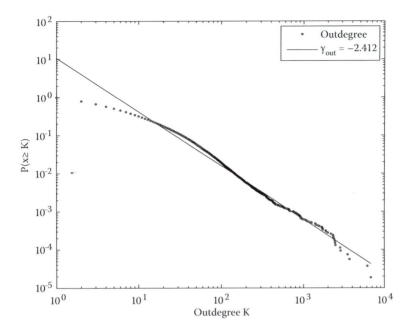

FIGURE 13.8 The out-degree distribution of Twitter. (Reproduced with the kind permission of Akshay Java, © 2008 Akshay Java (2008)).

EXERCISES AND POINTS TO PONDER

1. Consider your own Twitter account and review its contents over the period of a month or so. What might someone else make of the contents? Would it be possible to mine the information to find out more about what kind of person you are? Write a short article on the implications of this development in technology.

2. Microblogging services are increasingly being used via smartphones. In groups, discuss the differences between using such a service on a smartphone as opposed to a desktop PC. After the discussion, review the material provided in Perreault and Ruths (2011) and compare it with your own thoughts.

3. Write a PHP software module to use the Twitter API to publish a Tweet into your own timeline. The software should ask for the Twitter username and password, and the text of the Tweet and then use the API's update method (see: https://dev.twitter.com/docs/api/1/post/statuses/update).

4. (Group programming exercise). Read the paper by Bakshy et al. (2011) which discusses research into the role of influence on Twitter. Develop a program that uses the Twitter API and the method discussed in Section 4 of their paper to track the diffusion of posts across the Twittersphere. Note that this exercise might be helped by obtaining a ready-made dataset since Twitter has set up a number of restrictions on what can be done with the API (take a look at infochimps.com or http://twitter.mpi-sws.org/).

FURTHER READING

The speed and real-time nature of Twitter has been noted by a number of academics and commentators, namely McFedries (2009), Brian et al. (2010), and O'Reilly and Battelle (2009).

For more on information diffusion in Twitter see the work of Yang and Counts (2010) who look at the speed, scale and range of information cascades.

Further discussion of influence and the role of different types of users can be found in Cha et al. (2010). In particular they analyse three different forms of influence and present a top-200 list of influential users.

For further discussion on how Twitter is used, in particular the way in which the user imagines their audience, see Marwick and boyd (2011). This includes discussion of the way Twitter engenders what the authors call *micro-celebrity*.

For further discussion on the role of social media, such as blogs and Twitter, in political action and protest see Agarwal et al. (2011), Jisun An et al. (2011) and Shirky (2008).

In 2009 the mainstream media made much of a report that found 40% of content on Twitter to be "pointless babble". For a detailed review of this issue and other literature on content analysis see Stephen Dann's *First Monday* article (Dann 2010).

For a discussion of the temporal aspects of Twitter content see Shamma et al. (2011).

Akshay Java's PhD thesis presentation provides information on data mining in Twitter and the role of communities within social media services. See: http://ebiquity.umbc.edu/paper/html/id/429/Mining-Social-Media-Communities-and-Content

Web URI address shortening services and how they are used in Twitter and other social media are discussed further in Antoniades et al. (2011).

For more on Chinese microblogging see: http://www.slideshare.net/RockyFu/china-microblogging-weibo-statistics-feb-2011

For more on how to analyse Twitter see Leskovec (2011) and his online tutorial information at: http://snap.stanford.edu/proj/socmedia-www/index.html#info

III

Framework for the Future

Section III encompasses the base of the Web 2.0 'iceberg', exploring the technologies and standards that provide the foundations for the services outlined in Section II. The original framework of the Web, created by Tim Berners-Lee and based around a basic client-server model, has developed into a sophisticated and multi-layered architecture; and despite the pace of change the fundamental building blocks have, so far, remained the same Hypertext Markup Language (HTML), Uniform Resource Identifiers (URIs) and Hypertext Transfer Protocol (HTTP). However, technology does not stand still and new developments are taking place on almost a daily basis: new server-side frameworks; new interface technologies; Rich Internet Application (RIA) developments such as Flash and Silverlight. Combined with reduced costs to develop and distribute new services, the Web is evolving at a faster and faster rate.

Chapter 14 charts the development of Web technologies, exploring how and why the original model of the Web, based on the three core components of HTML, URIs and HTTP, has been extended to allow the development of more sophisticated and responsive services. It looks at the introduction of Ajax, critical to the development of Web 2.0; outlines in more detail how the Web as Platform concept is actually delivered; and covers some of the architectural aspects of designing services. It also introduces a number of technologies that have helped deliver the sorts of services we looked at in Section II such as Really Simple Syndication (RSS), authentication systems and widgets, as well as the database developments that have made it possible to handle the epic scale of data being produced. Finally, the chapter ends with a look at some of the technology standards that have delivered these developments: the different types that are available, how they are produced and how to evaluate them.

Chapter 15 looks to the future and asks 'What about Web 3.0?' There are contenders from all sections of the iceberg model, from the Semantic Web to the Internet of Things, but by this stage readers should be able to engage critically with the ideas and decide for themselves whether or not such a thing as Web 3.0 even exists.

## CHAPTER 14

Technology and Standards

I N SECTIONS I AND II WE CONSIDERED the powerful ideas and principles that are driving the Web's development and the online services that are the manifestations of those ideas. Underpinning all this are the Web's technologies and standards, which we will examine in this chapter.

The Web is essentially a client/server system on a global scale (Jazayeri 2007; Akritidis et al. 2011). Users view and interact with websites through Web browsers, which run on their client machines (whether this is a standard PC or Mac, games console or mobile device). These websites are held on Web servers, which sounds rather specialized, but which in fact may only consist of a standard PC hooked up to the Internet and running a piece of software called, appropriately, a Web server. However, most professional websites such as, say, the webpages of a university or the BBC, are held on specialist, dedicated server machines. These machines 'serve' webpage content in response to a request from the client machine's browser software. This client/server architecture in which one computer, the server, carries out a task on behalf of another—the client—is not unique to the Web and indeed Pressman argues that it now "dominates the landscape of computer-based systems" (Pressman 2000, 764). However, to most people the Web is the clearest everyday manifestation of the client/server model that they are likely to come across.

We begin with a brief review of the way that the Web works, looking at the three fundamental elements first developed by Tim Berners-Lee and his colleagues at CERN. We will then explore how the technology has evolved, looking in particular at a technique known as Ajax and reviewing the many server-side developments that have assisted in providing the sophisticated and responsive user interfaces that are a feature of the modern Web. We also examine the concept of the Web as Platform, as described by O'Reilly (2005b), and the technologies involved. Finally, we consider how the epic scale of data is processed and conclude by reviewing how Internet and Web technologies are standardized.

14.1 HOW THE WEB WORKS

The grand vision of the Internet age is that all computers in the world interconnect as one very large computing resource.

DAVE CRANE ET AL.
(*2006, 9*)

It is common for people to confuse the Web and the Internet, but as we have seen, the Internet is a network of networks that connects millions of different PCs, servers and other computing devices such as smartphones. It was first launched as ARPANet in September 1969, as a military research network that later developed into the worldwide network we know today. The Web, however, was created by Tim Berners-Lee in 1989 as part of his work at CERN, the European research laboratory. His vision was to connect documents on different machines using hypertext, so that people could read documents from any one of these machines. For this reason the Web is not held in any one place, but is scattered across millions of individual machines. Where the Internet is a global system of networked computing devices, the Web is a global system of linked hypertext documents that sits on top of the Internet.

HYPERTEXT

It is worth noting in passing that Tim Berners-Lee was not the originator of the concept of hypertext, which is usually attributed to computer pioneer Ted Nelson who first used the term in 1965.[*] Indeed, the World Wide Web was not even the first attempt at a widely usable hypertext system.[†] However, for various technical and cultural reasons, not least that CERN waived all intellectual property rights over the invention and that Berners-Lee has consistently refused to restrict its growth by commercialising the protocols, the Web has triumphed over other attempts to achieve the same end.

---

[*] Nelson outlined his vision of hypertext in a seminal book, *Literary Machines*, in 1981.
[†] For some of the other types of system see Berners-Lee et al. (1994).

The Web works because of a set of standards that define how webpages are formatted, how they are addressed and located, and how they are transferred between the server and the user's browser (Farrel 2004; W3C 2004). The formatting of the webpage is defined by the Hypertext Markup Language (HTML), addressing and location are handled by Universal Resource Locators (URLs[*]) and the key protocol involved in the delivery of webpages is the Hypertext Transfer Protocol (HTTP) (Berners-Lee et al. 1994). It was these three elements that Berners-Lee first proposed in 1989 while working at CERN (Gillies and Cailliau 2000).

---

[*] A URL is just one form of Uniform Resource Identifier (URI), in turn a wider conceptualization of the idea of a unique, global identifier. As discussed in the preface, the more widely accepted term URI has been used so far but in this instance it is more precise to use URL. There are other forms, see: http://en.wikipedia.org/wiki/Uniform_Resource_Identifier (15th August 2011).

14.1.1 Formatting the Web: The Hypertext Markup Language

Essentially, HTML allows a text file to be marked up with tags, to indicate how the browser should display the text. Thus, for example, if the creator of a document would like a line of the text to be displayed in bold they add the tag <b> before the text and the tag </b> after the text. However, as the name suggests, HTML is a hypertext markup language, not just a tagging system for presentation, and one of its key aims is to link documents to each other using a hypertext reference. On the visible webpage these usually appear as coloured, underlined words. Over the years, HTML has undergone a number of revisions and is currently at version 4.01, although work is currently being undertaken to produce a new standard, HTML5.*

14.1.2 Locating Web Documents: The Universal Resource Locator

When a user clicks on a hypertext link, the browser needs to know where to go to get the document being referenced. The URL, a unique global locator for an individual Web document, provides this information. It is a kind of universal postcode or zip code for Web documents. The basic layout of a URL is as follows:

http://<host name or IP address>[:<port>]/<path and file name>

The first part (http://) is known as the *scheme* and in this case it declares that the rest of the address should be interpreted as part of the hypertext transfer protocol.† The second part (<host name or IP address>) is the Internet Protocol address, or IP: essentially a number that acts as a computer's unique identifier on the Internet. However, these are not easy for humans to understand so the IP is usually given a hostname: a human-readable name for the target machine that is translated into the unique IP address. The final part is the path and filename, which define the exact document in question that has been identified by the host name or IP address.

In addition, the URL may also include tags that provide a way to pass information between the browser and the server. The *port* is one of these optional extras and it tells the browser which of the target machine's input/output ports to use (for the Web this is almost always port 80).

14.1.3 Delivering the Web: The Hypertext Transfer Protocol

The Hypertext Transfer Protocol facilitates the transfer of data between the client browser and the Web server. When the user wishes to display a new webpage (or refresh an existing one) the browser sends a request message using HTTP. The message is delivered to the server over the Internet using the underlying networking protocols such as TCP/IP, but the content of that message is defined by HTTP. The protocol has a number of what are called Methods: ways in which messages are exchanged between the client machine and the server. These include GET, POST, PUT and DELETE. The most common of these

---

* See Chapter 15 for more on HTML5 and also: http://dev.w3.org/html5/spec/Overview.html
† There are other communication protocols, such as FTP and Gopher, which have their own prefix. Descriptions of the other methods can be found at the URL specification site: http://www.ietf.org/rfc/rfc1738.txt

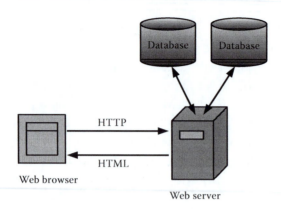

FIGURE 14.1   The client/server architecture of the Web. A client sends a request, in the form of HTTP, to the server. The server replies with information in the form of an HTTP response, which consists of a status message and a chunk of HTML for display in the browser (assuming the request was successful). Note that the server may use back-end databases to store some of its information. Full details at: http://www.ietf.org/rfc/rfc2616. (Illustration © 2011 by Intelligent Content Ltd Licensed under a Creative Commons Attribution-NonCommercial-NoDerivs 3.0 Unported license (CC BY-NR-ND 3.0))

is GET, which simply retrieves the data held at the resource identified by the URL. The process is shown in Figure 14.1. HTTP currently stands at version 1.1.

Initially the Web infrastructure was used to deliver HTML documents (Jazayeri 2007). Over time however, it became obvious that the URL could not only be used to identify a document resource but could also be used to identify a server script, which could run on behalf of the client. As long as the end result of this processing was itself an HTML document that could be returned to the client, then the overall architecture of the Web held together. Thus, in 1993, the **Common Gateway Interface**[*] (CGI) was introduced, formalizing the use of server-side scripts in this manner. This allowed database systems to be linked to the Web, usually through a PERL or PHP script and CGI interface standard, therefore vastly increasing the amount of information that could be made available (see Figure 14.1).

14.1.4 REST: An Architectural Model of the Web

Over time, the three architectural bases[†] of the Web—interaction using HTTP, identification via URLs and formatting with HTML—began to consolidate into a recognized architectural model: a sort of blueprint or abstraction of the way the Web works and the software components involved. This model, Representational State Transfer (REST), was expounded in detail by Roy Fielding as part of his doctoral thesis work at University of California, Irvine (Fielding 2000; Fielding and Taylor 2002). REST is not a standard per se, but rather describes an approach for understanding a client/server, stateless architecture whose most obvious implementation is the

---

[*] See: http://tools.ietf.org/html/rfc3875
[†] See: http://www.w3.org/TR/webarch/

Web.[*] It is an abstraction that provides developers and software architects with a way of telling good Web development practices from bad (Vlist et al. 2007). Somewhat obviously, there are two main concepts in REST, representation and state transfer.

14.1.4.1 Representation

In REST, every resource is identified by a URI, and HTTP is used to let the browser communicate its intentions through GET, POST, PUT, and DELETE requests. A request for a particular resource results in the return of a *representation* of that resource. Such a representation is formally defined as a sequence of bytes plus representation metadata to describe those bytes, but for the purpose of this discussion we can think of it simply as an HTML document or a string of Extensible Markup Language (XML). In the abstract world of REST, the representation is not the same thing as the resource itself. The representation is likely to be an HTML document or perhaps an image file or a video. Such documents and media files are representations of entities that exist outside the Web. This is a subtle concept but by way of example consider the weather forecast. This is a resource, but it may have more than one representation on the Web.

14.1.4.2 State Transfer

Most computer software systems need some way of being aware of what *state* they are in as well as some conception of moving from one state to another.[†] However, in order to cope with the scale of operating across the Internet, HTTP was developed without a notion of state (Berners-Lee et al. 1994). The upshot of this is that a Web server does not retain information about the state of the client browser between requests made through HTTP; rather, the client maintains its own record of what state it is in. The server simply returns the data that the browser is asking for at any particular time.

This means that even if there is a spike in traffic, the server does not have to burden itself with taking account of a complex collection of differing client states: an idea that Fielding and Taylor (2002) call *anarchic scalability*. However, this means that each request from client to server must contain all the information necessary to understand the request, and cannot take advantage of any stored context on the server. Although this means that the Web can operate at the Internet scale, it makes life difficult for developers who want their browser and server to work together, for example during the processing of an e-commerce credit card transaction. Although a number of technological 'kludges' have been tried over the years, for example by using cookies,[‡] the solution that gradually became accepted was

---

[*] In theory the same approach could be used in non-HTTP environments. One could build another hypertext system that follows the REST model, but is not the same as the Web. To date, however, nobody has done this. There is more discussion of this in the panel discussion at WS-REST 2010 listed in the Further Reading section.

[†] A state is any observable mode of behaviour within a system. A system will move between different states as time passes and events occur. Such a situation is often depicted in software engineering by state transition diagrams. Further details are in Chapter 12 of Pressman (2000).

[‡] A cookie is a tiny code or 'string' that the server initially sends to the client. The client stores the code and returns it when interacting with the server. The code can be used by the server to look up unique information about that particular user and their recent transactions with the server, for example, and most commonly, the state of any e-commerce transaction. In essence, the server is maintaining a record of the state. This way of doing things conflicts with REST architecture.

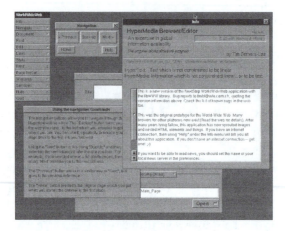

FIGURE 14.2   Tim Berners-Lee's original Web browser. Note the 'Edit' choice in the WorldWideWeb menu at the very top left hand corner of the figure. This was dropped from later versions which meant that the Web initially became a read-only medium. (Source: Wikimedia Commons. Authored by FedericoMP based on an image by Ck_mpk. This image is in the public domain. See: http://commons.wikimedia.org/wiki/File:WorldWideWeb.png)

based on the idea that the state transition takes place at the client end, i.e. in the browser. As the browser requests new resources, in the form of representations from the server, it moves from one state to another, hence the name REST. Essentially the process of transferring the representation acts as a transition to the next state.

14.1.5 A Read-Write Web?

There is one more point that needs to be made before we move to consider Web 2.0 and that is the common misconception that early Web browsers were designed to be read-only. If we look at the early history of the Web it is clear this was not the original intention. Tim Berners-Lee's first browser, WorldWideWeb, included a 'what-you-see-is-what-you-get', or WYSIWYG (pronounced wiz-ee-wig), editor (see Figure 14.2). However, during a series of ports to other machines from the original development computer, the ability to edit through the Web client was not included in order to speed up the process of adoption within CERN (Berners-Lee 1999). This attitude to the 'edit' function continued through subsequent Web browser developments such as ViolaWWW and Mosaic. Crucially, this left people thinking of the Web as a medium in which a relatively small number of people published and most browsed.

14.2 HOW WEB 2.0 SERVICES WORK

One of the key drivers behind the development of Web 2.0 services has been the roll-out of new Web-related technologies and standards. These have been underpinned by the powerful, though not particularly new, idea of the Web as Platform (Mikkonen and Taivalsaari 2008; Jazayeri 2007; Vossen 2011). Whereas in the past, software applications ran on the user's machine, handled directly by a desktop operating system such as MacOS, Windows or Linux, under the Web as Platform concept, software services are run within the window of the browser, communicating via the Internet to remote servers. This is part of a wider business and cultural change towards service-based models (Kazman and Chen 2009).

As we have already seen, Web 2.0 applications and services are very responsive and exhibit high levels of usability and interaction. Indeed, modern Web applications are more like desktop applications than traditional websites. The original model of the Web, based purely on request/response, HTTP/HTML architecture is not really capable of supporting this level of sophistication (Governor et al. 2009; Piero et al. 2010; Vossen and Hagemann 2007) and there are three main problems:

- The ability to present high-quality, dynamic graphics is limited.

- HTTP is limited to 'synchronous communications' when interacting with the server.

- There is limited data storage capability on the client (browser).

Although server-side scripting with CGI increased the amount of information that could be processed and accessed over the Web it did little to address these three issues. In the classical Web model, when the user clicks on something that requires the browser to redraw the screen, perhaps with new or modified information from the server, the whole page has to be redrawn and the user is left waiting, unable to interact with the webpage, whilst the request–response dance takes place (Ritchie 2007).

These technical limitations meant that websites built on original architecture principles did not look, feel or respond like desktop applications. The lack of sophisticated graphical user interface (GUI) components, which are common within desktop applications, and the requirement to return to the server and reload the whole webpage whenever the user clicked on a link meant that old-style Web applications increasingly came to be seen, by the early 2000s, as somewhat 'clunky' and unresponsive to the user. One often cited example is the lack of provision for drop-down menus. In the words of Crane et al. (2006), the original Web architecture was: "beginning to creak under the strain" (p. 4).

However, it is important to be clear that the underlying infrastructure of the Web has not changed (Vlist et al. 2007). The Web remains a global client/server hypermedia system based on the three fundamental protocols and format standards that Tim Berners-Lee outlined back in 1989. What has emerged in recent years is a number of technological improvements that have sought to resolve the problems with the traditional HTML/HTTP model. The most important of these is Ajax.

14.2.1 Ajax: The Key to Web 2.0

In February 2005, Jesse James Garrett of Adaptive Path LLC published a very influential online article called *Ajax: A New Approach to Web Applications* (Garrett 2005). In it he argued that a fundamental shift was taking place in Web technology and he described how his company had taken to calling this combination of technologies *Ajax*. Although the name is derived from the initial letters of Asynchronous JavaScript and XML, there were in fact a number of elements that had been converging which Garrett identified as:

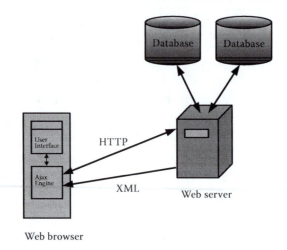

Web browser

FIGURE 14.3 Web 2.0 services make use of newer technologies such as XML and Ajax. (Illustration © 2011 by Intelligent Content Ltd Licensed under a Creative Commons Attribution-NonCommercial-NoDerivs 3.0 Unported license (CC BY-NR-ND 3.0)).

- Development of JavaScript to provide browser-based, client-side programming capabilities

- Standardized presentation techniques using Extensible HTML (XHTML) and Cascading Style Sheets (CSS)

- Dynamic display and interaction using the Document Object Model (DOM)

- Data interchange and manipulation using XML and Extensible Stylesheet Language Transformation (XSLT)

- Asynchronous data retrieval using XMLHttpRequest

With Ajax, the content of a webpage can be updated incrementally, as needed (see Figure 14.3). This is a profound break away from the original mechanism of the Web, which had to reload a whole page each time a part of that page needed to be changed.

Governor et al. (2009) claim that Ajax is probably the Web technique most closely associated with the emergence of Web 2.0, describing its development as a 'pivotal moment'. Johnson (2005) concurs, describing it as the 'crown jewel' of Web 2.0 which has allowed the development of key applications such as Flickr and Google Gmail.

14.2.1.1 JavaScript

In order to understand how Ajax came about we need to revisit a little Web history. In the mid- to late 1990s several developments took place that were intended to improve on the HTML/HTTP model of the Web. The first of these was JavaScript, a scripting language developed by Brendan Eich of Netscape, which allowed some of the processing to take place within the browser.* This resulted in a reduction in the number of trips back to the server to obtain updated information. An early, popular use for it was to validate data entered into Web forms, e.g. dates, telephone number etc. With JavaScript there was no need for the server to check that each box in the form had been filled in and that a date was, for example, in the expected format: this could all be done at the client end, prior to sending the data from the form to the server.

Although JavaScript was initially developed by Netscape, the process of overseeing its later development was handed over to ECMA (a standards body), and the standardized version is formally known as ECMAScript, although hardly anyone ever uses that term. Officially, JavaScript as developed by Netscape (and Microsoft's own version, Jscript) are referred to as *dialects* of ECMAScript. In reality, as is so often the case with the Web, the two proprietary versions provide additional functions not available in the official standard.

JavaScript is an interpreted, rather than a compiled, programming language. The code is in text form and converts to machine-executable code during runtime. This means that code can be generated dynamically.

14.2.1.2 Cascading Style Sheets

In 1996 the introduction of *Cascading Style Sheets* (CSS) allowed website designers to separate 'what' to display in a Web document from the 'how' of displaying it. These two developments improved the way that browsers rendered webpages and helped make them more responsive when new pages were loaded or refreshed.

14.2.1.3 Dynamic HTML

A further refinement that had a bearing on the development of Ajax was Microsoft's inclusion of *dynamic HTML* (DHTML) in their Explorer browser in 1997. DHTML allowed part of a page to be modified and re-rendered by the browser almost in real time, and it became particularly popular for animation within webpages. The introduction of JavaScript and DHTML, together with CSS, also meant that webpages could incorporate the graphical interface features that users were used to seeing on client applications, for example drop-down menus and clickable toolbar buttons.

14.2.1.4 Document Object Model

DHTML was further refined by the introduction of the *Document Object Model* (DOM) a single JavaScript object that represented the whole webpage and its constituent parts. Thus, JavaScript could be used to dynamically modify any aspect of the webpage as required. However, there have been problems with standardization (Vossen and Hagemann 2007). Although the World Wide Web Consortium (W3C) is officially responsible for a standard version of the DOM, many browsers still use slightly different object models.

---

* Despite the name, there is no connection with the popular programming language Java.

14.2.1.5 Hidden Frames

A later adjustment to the HTML/HTTP model was the concept of *frames*, which created the capability to split a webpage into a number of segments, each of which could be reloaded separately using JavaScript. This was further built upon by the introduction of hidden frames, an engineering kludge in which frames of zero pixels in size were embedded into the webpage for the sole purpose of allowing a form of communication back to the server without reloading anything visual on the screen.

Hidden frames were an early attempt at what is known as *asynchronous communication* with the server. By this we mean that the user can interact with the webpage whilst some processing takes place in the background without the user having to wait for the server to respond. This is an important concept in the development of Web 2.0 services. The Internet, being a network of networks, has what is known as *network latency*: the potential for small delays as messages are transferred from network to network. Introducing asynchronous communication meant that the user was less aware of these delays since the browser would continue to respond to actions.

14.2.1.6 XHTML

Around the time that these later developments were taking place, the W3C was introducing XHTML. This reformulated the HTML 4.0 standard as an XML-based format and both increased its interoperability with existing XML tools and provided for extensibility.

XML is a widely used, extensible, text-based markup language that allows developers to create their own document structures and data exchange formats. In many ways it is similar to HTML and uses the same tag concept with the familiar < > notation. However, the key difference is that XML, unlike HTML, is a generic markup language that enables developers to create their own markup languages. HTML has a defined set of tags, and if the developer uses a tag that is not in the defined set, then the browser simply ignores it. XML allows the developer to add new tags and other structures and elements. XHTML increased HTML's flexibility and this became important as Web 2.0–style services increased the demands made on the browser's rendering capabilities.

14.2.1.7 XMLHttpRequest

In 2001, following the widespread uptake of DHTML, DOM, hidden frames and XML, Microsoft introduced an ActiveX object called XMLHttp.[*] This was similar to an ad hoc HTTP request that could be controlled by JavaScript code within the browser. It allowed requests to be sent to the server and processed the returned data on an 'as needed' basis. In a nutshell it enabled JavaScript to make HTTP requests to a remote server without the need to reload the page (McLellan 2005). By only requiring small amounts of data to be exchanged with the server, the overall effect for the user was a more responsive

---

[*] Note the name is somewhat misleading since the request does not have to be made using the HTTP protocol (the more secure HTTPS can also be used).

Web experience. The new object was a success and was emulated by Mozilla with their introduction of XMLHttpRequest.[*] Standardization is now carried out by W3C.[†]

The data are normally exchanged in the form of XML, hence the name, but other text-based formats are possible, and indeed *JavaScript Object Notations* (JSON)[‡] is becoming popular amongst developers (Governor et al. 2009). The JavaScript code snippet below shows the basic idea. The first line creates a new XMLHttpRequest object. The second line prepares a new HTTP request, specifying that the HTTP GET method will be used and it will be sent to the Mozilla URI. It also indicates that the request will not be asynchronous. The third line does the actual sending.

```
# var req = new XMLHttpRequest();
# req.open('GET', 'http://www.mozilla.org/', false);
# req.send(null);
# if(req.status == 200)
# dump(req.responseText);
```

The synchronous/asynchronous parameter in the second line is important, since it determines whether or not the JavaScript code continues after sending the request to the server. When set to TRUE, the request is sent asynchronously and the code continues execution without waiting. The developer must set up an event handler, another piece of JavaScript code that watches for a response from the server. If the parameter is set to FALSE then the code sits where it is, awaiting the response. This means that the user cannot interact with the browser window. It is standard practice to use asynchronous, but there are occasions when a programmer might use the synchronous method. On completion, the XMLHttpRequest object will contain a string of text that represents changes required to be made to the DOM.[§]

14.2.1.8 Ajax as a Way of Working

Ajax is a direct descendant of XMLHttpRequest, combining its asynchronous communication with other developments such as JavaScript and DOM.

In its first incarnation, Ajax was known as AJAX because it was an acronym that referred to the names of the technologies being used. However, these days it can refer to any client-side script language. In a similar vein, XML may be substituted with JSON. It is therefore more accurate to think of Ajax as a way of working rather than a set of specific technologies (Richardson and Ruby 2007).

---

[*] Mozilla provides some useful guidance as to how this works at: https://developer.mozilla.org/En/XMLHttpRequest/Using_XMLHttpRequest

[†] See: http://www.w3.org/TR/XMLHttpRequest

[‡] JSON is a lightweight alternative to XML for data exchange and generally requires less data to be transferred between the server and the browser. See: http://www.json.org/ for further details.

[§] This is actually more complex than I have described here. There are several methods for obtaining the response in different formats. The responseText data is actually returned as a string of XML text which needs to be converted to a DOM object. The responseXML property of the XMLHttpRequest object will contain a DOM document object. See: http://www.w3.org/TR/XMLHttpRequest/#response for full details

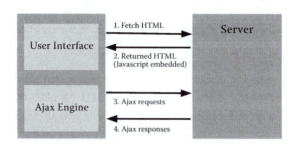

FIGURE 14.4 The Ajax engine in action. Once the Ajax engine has been downloaded and is running (steps 1 and 2) it can handle interaction with the server (steps 3 and 4). The Ajax responses can be in HTML or other languages such as JSON. (Illustration © 2011 by Intelligent Content Ltd Licensed under a Creative Commons Attribution-NonCommercial-NoDerivs 3.0 Unported license (CC BY-NR-ND 3.0))

14.2.1.8.1 Ajax Engine The key component of Ajax is what Jesse Garret (2005) called the *Ajax Engine*, a JavaScript object running within the client machine's browser that is called whenever information is needed from the server. When the user does something that requires part of the webpage to be redrawn, the Ajax Engine is called upon to schedule and execute the request. Effectively, the engine acts as a kind of intermediary between the browser and the server. Crucially, the request is made asynchronously. When the server returns with a response that contains data, usually in the form of XML, the engine parses this data and makes any changes required to the graphical information within the browser window.

Figure 14.4 shows how Ajax initially behaves like a standard webpage. An HTTP request is sent and HTML is returned; embedded within it is additional JavaScript code (including the engine) (Ousterhout and Stratmann 2010; Paulson 2005; Adobe 2005). Once the engine is running, it can issue requests back to the server and return data in the form of HTML, JSON etc. JavaScript event handlers deal with the interactions.

14.2.1.8.2 Ajax Toolkits As Ajax began to become popular, developers realized that they were implementing the same features over and over again. This led to the creation of various toolkits which included pre-coded modules and libraries for common features such as dropdown menus, tabs, toolbar buttons etc. These toolkits help to eliminate the more tedious aspects of developing Ajax applications and this is an active research and development area (Fraternali et al. 2010). There are a large number of such toolkits (the wiki AjaxPatterns[*] reports over 200), some of which are open source. An article in *Information World* (Wayner 2006) noted in particular: Dojo, Rico, Prototype, YUI, Kabuki and Google Web Toolkit. Becky Gibson (2007) provides a similar list and also notes how, increasingly, software integrated development environments (IDEs) are incorporating additional functionality to support the generation and debugging of Ajax-related code. A primary example is the Eclipse Ajax Tools Framework (ATF).

---

[*] See: http://ajaxpatterns.org/Frameworks

Also of interest is the OpenAjax Alliance, an organisation of vendors, open source projects and developers; and JQuery, a toolkit released in 2006 that has now become very popular.[*]

14.2.2 The Web as Platform

Web 2.0 represents the evolution of the web from a source of information to a platform.

DR. PRIYA NAGPURKAR ET AL.

(*2008, 109*)

Ajax was an important development in the history of the Web, but it is only one part of the Web 2.0 story as far as technology and standards are concerned. To complete the transition from a hypertext-oriented Web focused on content, to Web 2.0 services as we experience them today, required new technologies and standards that drew on ideas about the Web as Platform.

TECHNOLOGY PLATFORMS

A technology platform can be many things, but in computing it usually refers to the full stack of technologies that allow a piece of software to run (Feller 2010). This might include the computer's hardware and operating system as well as, perhaps, some specialist software such as a Java Runtime environment. All these components are sometimes represented as a *stack* of layers, with the layer on top reliant on what the layer below provides. So, when we say that the Web is acting as a platform, we usually mean that online services can be accessed and used through the browser, although the reality is that the browser itself runs on the PC or Mac desktop and therefore also relies on the computer's hardware and operating system.

However, as long as the online service can interact successfully with the technologies that the browser provides, it can operate on any browser that is running on any underlying software/hardware stack. In simple terms the online service no longer cares whether it is being accessed on a browser running within Apple MacOS, Microsoft Windows or on a smartphone. These issues have been 'abstracted' away.

The concept was pioneered by Netscape, the company that developed one of the first successful Web browsers back in the 1990s. In its marketing material Netscape pointed out that their browser could be seen as the next computing platform and described how it worked on many different computing hardware systems. Some existing companies— Microsoft in particular—saw this as a threat to their established desktop, shrink-wrapped[†] software businesses. Microsoft even started to develop its own browser, Internet Explorer, in response. This competition came to be known as the *browser wars* and was not without considerable controversy and legal shenanigans (see, for example, Auletta (2001) for further details). Although Netscape did not survive as a separate company after the dot-com bust of the early 2000s, the company's idea of the Web as Platform did survive.

---

[*] See: http://w3techs.com/technologies/overview/javascript_library/all
[†] This is shorthand for software that is licensed, put on a CD, shrink wrapped in plastic film and physically distributed.

One consequence of the Web as Platform is the emphasis on creating applications that provide an online *service*. A corollary of this is that there is much less emphasis on the software release cycle and, indeed, many well-known Web 2.0 services remain in perpetual beta (see Chapter 1).

As the Web as Platform concept has taken hold, the Web has metamorphosed from its beginnings as a global hypermedia system to a universal platform for delivering services and applications (Nyrhinen and Mikkonen 2009). Some technologists even argue that the browser is increasingly capable of acting as an operating system in its own right. This is a subject we will return to when we consider what is beyond Web 2.0.

So why has the idea of the Web as Platform become more feasible now? The answer is that browser technology has moved on to a new stage with the introduction of Rich Internet Applications.

14.2.2.1 Rich Internet Applications (RIAs)

Ajax was crucial to the development of Web 2.0. It was the first, and by far the most popular, attempt to tie together various Web technologies and standards in order to develop responsive, sophisticated websites that mimicked the behaviour of desktop applications, and in this sense it was pivotal. However, it is not the only approach to the problem and more recent attempts have been grouped together under the umbrella term of *Rich Internet Applications* (RIAs)(see Figure 14.5).

RIA is therefore a wide-ranging term which refers to a family of solutions that share the common goal of moving beyond the conventional hypertext-led Web (Fraternali et al. 2010; Bozzon et al. 2006). Indeed, Melia et al. (2010) argue that RIAs exist at the intersection of two competing development cultures: desktop clients and the Web.

The term Rich Internet Application was coined by Jeremy Allaire in 2002 in a document describing the benefits of a new version of the Adobe Flash plug-in. However, as Vossen and Hagemann (2007) have observed, like many Web developments this has been an evolutionary rather than revolutionary process and the ideas can be traced back to earlier developments such as JavaScript client-side scripting, Forrester's X-Internet report in 2001 (which described a kind of executable Internet[*]) and Webtops (a term introduced by the Santa Cruz Operation in 1994 for a Web-based interface to their Unix operating system).

One of the main advantages of RIAs is that they introduce new architectural ways of working by providing the client with both the ability to undertake considerable amounts of business logic and to provide data storage. With RIAs, the communication between the client and server follows a similar pattern to Ajax, except that both sides of the equation can initiate communication, making for a far more flexible environment. Finally, RIAs have also improved the graphical presentation and user interaction of client applications. Many of the Web 2.0 services and applications that we have discussed at length in this book make use of RIAs (Valverde and Pastor 2009; Linaje et al. 2007).

It is important to be clear that RIAs are more than Ajax. Firstly, other technologies and plug-ins attempt to better the effects of Ajax within the browser window. Examples, which we

---

[*] See: http://www.forrester.com/ER/Research/Report/Summary/0,1338,11282,FF.html

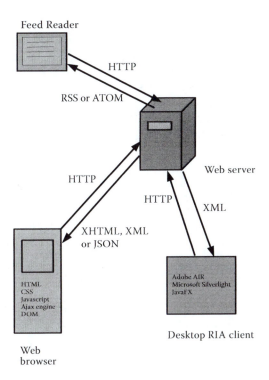

FIGURE 14.5   The complex ecosystem of Web technologies, including Rich Internet Applications and RSS/ATOM feeds. Note however that sturdy old HTTP still acts as the communications workhorse. (Illustration © 2011 by Intelligent Content Ltd Licensed under a Creative Commons Attribution-NonCommercial-NoDerivs 3.0 Unported license (CC BY-NR-ND 3.0))

will discuss further in a moment, include Adobe Flash, Microsoft's Silverlight, Open Laszlo and Flex. Secondly, technologies have been introduced that allow the concept of RIA to be moved beyond the browser window to allow Web-based applications to run as separate widgets or apps on the main PC or Mac desktop window. Examples include Adobe Air and Sun's JavaFX. This latter development is mainly due to the increasing importance of smartphones (where the browser experience is not as good as it is on a desktop computer), issues with browser security (as browsers often have, for security reasons, built-in limitations as to what data they can access on the desktop machine), the need to continue working off-line when broadband is not available (especially the case with mobile working) and the rising popularity of standalone widgets (see later in this chapter) (Hammond and Goulde 2007).

14.2.2.1.1 Deploying RIAs   There are currently three main options for delivering Web-based applications developed with RIAs: browser-based solutions, player-based solutions (using a browser plug-in), and client-based applications that are executed on the desktop as a set of runtime components (Hammond and Goulde 2007). Figure 14.6 shows the spectrum of possible solutions. Zeichick (2008b) notes that three major companies, Adobe, Microsoft and Sun Microsystems (now part of Oracle) are competing to be become dominant in RIA deployment.

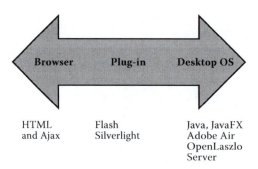

HTML · Flash · Java, JavaFX
and Ajax · Silverlight · Adobe Air
· · OpenLaszlo
· · Server

FIGURE 14.6   The spectrum of solutions available for the deployment of RIAs. (Illustration © 2011 by Intelligent Content Ltd Licensed under a Creative Commons Attribution-NonCommercial-NoDerivs 3.0 Unported license (CC BY-NR-ND 3.0))

14.2.2.1.1.1 Adobe Flash   Flash is a veteran in Web terms, having been a consistent presence since it was introduced by Macromedia in 1996 (the company has since been bought by Adobe). It was originally developed to deliver vector-based animation within the browser window via the use of a plug-in (the Flash Player). The Player is available for a range of desktop operating systems and browsers and it is widely accepted that at least 95% of Web users have the plug-in installed (Benninger 2006). These days it is widely used for animation and user interactivity, but it is also popular as a way of delivering video over the Web.

The Flash player supports a kind of programming language called ActionScript which creates interactivity within a Flash application (e.g. menu options when watching an animation). The Flash plug-in has also been used to bypass the cookie storage limitation on the client (Benninger 2006).

14.2.2.1.1.2 Adobe AIR   As we discussed in the previous section, RIAs are increasingly being deployed beyond the browser and on the PC or Mac desktop. One of the key tools that supports this development is the Adobe Air runtime system. It is not a system for developing code or applications, but a runtime module that allows Flash-, Ajax- or Flex-based Web applications to run on the desktop or on a mobile device (Vieriu and Tuican 2009). In order for a user to take advantage of an AIR application they must download the AIR runtime system. The runtime is installed once on the user's computer, and then AIR applications are installed and run just like any other desktop application.

14.2.2.1.1.3 Adobe Flex   Flex is an open source framework for the development and deployment of cross-platform RIAs based on the Adobe Flash platform and Adobe AIR runtime (Fukuda and Yamamoto 2008). It includes two languages, MXML (an XML-based language that developers use to define the interface of an application) and Flash's ActionScript. Flex also includes a component library with more than a hundred user interface components and an interactive application debugger. An application developed using Flex can run within the browser using the Flash plug-in or externally on a PC, Mac or Linux desktop, or smartphone using the AIR runtime system.

14.2.2.1.1.4 JavaFX Oracle's JavaFX is built around its recently acquired subsidiary company Sun Microsystems, which developed the Java language and environment. To build applications that run under JavaFX, developers use a combination of a scripting language, JavaFX Script, and Java code. The resulting application runs anywhere that the Java Runtime Environment (JRE) can run including smartphones, desktop machines, gaming consoles and TV set-top boxes. It was announced by Sun Microsystems in May 2007 and is currently at release JavaFX 1.3, although work is on-going on version 2.0. Some of the modules that support JavaFX have been released as open source under the GPL v2 licence.

14.2.2.1.1.5 Silverlight Microsoft's Silverlight is a cross-browser plug-in that works in a similar manner, and is a major competitor, to Adobe Flash. It delivers rich media, including video, and allows developers to build RIAs using Microsoft's .NET (pronounced 'dot net') framework with its associated tools and languages (such as C#), and thereby bring some of the flavour of the Windows world to the browser. It implements a full version of the .NET CLR (language runtime), and a subset of Windows Presentation Foundation (WPF)— Microsoft's core graphical subsystem for the Windows operating system. It also has its own markup language called Extensible Application Markup (XAML). The client plug-in runs under Windows and MacOS. Mobile devices are supported through Silverlight's integration into Windows Phone 7 and through an application for the Symbian system. A free software implementation, Moonlight, has been developed by Novell for support on Linux.

14.2.2.1.1.6 OpenLaszlo OpenLaszlo is an open source RIA development platform. The OpenLaszlo platform architecture is designed to accommodate multiple runtime rendering environments. Laszlo applications are developed in a language called LZX, a combination of JavaScript and XML. This code is then compiled into a variety of formats such as Flash (through use of the Small Web Format [SWF]) and Ajax/DHTML for use in the browser. Using special XML tags that form part of LZX, developers can create applications that take advantage of more advanced graphical elements such as buttons, drop-down menu items etc.

There are two ways that OpenLaszlo applications can be deployed: either as free-standing applications, which the company calls Solo, or on the OpenLaszlo Server. The former are simply Flash SWF files that have been compiled by the Laszlo system and can run in any browser that has the Flash plug-in installed. For the latter, the Web server needs to be running the OpenLaszlo Server as well as the standard HTTP server. The OpenLaszlo Server is implemented as a Java servlet and runs inside a servlet container or standard Java 2 Platform, Enterprise Edition (J2EE) application server such as Apache Tomcat, WebSphere or JBoss.

14.2.2.2 Scalable Vector Graphics

Closely related to RIAs, Scalable Vector Graphics (SVG) provide an easy way to program graphics and animation, which in turn has brought about a new generation of visually powerful, interactive Web services. It is increasingly being seen as an important adjunct to Ajax.

SVG is an XML standard for describing vector-based graphics that can be rendered by a modern Web browser (Quint 2003; Probets et al. 2001), and is being developed by the W3C.[*] It supports animation within the browser window with either JavaScript or Synchronized Multimedia Integration Language (SMIL),[†] and describes two-dimensional graphs using vectors rather than bitmap graph formats such as PNG and GIF. Vector formats are far more flexible; they make scaling and redrawing much easier and produce much smaller file sizes. Pictures are created from a series of objects or *primitives*, each of which is described by an XML tag. Available objects include line, rectangle, circle, ellipse, polyline and polygon. A typical XML tag might be:

```
<line x1="0" y1="100" x2="100" y2="0" stroke-width="2"/>
```

This draws a line of thickness '2' between the two co-ordinates, within the browser window.

There is an obvious role for SVG in the graphically rich user interfaces that are common in Web 2.0 but it has competition, including, as we discussed in the previous section, Adobe Flash and Microsoft's Silverlight. While it has an obvious advantage, in that it is an open standard, it is too soon to say whether this will be sufficient to establish it as the primary technology for handling graphics on the Web (Trébaol 2008; Ferraiolo 2008). On the one hand, Microsoft's Internet Explorer is yet to support the SVG standard, and on the other, SVG is increasingly seen as an important part of the future of Ajax, especially by the OpenAjax Alliance (the smartphone version, SVG Tiny, has achieved widespread deployment and adoption).

14.2.2.3 The Programmable Web: APIs, Mash-ups and REST

One of the key Web developments of recent years has been to expose and share data through Application Programming Interfaces (APIs). Developers use APIs to construct new services for their users and being able to reuse data from different sources has been critical for the emergence of Web 2.0 services. The ease with which they can be programmed and the enthusiasm of grassroots developers has ensured the widespread uptake of this way of working, often referred to as the *Programmable Web* (Maximilien and Ranabahu 2007). The combination of REST, APIs and a new generation of software development frameworks and toolkits has led to the emergence of data mash-ups: services that take data from a variety of sources and combine that data in new and interesting ways to produce novel Web 2.0 services.

14.2.2.3.1 APIs   De Souza et al. (2004, 222) define an API as a "well-defined interface that allows one software component to access programmatically another component infrastructure". The concept of exposing an API can be traced back to ideas about software development in the early 1970s. APIs facilitate what is known as *information hiding*, i.e. hiding the details of how a software module or service undertakes its task, but at the same time allowing developers sufficient information to enable them to make programmatic use of the service. This reduces the amount of detailed knowledge that a developer needs to have in order to use another piece of software and also means that the owner of the

---

[*] See: http://www.w3.org/Graphics/SVG/IG/resources/svgprimer.html
[†] See: http://www.w3.org/TR/REC-smil/

TABLE 14.1   The Set of Operations That Can Be Applied to a Resource
in the RESTful Way of Working

HTTP Method	Function
GET	Retrieve a representation of the current state of a resource.
PUT	Transfer a new state onto a resource or if the resource does not currently exist, create one.
DELETE	Delete the identified resource.
POST	Create a subordinate resource.

Source: Based on notes from Cesare Pautasso. 2009. RESTful webservice
composition with BPEL for REST. *Data & Knowledge Engineering*
68 (9) (September):851–866.

service can change internal details of the code without upsetting anyone who is relying on
it (assuming the details of the API itself do not change).

APIs are becoming very popular and as just one example, 75% of Twitter's traffic comes
from API calls rather than the standard Web interface.[*] Even the Bible has half a dozen
APIs.[†]

14.2.2.3.2 REST and Web 2.0   In Section 14.1.4 we explored the role of the REST architectural pattern in the development of the Web. More than 50% of Web 2.0 APIs use the REST
design architecture, according to ProgrammableWeb,[‡] and indeed, it is widely seen as a
kind of *de facto* standard (Battle and Benson 2008; Pierce et al. 2006).

As we have already seen REST leverages the three core Web standards: URLs, HTTP and
HTML. Taking a REST approach provides a way to organise and control access to the data
in a wide range of applications. It also facilitates interoperability between different Web-
based applications and provides an alternative to other techniques such as service-oriented
architecture (SOA) and Simple Object Access Protocol (SOAP)-based Web services (Pierce
et al. 2006; Vinoski 2008). This is often referred to as taking a RESTful approach to Web
2.0 development (Richardson and Ruby 2007).

The basic idea behind the RESTful approach is that resources on the server are referred
to using URLs, i.e. it is a resource-oriented approach (Overdick 2007; Kuuskeri and Turto
2010). Interaction with these resources takes place using the URI and the various HTTP
methods we discussed in the earlier section (see Table 14.1). REST does not mandate any
scheme for constructing URLs.

Put simply, these methods allow the client to undertake basic data processing tasks on
the server such as create a resource, read it, modify it and delete it. REST is structured
around every resource being accessed via a URI and a RESTful service exposes a URI for
every piece of data that the client's software might want to work on. This is often described
in terms of verbs and nouns. In the RESTful way of working, there is a small, fixed number

---

[*] See: http://www.forbes.com/2010/09/13/alcatel-lucent-mobile-technology-cio-network-api.html

[†] See: http://www.programmableweb.com/apitag/bible

[‡] See: http://blog.programmableweb.com/2011/03/08/3000-web-apis/

of verbs—*doing* words—and these are the methods of HTTP. There is no need to add to this basic list. However, everyone is free to add to the growing list of nouns by using new URIs. All the additional complexity occurs in the new resources. As Inoue et al. (2010, 329) write: "RESTful Web APIs have been gaining popularity because of their simplicity, interoperability, and scalability".

Using HTTP means that APIs which are overlaid on top of the URI structure create predictable and, to a certain extent, self-documenting APIs. The process of taking applications and turning them into addressable URIs allows for a process of using building blocks from across the Web to create new services (Raman 2009).

RESTful operation is often described in terms of the four basic operations of persistent storage, called create, read, update and delete (CRUD) (Pautasso 2009; Snell 2004). Recall that with REST, which is a resource-oriented service, a resource is identified by a URI and operations are carried out on that resource. Table 14.1 shows how these CRUD operations map to the HTTP operations.[*] These are fairly self-explanatory except for POST, which is used to modify subordinate resources. So, for example, a blogging software system might expose each of its hosted weblogs as a resource which can be manipulated using RESTful actions. The individual blog items would be subordinate resources, with the blog as their parent. To update a blog item, a POST is carried out to the parent blog.

Let's consider an example: the Twitter API. Twitter exposes some of its underlying data via its API, which is implemented in a manner that adheres to the REST principles (Makice 2009b). The API permits three kinds of HTTP request: GET, POST and DELETE. GET is used as a way of obtaining data, POST is used to change things, and DELETE is used to remove a resource from the Twitter server. The GET method accepts a URI and uses it to retrieve a resource from the server. For example:

GET https://twitter.com/statuses/show/id.xml HTTP/1.1

The response from the server will be to return the details of a single Twitter update message as given by its ID number. The data can be configured to be returned in either XML or JSON. So, for example, the use of the above GET method might return some XML code that looks a little like this:

```
<id>937108231</id>
<text>Sitting in a café discussing English prog rock with some
friends</text>
```

In fact, a lot more information than this is returned, including data about who has uploaded the message. However, what is important to grasp is the way in which a call to the API has, in effect, been embedded in the GET method of HTTP.[†]

We should also mention in passing that REST is not the only way to build Web-based services. An alternative approach is known as *Remote Procedure Call* (RPC). This relies on POST, and ignores the other HTTP methods. Only one URI is exposed—a kind of

---

[*] Further details of CRUD are also in Chapter 4 of Richardson and Ruby (2007).
[†] Further details can be found in (Makice 2009b).

application gateway to the available functions and data that the service is offering. The most popular way of working in RPC is *Simple Object Access Protocol* (SOAP), a kind of message format that is placed inside the HTTP message. Inside the SOAP envelope is the RPC call itself. SOAP is often used in what are called (uppercase) Web services, or sometimes more colloquially known as 'Big Web Services' (Richardson and Ruby 2007).

These provide an alternative architecture to REST and are formally defined by the W3C.* They comprise a number of technologies, organised into a layered standards stack including SOAP and Web Service Description Language (WSDL). However, this rather heavyweight way of working tends to be used by large corporate enterprises to handle their Web-based services and intranets and is not seen so widely in the Web 2.0 community.

Tim O'Reilly (2005b) refers to the two camps in his original paper on Web 2.0 and notes that Amazon offered both types of service: the SOAP system was used for high-value business-to-business transactions between suppliers and the company, but the lightweight REST offering was used for 95% of the interactions with the site. It is important to be aware, however, that there is perennial debate as to which way of working is best for the Web (Pautasso et al. 2008; Jazayeri 2007).†

14.2.2.3.3 Mash-ups   The Programmable Web allows developers to write applications that pull in data from other services and recombine it in a process known as a *mash-up* or *data mash-up* (Ingbert 2007; Yu et al. 2008; Maximilien et al. 2008; Benslimane et al. 2008).

As Ingbert (2007) argues, the successful Web 2.0 services that offer APIs provide access to enormous content repositories which: "no individual could gather on their own or afford to keep and maintain" (p. 2). Amazon is an example of an early pioneer of this way of working, providing an API to access its database of books. The Delicious Library application (unrelated to the Delicious social bookmarking system) was an early user of the Amazon API—mashing up book data with other information from the user (see Figure 14.7). It is important to remember however, that not all Web 2.0 services that provide APIs to access their data are fully open, nor do they allow complete access to all their data.

Formally we can say that a mash-up is: "an application development approach that allows users to aggregate multiple services, each serving its own purpose, to create a new service that serves a new purpose" (Lorenzo et al. 2009, 59). In general, data and services are made available to others through two principal methods: exposure via a Web API or as a data feed through Really Simple Syndication (RSS) or Atom. These services and feeds are basic 'ingredients' to be mixed and matched with others to form new applications.‡ The concept builds on an earlier, and far less effective, technique for extracting data from websites known as 'screen scraping' (Vossen and Hagemann 2007) in which data was taken or 'scraped' directly off websites and then recombined.

---

* See: http://www.w3.org/TR/2007/REC-wsdl20-primer-20070626/

† For further discussion see Chapter 10 of Richardson and Ruby (2007).

‡ The ProgrammableWeb website includes a directory of mash-ups.

FIGURE 14.7 The Delicious Library service. This was an early user of Amazon's API. (Source: Delicious Monster Software, LLC. All rights reserved.)

Map mash-ups, which combine data and geographic information, constitute nearly 50% of the total number of mash-ups (Anand et al. 2010). Map information can be combined with a variety of other data that have a geo-spatial element, for example house prices or pollution data. The pioneer in this regard was Google, which introduced its Google Maps Web service in 2005. The service integrates map, satellite and aerial imagery via a simple interface which includes Google's search facilities as well as what were, at the time, highly innovative *pan and zoom* or *slippy* maps (activated by clicking and dragging). Most importantly it includes a client-side API that allows users to customize the map backcloths by overlaying additional data and embedding the finished result into their own website.

14.2.2.3.3.1 Stable APIs The functionality of an API may be changed by the service provider either through the terms of use or by technical means, e.g. changing the way the API operates (Palfrey and Gasser 2007). Most Web 2.0 APIs are provided free of charge and thus the provider is under little obligation with regard to quality of service and may change the API functionality in the future as their business model evolves. However, developers who use an API have a certain expectation that there will not be too many changes to the interface. For example, an API may provide for a call, by another piece of software, to a module which has a number of parameters. If the owner of the API changes the number of parameters required, then all those developers who have used the API will have to change their own code.

The stability of an API is therefore an important factor for the reliability of data mash-ups (Souza et al. 2004; Fowler 2002). As Souza et al. write: "A stable API is not subject to frequent changes, therefore leveraging the promised independence between the API producers' and consumers' code" (p. 222).

14.2.2.3.3.2 Tools for Mash-up Development Yahoo! Pipes is a visual design tool for bolting together content feeds (in the form of RSS and Atom) and other sources of data, and is a key technology in the development of mash-ups. Other emerging development platforms in this area include IBM's Mashup Center, the Google App Engine, and MashLight* from the University of Politecnico do Milano.

14.2.2.3.4 Web Application Programming Languages and Frameworks   We have already discussed the large number of toolkits and frameworks that support the development of Ajax on the client side. In addition to these, there are a number of dynamic programming languages and application development frameworks that assist with software development on the server (Krämer et al. 2007; Casal 2005).

A framework is "a reusable, 'semi-complete' application that can be specialized to produce custom applications" (Fayad and Schmidt 1997, 32). Frameworks provide a skeletal support structure made of software components that new software applications can be quickly built on. A framework may include reusable code libraries, a scripting language, commonly used interface components, or other software packages that assist in gluing together different components of a software application (Shan and Hua 2006). Reusability, whereby generic components can be used in new applications, is a key characteristic. These systems significantly reduce the development time of Web-based services.

There are many such frameworks, with, for example, Shan and Hua (2006) listing more than thirty just for Java. This is partly because this aspect of Web application development overlaps with other, general-purpose systems development, including database access and management. For this reason many of the server-side support offerings relate to well-known enterprise development environments such as Java and .NET. In addition these frameworks support a diverse set of programming languages including C++, Java, Perl, PHP, Python and Ruby.

Key examples include Ruby on Rails and a number of Java-based frameworks including JavaServer Faces (JSF), Struts, Tapestry, Cocoon and SpringMVC. Non-Java examples include Django, which works with Python, and Seaside, which works with the highly influential object-oriented programming language SmallTalk (Jazayeri 2007).

14.2.2.3.4.1 Ruby on Rails   Due to its importance in Web 2.0 development we will take a closer look at the Ruby on Rails framework. Ruby, the programming language with which Rails is built, is a very important part of the framework's sophistication and power (Casal 2005). Ruby is a reflective, completely object-oriented scripting language, developed by Yukihiro Matsumoto.† It is interpreted rather than compiled and has a simple syntax that was partially inspired by languages such as Eiffel and Ada, but also includes features from Java, Python, Lisp and Smalltalk. It is widely perceived as a lightweight replacement for Java (Governor et al. 2009).

Ruby on Rails, an open source Web framework built using the Ruby programming language, is particularly factored to support the RESTful way of working—one of the

---

* There is an online video of MashLight in action at: http://home.dei.polimi.it/guinea/mashlight/demo.mov
† A reflective language allows the code to modify itself as it runs. See: http://en.wikipedia.org/wiki/Ruby_%28programming_language%29 [10th August 2011]

reasons for its popularity (Bachle and Kirchberg 2007; Wirdemann and Baustert 2007). It is structured around a software engineering architectural pattern known as Model-View-Controller (MVC), widely used in server systems, in which code that undertakes different tasks is clearly separated and demarcated (Ping et al. 2003). Thus all the business application logic is held in the Controller code and kept separate from code that handles how the data is presented to the user. The Model element contains core functionality such as the database access and control.

14.2.2.3.5 N-Tier   When working in an Ajax-supported, Web 2.0 environment, the server has two important roles. Firstly, it has to deliver the Web application to the client's browser. Secondly, it interacts with the browser while the application is being used. Traditionally, the client-server model consisted of two tiers: the client and the server. However, as systems have become more sophisticated, this has developed into what is known as the N-tier architecture. This is a well-known architectural model in distributed computing systems, where there is one client and a number of server-side tiers (for example, there may be a Web server and a database management server). Crane et al. (2006) argue that Ajax can be considered to be a further refinement of the N-tier model because it introduces a second tier at the client browser (i.e. the Ajax engine).

14.2.3 Syndication and Publication with RSS and Atom

Syndication feeds, used to broadcast information about the content of websites and services, are a key aspect of the Web as Platform since they contribute to the 'fluidity' between different services and sites, particularly with respect to user-generated content (Zakas et al. 2006; Vlist et al. 2007). A lot of blogging tools now create and publish syndication feeds automatically and webpages frequently display the familiar syndication icon that provides a quick way of registering for a feed (see Figure 14.8).

The feeds themselves have become so popular that feed reader (also known as *aggregator*) services have been built around them, with different levels of sophistication. More recently, publication techniques have been added with the introduction of the Atom Publishing Protocol.

The idea of syndication stems from the newspaper industry, where the concept of making an original article or cartoon available to a number of publications has been around since

FIGURE 14.8   The syndication icon. (Source: Mozilla Foundation. Licensed under Mozilla's MPL/GPL/LGPL tri-licence.)

the nineteenth century. Websites, particularly those that have frequent content changes, use syndication feeds to broadcast information about their new content. In this way, these feeds act as 'signals of change' (Hammond et al. 2004) and the advantage to the user is that instead of having to visit a number of, say, news sites, to see what has changed, they can subscribe to each site's feed and deploy an aggregator or reader to collate the information about the new content in one place.

The two key standards for syndication feeds are RSS and Atom, but for most users the differences are largely irrelevant as almost all feed readers and aggregators support both formats. In this section we will look at both RSS and Atom, and how they work, as well as the basics of aggregator services and the implications of the Atom Publishing Protocol.

14.2.3.1 RSS

Technically, RSS is an XML-based data format that enables websites to exchange publishing information and summaries of site contents. Indeed, in its earliest incarnation, RSS was understood to stand for Rich Site Summary (Doctorow et al. 2002). As it became more widely used for blog content syndication, later versions of RSS became known as Really Simple Syndication.

For a variety of historical reasons there are a number of RSS formats (RSS 0.91, RSS 0.92, RSS 1.0, RSS 2.0) and there are still issues of incompatibility (Sayre 2005). It is worth noting that RSS 2.0 is not simply a later version of RSS 1.0, but a different format. Despite this, RSS is still more popular than Atom, representing over 80% of feeds.[*]

14.2.3.2 Atom

In 2003 a new syndication system was developed to resolve some of the inconsistencies between the different RSS versions and clear up the problems with how they interoperated (Sayre 2005). This new system was called Atom and it consists of two standards: the Atom Syndication Format,[†] an XML language used for Web feeds, and the Atom Publishing Protocol,[‡] an HTTP-based protocol for creating and updating Web resources.

There is considerable discussion between proponents of RSS and Atom as to which is the best way forward for syndication. The two most important differences between them are: firstly, that the development of Atom is taking place through a formal, and open, standards process within the Internet Engineering Task Force (IETF); secondly, that the way Atom encodes the content of the feed item (known as the payload container) is more clearly defined (Sayre 2005). Atom can also enclose more than one podcast file at a time and so multiple file formats of the same podcast can be syndicated at once.

14.2.3.3 Syndication with RSS and Atom

Despite the presence of two formats (and the numerous versions of RSS) both have more or less similar structures (Snell 2005; Vossen and Hagemann 2007). The XML elements contained in a feed can be divided into two key areas: the channel, which provides metadata about the feed, and the individual feed items themselves. The following code fragment

---

[*] According to figures by Syndic8.com: http://www.syndic8.com/stats.php?Section=feeds#tabtable

[†] See: http://tools.ietf.org/html/rfc4287

[‡] See: http://tools.ietf.org/html/rfc5023

shows a truncated version of a typical RSS 2.0 feed (taken from my own blog). This is typical of the kind of code that is automatically generated by blogging software.

```
<?xml version="1.0" encoding="UTF-8"?>

<rss version="2.0"
        xmlns:content="http://purl.org/rss/1.0/modules/content/"
        xmlns:atom=http://www.w3.org/2005/Atom
        xmlns:dc="http://purl.org/dc/elements/1.1/"
        xmlns:sy="http://purl.org/rss/1.0/modules/syndication/"
        xmlns:slash="http://purl.org/rss/1.0/modules/slash/"
        >
<channel>
        <title>Tech Lunch</title>
<atom:link href="http://techlun.ch/feed/" rel="self"
type="application/rss+xml" />
        <link>http://techlun.ch</link>
        <description>Paul Anderson&#039;s technology blog</
description>
        <lastBuildDate>Tue, 07 Sep 2010 09:56:00 +0000</lastBuildDate>
        <language>en</language>
        <sy:updatePeriod>hourly</sy:updatePeriod>
        <sy:updateFrequency>1</sy:updateFrequency>
        <generator>http://wordpress.com/</generator>



<item>
            <title>Data mash-ups and the future of mapping</title>
            <link>http://techlun.ch/2010/09/07/data-mash-ups-
mapping/</link>
            <pubDate>Tue, 07 Sep 2010 09:56:00 +0000</pubDate>
            <dc:creator>pdanderson</dc:creator>
</item>
</channel>
</rss>
```

The key parts are in bold. The code is in XML and the first line declares what version of the W3C standard is being used. We can see that the fragment then has a declaration of the XML Namespaces (xmlns) that are going to be used within the rest of the code. Confusingly, the included namespaces include those used by the Atom format (it is common to find this kind of mix in syndication feeds*). We then see the Channel, which details some general information about the blog, for example, its title. This is then followed by a number of <items> (although in this case we have only shown one). Each item represents feed information for an individual blog item including the all-important URI of the blog post.

---

* Vossen (2011) states that this is done to cover up missing elements in the specification.

FIGURE 14.9 Google Reader RSS feed aggregator. Subscribed feeds are shown in the left hand pane. Next to this are the latest headlines for the feed being viewed. (Image courtesy of Google Inc., © 2011 Google Inc.)

14.2.3.4 Syndication Aggregators

As syndication has become increasingly popular, applications have built up around the techniques. These aggregator applications allow the user to subscribe to syndication feeds and then automatically poll the feed's server on a regular basis to see if new information has been made available. Wu and Li (2007) list three popular types of feed reader or aggregator:

1. Web-based aggregators: The primary examples are Google Reader and Newsgator. com.

2. Desktop-based aggregators: These are standalone client applications that need to be downloaded and run on the PC or Mac desktop. Primary examples include NetNewsWire, FeedReader and FeedDemon.

3. Web browsers: Most Web browsers have software that allows them to also act as feed readers. A number of e-mail clients also have feed-reading facilities.

The desktop-based readers offer the most sophisticated facilities, allowing the user to not only subscribe to feeds and view updates as they come in, but also to organise the feeds into groups and sub-groups, undertake searches and configure the time of the update process. Figure 14.9 shows a typical example of a Web-based aggregator, Google Reader.[*]

14.2.3.5 Atom Publishing Protocol

The Atom Publishing Protocol (APP or AtomPub) is an HTTP-based approach for creating and editing Web resources (Snell 2006). Where the syndication format handles what might be thought of as the consumption of Web content, APP handles publication (Kart et al. 2008). It is based around collections of resources such as webpages, podcast files or blog entries, which are represented by the Atom Syndication Format feed entries and held on a server. A client's software interacts with this collection using the CRUD-style,

---

[*] There are a large number of feed readers competing for a user's attention and Wikipedia lists dozens: http://en.wikipedia. org/wiki/Comparison_of_feed_aggregators

standard HTTP methods (GET, PUT, and DELETE). Thus, APP is an example of a RESTful service (Inoue et al. 2010).

AtomPub is used as a standard for Web 2.0 applications such as blog editing software (for example Wordpress allows users to manage blog posts using it[*]) and in some content management systems. Some people find the in-house text edit facilities provided by many hosted blogging services to be inadequate and would prefer to use a different client-based text editor to update the blog. If the blogging software's servers and the separate text editor in question both support AtomPub, then they can cooperate to allow the user to write and post blog items from the user's preferred editor.[†] Another example is Google Calendar, which will accept AtomPub-based posts[‡] and is based on Google's Data Protocol which makes use of AtomPub.[§]

14.2.4 Authentication Technologies

Using Web 2.0 services often requires the user to provide a good deal of profile information and despite a plethora of new technologies, username and password remain the dominant form of authentication on the Web (Bonneau and Preibusch 2010b). This has a number of inherent problems, not least the security risks of reusing the same password many times. In this section we briefly consider two emerging technologies that may help alleviate some of the issues around authentication on the Web. However, we should note Bonneau and Preibusch's reservations as to the likelihood of these systems becoming widely adopted. We should also note that there are a number of proprietary solutions such as Facebook's Connect and Google Friend Connect (Kim et al. 2010).

14.2.4.1 OpenID

Most websites ask for some personal information when a user registers to join the service. OpenID is a tool that lets users store this information with a trusted third party so that they do not need to re-enter it every time they register with a new site (Powell and Recordon 2007). Providers of OpenID third-party services include VeriSign and MyOpenID.

Basic profile information (such as name, date of birth and location) can be stored in an OpenID profile and used to pre-populate registration forms. It also allows a user to undertake a single-click login to a site that they have previously registered with (using a single code, based on an OpenID URI), and gives the user some control over how much information is shared with websites.

A number of well-known Web 2.0 services make use of OpenID including Google, Facebook, Yahoo! and MySpace. Figure 14.10 shows the OpenID login, which a user sees when they visit the registration page of a website that uses the OpenID system. The user

---

[*] See: http://codex.wordpress.org/AtomPub for details.

[†] Jesper G. Høy has a blog post describing this kind of task using Windows Live writer, a client blog editor which operates independently of the blog hosting software: http://www.jesperhoy.com/post/Publishing-content-to-ASPNET-web-sites-using-Windows-Live-Writer.aspx

[‡] See http://www.ibm.com/developerworks/xml/library/x-atompp2/

[§] See http://code.google.com/apis/gdata/

FIGURE 14.10 The OpenID logo. Reproduced with permission from the OpenID Foundation. (Reproduced with permission from OpenID Foundation. Copyright © 2006-2011 OpenID Foundation.)

only needs to enter their unique OpenID code and the rest of the registration process is handled by the OpenID system.

OpenID grew out of the blogging community where there was a need for people to take their blogging identity and use it when commenting on other people's blogs. It was originally developed in 2005 by Brad Fitzpatrick, chief architect of Six Apart, as Yadis (an acronym for 'yet another distributed identity system') and was first used on the LiveJournal blogging software.

14.2.4.2 OAuth

OAuth is an open standard for authorization within Web 2.0 applications and services. It is a tool for users to allow one service to share their information and resources (e.g. photos) with another service, but without handing over personal authorization details.

OAuth recognizes that in the Web 2.0 world there are more and more situations in which one service needs some kind of permission to access information about a user and share with another service. The problem is that if standard transactions are used to authenticate between these sites then the username and password have to be transmitted, something that is done by HTTP using Basic Access Authentication (effectively simply sending the username and password in a lightly encoded form). This has two problems. Firstly, it is easy to decode the encryption used in Basic Access and secondly, there is no mechanism for applying any limits as to what can be done once the authentication has taken place. OAuth gets around these problems by sharing tokens between sites rather than passing around the username and password. Tokens grant access to a specific site for specific resources and for a defined duration.

The formal specification[*] provides an example that explains the process. A Web user (i.e. the resource owner) can grant a printing service (the client) access to her private photos stored at a photo-sharing service (the server), without sharing her username and password with the printing service. Instead, she authenticates using username and password directly with the photo-sharing service which issues delegation-specific credentials to the printing service using tokens.[†]

---

[*] See: http://tools.ietf.org/html/rfc5849
[†] Further details can be found at: http://hueniverse.com/2007/10/beginners-guide-to-oauth-part-ii-protocol-workflow/

14.2.5 Interoperability and Data Portability: Online Social Networks

In Chapter 10 we looked at the social graph as a network of people and their connections. However, every social network site (SNS) has its own graph and an on-going debate centres on whether or not, and how, these graphs could be shared between different services. However, the data contained in a particular network's graph is the key data asset of the company that owns it and as such has immense value.

Breslin and Decker (2007) and Nguyen et al. (2009) both point out the difficulties that currently exist with achieving interoperability when many SNSs are keen to operate walled gardens. Razmerita et al. (2009) reviewed a number of leading SNSs and found that it was not possible to export/import user profile and relationship data between different networks and that the data that were made available were far less than the total data held by each network. The end result is that there are literally hundreds if not thousands of social graphs being constructed across the Web (Fitzpatrick 2007).

There is a particular tension within the Web 2.0 developer community over the role of the larger SNSs (Heyman 2008). Facebook, as the largest, attracts particular attention as it has created the most comprehensive social graph and yet this remains carefully controlled. Some open data activists even go so far as to argue that Facebook's social graph should be freed from any one company's control and made into a community asset along the lines of open source software (Fitzpatrick 2007; Gilbertson 2007). While Facebook's Open Graph protocol may sound as if it might be a step in the direction of freeing up its social graph, in fact it really just provides a way for other websites to tag their content so that it can be subsumed into Facebook.

Facebook's chief privacy officer Chris Kelly has defended the company by saying that although the idea of data portability is good in principle, the process of achieving it is more complex than some advocates suggest (Heyman 2008). This is not solely the view of one company; some academics argue, for example, that exchanging and aggregating user data poses privacy risks to individuals (Narayanan and Shmatikov 2009). In October 2010 Facebook announced a tool for users to download and save the data held about them. It is too early to say what the portability implications of this will be.

Despite what might be called political and business difficulties, a number of initiatives have begun to try and address these issues. One of these is the Data Portability project, which seeks to bring users and technology companies together in order to improve data porting between Web 2.0 services. This has become a much-debated issue, and a number of international conferences have emerged, such as the International Conference on Social Network Interoperability and the International Workshop on User Data Interoperability in the Social Web. The W3C has also set up the Federated Social Web Incubator group[*] to explore these kinds of issues. We will now consider two of the more technical solutions.

14.2.5.1 OpenSocial

OpenSocial is a collection of common APIs used by some SNSs. It was launched in 2007 by a group of companies, most notably Google and MySpace, to enable SNSs to share user

---

[*] http://www.w3.org/2005/Incubator/federatedsocialweb/

data, friend lists and other information with each other and with third-party developers.[*] Without an agreed, common API, all the different SNSs would provide their own unique set of interfaces, causing a headache for developers and slowing new developments. With OpenSocial however, each service develops its own implementation of the agreed common standard interface, and developers need only use the interface calls from the common API in order for their new applications to work with any site that offers OpenSocial. It makes use of a number of key standards and technologies including HTML, JavaScript, XML and Atom and is an example of RESTful architecture principles.[†]

14.2.5.2 Social Graph API

The Social Graph API[‡] was an attempt by Google to try and explore issues around data held in individual SNS graphs. It is based on working with two friendship-related standards, XFN and Friend-of-a-Friend (FOAF). XFN makes it possible for human relationships to be represented within hypertext links by including a REL attribute within an HTML href tag[§], e.g. <a href="http://jane-blog.example.org/" rel="sweetheart date met">Jane</a>. FOAF is a similar idea but designed for the emerging Semantic Web, which we will discuss later on. Google has created a resource, available to others, by crawling the Web and harvesting instances of these two formats.

14.2.6 Resource Description Framework in Attributes (RDFa) and Microformats

Another way in which Web 2.0 services demonstrate a marked progression in the development of the Web is to look at the way HTML is required to carry more information within its tagging structure. So far there have been two main approaches: RDFa, which is being slowly developed as a formal standard by the W3C and is designed to dovetail with the emerging Semantic Web, and microformats, which have emerged as a kind of grassroots response to the same problem but with little in the way of formal standardization.[¶]

14.2.6.1 RDFa

The RDFa embeds machine-readable metadata within a webpage.[**] In other words, it provides a way of adding extra information to a webpage that will not be read by a human user, but could be read and acted upon by another Web application or software program. Effectively the webpage is being augmented with additional information.

The W3C provides an easy-to-understand example:[††] if an author wishes to notify others that their webpage is available under the Creative Commons licence, he or she might

---

[*] Google has provided an introductory video, hosted on YouTube at: http://www.youtube.com/watch?v=9KOEbAZJTTk &feature=related

[†] See: http://docs.opensocial.org/display/OSD/OpenSocial+REST+Developer%27s+Guide+%28v0.9%29

[‡] See: http://code.google.com/apis/socialgraph/faq.html

[§] REL is an HTML attribute that describes a relationship between the current document and the one being referred to in the HTML hypertext link.

[¶] This is not to say that agreed microformats have not emerged through consensus. A well-used example is the hCard format, which allows business card metadata to be embedded in HTML. Indeed, this is itself based on a well-defined standard, the IETF's international business card standard, vCard.

[**] RDF is kind of universal language for expressing data and is a key component of the Semantic Web.

[††] See: http://www.w3.org/TR/xhtml-rdfa-primer/

put some text at the bottom of the page and provide a link to the licence. However, for a piece of software to understand what this link means, additional information needs to be included within the HTML file. This is what RDFa does. Essentially, for this example, one adds additional information within the hyperlink using the REL attribute. Thus the HTML code fragment would be:

```
All content on this site is licensed under
<a rel="license" href="http://creativecommons.org/licenses/
by/3.0/">
 a Creative Commons License
</a>
```

The hypertext link now contains an additional attribute, REL, and this is set to 'license'. How this is actually interpreted depends on what other Web application or software reads the page.

However, it is not only hypertext links that can be supplemented in this manner. RDFa allows other metadata to be embedded in many other HTML tags such as the heading (<h1>, <h2> etc.) or paragraph (<p>) tags. It also provides for a handful of additional attributes such as 'about', which provides for a URI that specifies the resource the metadata describes.

The real power however, comes from the fact that vocabularies can be used to define the exact metadata to be used with these attributes, which creates great flexibility. A number of vocabularies exist, notably Dublin Core, which provides ways to describe books and other documentation (e.g. author, title etc.). There are also a number that relate to people, their relationships and activities (e.g. FOAF, vCard and hCalendar). Furthermore, any user is free to create new vocabularies. The developer of a webpage that contains RDFa simply needs to tell the browser—by adding something in the HTML header—which vocabularies he plans to use within the rest of file. This can be seen in the following example:

```
<html xmlns="http://www.w3.org/1999/xhtml"
 xmlns:dc="http://purl.org/dc/elements/1.1/"
 version="XHTML+RDFa 1.0" xml:lang="en">
<head>
 <title>Paul's Home Page</title>
 <base href="http://example.org/pda/" />
 <meta property="dc:creator" content="Paul Anderson" />
</head>
```

In this example, by indicating an XML namespace (xmlns) in the first line, the browser is being told to make use of the Dublin Core vocabulary. The browser imports the namespace and associates it with the prefix 'dc'. Note that the browser is also told to use XHTML and RDFa version 1.0. From then on, whereever there is an RDFa attribute which uses the 'dc' prefix, the browser knows to make use of the Dublin Core vocabulary, e.g. in the penultimate line with: property="dc:creator".

14.2.6.2 Resource Description Framework (RDF)

The underlying model for the abstract representation of RDFa vocabularies is an important specification called the Resource Description Framework (RDF). RDF is a language for describing structured information, in particular meaning (*semantics*), which is being developed by the W3C and which has a major role to play in the Semantic Web. We will discuss the Semantic Web in the final chapter, but for now we will look at a few basic details of the RDF model since it plays a role not only in RDFa, but also RSS 1.0,[*] two technologies that already feature in Web 2.0 services.

RDF consists of three key concepts: resources, properties and statements. Resources are objects that we wish to make statements about and are identified by URIs. Properties describe the relationships between resources and thereby allow us to imbue meaning. Statements make assertions about the properties between resources. So for example a statement might be:

Paul Anderson is the author of a book about Web 2.0.

A statement is known as a *triple,* a concatenation of resource, a property and a value. That is, the property shows the relationship between the resource (the person in this case) and the object (or value) in question. These are sometimes referred to as subject, predicate and object triples (derived from predicate logic in mathematics, where these ideas originated), or simply as RDF triples.

An important, and powerful, feature of RDF is that properties are also identified by URIs. This provides a global naming scheme both for the objects we want to reason about and the relationships between them. In order to make RDF machine processable on the Web, these triples are written in a form of XML known as RDF/XML, which allows RDF to be exchanged across the Web.[†]

14.2.6.3 Microformats

Microformats are similar to RDFa in that metadata is added using the REL and CLASS attributes of existing HTML tags (Khare and Celik 2006; Khare 2006), but the approach to developing them is very different.[‡] XFN, which we have already mentioned, is a common example of a microformat. The following code, included in a blog post, uses the XFN format:

```
<a href="http://johnsmithweb.com" rel="friend met">John Smith</a>
```

It says that the words 'John Smith' will appear in the blog post as a hypertext link to the Johnsmith website. However, in addition, there are some metadata that define what kind of relationship there is between the blog owner and John Smith: in this case a friend they

---

[*] RSS 1.0 is based on the RDF/XML syntax.
[†] Further details from: http://www.w3.org/TR/rdf-syntax/
[‡] For a detailed look at the technical differences between RDFa and microformats see the report from Digital Enterprise Research Institute (Graf 2007).

have met in person. This additional information is not displayed by the browser, but might be used by another piece of social software.

14.2.7 Widgets

Widgets are small, client-side information applications that run either within the browser or separately on the desktop (Kaar 2007; Taraghi 2009; van Thuan et al. 2009). They are used to get quick access to frequently used, online information without the need to start up the Web browser and visit a specific page. They are a forerunner of apps, the smartphone client applications that are becoming so popular, and which we will discuss in more detail in the next chapter.

Also known as 'gadgets', the idea behind widgets builds on the RIAs discussed in the previous section, but with more of an emphasis on undertaking a small, self-contained task.[*] They started to appear in around 2003 and are being used to replace single-purpose, information-oriented applications such as stock-price tickers, weather forecasts, battery-life indicators etc. They are proving to be increasingly popular as they provide information, updated in real time, for as long as they are open. The service they present may appear to be simple but usually includes a complex mix of data 'mashed' from multiple sources.

The advantage they have over a webpage is that once a widget's code has been downloaded onto the device, there is no need to reload that code again, which saves on network traffic and makes them faster. Their development is relatively straightforward since they use popular Web technologies and standards.

In order to run a widget, a user requires a Widget user agent, which is either built into a Web browser or is a standalone application engine with similar functionality. Examples include Konfabulator, Windows Sidebar, Google Desktop, Apple Dashboard and Opera Widgets. An important development is the open source Wookie project,[†] currently being incubated by the Apache Foundation, which is building a Java server application to facilitate the deployment of W3C widgets (Wilson 2010).

To help developers to author widgets, the user agents provide APIs and support common Web standards and protocols such as JavaScript and Ajax. However there are interoperability problems between different user agents and engines (Mendes et al. 2009), and there have been issues with standardization. This has been particularly acute in the smartphone market, although an open standard is being developed by the W3C (W3C 2009a). A number of existing widget solution developers such as Opera have indicated that their proprietary systems will be aligned with W3C Widgets when the standard is finalized.[‡]

---

[*] The widget being discussed here is different to what are sometimes called 'Web widgets'. This is an unfortunate source of confusion. Web widgets are fragments of HTML/CSS/Javascript embedded into a webpage, which carry out a particular task. A good example is the Web widgets provided by Wordpress. The W3C Landscape study has more detail on the subtle differences (W3C 2008). The term 'W3C Widgets', the name of an emerging W3C Recommendation, is sometimes used to describe what we identify here as 'widgets' in order to distinguish them from 'Web widgets'.

[†] See: http://wiki.apache.org/incubator/WookieProposal

[‡] See, for example: http://dev.opera.com/sdk/

14.3 HANDLING THE EPIC SCALE OF DATA

We seem to always need more computers than we have.

JEFF DEAN
Google fellow (2007, 3:48)

In Chapter 4 we discussed how the collection and processing of large datasets has become one of the key principles underpinning Web 2.0. Although we have touched on how technical developments, particularly at Google, have facilitated this process, we will now consider this in more detail.

Collecting and searching through large amounts of data is an enormous computational task which is often referred to as working at the *peta-scale* (or 1,000,000 gigabytes—ten thousand times the average home PC's storage capacity) (Sankar et al. 2008). Although the average corporate database is much smaller (it is likely to be measured in terabytes [TB] i.e. 1,000 GB), petabyte levels of data handling are not uncommon on the Web. Google is understood to handle as much as 20 petabytes per day, eBay generates a petabyte a day in user activity log files alone and Facebook's photo storage totals at least 20 PB (Beaver et al. 2010; Dean and Ghemawat 2010). Datasets of this scale are sometimes referred to as Big Data,* and indeed the scale of the data is so big that, already, the petabyte is becoming somewhat inadequate. Industry commentators are starting to talk in terms of the exabyte (1,000 PB)(Watters 2010) and Internet networking technology is being implemented to address the realities of transferring data at this scale (Rizvi 2009).

Google's solution to the scalability issue is an enormous data structure called BigTable (Chang et al. 2008; Dean and Ghemawat 2010; Jia 2010). This works with Google's underlying file system (GFS) and something called BigDaddy, code that handles storage and access to the enormous amount of data that Google collects and sifts through (Ghemawat et al. 2003), as well as MapReduce, a distributed, parallel data processing algorithm (Dean and Ghemawat 2010, 2008). What is interesting about these kinds of algorithms is that the code is often not very long, but the scale of data being processed is enormous. For example, Sankar et al. (2008) quote figures of perhaps 200 or 300 lines of code for MapReduce, but it can handle data from one trillion URLs.

BigTable not only handles search, but also many of the company's other services including the Orkut SNS. The whole system is spread across a series of data centres which are themselves constructed from thousands of servers (Barroso et al. 2003; Carr 2008). Each of these is made from basic, commodity PCs running the Linux operating system. The individual machines also have large disk drives and very fast network connections so that they can exchange data rapidly.

BigTable is a bit like a gigantic Excel spreadsheet, although it is enormous: hundreds of terabytes in size. Like a spreadsheet, the table is made up of rows and columns that meet at junctions called cells, which in turn contain the individual items of data. Unlike a conventional spreadsheet, however, each cell in the table is accessed based on something called a

---

* See: http://www.economist.com/node/15557487

'triple' which consists of three references: the row, the column and a timestamp. The time element allows the system to look backwards and have a historical view of how individual data items have changed over time. The table is distributed across thousands of servers in a series of row ranges known as 'tablets' in order to balance the load across the system. Associated with BigTable is the BigTable API, which provides functions for controlling the table, creating rows, looking up information etc. (Chang et al. 2008; Jia 2010).

Google is not the only Web company developing these kinds of systems. Facebook makes use of a database system called Cassandra, which it has released as open source (Lakshman and Malik 2010), and a system called HayStack to handle its photo storage (Beaver et al. 2010). HayStack is based on a deep understanding of the precise requirements of delivering stored photos within the Facebook system. For example, the developers knew that users upload photos once and rarely delete them, but may access them many times. The priority then was to build a database system that was designed with these requirements in mind. Engineers at Facebook found that the metadata added to each photo caused bottlenecks and so they designed a system that reduced the need to store metadata on the hard disk. The system also uses clever caching mechanisms to store multiple photos in one file, which again improves access speeds.[*]

Not all this development is taking place behind closed doors. Open source developers have implemented projects that help to handle peta-scale computing, notably the Apache Hadoop project, which has replicated MapReduce in an open source form.[†] A number of Web 2.0 services use this software including Yahoo!, Twitter, Ning and LinkedIn.[‡] In addition, Facebook has launched the Open Compute project to make public more information about how it designs and builds its data centres (Judge 2011; Schneider 2011).

Web 2.0 companies have adopted a number of techniques to help improve the response times of their service operations and to cope with the large volume of users they see (Kim et al. 2010; Schneider 2011). Techniques that have been incorporated include HTTP traffic managers, which block unwanted traffic; traffic shapers, which control the flow of IP network communications; lightweight Web servers such as lighttpd. Sites also make use of load balancing technologies such as caching,[§] which control bottlenecks that form between servers (e.g. open source Squid reverse-proxy server). Major sites also separate more frequently accessed content into a different server farm which allows them to develop a specialist focus on performance criteria. The free, open source Memcached solution is also used extensively to cache database content within the main (faster) memory of servers (see Figure 14.11).

14.3.1 Database Technology

Today's relational database systems were designed for online transaction processing (OLTP)—critical data processing tasks such as credit card transactions. However, they are

---

[*] For more details see Beaver et al. (2010).

[†] By way of a public demonstration, in September 2010, a team of engineers at Yahoo! used Hadoop to calculate Pi to the 2,000,000,000,000,000th place—higher than anyone else has ever achieved (http://www.bbc.co.uk/news/technology-11313194).

[‡] Apache maintains a wiki-based list of major implementations: http://wiki.apache.org/hadoop/PoweredBy

[§] Caching is a process of keeping frequently requested Web content stored (cached) in faster computer memory.

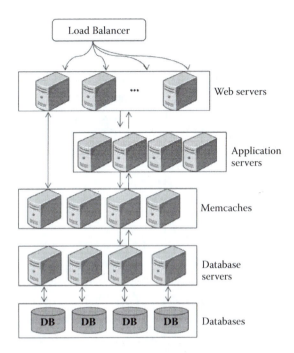

FIGURE 14.11 Typical infrastructure arrangement for a large Web 2.0 service. (Reprinted from Information Systems, 35(2), Kim, Won, Ok-Ran Jeong, and Sang-Won Lee, On social Web sites, p. 215-236. Copyright © 2010 with permission from Elsevier.)

not particularly good for Web 2.0–type tasks such as traversing a graph in an online social network (Kim et al. 2010). This means that database software has had to change to a distributed model in order to adapt to the peta-scale.

In order to guarantee the level of security and database integrity required for OLTP there are significant performance 'overheads'. Some Web 2.0 companies have not been prepared to accept these compromises as they affect the scalability and performance of their systems. Instead they work with databases in alternative ways and Kim et al. (2010, 225) argue that: "most, if not all, major sites do not guarantee the integrity and consistency of their databases". That is, they cannot guarantee that some data, e.g. a friend's comments, some news items, will not be lost from the site.

The traditional way of working with databases is to use SQL, and the open source MySQL system remains popular with developers of Web 2.0 systems. However, a new class of database, known as 'NoSQL' is emerging and examples include CouchDB, MongoDB, Membase, Neo4J and Redis (Eifrem 2009; Ghosh 2010; Watters 2010; Leavitt 2010). Of particular interest are graph databases: designed to follow the way data is used on the Web, for example, by storing it in a graph-like way that mirrors the way in which online social networks are structured (Angles and Gutierrez 2008; Eifrem 2009). Twitter has developed FlockDB, a database system designed for the kind of social graph tasks that they undertake (Adams 2010b), Google has developed Pregel (Malewicz et al. 2009) and Microsoft has its Trinity system. The latter is particularly interesting as it adopts a hypergraph model rather than a simple graph model. In a hypergraph a link connects a number of nodes, while in a simple graph a link connects two nodes only. Microsoft argues that this approach offers a better way of modelling complex relationships within a dataset.

Discussion of how to handle large datasets brings us to the emerging paradigm of cloud computing in which users tap into the 'cloud' of computing resources sitting on the Internet, almost as if they were using a utility. We will discuss this further in the last chapter, but for now we note Frischbier and Petrov (2010) who write that the cloud: "seems to be the future architecture to support especially large-scale and data-intensive applications" (p. 58).

14.4 STANDARDS

In a general sense, standards are commonly accepted agreements on ways to do or make things. Imagine how much easier life would be if we only needed one electricity charger for all our different gadgets. Establishing standards is therefore partly about ensuring interoperability between products but it also has additional benefits. Standards may establish a minimum level of quality for example, or reduce the amount of variety, allowing for economies of scale (imagine how difficult and expensive life would be if each charger needed to be plugged into its own type of wall socket).

Standards are the bedrock of technology development, but there can be significant differences between them. Open standards, for example, underpin the Internet and Web, but understanding what we mean when we describe a standard as being either open or closed first of all requires us to appreciate how standards come into being. In this section we will learn how standards are made, the processes that are involved in deciding how open a standard might be, and look at how standards are created for the Internet and Web. Finally, we will look at why standards are so important to the development of Web 2.0.

14.4.1 Determining a Standard

In order to understand the relative status that one set of standards may have over another it is important to understand the standards-making process. For example, most people are aware of organisations that produce standards in their own country such as the British Standards Institute (BSI; in the UK), the Deutsches Institut für Normung (DIN; in Germany), the Standardization Administration of China (SAC) and may even be aware of organisations that produce international standards, such as the International Organisation for Standardisation (ISO) and the Institute of Electrical and Electronics Engineers (IEEE) (pronounced 'eye-triple-ee'). These formal standards bodies have complex and often time-consuming processes, partly because some of the standards they ratify go on to form the basis for legal regulation within individual countries. Regulators are therefore expected to have a principled concern for the fullest democratic accountability during the development of what may become legally mandated requirements, particularly since formal standards are traditionally used in procurement decisions by central government departments and therefore involve spending taxpayers' money.

However, particularly in the computer industry, things are more complicated than this. In the past, the process of formal standards development was very time-consuming, with full ISO accreditation taking up to seven years (Cargill 1997a). In the late 1980s this became a problem for the fast-moving computer industry and led to the creation of faster-moving, industry-led consortia to act on standards development. Certainly, the technology area with greatest growth at the time, the early Internet and Web, did not seek any formal standards body activity, but chose to work through the IETF (Internet Engineering Task Force) and W3C (World Wide Web Consortium*) rather than the ISO.

Pedersen and Fomin (2005) report that there were over 400 fora relevant to the development and adoption of information and communications technologies (ICT) standards in 2005, all with their own blend of people representing different interests. A wide variety of national, international, and non-government agencies, as well as academics, researchers, business consortia, individual companies, and even individual people all get involved in the development of what might loosely be termed standards. The status of these other 'standards' often depends, in part, on the status of the organisation that produced them.

14.4.2 Open versus Closed Standards

Standards often start life as the ideas and technical specifications[†] of university researchers, professional bodies, learned societies or private companies rather than being created from scratch. In fact, the quality of the technical specification can also be used as a way of judging the quality of a standard. Different organisations have widely varying processes for the initiation, development and acceptance of a standard. The complexity of these processes is often a reflection of the number of stakeholders involved and the geographical reach of a standard. In addition, standardization is not simply a process of resolving technical issues; political, economic and administrative factors often also come into play (Jakobs et al. 1996). A wide variety of formats for document drafts, working groups, committees and ballot processes exist which attempt to form, in one way or another, a common agreement through some form of voting or consensus-seeking.

How open a standard is perceived to be will often depend on a combination of different factors. For example, proprietary standards (often known as *closed* standards) are created by individual companies for use within their organisation and by their customers who may be charged to use them. Over time, successful proprietary standards may develop, through the market, into what are called *de facto* standards. In this case, it is the 'fact' that a great many people, possibly everyone, is making use of a proprietary standard that makes it a standard: no scrutiny, through a formal standards-making process, has taken place.

At the other end of the spectrum, however, it is less easy to be clear about what constitutes openness (Cerri and Fuggetta 2007; Kelly 2006). Firstly, it is important to be clear that open standards are seen as a good thing and have been very important in the Web's success (Herman 2006). They allow different groups of technologists to work on different areas of

---

* The W3C was set up by Tim Berners-Lee to develop and maintain standards for the World Wide Web.

† Dargan (2005) defines a specification as: "essentially a white paper that provides sufficient detail to clearly describe the standard's detailed behaviour, features, functions, appearance, language and interface (API) to enable it to be successfully implemented" (p. 19).

the Internet and Web in parallel, confident that when systems are put together they will interoperate (recall the layered nature of the Internet and Web). Open standards also help to avoid the anti-competitive nature of *vendor lock-in*, where one company has too much power over a market because it controls a proprietary standard.

Tim Berners-Lee describes open standards in the context of the Web as: "standards that can have any committed expert involved in the design, that have been widely reviewed as acceptable, that are available for free on the Web, and that are royalty-free (no need to pay) for developers and users" (Berners-Lee 2010, 3). In this definition there is a focus on the breadth of expertise in the standards development process and making the standard available free of charge. Dargan offers a slightly different suggestion: "a public specification developed and maintained by consensus of a recognized standards body that defines interfaces and services for a computer system to perform, and that is made available to review and implement" (Dargan 2005, 11). Such a definition focuses on the idea of a formal process of consensus facilitated by a standards body (such as ISO or IEEE) and on the standard being open for review. Control over the development of the standard is also an important feature. As Cargill writes: "One of the elemental principles of standardization is that the future of a specification, once it is delivered to a standardization group, lies with the group and the market and not with a single vendor" (Cargill 1997b, 199).

The issue of intellectual property rights (IPR) is also crucial in standards work and can vary considerably as to the terms of any licensing, patents and royalties. Again, things vary and this is a highly complex area. The W3C provides its standards royalty free. However, the situation is often complicated by the fact that technology standards may pull together different technological areas, some of which may involve existing IPR (Cerri and Fuggetta 2007). In this case, 'open' in terms of IPR means that owners of any rights in technologies that are involved in an open standard agree to their use on what is known as Reasonable and Non-Discriminatory (RAND) terms. The IETF allows the inclusion of patented technologies within its standards provided they are released under RAND terms. In contrast, the W3C is stricter, refusing to approve standards where there is some existing IPR that the holder is not prepared to release under the same royalty-free terms.[*]

Clearly the degree of openness that a standard is deemed to possess is a nuanced concept involving several key elements: the process; the speed by which the standard is created (too fast and there is the danger that enough care has not been taken or that the processes have not been sufficiently democratic; too slow and the standard risks being irrelevant before it has even been published); the cost of accessing and using the standard; and any copyright or IPR impediments to implementing the standard.

14.4.3 Standardisation for the Internet and Web

The principle organisation for Internet standards is the Internet Society, an umbrella organisation that oversees the detailed technical work undertaken by the IETF,[†] which

---

[*] Although there is provision for exceptions—see: http://www.w3.org/Consortium/Patent-Policy-20040205/
[†] The Internet Society also oversees the work of a small number of other Internet-related standards bodies including the Internet Research Task Force (IRTF) Research Groups. See: http://www.isoc.org/standards/orgs.shtml

in turn oversees the development of key Internet technologies such as the TCP/IP protocol. It facilitates the publication of Requests for Comments (RFCs): technical memos by working engineers and researchers, which detail a development in the way the Internet operates. Most of these come from working groups set up by the IETF, but some can come from independent groups or lone engineers who happen to have a new idea. In a nutshell, when an RFC is issued, others comment on it and based on this feedback, it is revised and reissued. After a period of time, this iterative process may lead to a formal standard issued by the IETF.[*] There are also other standards groups, including IEEE, International Telecommunication Union (ITU) and the European Telecommunications Standards Institute (ETSI), which create and publish standards that relate to the Internet.

Of particular importance to the development of the Web are the standards developed by the W3C. It is this organisation, set up by Tim Berners-Lee in 1994, that is responsible for HTML, CSS and other key Web technologies. It oversees more than 100 standards and incorporates the work of more than 400 member organisations, about 60 staff and numerous expert individuals (Umapathy 2009).

The W3C standards are called Recommendations (W3C 2005). They begin life as working groups, which form around topics that are sufficiently interesting. Over time, the working group will issue various working documents and memos, and at some point a formal First Public Working Draft will be issued, which signals to the wider Web development community that it is time to take notice and engage in formal feedback. After a while a Last Call announcement is made indicating a deadline for final comments. If the work has reached an acceptable level of maturity then a Call for Review of a Proposed Recommendation is issued, offering a final chance for changes to be made before it becomes a W3C Recommendation. The Recommendations are under a royalty-free patent licence, allowing anyone to implement them.[†]

14.4.4 Standards and Web 2.0

Standards work! (especially the old ones ;-).

JOSÉ MANUEL ALONSO
W3C Spanish Office (Alonso 2006)

It is important to be clear that standards have played an essential role in the development of Web 2.0 (Kristaly et al. 2008). They have helped Web 2.0 services to be adopted because users and suppliers have been more confident in the market and the services themselves have been seen as likely to last longer and to interoperate better (Alonso 2006). The processes of working towards standards have also reduced research and development costs and have stimulated innovation. As Jay Kesan and Rajiv Shah write: "much of the success of the information age can be attributed to the use of standards ... when everyone uses the same standard, powerful network effects increase the utility of a technology" (Kesan and Shah 2008, 179).

---

[*] This can be a complex process and a more comprehensive explanation is available from the IETF's process guide at: http://tools.ietf.org/html/rfc2026

[†] For more details see: http://www.w3.org/2005/10/Process-20051014/intro

However, as we now know, the technologies, and therefore the standards, that underpin Web 2.0 services are really just part of the ongoing evolution of the Web. The most important of these, Ajax, is not one technology but a collection, for which most of the standards are provided by the W3C. Indeed, the key pieces of Ajax technology were in place and had been standardized before the Web 2.0 moniker gained credence in the mid 2000s (Alonso 2006).

The main exceptions are RSS and Atom. While Atom is being developed as a standard by the IETF, RSS is slightly different in that it is an example of what is sometimes called a *community standard*. This means it has been developed through a grassroots approach to interoperability led by individuals rather than organisations (Yuan 2010). Other such community standards include some authentication technologies and microformats.*

This is not to say that everything is straightforward with respect to Web 2.0 and standards. As we have already noted there is considerable tension over the role of user data obtained from the social graph and it is unclear how far standardization and interoperability will be able to assist in this respect. There are also worries about how the Web's universal model is being undermined in the smartphone market by the introduction of native applications based on proprietary standards (an issue we will return to in our final chapter). For these reasons it is clear that keeping an eye on developments in Web and Internet standards will remain important for any student of Web 2.0.

EXERCISES AND POINTS TO PONDER

1. Review the material from the W3C workshop on the Future of Social Networking in January 2009, hosted in Barcelona by Universitat Politècnica de Catalunya (http://www.w3.org/2008/09/msnws/report.html). Discuss the benefits and potential drawbacks to the development of social network architectures that are less centralized and more distributed. What are the barriers to the sharing of data between social networks?

2. **Read about the FOAF format and then develop a FOAF profile for you and for a group** of colleagues on the same course or in another department.

3. Follow the instructions given in Yu and Woodward (2009) to mine data from ProgrammableWeb's database and map the usage of APIs to mash-ups. The paper states that the long tail of the power law is shorter than in other fields of Web 2.0. Can you recreate their results? This task requires NetDraw (which is free): http://www.analytictech.com/netdraw/netdraw.htm

4. Wang et al. (2009) and Yu and Woodward (2009) both discuss how real-world social network analysis can be applied to the network of APIs and mash-ups. Read these papers and write about the clustering and network properties that are exhibited by the API ecosystem. Is the ecosystem a small world network? What are the implications of your conclusions?

---

* For example, XFN was a product of the Global Multimedia Protocols Group, a club consisting of a few designers who borrowed their name from Neal Stephenson's novel, *Snow Crash* (Khare 2006).

5. Read and discuss Moriyoshi et al. (2009) and Nagpurkar et al. (2008) who both debate the workload of Web 2.0 applications and their impact on server-side technologies. Write about how Web 2.0's impact on the server differs from the impact of the original Web model. What can be done to alleviate any difficulties?

6. Try creating your own XFN code by using the XFN generator: http://www.gmpg.org/xfn/creator

FURTHER READING

Section 14.1: How the Web Works

For a detailed review of the early history of the Web, including many explanations of how the basic technology works, see *How the Web was Born* by Gillies and Cailliau (2000). For further information about the very earliest days of the Web see Reid (1997b).

Many commentators note the importance of the ideas of Vannevar Bush and his Memex machine, first outlined in 1945, in inspiring hypertext pioneers (see, for example, Naughton 1999).

Section 14.2: How Web 2.0 Services Work

Pressman (2000), Chapter 28, details client-server models and discusses different ways of implementing them, in particular the N-tiered system, which is becoming increasingly common.

Readers who wish to see a DOM in action can add the additional Inspector module into Firefox (https://developer.mozilla.org/En/DOM_Inspector).

For a basic introduction to programming with REST see:

http://www.ibm.com/developerworks/webservices/library/ws-restful/. For a tutorial on REST see Costello (2002).

For more on the debate between those who support heavy-weight Web services and those who support REST see: http://www.w3.org/2007/01/wos-ec-program.html

There is an MP3 recording of a panel at the First International Workshop on RESTful Design discussing REST and other architectural styles at: http://www.ws-rest.org/2010/

See Ohara (2010) for more on how REST works with regard to the load on a server and techniques to aggregate requests between clients and server.

Read the thoughts of David Stutz on software and platforms including references to the ideas of Clay Christensen and Ray Ozzie on innovation in software: http://www.synthesist.net/writing/software_platforms.html

For more discussion on the Web as Platform concept, and in particular debates about the future role of native apps within the concept see Mikkonen and Taivalsaari (2011) and Charland and Leroux (2011).

For a discussion on how the use of APIs differs from conventional software development, and an analysis of metrics that might be used to determine quality, see Koschmider et al. (2010).

To see the smorgasbord that is Google's array of APIs visit: http://code.google.com/more/table/

For more discussion of the way that SNSs make use of APIs such as Google Friend Connect see Kim et al. (2010).

For detailed advice on best practice for making use of third-party Web 2.0 APIs (and for providing one's own) see JISC UKOLN's Good Practice for Provision of APIs project (http://blogs.ukoln.ac.uk/good-apis-jisc/good-practice-for-provision-of-apis/).

For further discussion of mash-ups see Yu et al. (2008). Intel has some videos of its MashMaker tool in action at: http://software.intel.com/en-us/articles/intel-mash-maker-videos-and-example-mashups/. For more on enterprise-related mash-ups see the Open Mashup Alliance (http://www.openmashup.org/) and their work on a development language—Enterprise Mashup Markup Language (EMML).

For an introduction to microformats see Emily Lewis's articles, http://ablognotlimited.com/index.php/articles/getting-semantic-with-microformats-introduction/ and see also UKOLN's introductory guide to microformats: http://www.ukoln.ac.uk/cultural-heritage/documents/briefing-71/html/

For details of SVG, and in particular further information on how animation works, see Quint (2003).

See Thomas Ullman's online tutorial on how to build a widget: http://people.kmi.open.ac.uk/ullmann/tutorials/wookie/widget.htm

For more on widgets and their relationship with manufacturers' own attempts at similar solutions see Scott Wilson's April 2010 presentation to the London Android Group: http://skillsmatter.com/podcast/os-mobile-server/scott-wilson-w3c-widgets-and-android

Section 14.3: Handling the Epic Scale of Data

LinkedIn's development team has an interesting blog and website with links to various talks and software projects. See: http://sna-projects.com/sna/ and http://sna-projects.com/blog/

For more detailed discussion of the idea of NoSql databases see Leavitt (2010) and read some of the debate between those in favour of this approach and those who have reservations, at Daniel Abadi's blog (http://dbmsmusings.blogspot.com/2010/08/problems-with-acid-and-how-to-fix-them.html) and in Harris (2011).

For details of data centre infrastructure see the video at Facebook's Open Compute initiative: http://opencompute.org/

A video on how YouTube scaled to handle large numbers of users is at: http://video.google.com/videoplay?docid=-6304964351441328559#

For more on how Google builds its data centres as well as an explanation of MapReduce see Jeff Dean's talk to the Seattle scalability conference, 2007: http://video.google.com/videoplay?docid=-6304964351441328559#docid=-2727172597104463277

Pujol et al. (2010) provide further information on details of how to scale Web infrastructure for **online social network systems**.

Section 14.4: Standards

Read Victor Stango (2004) on the economic importance of standards and the role of network effects.

## CHAPTER 15

Beyond Web 2.0

The computer industry is driven by the furious pace of technological innovation. It is not surprising then that not long after Tim O'Reilly started to promote the idea of Web 2.0, people began to wonder what 'Web 3.0' might look like. Indeed, within a few months of the first Web 2.0 conference in 2004, trade magazines were beginning to speculate on the next version of the Web (see, for example, ZDNet[*] and Dan Gilmour in the *Financial Times*[†]). Others, however, were not so sure that these speculations were valid.[‡]

As time passed a consensus seemed to emerge that 'Web 3.0' was the Semantic Web, Tim Berners-Lee's vision for imbuing the Web with meaning in order to allow far more information to be processed by machines (Hendler 2009). This third 'version' of the Web would be able to express a kind of intelligence by incorporating new ideas from artificial intelligence, natural language processing and data mining techniques. Indeed, when questioned at the WWW 2006 conference in Edinburgh, Berners-Lee stated that Web 3.0 (although he objected to the term) was likely to be a combination of the Semantic Web and high-powered graphics using the (then new) SVG format.

This is not to say that the Semantic Web is the only contender for 'What's next on the Web'. A survey by the Institute of Electrical and Electronics Engineers (IEEE) in mid-2011, of two dozen leading Web academics, entrepreneurs and analysts, pointed to at least five technology contenders for the title (Ackerman and Guizzo 2011). These included mobile technologies, the convergence of TV with the Internet and new forms of voice and gesture interfaces.

Smartphone and other mobile technology is an area that many commentators and academics agree will dramatically alter the way we use the Web over the next few years. As Mike Jones, CEO of MySpace told the 2010 LeWeb conference in Paris: "When I think about the definition of Web 2.0 and I think about the change into Web 3.0, I get very transfixed on both mobile and portable devices and the application of social technologies to digital experiences" (Jones 2010, 7:00). Others point to the arrival of location-based technologies such as handheld global positioning system (GPS) and the subsequent explosion

---

[*] See: http://www.zdnet.com/blog/saas/what-to-expect-from-web-30/68
[†] See: http://dangillmor.typepad.com/dan_gillmor_on_grassroots/2005/04/web_20_try_30.html
[‡] See: http://edgeperspectives.typepad.com/edge_perspectives/2005/12/ready_for_web_3.html

of geospatial-related applications, services and games as another area of interest (Batty et al. 2010). Such technologies feed into the development of the kind of real-time Web that Twitter and other microblogging services first created, and the authors argue the ensuing "moment-relevant Internet ... is likely to produce new ways of visualizing space and time" (p. 12). Others, including Tim O'Reilly, believe that the widespread introduction of sensor technologies and the emergence of what is known as the Internet of Things will drive the evolution of the Web (O'Reilly and Battelle 2009).[*]

On the other hand, so-called Web 3.0 might simply be a continuation of existing developments. Many people involved in the development of online social networks argue that we have yet to understand or take advantage of the true power of the emerging digital social graph and the vast amount of personal data that are being collected by the companies involved. A whole new raft of applications is likely, which could leverage these resources in ways that have yet to be thought of.

In the remaining part of this book we will consider each of these and offer an introduction to the key ideas and technologies. We will also look at some other interesting technologies, such as HTML5, which will play a major role in whatever future emerges on the Web. Whether 'Web 3.0' is an appropriate term for any or all of these I leave to you to decide. Which of these will come to dominate remains to be seen, or indeed, it may even be something that has not yet left the laboratory. Perhaps 'Web 3.0' is some combination of some or all of these ideas and technologies: Vossen and Hagemann (2007), for example, argue that a process by which Semantic Web and Web 2.0 services grow together might be called 'Web 3.0' (p. 283).

Perhaps, as Jim Hendler told the *Communications of the ACM* magazine in March 2010, the best approach is to adopt the suggestion of Nova Spivack, a Semantic Web entrepreneur, and consider the version numbers as representing the passage of time. He says: "I tend to like Nova Spivack's idea that the version numbers correspond more to Web decades than to specific technologies, and that 3.0 will be the term used for all the new technologies emerging over the coming third decade of the Web" (Kroeker 2010, 16).

15.1 THE SEMANTIC WEB

A serious contender for the long-term future of the Web is the *Semantic Web*, a grand vision for creating online content that can be processed automatically by computers (Berners-Lee et al. 2001) (see Figure 15.1). The basic idea is to add meaning (hence *semantics*) to Web content in such a way that computers can process the content to execute tasks using powerful new applications and services.[†] Currently, humans read, listen, watch, fill in forms and send messages to each other. The vision of the Semantic Web is that at least some of this will be done by computers on our behalf; that is, the Web will become 'machine-processable'.

---

[*] See also: http://www.guardian.co.uk/technology/2011/mar/15/sxsw-2011-internet-online

[†] The vast majority of the content on the Web is for human use—it consists of text, pictures, video and audio, all of which require human sensory capacity and reasoning in order to process and make use of it. Even the databases that are currently made available via the Web tend to be there so that humans can access the data within them and undertake some kind of task.

FIGURE 15.1   The W3C's Semantic Web logo, which is seen across the Web more and more as the technologies mature. According to the W3C the three sides of the tri-colour cube evoke the triplet of the RDF model whilst the peeled back lid invites you to '**open your data**' to the Semantic Web. (Semantic Web logo used with kind permission from the World Wide Web Consortium (w3.org).*)

---

* See: http://www.w3.org/2007/10/sw-logos.html

Since data are so important to this vision, the Semantic Web is increasingly referred to as the 'Web of Data',* and this might represent a nod towards pragmatism on the part of the Semantic Web's proponents. Whereas the original vision focused on the role of automatic, intelligent agents undertaking tasks on behalf of humans, more recent material tends to focus at least as much on data integration, in which "data in various locations and various formats can be integrated in one, seamless application" (W3C 2009c, webpage), as it does on intelligent agents.

Google's Rich Snippets is a good example. When search results are presented, the Google engine looks for additional, marked-up information within the hypertext of the webpage, which provides extra information for the results. So for example, a snippet might include some indication of a rating (see Figure 15.2).

This extra information has been added to the webpage in the form of additional tags, usually in the form of an Resource Description Framework in Attributes (RDFa), which provide structured data over and above what is required to display the webpage content. These extra tags are the way semantic content is added to the Web.

Sometimes people who come across the Semantic Web say that this is what they thought Web 2.0–style data mash-ups were all about: allowing data from different sources to be pulled together and used by new applications and services. This is true to an extent, but a fundamental difference is that mash-ups make use of Web services' proprietary APIs which act as gatekeepers and limit access to the full data collection. In addition, these data collections are not the standardized form of structured data, embedded within the Extensible Markup Language (XML) of the webpage itself, that is proposed by the Web of Data concept (Herman 2009a).

The Semantic Web is, at least in part, an attempt to represent knowledge in a way that allows computers to automatically come to conclusions and make decisions as a result of a certain type of reasoning. This sometimes leads to the misconception that it is an attempt to bring artificial intelligence (AI) to the Web. In fact, Tim Berners-Lee's (2001) article makes it clear that great gains might be possible without resorting to high levels of artificial intelligence: "on the scale of *2001*'s HAL or *Star Wars*'s C-3PO" (p. 37). The goal is not so much about building a software agent that will fully understand a given situation, in a human way, but something that will "assist human users in their day-to-day activities" (Antoniou and Harmelen 2004, 16).

---

* See, for example, the W3C's introduction to the subject: http://www.w3.org/2001/sw/

FIGURE 15.2   Google's Rich Snippets. Additional information, in this case review stars, is provided to the searcher beneath the name of the search result. (Image courtesy of Google Inc.)

The problem with the idea of bringing AI to the Web is that the record of the AI community has been patchy, certainly in its overall goal of replicating human intelligence. Antoniou and Harmelen (2004) have written: "one might worry that, in the worst case, the Semantic Web will repeat AI's errors: big promises that raise too high expectations, which turn out not to be fulfilled (at least not in the promised time frame)" (p. 16). This is perhaps another reason why Semantic Web researchers have, of late, begun to refer to this work as the 'Web of Data'.

This is not to say that the work that has gone into AI research over the last fifty years is being ignored. The World Wide Web Consortium (W3C) have written that: "Some parts of the Semantic Web technologies are based on results of Artificial Intelligence research" (W3C 2009b, webpage) and they single out knowledge representation and logic as two key areas that draw on this heritage. Shadbolt et al. (2006) have written: "it [Semantic Web] will draw on some key insights, tools, and techniques derived from 50 years of AI research" (p. 96).

15.1.1 Linked Data

Perhaps the most important on-going development with respect to the Semantic Web is that of linked data (Bizer 2009; Bizer et al. 2009). This has the overall goal of supporting the development of a Web of Data (and therefore ultimately contributing to the Semantic Web vision) by exposing as many data sources as possible using the Resource Description Framework (RDF) (see Chapter 14). The idea is that if everyone does their bit to mark up the data that they have control over, and publish it to the wider Web, then, in much the same way as the Web of Hypertext Markup Language (HTML) documents was created, a new Web of Data will emerge. A set of principles* has been developed to help overcome technical barriers to the sharing of data with the long-term goal of moving towards a single global data space. These build on fundamental principles of the Web and key standards such as Uniform Resource Identifiers (URIs) and Hypertext Transfer Protocol (HTTP). Data that conforms to these principles, makes use of non-proprietary standards such as RDF, and is made openly available on the Web, is known colloquially as 'five star' data.

This process has already begun and the rate of publication of linked data has increased rapidly in the last few years—an annual rate of 300%—and a large number of companies, scientific agencies, research organisations, libraries and media publishers have contributed (Bizer et al. 2011). A loose, grassroots movement is partially coordinated by the W3C and

---

* See: http://www.w3.org/DesignIssues/LinkedData.html

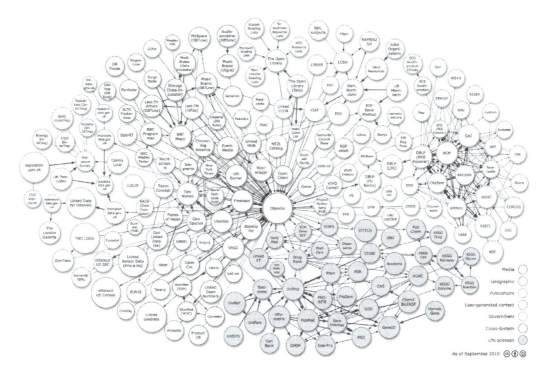

FIGURE 15.3 (See colour insert.) The Linked Data Cloud showing datasets that are published in Linked Data format and interlinked with other datasets in the cloud. As of September 2010. (From Wikimedia Commons, image by Anjeve and Richard Cyganiak. Attribution-ShareAlike 3.0 Unreported (CC BY-SA 3.0).*)

---

* See: http://en.wikipedia.org/wiki/File:Lod-datasets_2010-09-22_colored.png

the resultant network of interlinked datasets is sometimes portrayed in a 'data cloud' (see Figure 15.3).*

Work in this area has been supported, in the United States and United Kingdom, by a movement to open up government and other public sector data. Tim Berners-Lee, Nigel Shadbolt and other leading members of the W3C have been active in efforts to persuade governments that they should open their data up to the Web and make it 'five star' (Shadbolt 2010; Sheridan and Tennison 2010).

15.1.1.1 DBpedia: An Example of Linked Data

An important derivative of Wikipedia, and a prime example of linked data, is the DBpedia project. It was set up in 2007 by the University of Leipzig and Free University, Berlin, and provides a source of structured data that has been extracted from the main Wikipedia site. Although much of Wikipedia is free text, there are various forms of structured information which are marked up using wikicode (for example, quite a lot of data are held in

---

* The latest news on the state of the cloud can be seen at: http://www4.wiwiss.fu-berlin.de/lodcloud/state/

what are called infoboxes*). DBpedia extracts this and turns it into a knowledge base that contains data on, for example, people (including name, birthplace, birth date etc.) and buildings (latitude, longitude, architect, style etc.).

The extraction process makes use of Wikipedia's live article feed and therefore is automatically updated on a regular basis.[†] The data are organised into millions of RDF triples, ready for the Semantic Web, and there are already over a billion of them.

15.1.2 Semantic Web versus semantic web

The Semantic Web vision and its proposed implementation through standards development at the W3C has been criticized by some Web developers as overly ambitious and unsuited to the needs of today's applications (Hitzler et al. 2010, 14). A recurring issue is how all the required extra data is to be added to existing webpages. Gartner, for example, predicts it will be 2017 before the majority of webpages have some form of semantic metadata (Herman 2009b). There has been considerable debate around the best way forward and a number of ad hoc ways of adding machine-processable data have emerged. These techniques are sometimes known as 'semantic web' (lowercase) in order to differentiate them from the loftier goals of the Semantic Web (uppercase) vision (Khare 2006). Examples of the lowercase approach include microformats, which embed small chunks of semantic data within the HTML of a webpage (see Chapter 14).

15.1.3 Web 2.0 and the Semantic Web

Although the Semantic Web is seen as the next important phase of the Web's development, there has also been some speculation as to how Web 2.0 may work with semantic technologies (Hendler and Golbeck 2008; Battle and Benson 2008; Thomas and Sheth 2011; Kinsella et al. 2009; Breslin et al. 2009). Such combinations are often called the Social Semantic Web (Figure 15.4).

Hendler and Golbeck (2008) argue that Web 2.0 can bring social dynamics to the Semantic Web, in particular the powerful network effects demonstrated by services such as Facebook and YouTube. They argue that to date, Semantic Web work has focused too much on developing expert-like knowledge systems that take advantage of semantics within particular domains but do not take advantage of the wider dynamic power of the social Web. They cite the example of RealTravel.com as a site that shows the way forward. This combines Web 2.0–style, user-generated content and social networking information related to travel, with behind-the-scenes use of semantic technologies such as an ontology for place names and locations.[‡]

---

* An infobox is a fixed-format table designed to be added to the top right-hand corner of articles to contain a summary of some of the key points of the article.
† Wikipedia provides a Wikipedia OAI-PMH (Open Archives Initiative Protocol for Metadata Harvesting) feed. This is a protocol for harvesting metadata descriptions of records in an archive. It is widely used by many libraries, institutional repositories and archives. Data providers provide their metadata in XML Dublin Core format, although other formats can be used.
‡ You can read more about RealTravel.com from Tom Gruber's 2007 talk: http://tomgruber.org/writing/social-web-meets-semantic-web.ppt

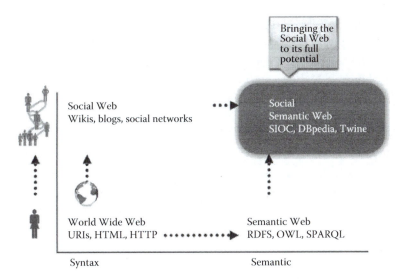

FIGURE 15.4   The Social Semantic Web is a combination of Web 2.0 social dynamics and the knowledge representation powers of the Semantic Web. (Reprinted from Advances in Computers, KINSELLA, Sheila; Alexandre PASSANT, John G. BRESLIN, Stefan DECKER, Ajit JAOKAR, and V. Zelkowitz MARVIN, *The Future of Social Web Sites: Sharing Data and Trusted Applications with Semantics*, p.125, Copyright © 2009, with permission from Elsevier.)

Hendler and Golbeck argue that this is a start, but more power will come when *different* Web 2.0 sites are linked behind the scenes using the power of semantic technologies. The ability to make connections between different sites' interpretations of essentially the same data is achieved by using the same word or ontological reasoning; for example, use of the word 'Paris' on two different websites or use of 'Paris' on one and 'Capital of France' on another. Semantic technologies provide the capability for this kind of connection.

Hendler and Golbeck (2008) also argued that there is much the Semantic Web community can learn from the experience of creating tagging systems based on folksonomies. They conclude: "the integration of [online] social networks, semantics and content has the potential to revolutionize web interaction" (p. 10). Battle and Benson (2008) concurred with these views, arguing that: "the absence of semantic data descriptions on Web 2.0 has put a low ceiling on the complexity that these sites can achieve" (p. 1). Both developments, they note, need each other. They argue that integration can be achieved through Representational State Transfer (REST) architecture; since REST uses URIs as resource identifiers, it is clearly in alignment with the technical direction of the Semantic Web. The operations that REST allows for— create, read, update and delete (CRUD)—also fit neatly with Semantic Web. The authors provide further technical details and an example in their paper.

Other researchers are thinking about the differences between formal ontologies and the folksonomies and collaborative tagging collections that many Web 2.0 services help to create (Limpens et al. 2008). Exploring the synergies between these ways of working and developing potential bridges between the two may bring benefits to the Web.

15.2 SMARTPHONES AND THE RISE OF APPS

It is important to be aware of the role that smartphones are playing in the use and technical development of Web 2.0 services. These increasingly sophisticated devices are more computer than telephone and when combined with fast, 4G and wireless broadband access, provide a new hardware platform for using the Web. Many of these devices also include a range of sensors, motion detectors and GPS navigation systems turning them into sensory devices for a new range of location-based services. Taken together, these developments are often referred to as the 'mobile Web' (Sankar et al. 2008). Analysts predict that within a few years more users will access the Internet from such mobile devices than from desktop PCs. Ofcom's (2011) report details the scale of use of the mobile Web (in the UK at least), particularly in order to interact with Web 2.0 services. As Tim O'Reilly and John Battelle have written: "the smartphone revolution has moved the Web from our desks to our pockets" (O'Reilly and Battelle 2009, 1).

However, the mobile Web is increasingly being used not through a Web browser, but by interacting with individual client applications that run directly on the phone's operating system. These are collectively known as 'native' or 'dedicated' apps, and there has been huge growth in their use since the early 2010s. As Chris Anderson, editor in chief of *Wired* magazine wrote in a widely read essay: "Over the past few years, one of the most important shifts in the digital world has been the move from the wide-open web to semi-closed platforms that use the internet for transport but not the browser for display" (Anderson 2010, 129).

This position is not without its critics. Charland and Leroux (2011) argue that things are more evenly balanced between native and Web apps (see Chapter 14 for an explanation of Web apps) particularly when it concerns the development of the software, and they point out the difficulties of developing and supporting a version of an app's software for each of the main mobile operating systems. However, although it may be true that the performance of native apps is currently better, they write: "The Web technology stack has not achieved the level of performance we can attain with native code, but it's getting close" (p. 53). Mikkonen and Taivalsaari (2011) concur, arguing that although native apps are currently in the ascendancy, this is likely to be a fairly temporary position and "the use of open Web applications will eventually surpass the use of custom native applications on mobile devices" (p. 30). This is partly due to the process of 'catch-up' that is taking place with the performance and capabilities of Web technologies through the introduction of new standards such as HTML5, JavaScript 2.0* and WebGL (Anttonen et al. 2011).

These differences of opinion are likely to be a source of conflict over the next few years. As Web 2.0 services migrate from the desktop to the mobile platform, this debate is going to be key in terms of affecting the future direction of their development. In many respects these issues echo the power of the idea of openness in the development of the Internet and Web, which we discussed in Chapter 6. Tim Berners-Lee, for example, has spoken

---

* This term is used as a shorthand term for the next version of JavaScript, which formally consists of ECMAScript 5 and ECMAScript Harmony standards.

out about the need to avoid the 'closed worlds' created by native apps (Berners-Lee 2010). Others, including Wikipedia's Jimmy Wales, worry about the way in which native apps tend to be distributed through a centralized resource, or 'app store', controlled by a particular company (Charlesworth 2011). Two important players in this, aside from the smartphone manufacturers, are Mozilla (with their Web Apps project) and Google, who are working on the Android and Chrome apps development projects.

15.2.1 Location-Based Web 2.0 Services

In an update report on Web 2.0 published in 2009, Tim O'Reilly makes a number of points about what has changed in the five years since the idea was first proposed (O'Reilly and Battelle 2009). One of the most important changes is the arrival of the smartphone, and in particular its location-detecting capabilities powered principally by GPS.

Knowledge about a person's physical location is such a profoundly important concept in human society that being able to collect reasonably precise location data via a Web-based service is triggering a vast array of new applications. These Web 2.0 location-based services (LBSs), also known as 'geosocial' services, range from guide map applications to new forms of multi-player games (Zickuhr and Smith 2010; Benford 2005; Dey et al. 2010). They build on a history of early experimentation, within what is known as pervasive (or ubiquitous) computing research, with ascertaining and using a person's location. They integrate with a growing network of online geospatial data sources, Web 2.0 social network sites (SNSs), mash-ups and mapping applications, which together form what is sometimes called the 'GeoWeb' or 'Where 2.0' (Küpper and Treu 2010). Table 15.1 presents a summary of some well-known examples.

The basic process of a Web 2.0 LBS is illustrated in Figure 15.5. In simple terms, the smartphone determines its location using a variety of inputs depending on the context and local environment. This is then communicated to an LBS, which in turn combines it with other data from a variety of sources, for example a map database and an SNS, in order to deliver some kind of new service. As the user moves around, this process is continuously repeated, forming a kind of real-time process that gives a sense of using a responsive service (for example, an online guide book on a smartphone that updates its information in response to changes in location).

Dhar and Varshney (2011) argue that although much progress has been made, considerable technical and business model challenges remain. Technically, location detection involves a number of technologies (GPS, Local Area Network (LAN) detection, mobile phone cell triangulation), each of which is only accurate to a certain degree, and successfully combining them is still an active research area. This is particularly relevant for indoor location detection as GPS often only functions outside since it needs a line of sight to the satellites involved. There are also ongoing issues with the processing power, memory size, battery capacity, data transmission rates and screen sizes of the mobile devices being used, and much work is needed in these areas over the next few years. A number of bodies are involved in the development of technologies and standards including W3C, Open Mobile Alliance, Open Geospatial Consortium and Internet Engineering Task Force.

TABLE 15.1   Notable Examples of Location-based Services

Type	Description	Notable Examples
Guides and recommendations	Helps a person navigate and suggests places to visit, eat etc.	NileGuide Where
Locating friends	Shows the location of a user's friends on a smartphone map. Often integrated with an SNS.	Buzzd Facebook Places Google Latitude Loopt
Sharing information	Used to communicate with people currently in the same location or leave messages for future visitors	Blockboard Flook Points of Interest
Virtual check-in	A form of game in which users 'check in' to their current physical location, tell their friends where they are and collect badges or stickers	Four Square Gowalla Yelp
Geotagging photos	Automatically tags photos with geospatial data and uploads to their Web 2.0 service	Flickr Maps Mopho.to
Location-based games	Role-playing games that involve the physical environment, location and interaction with other players.	Can You See Me Now Geo Caching Parallel Kingdom Scvngr
Augmented Reality	Overlays the image in a phone's camera viewfinder with contextual information about the location (see Figure 15.6).	Layar Wikitude
Citizen Sensor networks	Enables members of the public to act as 'sensors' by using their smartphones to feed data about a location back to the service provider.	SeeClickFix MetroSense

It probably goes without saying that in addition to the technical challenges outlined previously, there are substantial social concerns associated with the widespread adoption of location-based services, in particular some very considerable privacy issues (Dey et al. 2010; Zafeiropoulou et al. 2011). This is an area that is still to be adequately explored, but which builds on research already undertaken in the field of ubiquitous computing. Importantly, privacy connected to location is not simply a question of whether a user chooses to share their position with others. Users may not fully realise that a great deal of personal, contextual information can be inferred from the data collected by these sorts of location-based services.

15.3 LEVERAGING THE SOCIAL GRAPH

Perhaps the more interesting developments, in terms of far-reaching consequences, will involve leveraging the social graph. This will enable Web 2.0 companies to develop new services and, most importantly for investors, to monetize the vast datasets that have been collected.

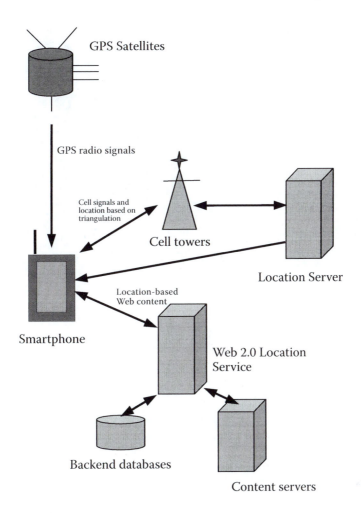

GPS Satellites

GPS radio signals

Cell signals and
location based on
triangulation

Cell towers

Location Server

Smartphone

Location-based
Web content

Web 2.0 Location
Service

Backend databases

Content servers

FIGURE 15.5   Typical set-up for a Web 2.0 location based service interacting with a smartphone. Location data is provided either by GPS or by triangulation from information from the cell phone masts, or some combination of each. The location data is then used to provide location-related content. (Illustration © 2011 by Intelligent Content Ltd Licensed under a Creative Commons Attribution-NonCommercial-NoDerivs 3.0 Unported license (CC BY-NR-ND 3.0)).

One example is IBM's SmallBlue project (Chi et al. 2011). This recognizes that people rely on a trusted network of friends and colleagues to obtain a great deal of the information they use in everyday work settings. The project builds on this by creating a dataset from the e-mail and social media interactions (blogs, wikis, intranet messaging etc.) of tens of thousands of employees. This data can then be mined to help employees to find others with a certain expertise or knowledge.[*]

Another aspect of leveraging the social graph is the changing role of advertising on the Web (Karimzadehgan et al. 2009; Hof 2011). Social network sites (SNSs), Facebook in

---

[*] See: www.research.ibm.com/smallblue/ (includes a video). Note that the commercial version of the project is called Atlas.

FIGURE 15.6   An example of a type of augmented reality location-based service. (From Wikitude by MR3641, hosted by Wikimedia Commons, licenced as Creative Commons: Attribution ShareAlike 3.0 Unreported [CC BY-SA 3.0])

particular, are investing huge resources into turning the social graph into a mechanism for advertising and developing product brands. Building on the age-old view that word of mouth is the best sales technique, these sites are developing an infrastructure to deliver 'social ads'. These combine data about a user's actions on the site (for example, making a purchase) with an advertiser's message, and then broadcasting the result across the user's online network of friends. The theory is that advertising and promotion that is propagated through a social network is seen as inherently more trustworthy by users who value their friends' and colleagues' judgment.

In Facebook's case the 'Like' button has become a powerful tool, allowing users to signal their approval of a product or service and pass that signal along to the rest of their social graph. The company's Open Graph technology means that the 'Like' button has now migrated away from the Facebook site to thousands of partner sites. Information from these partners is fed back to Facebook so that users can see what friends have been doing and purchasing on other sites. There are, of course, considerable privacy issues with this development and it helps to emphasize the growing concern about the vast datasets that Web 2.0 companies are building about their users.

A further development is that of social search, which makes particular use of the social graph (McDonnell and Shiri 2011; Carmel et al. 2009). These new techniques use information about the user's interests and preferences, gathered from their interactions with SNSs and other Web 2.0 services, to enhance the quality of search results. A further refinement being explored by Facebook, Google, Twitter and others, is to also mine the interests and preferences of a user's friends, since they are likely to have some things in common

(Simonite 2011). A related trend is that of 'social browsing'—making use of one's network of online friends as a filter for what's happening in the world.*

An important component in any discussion of the future of SNSs must be the issue of data portability we explored in Chapter 10. It is argued that users have too little control over their own data and what is done with it, and that they become frustrated at the way in which different systems lock up their data in information 'silos'. One possible way forward is decentralisation (Yeung et al. 2007; Datta et al. 2010), which involves exporting a user's data from existing SNSs (in new Semantic Web data formats, such as RDF) and storing it with third parties (i.e. away from the main SNS). Proponents argue that users are likely to have more control over their data if it is held by third parties who use the latest standards and languages for controlling access to data.

15.3.1 Social Network Sites as Platforms

In Chapter 2 we discussed the concept of the Web as Platform, the idea that applications and services are accessed through the browser and delivered across the Web. As SNSs grow, in terms of both the number of users and the sophistication and scalability of their technical infrastructure, researchers and commentators are beginning to wonder whether they might become the next 'platform' (Cusumano 2011; Gottron et al. 2011). Such a development is related to the idea of the Web as an operating system which we discuss next, potentially providing a new runtime environment for socially-oriented applications and services (Häsel 2011). Companies such as Facebook, Google and Twitter are using the power of network effects to build enormously popular technology platforms that others are keen to integrate with in order to develop new services. Important developments include Facebook's Platform and Google's OpenSocial. It is likely that a power struggle will take place over coming years between major IT companies, in order to establish the most successful platform.

However, as you would expect, this is not without its detractors, not least those who worry about privacy and campaign for digital rights. Important work in this respect is being conducted by those groups who want to see far more open online social networks that are not owned by private companies, something that is often referred to as the *federated social Web* (Passant et al. 2011; Bleicher 2011). Important projects in this include Diaspora and GNU Social.

15.4 WEBOS AND THE BROWSER AS OPERATING SYSTEM

The Web as Platform idea is likely to be taken towards a vision that is commonly referred to as the Web Operating System (WebOS). This is not so much a specific set of technologies but a vision of a new way of working.

Traditionally, a computer's operating system was its primary workhorse, controlling hardware such as the hard disk and overseeing how different software applications, user interfaces and device drivers within the machine all interacted with each other. An

---

* See, for example, Henry Copeland's contribution to a panel at the FutureWeb conference (part of WWW2010). See: http://www.elon.edu/e-web/predictions/futureweb2010/future_social_networks.xhtml

operating system (OS) is a highly complex piece of software (Microsoft's Windows XP, for example, runs to over 45 million lines of code) and is very tightly integrated with the underlying hardware. This integration has meant that OSs are built with the understanding that almost all of the software and hardware they interact with is held on the same machine. However, the Web as Platform envisions a very different approach—online services, which can come from anywhere on the Internet, are run within the browser window. The WebOS vision takes this further, going beyond applications to ask: Why limit the operating system itself to a single computer? On the desktop, applications run on top of the operating system; if Web services run on top of the browser then perhaps the browser can be considered as some sort of operating system. It is an idea that further blurs the boundaries between a single machine and the wider network and, of course, fits neatly with many of the ideas behind cloud computing. As Weiss (2005, 20) writes: "The WebOS vision explodes the operating system itself, outside the physical bounds of a box, and across the Internet".

As we saw in Chapter 14, when we discussed the emergence of Ajax and Rich Internet Applications (RIAs) as a means to help Web-based applications to both behave and look like desktop applications, the gap between desktop, native applications and Web services is continually narrowing. Technologies that will help this process include Microsoft's Xax, Google's Native Client and HTML5. A number of browser developers are working on new developments that take the WebOS concept forward including Google (Chrome) and Microsoft (Explorer 8). Other experimental systems include Gazelle, Mozilla's Electrolysis project, and the Opus Palladianum (OP) browser being developed by the University of Illinois at Urbana-Champaign. There is still much work to be done, and Mikkonen and Taivalsaari (2011) argue that a major round of standardization will need to take place over the next five years or so in order to establish a more complete platform. A critical part of this will be work on technologies that will "more comprehensively 'virtualize' the underlying operating system and device capabilities, as well as ensure that the necessary security mechanisms are in place" (p. 35).

15.4.1 HTML5

Beneath the surface, this "Web 2.0" era required a lot of tape and glue.

BOBBY JOHNSON
MIT Technology Review (2010, 46)

Today's Web has evolved far beyond static HTML documents and its next major technical development will be the introduction of HTML5, a major revision of the Web markup language.[*] It has been a slow process, subject to splits within the computer industry over what direction to take (Johnson 2010; Pilgrim 2011). However, browser companies are already supporting parts of the emerging standard and it is seen by some commentators as likely to tip the balance back in favour of Web-based apps over native ones (Lohr 2011).

---

[*] See: http://dev.w3.org/html5/spec/Overview.html

The main reason to embark on such an undertaking is to rejuvenate the markup standard so that it can cope far better with the Web as Platform paradigm. There will be new tags for video and audio, a 'canvas' tag for animation, better integration of SVG, new document structure elements (e.g. article, section, header), enhanced security features and support for new, user interface features such as 'drag and drop'. In addition, new features will reinforce the idea of the browser as an operating system, in particular, allowing the browser to store large amounts of data (proposed to be around 5 megabytes) on the host computer's system.*

Although HTML5 is the name of a standard, as a term it is increasingly being used as a kind of tagline for a general collection of improvements to Web technology that will allow it to compete with existing RIA technologies such as Flash, and also with the new generation of native apps on mobile phones. Some even argue that 'HTML5' is becoming a shorthand answer to the question—what is Web 3.0? (Hontz 2011).

15.5 CLOUD COMPUTING

In Chapter 4 we discussed the enormous data centres that the main Web 2.0 service providers have built in an effort to keep up with the rapid growth in demand for their services. In recent years, the giants of Web 2.0 have begun to make their infrastructure available for others to use in the same way that we use a utility such as electricity or gas—an infrastructure commonly known as 'cloud computing' (Carr 2008; Grossman 2009).

Unfortunately, like many computer industry terms its meaning has become somewhat blurred with use (Frischbier and Petrov 2010). Although many people use the term to refer to the commercial offering of computer resources as a utility, others use it to refer to a more general process of migrating users' data (for example, music files) away from their desktop PC or smartphone and into a third party's storage system. Indeed, it can be argued that 'the cloud' as a term is starting to be used in place of 'the Internet', giving rise to expressions such as 'users are living in the cloud', to mean spending significant amounts of time online. Thus, on the one hand we have Apple's iCloud project, which aims to provide remote data storage for its iTunes music service, and on the other, we have Amazon's Elastic Compute Cloud (Amazon EC2), which provides utility computing.

Despite this confusion, the US National Institute of Standards and Technology (NIST) has attempted a formal definition and this is beginning to gain some traction in the industry (Pallis 2010, 70):

> Cloud Computing is a model for enabling convenient, on-demand network access to a shared pool of configurable computing resources (e.g., networks, servers, storage, applications and services) that can be rapidly provisioned and released with minimal management effort or service provider interaction.

Kraan and Yuan (2010) further refine this by arguing that there are five key characteristics to a cloud computing service: rapid elasticity, ubiquitous access over the network,

---

* See: http://dev.w3.org/html5/webstorage/

location-independent data centres (the user is unaware of which physical data centre is handling their data), a pay-per-use business model, and a self-service approach that allows third parties to set up and run systems using the cloud resource. A large number of companies are offering such services and there is a rapidly developing research agenda looking at the technicalities of providing them as well as considerable interdisciplinary work on issues such as business models, privacy, legal debates, service level agreements and standards for interoperability. It is also worth remembering that much of this work builds on previous generations of computer technology and tacit knowledge gained from developing mainframe timeshare systems, virtualization systems, high-performance computing and grid computing.

How does this relate to Web 2.0? Firstly, many of the key players in the cloud computing market are also notable in the Web 2.0 world—companies like Amazon, Google and Microsoft. Building the infrastructure to cope with Internet-scale operations has led these companies to make discoveries that others can use (e.g. Google's BigTable data structures). Indeed, Sankar et al. (2008) have argued that cloud computing concepts have proved "fundamental" to the infrastructure of Web 2.0. Also, many Web 2.0 companies, especially start-ups, make use of cloud facilities and indeed it can be argued that the ease with which such services can scale has been an important factor in recent innovation on the Web.

Secondly, a new technical agenda, known as Cloud 2.0, is looking to integrate online social networking, Web 2.0–style user-generated content and cloud computing infrastructure in innovative ways (Pallis 2010). Early examples include a proposal to make use of the trust relationships that exist between users of SNSs to help distribute computing resources (Chard et al. 2010), and an improved recommendation system (e.g. best restaurant in the area) based on gathering 'social intelligence' from SNSs and processing it in the cloud (Hu et al. 2010). Others argue that the cloud's remote computing power will be harnessed with smartphones to develop new Web-based social applications that demonstrate elements of artificial intelligence such as speech recognition (Gruber 2009). It is clearly an area that is going to be important in coming years.

15.6 BIG DATA

We are currently in the midst of an explosion of Web-based data, driven by new Web 2.0–style technologies and developments such as smartphones, location-based systems and the Internet of Things (see Section 15.7). As new devices and smart objects join the network and Web services become even more popular, a veritable flood of data is pouring from the Internet, and the industry has labelled this 'Big Data' (Ackerman and Guizzo 2011; Jacobs 2009; Bollier 2010). Unsurprisingly, it is not always clear what precisely is being discussed, but it generally refers to situations in which Internet-scale levels of data[*] are being created and processed by Web-based services. In order to handle this level of data a whole new generation of technologies is emerging, including Hadoop and MapReduce, and in addition, statisticians and data scientists are in demand as companies scramble to acquire new

---

[*] Jacobs (2009) argues that it is any situation in which the scale of data being handled is at the limit of what current technology can cope with.

skill sets. As part of this process researchers are beginning to explore new algorithms and innovative chip designs for processing large datasets (Shneiderman et al. 2011).

Speculation on the consequences of Big Data builds on Tim O'Reilly's original point about data as the next Intel Inside (see Chapter 4): the crucible of Web innovation is becoming the creation and exploitation of datasets. Companies are racing both to create and exclusively own these new datasets, and to develop new analytical and visualization techniques to mine them and develop new markets and businesses. This is not restricted to business alone: scientists are exploring what can be done with gigantic datasets that are being collected by new experimental infrastructures like the CERN Large Hadron Collider; public agencies are looking at new ways to make use of the data they collect about citizens; security services are investigating what large datasets can tell them about crime and terrorism.

15.7 THE INTERNET OF THINGS

On the Internet nobody knows you are a light bulb.

NEIL GERSHENFELD
MIT's Center for Bits and Atoms (Gershenfeld 2005, Slide 3).

Although rarely commented on in the popular media, I believe the Internet of Things (IoT)* is likely to be one of the most important developments in the history of the Internet and is a strong contender for the title of 'Web 3.0'.

The IoT is about connecting physical objects to the Web/Internet and one way of understanding it is that if Web 2.0 is all about connecting people, then version 3.0 might be about connecting things to things and people to things. In one sense it is an aspect of the remorseless logic of the link—first of all reaching across webpages and documents, then encompassing graphics, audio and video, moving on to people (through Web 2.0), and now taking in the physical world. It is likely to have profound consequences for society as Andreas Schaller and colleagues at Motorola have written: "By enabling connectivity for virtually any physical object that can potentially offer a message, the Internet of Things will affect every aspect of life and business in ways that used to be the realm of fantasy" (Schaller et al. 2008, 82).

Although the term was coined in the 1990s the technology being used to build IoT can be traced back to the development of radar during the Second World War. Principle among these is Radio Frequency Identification (RFID), a technique for identifying an object at a distance via radio waves (Ward et al. 2006). In simple terms, RFID consists of a microchip (tag) and a 'reader'. The tag is attached to a physical object and returns an identifying radio signal when interrogated by the reader. It is a technique that has been steadily refined over the last twenty years or so and is now used widely in the manufacturing and retail supply chains, where it has proven to be invaluable for product tracking and other logistical tasks.

RFID tags as used in the supply chain are very simple devices consisting of an integrated circuit embedded with the identification code and a tiny antenna that can send and receive

---

* Sometimes Web of Things or T2T (Thing to Thing network).

radio waves. They can only do one task—transmit their code—and are becoming increasingly cheap to mass-produce. They are so small and thin that they can be embedded within packaging, sown into the fabric of clothing, or even 'printed' on the side of pallets.

The IoT builds on RFID by increasing the sophistication of the computational capabilities of the microchip so that it can interact with the Internet through technologies such as WiFi. In fact, these tags can do more than interact with the Internet. In many cases they also include some form of sensor technology, perhaps location awareness via GPS, temperature gauges and so forth. Thanks to miniaturization and developments in electronics and software, quite complex computing systems can now be held on a tag no bigger than a thumbnail. A physical object tagged with this kind of microchip is known as a smart object (Mulligan 2010).

These developments bring RFID into contact with another strand of computer science with a long pedigree—ubiquitous computing. In the ubiquitous (ubicomp) or pervasive computer vision there will be a multitude of small—sometimes invisible to the human eye—but computationally capable devices that will be scattered throughout our environments, operating silently and largely unseen.

In the coming decade we will see widespread use of RFID technologies, embedded sensors and other IoT techniques and this is likely to profoundly alter what the Internet/Web is capable of doing. As sensors become prevalent in our working and home environments, a new and enormous set of real-time data will be made available to the Web (Ackerman and Guizzo 2011). We will see a myriad of new applications and innovations from microwave ovens that can set their own cooking time (based on the information embedded in the tag attached to a ready-meal), to temperature-controlled homes and 'smart' energy meters. Our homes, offices, cars, public transport systems and other urban infrastructure will be increasingly 'aware' of their operating environment and the movements of people within them. This will offer tremendous opportunities for new Web-based services and ideas, but also present new challenges in social issues such as privacy and surveillance.

15.8 WEB SCIENCE

We conclude this chapter with a brief look at an emerging agenda in academic computer science which is likely to become very significant. Web Science is an evolving programme of interdisciplinary study to understand the Web as an information artefact in its own right (Berners-Lee et al. 2006; Hendler et al. 2008). It arose out of a collaboration between the universities of Southampton (UK), and the Massachusetts Institute of Technology (MIT; USA) in 2006. This has since developed into a charitable trust—The Web Science Trust—whose mission is to guide the development of this new area of research. At its heart is a study of the Web as a phenomenon: a complete system, an almost physical entity that can be surveyed and explored much as a geographer might study a new landmass (see figure 15.7).

We have already touched upon some of the ideas and methods that this approach uses: Web graphs, Network Effects and the manifestations of the power law. Web science seeks to explore how Web services work as 'social machines'—something more than pieces of engineering, and more like entities with a social dynamic. So, for example, Wikipedia is more

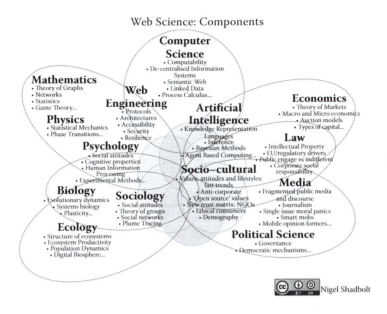

FIGURE 15.7 The interdisciplinary nature of Web Science. (From Nigel Shadbolt, University of Southampton. Creative Commons CC BY-SA 2.0)

than the MediaWiki code, it is also the collective action of millions of users, supported by an online community with rules, policies and organisational factors. How do these interplay with each other? It is a question that requires more than computer science and the answers lie in working across traditional subject boundaries, pulling together the ideas of computing, sociology, law, psychology, philosophy, physics, biology and many others.

Web science is seen as an important endeavour because the Web is becoming so intrinsic to modern societies. As Hendler et al. (2008) have written: "the future of human society is now inextricably linked to the future of the Web" (p. 68). It is only by carefully studying how the Web is developing that we can make meaningful, and shared, contributions as to its future development.

In a similar vein, the US National Science Foundation (NFS) is exploring how the academic research agenda is being changed by the rapid adoption of Web 2.0 by so many people (Pirolli et al. 2010; Shneiderman et al. 2011). Not only do social media suggest dramatic transformation across many aspects of society (business, healthcare, education and so forth), but realizing its full value will require a whole gamut of new, interdisciplinary research agendas.

EXERCISES AND POINTS TO PONDER

1. Read about the Friend-of-a-Friend (FOAF) RDF system for the Semantic Web. See: http://www.foaf-project.org/ and http://xmlns.com/foaf/spec/ Using what you've learned, create RDF data for a group of friends in your class.

2. At WWW2010, Zeynep Tufekci talked about how the lack of a physical space in Web 2.0 changes communication. See a video extract of her talk at: http://www.elon.

edu/e-web/predictions/futureweb2010/default.xhtml. Discuss in class the consequences of moving to this new way of communicating. After your discussion, have a
look at danah boyd discussing this issue at the same conference and compare: http://
www.elon.edu/e-web/predictions/futureweb2010/danah_boyd_lee_rainie.xhtml

3. Read Luciano Floridi's comment, "the full Semantic Web is a well-defined mistake,
whereas the Web 2.0 is an ill-defined success", in Floridi (2009) and then discuss in
class. Do you agree? Is the Semantic Web too ambitious?

FURTHER READING

Web 3.0

For links to a series of presentations by a variety of analysts and academics on 'What is Web 3.0' see the
blog post by Amit Agarwal: http://www.labnol.org/internet/web-3-concepts-explained/8908/
For more on the future of the Web in general and various ideas about Web 3.0 see: http://www.elon.
edu/e-web/predictions/futureweb2010/default.xhtml

Section 15.1: The Semantic Web

For a simple explanation of the Semantic Web see Herman (2009a).
Use cases for Semantic Web: http://www.w3.org/2001/sw/sweo/public/UseCases/
For more on trust issues related to the Semantic Web see Artz and Gil (2011).
For more on how technology can be used to marry Web 2.0 and the Semantic Web see Kinsella et al.
(2009).
Explore the UK's Linked Government data project at: http://data.gov.uk/
See Tim Berners-Lee's talk on linked data at TED 2009 conference: http://www.ted.com/talks/view/
lang/eng//id/484
For more discussion of folksonomy and ontology see Limpens (2009).
For more on the social Semantic Web see John Breslin's presentation to IET Ireland Network and
NUI Galway CompSoc, DERI, NUI Galway, 27th November 2008: http://www.slideshare.net/
Cloud/the-social-semantic-web-presentation
For a detailed review of the Semantic Web and its relationship to artificial intelligence research see
Alesso and Smith (2006).

Section 15.2: Smartphones and the Rise of Apps

For a discussion on the performance shortcomings of Web apps in comparison with native apps see
Anttonen et al. (2011).
For a review of how native apps compare with the founding ideas and principles of Web 2.0 as
first outlined by Tim O'Reilly see John Battelle's blog entry: http://battellemedia.com/
archives/2011/03/a_report_card_on_web_2_and_the_app_economy.php
For further discussion of the advantages of developing mobile Web apps rather than native apps see
the JISC CETIS briefing paper: http://t.co/EbRDrS3
For a further look into the potential future of Web services on mobile phones see the CleanSlate
project at Stanford University: http://cleanslate.stanford.edu/research_project_pomi.php
For more on the battleground between Web and native apps and in particular the role of HTML5
see: http://www.nytimes.com/2011/03/27/business/27unboxed.html

For a summary of the various W3C standards involved in Web app development see (http://www.w3.org/2011/02/mobile-web-app-state.html); and the EU project: (http://mobiwebapp.eu/objectives/); and the W3C mobile best practice guide: http://www.w3.org/2010/09/MWABP/Overview.html.en

For far more technical detail on how a Web 2.0 service interacts with a smartphone in order to run an LBS see Küpper and Treu (2010).

For more on the history of LBSs and how they might develop in the next few years see Bellavista et al. (2008).

For more on citizen sensor networks see Sheth (2009), Campbell et al. (2008) and Nagarajan et al. (2009; 2011).

Section 15.3: Leveraging the Social Graph

For more on Social Search, including a taxonomy of the different approaches see McDonnell and Shiri (2011).

For more on social advertising and how it fits into a wider subject known as Computational Advertising see lecture notes from Andrei Broder at Stanford University: http://www.stanford.edu/class/msande239/

For more on the federated social Web see Dhekane and Vibber (2011).

Section 15.4: WebOS and the Browser as Operating System

See Tim O'Reilly's thoughts on how the Internet is becoming an operating system: http://radar.oreilly.com/2010/03/state-of-internet-operating-system.html

An excellent, detailed outline of HTML5 is provided by Mark Pilgrim's Dive into HTML5 website (http://diveintohtml5.info/) the contents of which form the backbone of his book on the same subject (Pilgrim 2011).

Section 15.5: Cloud Computing

For more on the future directions of cloud computing see the EU Commission's report, *The Future of Cloud Computing*: http://cordis.europa.eu/fp7/ict/ssai/docs/cloud-report-final.pdf

For an accessible introduction to the background, history and discussion of key ideas behind the cloud see Nicholas Carr's book, *The Big Switch* (Carr 2008).

Section 15.6: Big Data

For further discussion of the economic and social issues surrounding the ideas of Big Data see Bollier (2010), and the O'Reilly data blog: http://radar.oreilly.com/data/

Section 15.7: The Internet of Things

For more on RFID see JISC Technology & Standards Watch report (Ward et al. 2006), and Yan et al. (2008) and Ahson and Ilyas (2008).

For further discussion of Smart Objects see Kortuem et al. (2010).

The workshop discussion at Pervasive 2010 has more on the new services that might be introduced through IoT (Michahelles et al. 2010).

Section 15.8: Web Science

There is a lot more information, including papers and videos of talks, at the Web Science Trust website: http://webscience.org/

Further details on the US National Science Foundation sponsored workshops on Technology Mediated Social Participation: http://www.tmsp.umd.edu/

Epilogue

BUBBLE 2.0?

There is clearly a bubble inflating … and when it does burst most of the money that has been invested will be lost. But there will be some winners and that's what sort of draws us all in—the hope that we are smart enough to be among the winners.

BOB METCALFE
Interviewed on BBC TV's Newsnight Programme 4th April 2011 [33:00]

We end this book as it began with a discussion of a bubble. Web 2.0 was born out of the wreckage of the dot-com bust of 2000, an umbrella term that sought to capture the excitement being generated by those companies and their thousands of users who had not only survived but thrived. As I write, a second dot-com bubble, inevitably labelled Bubble 2.0, is being widely discussed in the media. LinkedIn has been floated on the stock market for US$8.5 billion, Twitter is believed to be worth as much as US$10 billion and Facebook is preparing for flotation in 2012 at a value in excess of the Ford Motor Company (Rushe 2011). It seems ironic that only a decade later we may have come full circle.

If there is a bust, there will be survivors and the technologies and ideas that have helped them survive will become part of the evolving Web. It is too early to say what this might be, or even whether a term such as 'Web 3.0' will be used to describe it. However, I will make two predictions. Firstly, the design of new Web technologies is going to have to pay far more attention to social and ethical issues, such as users' privacy, as we become increasingly aware of the power of the Internet. As Pink Floyd's Roger Waters put it: "What it comes down to for me is this: Will the technologies of communication in our culture serve to enlighten us and help us to understand one another better, or will they deceive us and keep us apart?" (Waters 2011, webpage).

Secondly, new ideas, theories and ways of working will emerge from Web science. To take one example: a recurring theme in this book has been the prevalence of the power law throughout the ecosystem of Web 2.0 services. The implications of this are yet to be properly explored let alone used to develop new ways of working. The successful companies of tomorrow are likely to be the ones who make use of this kind of knowledge to develop new services. As Tim Berners-Lee said during a panel organised to celebrate the twentieth anniversary of the Web: "the Web, in the sense of a wonderful read/write collaborative space which I originally envisaged, I haven't seen it yet. We are still working on it" (Berners-Lee et al. 2009, 7:20).

In the end companies come and go, services flit into being and are then forgotten, code is used and reused. The computer industry is known for its Darwinian economics and Schumpter-style capitalism of creative destruction and rebirth. The enduring ideas of the Web, the key principles and platform standards such as HTML are likely, however, to be with us for a long time. They will endure long after the Web 2.0 moniker has faded.

References

Abelson, Hal, L. Ken Ledeen, and Harry Lewis. 2008. *Blow to Bits Your Life, Liberty, and Happiness after the Digital Explosion*. Boston: Pearson Educational.

Ackerman, Elise, and Erico Guizzo. 2011. 5 Technologies that will shape the Web. *IEEE Spectrum* 48 (6) (June):32–36.

Acquisti, Alessandro, and Ralph Gross. 2006. Imagined communities: Awareness, information sharing, and privacy on the Facebook. In *Privacy Enhancing Technologies*, edited by G. Danezis and P. Golle. Berlin/Heidelberg: Springer.

Adamic, Lada, Serge Abiteboul, and Anne-Marie Vercoustre. 1999. The small world Web. In *Research and Advanced Technology for Digital Libraries*, edited by S. Abiteboul and A.-M. Vercoustre. Berlin/Heidelberg: Springer.

Adamic, Lada, and Bernado Huberman. 2002. Zipf's law and the Internet. *Glottometrics* 3:143–150.

Adams, John. 2010a. In the belly of the whale: Operations at Twitter. YouTube. 25th June 2010. http://www.youtube.com/watch?v=_7KdeUIvlvw

Adams, John. 2010b. Billions of Hits: Scaling Twitter. Presentation made to *CHIRP 2010*, 14th–15th April, at San Francisco. http://www.slideshare.net/netik/billions-of-hits-scaling-twitter

Adams, Paul. 2010. The real life social network. Presentation made to Voices that Matter: Web Design Conference, 28th June 2010, at Mission Bay Center, San Francisco, CA. http://www.slideshare.net/padday/bridging-the-gap-between-our-online-and-offline-social-network

Adler, B. Thomas, and Luca de Alfaro. 2006. *A Content-Driven Reputation System for the Wikipedia*. Report UCSC-CRL-06-18. School of Engineering, University of California, Santa Cruz. Santa Cruz, CA: University of California.

Adler, B. Thomas, Luca de Alfaro, Ian Pye, and Vishwanath Raman. 2008. Measuring author contributions to the Wikipedia. WikiSym'08, 8th–10th September, at Porto, Portugal. Proceedings published by the Association for Computing Machinery.

Adobe. 2005. *How does AJAX work?* Adobe Systems Romania, 10th November. http://www.interaktonline.com/Support/Articles/Details/AJAX%3A+Asynchronously+Moving+Forward-Introduction.html?id_art=36 (accessed 18th August).

Adomavicius, Gediminas, Ramesh Sankaranarayanan, Shahana Sen, and Alexander Tuzhilin. 2005. Incorporating contextual information in recommender systems using a multidimensional approach. *ACM Trans. Inf. Syst.* 23 (1):103–145.

Adomavicius, Gediminas, and Alexander Tuzhilin. 2005. Toward the next generation of recommender systems: A survey of the state-of-the-art and possible extensions. *IEEE Transactions on Knowledge and Data Engineering* 17 (6):734–749.

Agarwal, N., S. Kumar, H. Liu, and M. Woodward. 2009. Blogtrackers: A tool for sociologists to track and analyze blogosphere. 3rd International AAAI Conference on Weblogs and Social Media (ICWSM), 17th–20th May, at San Jose, CA. Proceedings published by Association for the Advancement of Artificial Intelligence (AAAI).

Agarwal, Nitin, and Huan Liu. 2008. Blogosphere: Research issues, tools, and applications. *SIGKDD Explor. Newsl.* 10 (1):18–31.

Agarwal, Nitin, and Huan Liu. 2009. Modeling and data mining in blogosphere. In *Synthesis Lectures on Data Mining and Knowledge Discovery*, edited by R. Grossman. San Rafael, CA: Morgan & Claypool.

Agarwal, Nitin, Magdiel Galan, Huan Liu, and Shankar Subramanya. 2010. WisColl: Collective wisdom based blog clustering. *Information Sciences* 180 (1) (2nd January):39–61.

Agarwal, Nitin, Merlyna Lim, and Rolf T. Wigand. 2011. Collective action theory meets the blogosphere: A new methodology. In *Networked Digital Technologies*, edited by S. Fong. Berlin/ Heidelberg: Springer.

Agichtein, Eugene, Carlos Castillo, Debora Donato, Aristides Gionis, and Gilad Mishne. 2008. Finding high-quality content in social media. International Conference on Web Search and Web Data Mining (WSDM 2008), 11th–12th February, at Palo Alto, CA. Proceedings published by the Association for Computing Machinery.

Ahern, Shane, Dean Eckles, Nathaniel S. Good, Simon King, Mor Naaman, and Rahul Nair. 2007. Over-exposed? Privacy patterns and considerations in online and mobile photo sharing. SIGCHI Conference on Human Factors in Computing Systems, 28th April–3rd May, at San Jose, CA. Proceedings published by the Association for Computing Machinery.

Ahn, Luis von, and Laura Dabbish. 2008. Designing games with a purpose. *Communications of the ACM* 51 (8):58–67.

Ahn, Yong-Yeol, Seungyeop Han, Haewoon Kwak, Sue Moon, and Hawoong Jeong. 2007. Analysis of topological characteristics of huge online social networking services. 16th International World Wide Web Conference (WWW'07), 8th–12th May, at Banff, Alberta, Canada. Proceedings published by the Association for Computing Machinery.

Ahson, Syed A., and Mohammad Ilyas. 2008. *RFID Handbook: Applications, Technology, Security, and Privacy* Boca Raton, FL: CRC Press.

Akritidis, Leonidas, Dimitrios Katsaros, and Panayiotis Bozanis. 2011. Modern Web technologies. In *New Directions in Web Data Management 1*, edited by A. Vakali and L. Jain. Berlin/Heidelberg: Springer.

Alag, Satnam. 2009. *Collective Intelligence in Action*. Greenwich, CT: Manning Publications Co.

Albert, R. , H. Jeong, and A.-L. Barabasi. 1999. Internet: Diameter of the World-Wide Web. *Nature* 1999 (6749):130.

Alesso, H. Peter, and Craig F. Smith. 2006. *Thinking on the Web*. Hoboken, NJ: Wiley.

Alfaro, Luca de, Ashutosh Kulshreshtha, Ian Pye, and B. Thomas Adler. 2011. Reputation systems for open collaboration. *Communications of ACM* 54 (8) (August 2011):81–87.

Allen, Matthew. 2008. Web 2.0: An argument against convergence. *First Monday* 13 (3). http://firstmonday.org/htbin/cgiwrap/bin/ojs/index.php/fm/article/view/2139/1946 (accessed 11th July 2011).

Almeida, Rodrigo B., Barzan Mozafari, and Junghoo Cho. 2007. On the evolution of Wikipedia. International Conference on Weblogs and Social Media (ICWSM'2007), 26th–28th March, at Boulder, CO. Proceedings published by conference organisers.

Alonso, José Manuel. 2006. Analyzing the role of standards in Web 2.0. Presentation made to Sixth Internet Next Generation Workshop, 18th October 2006, at Madrid, Spain. http://www.w3c.es/ Presentaciones/2006/1018-newWeb-JA/

Amaral, L. A. N., A. Scala, M. Barthélémy, and H. E. Stanley. 2000. Classes of small-world networks. *Proceedings of the National Academy of Sciences of the United States of America* 97 (21) (10th October):11149–11152.

Ammann, Rudolf. 2009. Jorn Barger, the newspage network and the emergence of the weblog community. 20th ACM Conference on Hypertext and Hypermedia, 29th June, at Torino, Italy. Proceedings published by the Association for Computing Machinery.

Anand, Suchith, Michael Batty, Andrew Crooks, Andrew Hudson-Smith, Mike Jackson, Richard Milton, and Jeremy Morley. 2010. Data mash-ups and the future of mapping. Horizon Scanning Report 10_01. JISC Technology & Standards Watch. Bristol, UK: JISC. September. http://www. jisc.ac.uk/whatwedo/services/techwatch/reports/horizonscanning/hs1001.aspx

Anderson, Chris. 2006. *The Long Tail*. London: Random House Business Books.

Anderson, Chris. 2010. The Web is dead. *Wired*, October 2010, 129–131.

Anderson, Paul. 2009. Meritocrats, cluebats and the open development method: An interview with Justin Erenkrantz. OSSWatch. Oxford, UK: University of Oxford. February 2009. http://www.oss-watch.ac.uk/resources/erenkrantz.xml

Angeletou, Sofia, Marta Sabou, Lucia Specia, and Enrico Motta. 2007. Bridging the gap between folksonomies and the semantic Web. 4th European Semantic Web Conference, 7th June, at Innsbruck, Austria. Proceedings published by University of Kassel.

Angles, Renzo, and Claudio Gutierrez. 2008. Survey of graph database models. *ACM Computing Surveys* 40 (1):1–39.

Anthony, Denise, Sean W. Smith, and Tim Williamson. 2005. Explaining quality in Internet collective goods: Zealots and good Samaritans in the Case of Wikipedia. Fall 2005 MIT Innovation & Enterpreneurship Seminar, at MIT. Proceedings published by MIT.

Antoniades, Demetris, Iasonas Polakis, Georgios Kontaxis, Elias Athanasopoulos, Sotiris Ioannidis, Evangelos P. Markatos, and Thomas Karagiannis. 2011. we.b: The web of short urls. Proceedings of the 20th International Conference on World Wide Web. 28th March–1st April, at Hyderabad, India. Proceedings published by the Association for Computing Machinery.

Antoniou, Grigoris, and Frank van Harmelen. 2004. *A Semantic Web primer*. Cambridge, MA: MIT Press.

Anttonen, Matti, Arto Salminen, Tommi Mikkonen, and Antero Taivalsaari. 2011. Transforming the Web into a real application platform: New technologies, emerging trends and missing pieces. 2011 ACM Symposium on Applied Computing (SAC 2011), 21st–24th March, at TaiChung, Taiwan. Proceedings published by the Association for Computing Machinery.

ARC. 2010. *The Internet in Australia. ARC Centre of Excellence for Creative Industries and Innovation*. Queensland, Australia: Queensland University of Technology. 17th May. http://www.cci.edu.au/sites/default/files/sewing/CCi%20Digital%20Futures%202010%201.pdf

Arjan, Rajiv, Ulrike Pfeil, and Panayiotis Zaphiris. 2008. Age differences in online social networking. Conference on Human Factors in Computing Systems (CHI '08), 5th–10th April, at Florence, Italy. Proceedings published by the Association for Computing Machinery.

Artz, Donovan, and Yolanda Gil. 2011. A survey of trust in computer science and the Semantic Web. *Journal of Web Semantics* 5 (2):58–71.

Auletta, Ken. 2001. *World War 3.0: Microsoft and Its Enemies*. London: Random House.

Bachle, M., and P. Kirchberg. 2007. Ruby on Rails. *IEEE Software* 24 (6):105–108.

Backstrom, Lars, Dan Huttenlocher, Jon Kleinberg, and Xiangyang Lan. 2006. Group formation in large social networks: membership, growth, and evolution. 12th ACM SIGKDD International Conference on Knowledge Discovery and Data Mining, 20th–23rd August, at Philadelphia, PA. Proceedings published by the Association for Computing Machinery.

Baeyer, Hans Christian von. 2003. *Information: The New Language of Science*: Weidenfeld & Nicolson.

Bakhshandeh, Reza, Mehdi Samadi, Zohreh Azimifar, and Jonathan Schaeffer. 2011. Degrees of separation in social networks. The Fourth International Symposium on Combinatorial Search (SoCS-2011), 15th July, at Castell de Cardona, Barcelona, Catalonia, Spain. Proceedings published by AAAI Press.

Bakshy, Eytan, Jake M. Hofman, Winter A. Mason, and Duncan J. Watts. 2011. Everyone's an influencer: Quantifying influence on Twitter. Fourth ACM International Conference on Web Search and Data Mining (WSDM'11), 9th–12th February, at Hong Kong, China. Proceedings published by the Association for Computing Machinery.

Baldi, Pierre, Paolo Frasconi, and P. Smyth. 2003. *Modelling the Internet and the Web*. Chichester, UK: Wiley.

Baldwin, Carliss Y., and Kim B. Clark. 2006. The architecture of participation: Does code architecture mitigate free riding in the open source development model? *Management Science* 52:1116–1127.

Ball, Philip. 2005. *Critical Mass: How One Thing Leads to Another*. London: Arrow Books.

Banerjee, A., M. Faloutsos, and L. N. Bhuyan. 2008. Profiling podcast-based content distribution. INFOCOM Workshops 2008, 13th–18th April, at Phoenix, AZ. Proceedings published by the Institute of Electrical and Electronics Engineers.

Bangman, Eric. 2007. Google cites Safe Harbour, fair use in *Viacom v. YouTube* defense. *Law and Disorder*. http://arstechnica.com/tech-policy/news/2007/05/google-cites-safe-harbor-fair-use-in-viacom-v-youtube-defense.ars

Bansal, Nilesh, Fei Chiang, Nick Koudas, and Frank Wm. Tompa. 2007. Seeking stable clusters in the blogosphere. 33rd International Conference on Very Large Databases, 23rd–27th September, at Vienna, Austria. Proceedings published by VLDB Endowment.

Bansal, Nilesh, and Nick Koudas. 2007a. BlogScope: A system for online analysis of high volume text streams. 33rd International Conference on Very Large Data Bases, 23rd–27th September, at University of Vienna, Austria. Proceedings published by the Association for Computing Machinery.

Bansal, Nilesh, and Nick Koudas. 2007b. Searching the blogosphere. 10th International Workshop on Web and Databases, 15th June, at Beijing, China. Proceedings published by the Association for Computing Machinery.

Barabási, Albert-László. 2002. *Linked: The New Science of Networks*. Cambridge, MA.: Perseus Publishing.

Barabási, Albert-László. 2009. Scale-free networks: A decade and beyond. *Science* 325 (5939) (24th July 2009):412–413.

Barabási, Albert-László, and Réka Albert. 1999. Emergence of scaling in random networks. *Science* 286 (5439):509–512.

Barabási, Albert-László, and Eric Bonabeau. 2003. Scale-free networks. *Scientific American*, May.

Baran, Paul. 2009. *Forerunner of the Internet: Early RAND Work in Distributed Networks and Packet Switching (1960–1965)*. RAND Video. http://www.rand.org/multimedia/video/2009/10/06/distributed_communications_and_packet_switching.html

Bar-Ilan, Judit. 2004. An outsider's view on "topic-oriented blogging". In *Proceedings of the 13th International Conference on World Wide Web—Alternate Track Papers & Posters, WWW 2004, New York, NY, 17th–20th May*. New York: Association for Computing Machinery.

Barlow, Aaron. 2007. *The Rise of the Blogosphere*. Westport, CT: Praeger.

Barnes, Susan B. 2006. A privacy paradox: Social networking in the United States. *First Monday* 11 (9) (September 2006). http://firstmonday.org/htbin/cgiwrap/bin/ojs/index.php/fm/article/view/1394/1312

Barrett, Daniel J. 2009. *Media Wiki*. Sebastopol, CA: O'Reilly Media Inc.

Barroso, Luiz, Jeffrey Dean, and Urs Hölzle. 2003. Web search for a planet. *IEEE Micro* 23 (2) (March–April):22–28.

Battelle, John. 2005. *The Search*. London: Nicholas Brealey Publishing.

Battle, Robert, and Edward Benson. 2008. Bridging the Semantic Web and Web 2.0 with Representational State Transfer (REST). *Web Semantics: Science, Services and Agents on the World Wide Web* 6 (1):61–69.

Batty, Michael, Andrew Hudson-Smith, Richard Milton, and Andrew Crooks. 2010. Map mashups: Web 2.0 and the GIS revolution. *Annals of GIS* 16 (1):1–13.

Beaver, Doug, Sanjeev Kumar, Harry C. Li, Jason Sobel, and Peter Vajgel. 2010. Finding a needle in Haystack: Facebook's photo storage. 9th USENIX Symposium on Operating System Design and Implementation (OSDI), 4th–6th October, at Vancouver, BC, Canada. Proceedings published by USENIX.

Bell, Gavin. 2009. *Building Social Web Applications*. Sebastopol, CA: O'Reilly Media Inc.

Bellavista, P., A. Kupper, and S. Helal. 2008. Location-based services: Back to the future. *Pervasive Computing, IEEE* 7 (2):85–89.

Benevenuto, Fabricio, Fernando Duarte, Tiago Rodrigues, Virgilio A. F. Almeida, Jussara M. Almeida, and Keith W. Ross. 2008. Understanding video interactions in YouTube. 16th ACM International Conference on Multimedia, 26th–31st October, at Vancouver, British Columbia, Canada. Proceedings published by the Association for Computing Machinery.

Benevenuto, Fabricio, Tiago Rodrigues, Meeyoung Cha, and Virgio Almeida. 2009. Characterizing user behavior in online social networks. 9th ACM SIGCOMM Conference on Internet Measurement, 4th–6th November, at Chicago, IL. Proceedings published by the Association for Computing Machinery.

Benford, Steve. 2005. Future location-based experiences. JISC Technology & Standards Watch. Bristol, UK: JISC. January. http://www.jisc.ac.uk/whatwedo/services/techwatch/reports/archive.aspx

Benjamin, Louise M. . 1993. In search of the Sarnoff radio music box memo. *J. Broadcast & Electronic Media* 37 (3):325.

Benkler, Yochai. 2006. *The Wealth of Networks*. New Haven: Yale University Press.

Benninger, Corey. 2006. *AJAX Storage: A Look at Flash Cookies and Internet Explorer*. Persistence Foundstone Professional Services & Education. Santa Clara, CA: I. McAfee.

Benslimane, D., S. Dustdar, and A. Sheth. 2008. Services mashups: The new generation of Web applications. *IEEE Internet Computing* 12 (5):13–15.

Bergsma, Mark. 2007. Wikimedia architecture. http://www.nedworks.org/~mark/presentations/san/Wikimedia%20architecture.pdf

Bermingham, Adam, and Alan F. Smeaton. 2010. Crowdsourced real-world sensing: Sentiment analysis and the real-time Web. Sentiment Analysis Workshop at Artificial Intelligence and Cognitive Science (AICS 2010) 30th August–1st September, at Galway, Ireland. Proceedings published by Science Foundation Ireland.

Berners-Lee, Tim. 1998. *Axioms of Web Architecture*. W3C, January 1998. http://www.w3.org/DesignIssues/Model.html (accessed 14th July 2011).

Berners-Lee, Tim. 1999. *Weaving the Web*. London: Orion Business Books.

Berners-Lee, Tim. 2010. Long live the Web. *Scientific American*, 22nd Nov.

Berners-Lee, Tim, Robert Cailliau, Vinton G. Cerf, Dale Dougherty, Mike Shaver, and Wendy Hall. 2009. Web 20th Anniversary Panel. VideoLectures.net. April. http://videolectures.net/www09_hall_panel/

Berners-Lee, Tim, Robert Cailliau, Ari Luotonen, Henrik Frystyk Nielsen, and Arthur Secret. 1994. The World-Wide Web. *Communications of the ACM* 37 (8):76–82.

Berners-Lee, Tim, Wendy Hall, James A. Hendler, Kieron O'Hara, Nigel Shadbolt, and Daniel J. Weitzner. 2006. A framework for Web science. *Foundations and Trends in Web Science* 1 (1):1–130.

Berners-Lee, Tim, James Hendler, and Ora Lassila. 2001. The Semantic Web. *Scientific American*, 17th May.

Besser, Jana, Katja Hofmann, and Martha Larson. 2008. An exploratory study of user goals and strategies in podcast search. Workshop Information Retrieval (WIR) 2008, 6th–8th October, at University of Würzburg, Germany. Proceedings published by Special Interest Group on Information Retrieval.

Biel, Joan-Isaac, and Daniel Gatica-Perez. 2009. Wearing a YouTube hat: Directors, comedians, gurus, and user aggregated behavior. 17th ACM International Conference on Multimedia (ACMMM09), 19th–24th October, at Beijing, China. Proceedings published by the Association for Computing Machinery.

Biel, Joan-Isaac, and Daniel Gatica-Perez. 2011. Call me guru: User categories and large-scale behavior in YouTube. In *Social Media Modeling and Computing*, edited by S. C. H. Hoi, J. Luo, S. Boll, D. Xu, R. Jin and I. King. London: Springer.

Birdsall, William F. 2007. Web 2.0 as a social movement. *Webology* 4 (2). http://www.webology.ir/2007/v4n2/a40.html (accessed 11th July 2011).

Bizer, Christian. 2009. The emerging Web of linked data. *IEEE Intelligent Systems* 24 (5):87–92.

Bizer, Christian, Tom Heath, and Tim Berners-Lee. 2009. Linked data—The story so far. *International Journal on Semantic Web* 5 (3).

Bizer, Christian, Tom Heath, Tim Berners-Lee, and Michael Hausenblas. 2011. Overview of the State of the Data Web. Linked Data on the Web (LDOW2011) (at WWW 2011), 29th March, at Hyderabad, India. Proceedings published by the Association for Computing Machinery.

Bleicher, Ariel. 2011. The Anti-facebook. *IEEE Spectrum* 48 (6) (June):47–51.

Blood, Rebecca. 2000. *Weblogs: A History and Perspective*, 7th September 2000. http://www.rebeccablood.net/essays/weblog_history.html (accessed 20th July 2011).

Blood, Rebecca. 2004. How blogging software reshapes the online community. *Communications of the ACM* 47 (12):53–55.

Bogers, Toine, and Antal van den Bosch. 2008. Recommending scientific articles using Citeulike. 2nd ACM Conference on Recommender Systems, 23rd–25th October, at Lausanne, Switzerland. Proceedings published by the Association for Computing Machinery.

Bojars, Uldis, Alexandre Passant, John G Breslin, and Stefan Decker. 2008. Social network and data portability using semantic web technologies. 2nd Workshop on Social Aspects of the Web SAW 2008 at BIS2008, 5th–7th May, at Innsbruck, Austria. Proceedings published by conference organisers.

Bollen, Johan, Huina Mao, and Alberto Pepe. 2011. Modeling public mood and emotion: Twitter sentiment and socio-economic phenomena. International AAAI Conference on Weblogs and Social Media (ICWSM-11), 17th–21st July, at Barcelona, Spain. Proceedings published by AAAI Publications.

Bollen, Johan, Huina Mao, and Xiaojun Zeng. 2011. Twitter mood predicts the stock market. *Journal of Computational Science* 2 (1):1–8.

Bollier, David. 2010. *The Promise and Peril of Big Data*. The Aspen Institute. Washington, DC: The Aspen Institute. 1st January. http://www.aspeninstitute.org/publications/promise-peril-big-data

Bonato, Anthony, Jeannette Janssen, and Paweł Prałat. 2010. A geometric model for on-line social networks. 3rd Workshop on Online Social Networks (WOSN 2010), 22nd June, at Boston, MA. Proceedings published by Usenix.

Bonneau, Joseph, and Sören Preibusch. 2010a. The privacy jungle: On the market for data protection in social networks. In *Economics of Information Security and Privacy*, edited by T. Moore, D. Pym and C. Ioannidis. New York: Springer.

Bonneau, Joseph, and Sören Preibusch. 2010b. The password thicket: Technical and market failures in human authentication on the Web. The Ninth Workshop on the Economics of Information Security (WEIS 2010) 7th–8th June, at Harvard University, Cambridge, MA. Proceedings published by Conference Organisers.

Boratto, Ludovico, Salvatore Carta, Eloisa Vargiu, Tommaso Di Noia, and Francesco Buccafurri. 2009. RATC: A robust automated tag clustering technique e-commerce and web technologies. In *E-Commerce and Web Technologies*, edited by T. Di Noia and F. Buccafurri. Berlin/Heidelberg: Springer.

Borland, John. 2008. Twitter's growing pains. *MIT Technology Review*, 21st July. http://www.technologyreview.com/business/21103/

Bornholdt, Stefan, and Heinz Georg Schuster. 2002. *Handbook of Graphs and Networks: From the Genome to the Internet*. Weinheim, Germany: Wiley VCH.

Boulton, Clint. 2010. Twitter builds data centre to combat outages. *eWeek*, 23rd July. http://www.techweekeurope.co.uk/news/twitter-builds-data-centre-to-combat-outages-8582

boyd, danah. 2006. The significance of social software. Presentation made to BlogTalk Reloaded, 2nd October, at Vienna, Austria. http://www.danah.org/papers/BlogTalkReloaded.html

boyd, danah. 2008a. Taken out of context: American teen sociality in networked publics. PhD diss., Information Management and Systems, University of California, Berkeley, CA.

boyd, danah. 2008b. Why youth love social network sites. In *Youth, Identity, and Digital Media*, edited by D. Buckingham. Cambridge, MA: MIT Press.

boyd, danah, and N. Ellison. 2007. Social network sites: Definition, history, and scholarship. *Journal of Computer-Mediated Communication* 13 (1) (2007):210–230.

boyd, danah, and Eszter Hargittai. 2010. Facebook privacy settings: Who cares? *First Monday* 15 (8) (August).

boyd, danah, Scott Golder, and Gilad Lotan. 2010. Tweet, Tweet, retweet: Conversational aspects of retweeting on Twitter. 43rd Hawaii International Conference on System Sciences, 5th–8th January, at Hawaii. Proceedings published by the Institute of Electrical and Electronics Engineers.

Boyle, James. 2008. *The Public Domain: Enclosing the Commons of the Mind*. New Haven: Yale.

Bozzon, Alessandro, Sara Comai, Piero Fraternali, and Giovanni Toffetti Carughi. 2006. Conceptual modeling and code generation for Rich Internet Applications. 6th International Conference on Web Engineering (ICWE 2006), 11th–14th July, at Palo Alto, CA. Proceedings published by the Association for Computing Machinery.

Bray, Tim. 2005. Not 2.0. ongoing. 4th August 2005. http://www.tbray.org/ongoing/When/200x/2005/08/04/Web-2.0 (accessed 11th July 2011).

Bray, Tim. 2006. OSCON—Open Data. ongoing. 30th July. http://www.tbray.org/ongoing/When/200x/2006/07/28/Open-Data.

Breen, Jason C. 2007. YouTube or YouLose: Can YouTube survive a copyright infringement lawsuit. *Texas Intellectual Property Law Journal* 16:151.

Breslin, John, and Stefan Decker. 2007. The future of social networks on the Internet: The need for semantics. *IEEE Internet Computing* 11 (6) (November/December):86–90.

Breslin, John G., Alexandre Passant, and Stefan Decker. 2009. *The Social Semantic Web*. Berlin: Springer.

Brian, P. Blake, Agarwal Nitin, T. Wigand Rolf, and D. Wood Jerry. 2010. Twitter quo vadis: Is Twitter bitter or are Tweets sweet? Seventh International Conference on Information Technology, 12th–14th April, at Las Vegas, Nevada. Proceedings published by the Institute of Electrical and Electronics Engineers.

Brin, Sergey, and Lawrence Page. 1998. The anatomy of a large-scale hypertextual Web search engine. *Computer Networks and ISDN Systems* 30 (1–7):107–117.

Briscoe, B., A. Odlyzko, and B. Tilly. 2006. Metcalfe's law is wrong: Communications networks increase in value as they add members—but by how much? *IEEE Spectrum* 43 (7):34–39.

Broder, A., Ravi Kumar, Farzin Maghoul, Prabhakar Raghavan, Sridhar Rajagopalan, Raymie Stata, Andrew Tomkins, and Janet Wiene. 2000. Graph structure in the web. The Ninth International World Wide Web Conference (WWW '9), 15th–19th May, at Amsterdam. Proceedings published by IW32C.

Broughton, John. 2008. *Wikipedia: The Missing Manual*. Sebastopol, CA: O'Reilly Media Inc.

Bruns, Axel. 2008. *Blogs, Wikipedia, Second Life, and Beyond: From Production to Produsage*. New York: Peter Lang Publishing, Inc.

Bryant, Susan L., Amy Bruckman, and Andrea Forte. 2005. Becoming Wikipedian: Transformation of participation in a collaborative online encyclopedia. Group'05, 6th–9th November, at Sanibel Island, FL. Proceedings published by the Association for Computing Machinery.

Bull, Andy. 2010. Twins put Facebook billions on hold to focus on boat race. *The Guardian*, 3rd April.

Burgess, Jean 2007. Vernacular creativity, cultural participation and new media literacy: Photography and the Flickr network. Internet Research 7.0, 27th–30th September, at Brisbane, Australia. Proceedings published by Association of Internet Researchers.

Buriol, Luciana S., Carlos Castillo, Debora Donato, Stefano Leonardi, and Stefano Millozzi. 2006. Temporal analysis of the wikigraph. 2006 IEEE/WIC/ACM International Conference on Web Intelligence, 18th–22nd December, at Hong Kong, China. Proceedings published by the Institute of Electrical and Electronics Engineers Computer Society.

Busch, Michael. 2010. Twitter's new search architecture. Twitter Engineering. http://engineering. twitter.com/2010/10/twitters-new-search-architecture.html (accessed 8th August 2011).

Cadenhead, Roger. 2005. *Movable Type 3 Bible*. Indianapolis, IN: Wiley Publishing, Inc.

Cairns, Paul, and Mark Blythe. 2010. Research methods 2.0. In *Social Computing and Virtual Communities*, edited by P. Zaphiris and C. S. Ang. Boca Raton, FL: CRC Press.

Campbell, Andrew, Shane B. Eisenman, Nicholas D. Lane, Emiliano Miluzzo, Ronald A. Peterson, Hong Lu, Xiao Zheng, Mirco Musolesi, Kristof Fodor, and Gahng-Seop Ahn. 2008. The rise of people-centric sensing. *IEEE Internet Computing* 12 (4):12–21.

Campbell, Gardner. 2005. There's something in the air: Podcasting in education. *EDUCAUSE Review* 40 (6) (November/December):32–47.

Campbell, Laura E., and Beth Dulabahn. 2010. Digital preservation: NDIIPP and the Twitter archives. 7th International Conference on Preservation of Digital Objects 19th–24th September, at Vienna, Austria Proceedings published by conference organisers.

Campbell, Sara L., and Javier M. G. Duarte. 2008. Poisson statistics of radioactive decay. Preprint. MIT Department of Physics.

Canaves, Sky. 2001. China's social networking problem. *IEEE Spectrum* 48 (6) (June):66–69.

Capocci, A., V. D. P. Servedio, F. Colaiori, L. S. Buriol, D. Donato, S. Leonardi, and G. Caldarelli. 2006. Preferential attachment in the growth of social networks: The case of Wikipedia. American Physical Society, March Meeting, at Baltimore, MD. Proceedings published by American Physical Society.

Capocci, Andrea, Andrea Baldassarri, Vito D.P. Servedio, and Vittorio Loreto. 2009. Statistical properties of inter-arrival times distribution in social tagging systems. 20th ACM Conference on Hypertext and Hypermedia (Hypertext 2009), 29th June–1st July, at Torino, Italy. Proceedings published by the Association for Computing Machinery.

Cargill, Carl F. 1997a. Section 1. Prelude. *StandardView* 5 (4):128–132.

Cargill, Carl F. 1997b. Section 13. Conclusion and analysis. *StandardView* 5 (4):198–200.

Carmel, David, Naama Zwerdling, Ido Guy, Shila Ofek-Koifman, Nadav Har'el, Inbal Ronen, Erel Uziel, Sivan Yogev, and Sergey Chernov. 2009. Personalized social search based on the user's social network. 18th ACM Conference on Information and Knowledge Management (CIKM 2009), 2nd–6th November, at Hong Kong, China. Proceedings published by the Association for Computing Machinery.

Carr, Nicholas. 2008. *Big Switch: Rewiring the World, from Edison to Google*. New York: W.W. Norton & Company, Inc.

Carr, Nicholas. 2010. Real-time search. *MIT Technology Review*, June, pp. 46–47.

Casal, David. 2005. Advanced Software Development for Web Applications. HS 0505. JISC Technology & Standards Watch. Bristol, UK: JISC, December. http://www.jisc.ac.uk/what-wedo/services/techwatch/reports/horizonscanning/hs0505.aspx

Cass, Stephen. 2011. Social machinery. *MIT Technology Review*, August, 68–69.

Cassidy, John. 1999. The woman in the bubble. *The New Yorker*, 26th April, p. 48.

Cassidy, John. 2002. *Dot.con*. London: Allen Lane.

Castellanos, Malu, Riddhiman Ghosh, Yue Lu, Lei Zhang, Perla Ruiz, Mohamed Dekhil, Umeshwar Dayal, and Meichun Hsu. 2011. LivePulse: Tapping social media for sentiments in real-time. 20th International Conference Companion on World Wide Web (WWW2011), 28th March–1st April, at Hyderabad, India. Proceedings published by the Association for Computing Machinery.

Castells, Manuel. 2000. *The Rise of the Network Society*. 2nd ed. Vol. 1. Malden, MA: Blackwell Publishing.

Castells, Manuel. 2001. *The Internet Galaxy*. Oxford: Oxford University Press.

Cattuto, Ciro, Vittorio Loreto, and Luciano Pietronero. 2007a. Semiotic dynamics and collaborative tagging. *Proceedings of the National Academy of Sciences* 104 (5) (January 30, 2007):1461–1464.

Cattuto, Ciro, Christoph Schmitz, Andrea Baldassarr, and Vito D. P. Servedio. 2007b. Network properties of folksonomies. *AI Communications* 20 (4) (8th November):245–262.

Caverlee, James, and Steve Webb. 2008. A large-scale study of MySpace: Observations and implications for online social networks. Second International Conference on Weblogs and Social Media, 30th March–2nd April, at Seattle, Washington. Proceedings published by The AAAI Press, Menlo Park, California.

Cerf, Vint. 2009. WWW 2009 Conference—20th Anniversary Panel Video Lectures.Net. April 2009. http://videolectures.net/www09_hall_panel/

Cerri, Davide, and Alfonso Fuggetta. 2007. Open standards, open formats, and open source. *Journal of Systems and Software* 80 (11):1930–1937.

Cha, Meeyoung, Hamed Haddadi, Fabricio Benevenuto, and Krishna P. Gummadi. 2010. Measuring user influence in Twitter: The million follower fallacy. 4th International Conference on Weblogs and Social Media (ICWSM-10), 23rd–26th May, at George Washington University, Washington, DC. Proceedings published by Association for the Advancement of Artificial Intelligence.

Cha, Meeyoung, Haewoon Kwak, Pablo Rodriguez, Yong-Yeol Ahn, and Sue Moon. 2007. I tube, you tube, everybody tubes: Analyzing the world's largest user generated content video system. 7th ACM SIGCOMM Conference on Internet Measurement, 24th–26th October, at San Diego, CA. Proceedings published by the Association for Computing Machinery.

Cha, Meeyoung, Alan Mislove, and Krishna P. Gummadi. 2009. A measurement-driven analysis of information propagation in the Flickr social network. 18th International Conference on World Wide Web (WWW '09), 20th–24th April, at Madrid, Spain. Proceedings published by the Association for Computing Machinery.

Chakrabarti, Soumen, Mukul M. Joshi, Kunal Punera, and David M. Pennock. 2002. The structure of broad topics on the web. 11th International Conference on World Wide Web, 7th–11th May, at Honolulu, Hawaii. Proceedings published by the Association for Computing Machinery.

Chang, Fay, Jeffrey Dean, Sanjay Ghemawat, Wilson C. Hsieh, Deborah A. Wallach, Mike Burrows, Tushar Chandra, Andrew Fikes, and Robert E. Gruber. 2008. Bigtable: A distributed storage system for structured data. *ACM Transactions on Computer Systems* 26 (2):1–26.

Chard, Kyle, Simon Caton, Omer Rana, and Kris Bubendorfer. 2010. Social Cloud: Cloud Computing in Social Networks. IEEE 3rd International Conference on Cloud Computing (CLOUD 2010), 5th–10th July, at Miami, FL. Proceedings published by the Institute of Electrical and Electronics Engineers Computer Society.

Charland, Andre, and Brian Leroux. 2011. Mobile application development: Web vs. native. *Communications of the ACM* 54 (5):49–53.

Charlesworth, Andrew. 2011. Apple "biggest threat to open Internet" says Wikipedia founder. *Computing*, 13th January. http://www.computing.co.uk/ctg/news/1937050/apple-biggest-threat-internet-wikipedia-founder

Chatterjee, Patrali, Donna L. Hoffman, and Thomas P. Novak. 2003. Modeling the clickstream: Implications for Web-based advertising efforts. *Marketing Science* 22 (4) (Autumn 2003):520–541.

Chen, Xi, and Shuo Shi. 2009. A literature review of privacy research on social network sites. Paper read at Multimedia Information Networking and Security, International Conference on, at Los Alamitos, CA. Proceedings published by the Institute of Electrical and Electronics Engineers Computer Society.

Cheng, Xu, Cameron Dale, and Jiangchuan Liu. 2008. Statistics and social network of YouTube videos. 16th International Workshop on Quality of Service (IWQoS 2008), 2nd–4th June, at University of Twente, Enschede, The Netherlands. Proceedings published by the Institute of Electrical and Electronics Engineers.

Cheng, Zengyan, Yinping Yang, and John Lim. 2009. Cyber migration: An empirical investigation on factors that affect users' switch intentions in social networking sites. Hawaii International Conference on System Sciences, 4th–7th January, at Grand Wailea, Maui. Proceedings published by the Institute of Electrical and Electronics Engineers Computer Society.

Chesney, Thomas. 2006. An empirical examination of Wikipedia's creditability. *First Monday* 11 (11). http://firstmonday.org/htbin/cgiwrap/bin/ojs/index.php/fm/article/view/1413/1331 (accessed 1st August 2011).

Cheswick, Bill, Hal Burch, and Steve Branigan. 2000. Mapping and visualizing the Internet. USENIX Annual Technical Conference, 18th–20th June, at San Diego, CA. Proceedings published by USENIX Association.

Chew, Monica, Dirk Balfanz, and Ben Laurie. 2008. (Under)mining privacy in social networks. W2SP 2008: Web 2.0 Security and Privacy 2008, 22nd May, at Oakland, CA. Proceedings published by the Institute of Electrical and Electronics Engineers.

Chi, Changyan, Qinying Liao, Yingxin Pan, Shiwan Zhao, Tara Matthews, Thomas Moran, Michelle X. Zhou, David Millen, Ching-Yung Lin, and Ido Guy. 2011. Smarter social collaboration at IBM research. ACM 2011 Conference on Computer-Supported Cooperative Work (CSCW 2011), 19th–23rd March, at Hangzhou, China. Proceedings published by the Association for Computing Machinery.

Chirita, Paul-Alexandru, Stefania Costache, Wolfgang Nejdl, and Siegfried Handschuh. 2007. P-TAG: Large-scale automatic generation of personalized annotation tags for the Web. 16th International Conference on World Wide Web, at Banff, Alberta, Canada. Proceedings published by the Association for Computing Machinery.

Chung, Sukwon, Dungjit Shiowattana, Pavel Dmitriev, and Su Chan. 2009. The web of nations. 18th International Conference on World Wide Web, at Madrid, Spain. Proceedings published by the Association for Computing Machinery.

Clark, Dave. 1992. A cloudy crystal ball—Visions of the future. Paper read at 24th Meeting of the Internet Engineering Task Force (IETF), 13th–17th July at Cambridge, MA. Proceedings published by Corporation for National Research Initiatives

Clarke, Barbie 2009. BFFE (Be Friends Forever): The way in which young adolescents are using social networking sites to maintain friendships and explore identity. WebSci'09: Society On-Line, 18th–20th March, at Athens, Greece. Proceedings published by Web Science Trust.

Clauset, Aaron, Cosma R. Shalizi, and M. E. J. Newman. 2009. Power-law distributions in empirical data. *SIAM Review* 51 (4) (Feb):661–703.

Coates, Tom. 2003. On permalinks and paradigms … Plasticbag.org. 11th June 2003. http://www.plasticbag.org/archives/2003/06/on_permalinks_and_paradigms/ (accessed 21st July 2011).

Comerford, R. 1992. How DEC developed Alpha. *Spectrum, IEEE* 29 (7):26–31.

Constantinides, Efthymios, and Stefan J Fountain. 2008. Web 2.0: Conceptual foundations and marketing issues. *Journal of Direct, Data and Digital Marketing Practices* 9 (3):231–244.

Cook, Blaine. 2007. Big Bird (Scaling Twitter). Presentation made to SDForum Silicon Valley Ruby Conference 2007, 21st April, at San Jose, CA. http://www.slideshare.net/Blaine/scaling-twitter

Cormode, Graham, and Balachander Krishnamurthy. 2008. Key differences between Web 1.0 and Web 2.0. *First Monday* 13 (6). http://firstmonday.org/htbin/cgiwrap/bin/ojs/index.php/fm/article/view/2125/1972 (accessed 12th July 2011).

Costello, Roger L. 2002. *XFront: Building Web Services the REST Way.* http://www.xfront.com/REST-Web-Services.html (accessed 9th August 2011).

Couvering, E. 2008. The history of the Internet search engine: Navigational media and the traffic commodity. In *Web Search*, edited by A. Spink and M. Zimmer. Berlin/Heidelberg: Springer.

Cox, Andrew, Paul Clough, and Stefan Siersdorfer. 2011. Developing metrics to characterise Flickr groups. *Journal of the American Society for Information Science and Technology* 62 (3):493–506.

Cox, Andrew M. 2008. Flickr: A case study of Web 2.0. *Aslib Proceedings* 60 (5):493–516.

Crandall, David J., Lars Backstrom, Daniel Huttenlocher, and Jon Kleinberg. 2009. Mapping the world's photos. 18th International Conference on World Wide Web (WWW'09), 20th–24th April, at Madrid, Spain. Proceedings published by the Association for Computing Machinery.

Crane, Dave, Eric Pascarello, and Darren James. 2006. *Ajax in Action*. Greenwich, CT: Manning Publications Co.

Crofts, Sheri, Jon Dilley, Mark Fox, Andrew Retsema, and Bob Williams. 2005. Podcasting: A new technology in search of viable business models. *First Monday* 10 (9) (5th September).

Crovella, M. E., and A. Bestavros. 1997. Self-similarity in World Wide Web traffic: Evidence and possible causes. *Networking, IEEE/ACM Transactions on* 5 (6):835–846.

Crowd Sciences. 2009. Social media insights: Twitter. Crowd Sciences. Mountain View, CA: Crowd Science Inc. 4th September. http://www.crowdscience.com/research/twitter_research_study

Cusumano, Michael, Yiorgos Mylonadis, and Richard Rosenbloom. 1992. Strategic maneuvering and mass-market dynamics: The triumph of VHS over Beta. *The Business History Review* 66 (1) (Spring 1992):51–94.

Cusumano, Michael A. 2011. Platform wars come to social media. *Communications of the ACM* 54 (4):31–33.

Dalsgaard, Christian, and Elsebeth Korsgaard Sorensen. 2008. A typology for Web 2.0. Paper read at The 7th European Conference on e-Learning, 6th–7th November, at Grecian Bay Hotel, Agia Napa, Cyprus. Proceedings published by Academic Publishing Ltd.

Dann, Stephen. 2010. Twitter content classification. *First Monday* 15 (12) (6th December).

Dargan, P.A. 2005. *Open Systems and Standards*. Norwood, MA: Artech House, Inc.

Datta, Anwitaman, Sonja Buchegger, Le-Hung Vu, Thorsten Strufe, and Krzysztof Rzadca. 2010. Decentralised online social networks. In *Handbook of Social Network Technologies and Applications*, edited by B. Furht. New York: Springer.

Davidov, Dmitry, Oren Tsur, and Ari Rappoport. 2010. Semi-supervised recognition of sarcastic sentences in Twitter and Amazon. 14th Conference on Computational Natural Language Learning, 15th–16th July, at Uppsala, Sweden. Proceedings published by Association for Computational Linguistics.

Dean, Jeff. 2007. *Building a Computer System for the World's Information*. Google Video. 23rd June. http://video.google.com/videoplay?docid=-6304964351441328559#docid=-2727172597104463277

Dean, Jeffrey, and Sanjay Ghemawat. 2010. MapReduce: A flexible data processing tool. *Communications of the ACM* 53 (1):72–77.

Dean, Jeffrey, and Sanjay Ghemawat. 2008. MapReduce: Simplified data processing on large clusters. *Communications of the ACM* 51 (1):107–113.

Deering, Steve. 2001. Watching the waist of the Protocol Hourglass. Presentation made to IETF 51, August 2001, at London.

Denham, Elizabeth. 2009. Report of findings into the complaint filed by the Canadian Internet Policy and Public Interest Clinic (CIPPIC) against Facebook Inc. under the Personal Information Protection and Electronic Documents Act. Office of the Privacy Commissioner of Canada. Ottawa, Ontario: The Privacy Commissioner of Canada. http://www.priv.gc.ca/cf-dc/2009/2009_008_0716_e.cfm

De Souza, Cleidson R. B., David Redmiles, Li-Te Cheng, David Millen, and John Patterson. 2004. How a good software practice thwarts collaboration: The multiple roles of APIs in software development. *SIGSOFT Software Engineering Notes* 29 (6):221–230.

Dey, Anind, Jeffrey Hightower, Eyal de Lara, and Nigel Davies. 2010. Location-based services. *IEEE Pervasive Computing* 9 (1):11–12.

Dhar, Subhankar, and Upkar Varshney. 2011. Challenges and business models for mobile location-based services and advertising. *Communications of the ACM* 54 (5):121–128.

Dhekane, Ruturaj, and Brion Vibber. 2011. Talash: Friend finding in federated social networks. Linked Data on the Web (LDOW2011), 29th March, at Hyderabad, India. Proceedings published by the Association for Computing Machinery.

Dill, Stephen, Ravi Kumar, Kevin S. Mccurley, Sridhar Rajagopalan, D. Sivakumar, and Andrew Tomkins. 2002. Self-similarity in the web. *ACM Trans. Internet Technol.* 2 (3):205–223.

Ding, Ying, Elin K. Jacob, Zhixiong Zhang, Schubert Foo, Erjia Yan, Nicolas L. George, and Lijiang Guo. 2009. Perspectives on social tagging. *Journal of the American Society for Information Science and Technology* 60 (12):2388–2401.

DiNucci, D. 1999. Design & new media: Fragmented future—Web development faces a process of mitosis, mutation, and natural selection. *Print* 53 (4):32–35

Doctorow, Cory, Rael Dornfest, J. Scott Johnson, Shelley Powers, Benjamin Trott, and Mena Trott. 2002. *Essential Blogging.* Sebastopol, CA: O'Reilly & Associates Inc.

Dohler, M., T. Watteyne, F. Valois, and J. L. Lu. 2008. Kumar's, Zipf's and other laws: How to structure a large-scale wireless network. *Annals of Telecommunications* 63 (5):239–251.

Domingos, Pedro. 2005. Mining social networks for viral marketing. *IEEE Intelligent Systems* 20 (1) (Jan/Feb 2005):80–82.

Donath, J, and d. boyd. 2004. Public displays of connection. *BT Technology Journal* 22 (4) (October):71–82.

Donato, Debora, Luigi Laura, Stefano Leonardi, and Stefano Millozzi. 2007. The Web as a graph: How far we are. *ACM Trans. Internet Technology* 7 (1).

Donato, Debora, Stefano Leonardi, Stefano Millozzi, and Panayiotis Tsaparas. 2008. Mining the inner structure of the Web graph. *Journal of Physics A: Mathematical and Theoretical* 41 (22):224017.

Dorogovtsev, and Mendes. 2000. Evolution of networks with aging of sites. *Physical Review Series E* 62 (2): 1842–1845.

Drezner, D. W., and H. Farrell. 2004. The power and politics of blogs. *Public Choice* 134 (1):15–30.

Du, Helen S,, and Christian Wagner. 2005. Success in the "blogosphere": Exploring the role of technology. 9th Pacific Asia Conference on Information Systems, 7th–10th July, at Bangkok, Thailand. Proceedings published by PACIS.

Dutton, W. H, and E. J. Helsper. 2007. *The Internet in Britain 2007.* Oxford Internet Institute. Oxford, UK: University of Oxford. http://www.oii.ox.ac.uk/research/oxis/oxis2005_report.pdf

Easley, David, and Jon Kleinberg. 2010. *Networks, Crowds and Markets.* Cambridge, UK: Cambridge University Press.

Ebersbach, Anja, Markus Glaser, and Richard Heigl. 2006. *Wiki: Web Collaboration.* Berlin: Springer Verlag.

Edirisingha, Palitha, and Gilly Salmon. 2007. Pedagogical models for podcasts in higher education. EDEN Conference, 13th–16th June, at Naples, Italy. Proceedings published by EDEN.

Edirisingha, Palitha, and Gilly Salmon. 2008. *Podcasting for Learning in Universities.* Milton Keynes, UK: Open University Press.

Edirisingha, Palitha, Matthew Mobbs, Richard Mobbs and Gilly Salmon. 2008. *How to Create Podcasts for Education.* Open University Press.

Efimova, Lilia, and Aldo de Moor. 2005. Beyond personal web publishing: An exploratory study of conversational blogging practices. 38th Annual Hawaii International Conference on System Sciences (HICSS'05) 3rd–6th January, at Big Island, Hawaii. Proceedings published by the Institute of Electrical and Electronics Engineers Computer Society.

Eger, Jonathan. 2011. The number of photos on Facebook is exploding. *Photo Weekly*, 21st February.

Eifrem, Emil. 2009. Neo4j: The benefits of graph databases. Presentation made to OSCON 2009, 20th–24th July, at San Jose, CA. http://www.slideshare.net/emileifrem/neo4j-the-benefits-of-graph-databases-oscon-2009

Elliott, Stuart. 2007. 'Intel inside' ad campaign shifts focus to the Web. *New York Times*, 11th October, 2007. http://www.nytimes.com/2007/10/11/technology/11iht-adco.4.7856566.html?_r=1 (accessed 12th July 2011).

Ellison, Nicole B., Cliff Lampe, and Charles Steinfield. 2009. Social network sites and society: Current trends and future possibilities. *Interactions* 16 (1):6–9.

Ellison, Nicole B., Charles Steinfield, and Cliff Lampe. 2007. The benefits of Facebook "friends": Social capital and college students' use of online social network sites. *Journal of Computer-Mediated Communication* 12 (4):1143–1168.

Estrin, Daniel. 2011. *Wikipedia says it's losing contributors*. MSNBC, 4th August. http://www.msnbc.msn.com/id/44027246/ns/technology_and_science-tech_and_gadgets/t/wikipedia-says-its-losing-contributors/ (accessed 18th September 2011).

Etling, Bruce, John Kelly, Robert Faris, and John Palfrey. 2009. *Mapping the Arabic Blogosphere*. Berkman Center for Internet and Society. Cambridge, MA: Harvard University. June 2009. http://cyber.law.harvard.edu/sites/cyber.law.harvard.edu/files/Mapping_the_Arabic_Blogosphere.pdf

Evans, Alan, and Diane Coyle. 2010. *Introduction to Web 2.0*. Boston: Prentice Hall.

Evans, David S., Andrei Hagiu, and Richard Scmalensee. 2006. *Invisible Engines*. Cambridge, MA: MIT Press.

Evans, Mike. 2006. The evolution of the Web: From Web 1.0 to Web 4.0. Presentation made to Centre for Security, Communications and Network Research Internal Seminar, 8th November 2006, at University of Plymouth. http://www.cscan.org/default.asp?page=cscan-seminars

Faloutsos, Michalis, Petros Faloutsos, and Christos Faloutsos. 1999. On power-law relationships of the Internet topology. Applications, technologies, architectures, and protocols for computer communication, 31st August–3rd September, at Cambridge, MA. Proceedings published by the Association for Computing Machinery.

Farooq, Umer, Thomas G. Kannampallil, Yang Song, Craig H. Ganoe, John M. Carroll, and Lee Giles. 2007. Evaluating tagging behavior in social bookmarking systems: Metrics and design heuristics. 2007 International ACM Conference on Supporting Group Work (Group '07), 4th–7th November, at Sanibel Island, FL. Proceedings published by the Association for Computing Machinery.

Farrel, Adrian. 2004. *The Internet and Its Protocols*. Waltham, MA: Morgan Kaufman.

Fayad, Mohamed, and Douglas C. Schmidt. 1997. Object-oriented application frameworks. *Communications of the ACM* 40 (10):32–38.

Feller, Joseph. 2010. *"The Web as Platform": What Does It Mean?—Part I* (Vol. 10, No. 2). Cutter Consortium. http://www.cutter.com/content-and-analysis/resource-centers/business-technology-trends/sample-our-research/bttu0902.html (pay to see). (accessed 9th August 2011).

Felt, Adrienne, and David Evans. 2008. Privacy protection for social networking platforms. W2SP 2008: Web 2.0 Security and Privacy 2008, 22nd May, at Oakland, California. Proceedings published by the Institute of Electrical and Electronics Engineers.

Feng, Shi, Jun Pang, Daling Wang, Ge Yu, Feng Yang, and Dongping Xu. 2011. A novel approach for clustering sentiments in Chinese blogs based on graph similarity. *Computers & Mathematics with Applications*, 62(7): 2770–2778.

Ferraiolo, Jon. 2008. How Ajax changes the game for SVG. 6th International Conference on Scalable Vector Graphics, 26th–28th August, at Nuremberg, Germany. Proceedings published by conference organisers.

Fielding, Roy T., and Richard N. Taylor. 2002. Principled design of the modern Web architecture. *ACM Transactions on Internet Technology* 2 (2):115–150.

Fielding, Roy Thomas. 2000. Architectural styles and the design of network-based software architectures. PhD diss., Information and Computer Science, University of California, Irvine.

Figueiredo, Flavio, Fabiano Belém, Henrique Pinto, Jussara Almeida, Marcos Gonçalves, David Fernandes, Edleno Moura, and Marco Cristo. 2009. Evidence of quality of textual features on the Web 2.0. 18th ACM Conference on Information and Knowledge Management (CIKM 2009), 2nd–6th November, at Hong Kong, China. Proceedings published by the Association for Computing Machinery.

Fitzpatrick, Brad. 2007. Thoughts on the social graph. bradfitz.com. 17th August 2007. http://bradfitz.com/social-graph-problem/ (accessed 9th August 2011).

Fletcher, Sara. 2010. Royal Society Web Science meeting—a (semi) live blog. A different wavelength: A Nature network blog. 27th September 2010. http://blogs.nature.com/sara/2010/09/27/royal-society-web-science-meeting---a-semi-live-blog (accessed 8th September 2011).

Flew, Terry. 2005. Creative commons and the creative industries. *Media and Arts Law Review* 10 (4) (December 2005):257–264.

Floridi, Luciano. 2009. Web 2.0 vs. the Semantic Web: A philosophical assessment. *Episteme* 6 (February):25–37.

Fogg, B.J., and Daisuke Iizawa. 2008. Online persuasion in Facebook and Mixi: A cross-cultural comparison. *Persuasive Technology* 5033/2008 (June):35–46.

Fowler, M. 2002. Public versus published interfaces. *IEEE Software* 19 (2):18–19.

Fraser, Matthew, and Soumitra Dutta. 2009. *Throwing Sheep in the Boardroom: How Online Social Networking Will Transform Your Life, Work and World.* Chichester, UK: John Wiley & Sons Ltd.

Fraternali, Piero, Gustavo Rossi, and Fernando Sanchez-Figueroa. 2010. Rich Internet Applications. *IEEE Internet Computing* 14 (3):9–12.

Frischbier, Sebastian, and Ilia Petrov. 2010. Aspects of data-intensive cloud computing. In *From Active Data Management to Event-Based Systems and More*, edited by K. Sachs, I. Petrov and P. Guerrero. Berlin/Heidelberg: Springer.

Fu, Feng, Lianghuan Liu, and Long Wang. 2008. Empirical analysis of online social networks in the age of Web 2.0. *Physica A: Statistical Mechanics and Its Applications* 387 (2–3):675–684.

Fukuda, H., and Y. Yamamoto. 2008. A system for supporting development of large-scaled Rich Internet Applications. 23rd IEEE/ACM International Conference on Automated Software Engineering, 15th–19th September, at L'Aquila, Italy. Proceedings published by IEEE Computer Society.

Gamma, E, R Helm, R Johnson, and J Vlssides. 1994. *Design Patterns: Elements of Reusable Object-Oriented Software*. Boston: Addison Wesley.

Gannes, Liz. 2011. Facebook "deprecates" FBML tomorrow (Aw, Poor FBML!). AllThingsD. 9th March. http://allthingsd.com/20110309/facebook-deprecates-fbml-tomorrow-aw-poor-fbml/ (accessed 9th September 2011).

Gao, Hongyu, Jun Hu, Tuo Huang, Jingnan Wang, and Yan Chen. 2011. Security issues in online social networks. *IEEE Internet Computing* 15 (4):56–63.

Gao, Wen, Yonghong Tian, Tiejun Huang, and Qiang Yang. 2010. Vlogging: A survey of videoblogging technology on the web. *ACM Computing Surveys* 42 (4):1–57.

Garrett, Jesse James. 2005. *Ajax: A New Approach to Web Applications*. Adaptive Path LLC, 18th February. http://www.adaptivepath.com/ideas/essays/archives/000385.php (accessed 9th August 2011).

Geer, David. 2010. Is it really time for real-time search? *Computer* 43 (3) (March 2010):16–19.

Geiger, R. Stuart, and David Ribes. 2010. The work of sustaining order in Wikipedia: The banning of a vandal. 2010 ACM Conference on Computer Supported Cooperative Work (CSCW 2010), 6th–10th February, at Savannah, GA. Proceedings published by the Association for Computing Machinery.

Geoghegan, Michael Woodland, and Dan Klass. 2005. *Podcast Solutions: The Complete Guide to Podcasting*: APress.

Gershenfeld, Neil. 2005. Internet 0. Presentation made to Center for Bits and Atoms Internal Workshop, at MIT, Cambridge, MA.

Ghemawat, Sanjay, Howard Gobioff, and Shun-Tak Leung. 2003. The Google file system. *SIGOPS Operating Systems Review* 37 (5):29–43.

Ghosh, Debasish. 2010. Multiparadigm data storage for enterprise applications. *IEEE Software* 27 (5):57–60.

Gibson, Becky. 2007. Enabling an accessible Web 2.0. 2007 International Cross-Disciplinary Conference on Web Accessibility (W4A), 7th May, at Banff, Canada. Proceedings published by the Association for Computing Machinery.

Gilbert, Eric, and Karrie Karahalios. 2009. Predicting tie strength with social media. 27th International Conference on Human Factors in Computing Systems, at Boston, MA. Proceedings published by the Association for Computing Machinery.

Gilbertson, Scott. 2007. Slap in the Facebook: It's time for social networks to open up. *Wired*, 6th August.

Gilder, George. 2006. The information factories. *Wired*, October 2006. http://www.wired.com/wired/archive/14.10/cloudware.html

Giles, Jim. 2005. Special report: Internet encyclopaedias go head to head. *Nature* (438) (15th December):900–901.

Gill, Phillipa, Martin Arlitt, Zongpeng Li, and Anirban Mahanti. 2007. YouTube traffic characterization: A view from the edge. 7th ACM SIGCOMM Conference on Internet Measurement, 24th–26th October, at San Diego, CA. Proceedings published by the Association for Computing Machinery.

Gillies, James, and Robert Cailliau. 2000. *How the Web was Born*. Oxford: Oxford University Press.

Gilmour, Dan. 2004. *We the Media: Grassroots Journalism by the People, for the People*. Sebastopol, CA: O'Reilly Media Inc.

Gjoka, M., M. Kurant, C. T. Butts, and A. Markopoulou. 2010. Walking in Facebook: A case study of unbiased sampling of OSNs. INFOCOM, 14th–19th March, at San Diego, CA. Proceedings published by the Institute of Electrical and Electronics Engineers.

Glance, Natalie S., Matthew Hurst, and Takashi Tomokiyo. 2004. BlogPulse: Automated trend discovery for weblogs. 13th International World Wide Web Conference (WWW'04), 17th–22nd May, at Sheraton, New York, NY. Proceedings published by the Association for Computing Machinery.

Goad, Robin. 2011. Experian Hitwise China launch and micro-blogging in China. Experian Hitwise. 25th May. http://weblogs.hitwise.com/robin-goad/2011/05/experian_hitwise_china_launch.html (accessed 8th August 2011).

Goetz, M., J. Leskovec, M. McGlohon, and C. Faloutsos. 2009. Modeling blog dynamics. AAAI Conference on Weblogs and Social Media (ICWSM), 17nd–20th May, at San Jose, CA, Proceedings published by Association for the Advancement of Artificial Intelligence.

Golbeck, Jennifer. 2007. The dynamics of web-based social networks: Membership, relationships, and change. *First Monday* 12 (11). http://firstmonday.org/htbin/cgiwrap/bin/ojs/index.php/fm/article/view/2023/1889 (accessed 20th May 2010).

Goldberg, David, David Nichols, Brian M. Oki, and Douglas Terry. 1992. Using collaborative filtering to weave an information tapestry. *Communications of the ACM* 35 (12):61–70.

Golder, S., and B. A. Huberman. 2005. The structure of collaborative tagging systems. Information Dynamics Lab, HP Labs. http://www.hpl.hp.com/research/idl/papers/tags/

Golder, Scott, Dennis Wikinson, and Bernardo Huberman. 2007. Rhythms of social interaction: Messaging within a massive online network. In *Communities and Technologies 2007*, edited by C. Steinfield, B. T. Pentland, M. Ackerman and N. Contractor. London: Springer.

Golder, Scott A., and Bernardo A. Huberman. 2006. Usage patterns of collaborative tagging systems. *Journal of Information Science* 32 (2):198–208.

Goldfarb, Avi, and Catherine Tucker. 2011. Online advertising. In Marvin Zelkowitz (ed.), *Advances in Computers* (Vol. 81). Elsevier, pp. 289–315.

Goldman, Jay. 2009. *Facebook Cookbook*. Sebastopol, CA: O'Reilly Media Inc.

Gottron, Thomas, Jérôme Kunegis, Ansgar Scherp, and Steffen Staab. 2011. One community does not rule them all. Web Science 2011, 14th–17th June, at Koblenz. Proceedings published by the Association for Computing Machinery.

Governor, James, Dion Hinchcliffe, and Duane Nickull. 2009. *Web 2.0 Architectures*. Sebastopol, CA: O'Reilly Media Inc.

Grace, Julia H., Dejin Zhao, and danah boyd. 2010. Microblogging: What and how can we learn from it? 28th International Conference on Human Factors in Computing Systems (CHI '10), 10th–15th April, at Atlanta, GA. Proceedings published by the Association for Computing Machinery.

Graf, Alexander. 2007. *RDFa vs. Microformats DERI*. Technical Report 2007-04-10. Digital Enterprise Research Institute (DERI). Galway, Ireland: DERI.

Graham, Brad L. 1999. Friday 10th September, 1999: It's Peter's fault. Must See HTTP://. http://www.bradlands.com/weblog/comments/september_10_1999/ (accessed 10th August 2011).

Graham, Jefferson. 2006. Flickr of idea on a gaming project led to photo website. *USA Today*, 28th February. http://www.usatoday.com/tech/products/2006-02-27-flickr_x.htm

Greenspan, Alan. 1996. The challenge of central banking in a democratic society. Presentation made to *Annual Dinner and Francis Boyer Lecture of The American Enterprise Institute for Public Policy Research*, 5th December 1996, at Washington, DC. http://www.federalreserve.gov/boarddocs/speeches/1996/19961205.htm

Gregg, Dawn G. 2010. Designing for collective intelligence. *Communications of the ACM* 53 (4) (April 2010):134–138.

Gregorio, Joe. 2005. What do you see in Web 2.0? *BitWorking*. 8th Sept 2005. http://bitworking.org/news/What_do_you_see_in_Web_2_0_ (accessed 12th July 2011).

Grieve, J., D. Biber, E. Friginal, and T. Nekrasova. 2010. Variation among blogs: A multi-dimensional analysis. In *Genres on the Web*, edited by A. Mehler, S. Sharoff and M. Santini. New York: Springer-Verlag.

Gross, Ralph, and Alessandro Acquisti. 2005. Information revelation and privacy in online social networks. 2005 ACM Workshop on Privacy in the Electronic Society, 7th November, at Alexandria, VA. Proceedings published by the Association for Computing Machinery.

Grossman, Lev. 2006. You — Yes, You — Are TIME's Person of the Year. *Time*, 25th December.

Grossman, R. L. 2009. The case for cloud computing. *IT Professional* 11 (2):23–27.

Gruber, Tom. 2008. Collective knowledge systems: Where the social Web meets the semantic Web. *Web Semantics: Science, Services and Agents on the World Wide Web* 6 (1):4–13.

Gruber, Tom. 2009. Big think. Presentation made to Web 3.0, 27th January, at Santa Clara, CA. http://www.slideshare.net/mediabistro/web-3-tom-gruber

Gruber, Thomas. 2007. Ontology of folksonomy: A mash-up of apples and oranges. *International Journal on Semantic Web and Information Systems* 3 (1):1–11.

Gruhl, Daniel, R. Guha, David Liben-Nowell, and Andrew Tomkins. 2004. Information diffusion through blogspace. 13th International Conference on World Wide Web (WWW'04), 17th–22nd May, at New York, NY. Proceedings published by the Association for Computing Machinery.

Gunawardena, Dinan, Thomas Karagiannis, Alexandre Proutiere, and Milan Vojnovic. 2009. Characterizing podcast services: Publishing, usage, and dissemination. 9th ACM SIGCOMM Conference on Internet Measurement, 4th–6th November, at Chicago, IL. Proceedings published by the Association for Computing Machinery.

Guy, Marieke, and Emma Tonkin. 2006. Folksonomies. *D-Lib Magazine* 12 (1). http://www.dlib.org/dlib/january06/guy/01guy.html (accessed 14th July 2011).

Hagemann, Stephan, and Gottfried Vossen. 2009. Categorizing user-generated content. WebSci'09, 18th–20th March, at Athens, Greece. Proceedings published by Web Science Trust.

Halpin, Harry. 2008. Foundations of a philosophy of collective intelligence. AISB 2008 Convention on Communication, Interaction and Social Intelligence, 1st–4th April 2008, at Aberdeen, Scotland. Proceedings published by AISB.

Halpin, Harry, Andy Clark, and Michael Wheeler. 2010. Towards a philosophy of the Web: Representation, enaction, collective intelligence. WebSci10, 26th–27th April, at Raleigh, NC. Proceedings published by Web Science Trust.

Halpin, Harry, Valentin Robu, and Hana Shepherd. 2007. The complex dynamics of collaborative tagging. 16th International Conference on World Wide Web (WWW 2007), 8th–12th May, at Banff, Alberta, Canada. Proceedings published by the Association for Computing Machinery.

Halvey, Martin J., and Mark T. Keane. 2007. Analysis of online video search and sharing. Eighteenth Conference on Hypertext and Hypermedia, 10th–12th September, at Manchester, UK. Proceedings published by the Association for Computing Machinery.

Hammersley, Ben. 2003. *Content Syndication with RSS*. Sebastopol, CA: O'Reilly Media Inc.

Hammond, Jeffrey, and Michael Goulde. 2007. Rich Internet apps move beyond the browser. Forrester Research Inc. Cambridge, MA: Forrester Research Inc. 27th June. http://www.forrester.com/rb/Research/rich_internet_apps_move_beyond_browser/q/id/42708/t/2

Hammond, Tony, Timo Hannay, and Ben Lund. 2004. The role of RSS in science publishing. *D-Lib Magazine* 10 (12) (December).

Hammond, Tony, Timo Hannay, Ben Lund, and Joanna Scott. 2005. Social bookmarking tools (I)—A general review. *D-Lib Magazine* 11 (4). http://www.dlib.org/dlib/april05/hammond/04hammond.html (accessed 12th July 2011).

Harding, William T., Anita J. Reed, and Robert L. Gray. 2001. Cookies and Web bugs: What they are and how they work together. *Information Systems Management* 18 (3) (2011/07/20):17–24.

Harkin, James. 2009. *Cyburbia*. London: Little Brown.

Harris, Derrick. 2011. Facebook trapped in MySQL 'fate worse than death'. GigaOM. http://gigaom.com/cloud/facebook-trapped-in-mysql-fate-worse-than-death/ (accessed 22nd August 2011).

Harris, Howard, and Sungmin Park. 2008. Educational usages of podcasting. *British Journal of Educational Technology* 39 (3):548–551.

Harrod, Horatia. 2009. Flickr: The world's photo album. *The Daily Telegraph*, 26th March. http://www.telegraph.co.uk/culture/5048643/Flickr-the-worlds-photo-album.html

Hartl, Michael, and Aurelius Prochazka. 2007. *Railsspace: Building a Social Networking Website with Ruby on Rails*. Boston: Addison Wesley.

Häsel, Matthias. 2011. Opensocial: An enabler for social applications on the Web. *Communications of the ACM* 54 (1):139–144.

Hauben, Michael, and Ronda Hauben. 1998. On the early days of Usenet: The roots of the cooperative online culture. *First Monday* 3 (8) (August).

Head, Alison J., and Michael B. Eisenberg. 2010. How today's college students use Wikipedia for course-related research. *First Monday* 15 (3). http://firstmonday.org/htbin/cgiwrap/bin/ojs/index.php/fm/article/viewArticle/2830/2476 (accessed 1st August 2011).

Hearst, Marti, Matthew Hurst, and Susan T. Dumais. 2008. What should blog search look like? ACM Workshop on Search in Social Media, 30th October, at Napa Valley, CA. Proceedings published by the Association for Computing Machinery.

Heckner, Markus, Michael Heilemann, and Christian Wolff. 2009. Personal information management vs. resource sharing: Towards a model of information behavior in social tagging systems. 3rd International AAAI Conference on Weblogs and Social Media, 17th–20th May, at San Jose, California. Proceedings published by AAAI Digital Library.

Heilemann, John. 2006. Tag sale. *Business 2.0*, 31st January.

Hendler, J. 2009. Web 3.0 emerging. *Computer* 42 (1):111–113.

Hendler, James, and Jennifer Golbeck. 2008. Metcalfe's law, Web 2.0, and the semantic Web. *Web Semantics: Science, Services and Agents on the World Wide Web* 6 (1):14–20.

Hendler, James, Nigel Shadbolt, Wendy Hall, Tim Berners-Lee, and Daniel Weitzner. 2008. Web science: An interdisciplinary approach to understanding the web. *Communications of the ACM* 51 (7):60–69.

Herman, Ivan. 2006. W3C and open standards. Presentation made to *LinuxAsia Conference & Expo*, 10th February, at Delhi, India. http://www.w3.org/2006/Talks/0210-Delhi-IH/

Herman, Ivan. 2009a. Introduction to the Semantic Web. Presentation made to Talk at the Labs of Deutsche Telekom, 14th December, at Darmstadt, Germany. http://www.w3.org/2009/Talks/1214-Darmstadt-IH/

Herman, Ivan. 2009b. Semantic Web: What is being done today. Presentation made to Talk at the Labs of Deutsche Telekom, 14th December, at Darmstadt, Germany. http://www.w3.org/2009/Talks/1214-Darmstadt-IH/

Hernando, A., D. Villuendas, C. Vesperinas, M. Abad, and A. Plastino. 2009. Unravelling the size distribution of social groups with information theory on complex networks. *qrXiv* (16th September). This is a prepress available online at: http://arxiv.org/abs/0905.3704

Herring, S., C. Kouper, and L. Scheidt. 2004. Women and children last: The discursive construction of weblogs. In *Into the Blogosphere*, edited by L. Gurak. St. Paul, MN: University of Minnesota.

Herring, Susan C. 2010. Web content analysis: Expanding the paradigm. In *The International Handbook of Internet Research Policy*, edited by J. Hunsinger and L. Klastrup. Amsterdam: Springer Netherlands.

Herring, Susan C., Inna Kouper, John C. Paolillo, Lois Ann Scheidt, Michael Tyworth, Peter Welsch, Elijah Wright, and Ning Yu. 2005. Conversations in the blogosphere: An analysis "from the bottom up". Paper read at 38th Annual Hawaii International Conference on System Sciences (HICSS'05), Track 4, at Hawaii. Proceedings published by the Institute of Electrical and Electronics Engineers.

Herring, Susan C., Lois Ann Scheidt, Sabrina Bonus, and Elijah Wright. 2004. Bridging the Gap: A genre analysis of Weblogs. 37th Hawaii International Conference on System Sciences, 5th–8th January, at Hilton Waikoloa Village, Hawaii. Proceedings published by the Institute of Electrical and Electronics Engineers.

Herring, Susan C., Lois Ann Scheidt, Inna Kouper, and Elijah Wright. 2006. A longitudinal content analysis of Weblogs: 2003–2004. In *Blogging, Citizenship and the Future of Media*, edited by M. Tremayne. London, UK: Routledge.

Hertogh, Steven De, Stijn Viaene, and Guido Dedene. 2011. Governing Web 2.0. *Communications of the ACM* 54 (3):124–130.

Heylighen, Francis. 1999. Collective intelligence and its implementation on the Web: Algorithms to develop a collective mental map. *Computational & Mathematical Organisation Theory* 5 (3):253–280.

Heyman, K. 2008. The move to make social data portable. *Computer* 41 (4):13–15.

Hinchcliffe, Dion. 2006. Riding the hockey stick: Scaling Web 2.0 software. *Enterprise Web 2.0*. 16th July 2006. http://www.zdnet.com/blog/hinchcliffe/riding-the-hockey-stick-scaling-web-20-software/54 (accessed 5th August 2011).

Hitzler, Pascal, Markus Krötzsch, and Sebastian Rudolph. 2010. *Foundations of Semantic Web Technologies*. Boca Raton, FL: CRC Press.

Hochheiser, Harry, and Ben Shneiderman. 2010. From bowling alone to tweeting together: Technology-mediated social participation. *Interactions* 17 (2) (March/April 2010).

Hof, Robert D. 2011. You are the Ad. *MIT Technology Review*, May/June, pp. 64–69.

Honey, C., and S. C. Herring. 2009. Beyond microblogging: Conversation and collaboration via Twitter. 42nd Hawaii International Conference on System Sciences (HICSS '09), 5th–9th January, at Hilton Waikoloa Village Resort, Hawaii. Proceedings published by the Institute of Electrical and Electronics Engineers.

Hontz, Paul. 2011. Why two engineers left Apple to build a Flash alternative: The Hype (YC W11) story. *The Startup Foundry*. 23rd May. http://thestartupfoundry.com/2011/05/23/why-two-engineers-left-apple-to-build-a-flash-alternative-the-hype-yc-w11-story/ (accessed 19th August 2011).

Hotho, Andreas, Robert Jäschke, Christoph Schmitz, and Gerd Stumme. 2006. Trend detection in folksonomies. In *Semantic Multimedia*, edited by Y. Avrithis, Y. Kompatsiaris, S. Staab and N. O'Connor. Berlin/Heidelberg: Springer.

Howe, Jeff. 2006. The rise of crowdsourcing. *Wired*, June. http://www.wired.com/wired/archive/14.06/crowds.html

Hu, D. H., Wang Yinfeng, and Wang Cho-Li. 2010. BetterLife 2.0: Large-scale social intelligence reasoning on cloud. 2010 IEEE Second International Conference on Cloud Computing Technology and Science (CloudCom), 30th November–3rd December, at Indianapolis, IN. Proceedings published by the Institute of Electrical and Electronics Engineers.

Huang, Jeff, Katherine M. Thornton, and Efthimis N. Efthimiadis. 2010. Conversational tagging in Twitter. 21st ACM Conference on Hypertext and Hypermedia, 13th–16th June, at Toronto, Ontario, Canada. Proceedings published by the Association for Computing Machinery.

Huberman, Bernardo A. 2001. *The Laws of the Web*. Boston, MA.: The MIT Press.

Huberman, Bernardo A., and Lada A. Adamic. 1999. Growth dynamics of the World-Wide Web. *Nature* 401 (6749) (September):131.

Huberman, Bernardo A., Daniel M. Romero, and Fang Wu. 2008a. Social networks that matter: Twitter under the microscope. *arXiv* (December). http://arxiv.org/abs/0812.1045

Huberman, Bernardo, Daniel M Romero, and Fang Wu. 2008b. Social networks that matter: Twitter under the microscope. *First Monday* 14 (1) (20th December). http:// firstmonday.org/htbin/ cgiwrap/ bin/ojs/index.php/fm/article/view/2317/2063

Ingbert, R. Floyd. 2007. Web mash-ups and patchwork prototyping: User-driven technological innovation with Web 2.0 and open source software. 40th Annual Hawaii International Conference on System Sciences (HICSS 2007), 3rd–6th January, at Waikoloa, HI. Proceedings published by the Institute of Electrical and Electronics Engineers.

Inoue, Takeru, Hiroshi Asakura, Yukio Uematsu, Hiroshi Sato, and Noriyuki Takahashi. 2010. Rapid development of Web applications by introducing database systems with Web APIs. In *Database Systems for Advanced Applications*, edited by H. Kitagawa, Y. Ishikawa, Q. Li, and C. Watanabe. Berlin/Heidelberg: Springer.

Iyer, B., and T.H. Davenport. 2008. Reverse engineering Google's innovation machine. *Harvard Business Review* 86 (4) (April 2008):58–69.

Jackson, Samuel. 2010. Chinese youth and the social web. Published by M. Research. 15th May. http://www.samjackson.org/college/2010/05/18/chinese-youth-and-the-social-web/

Jacobs, Adam. 2009. The pathologies of big data. *Communications of the ACM* 52 (8):36–44.

Jacobs, Neil. 2006. *Open Access: Key Strategic, Technical and Economic Aspects*. Oxford: Chandos Publishing (Oxford) Ltd.

Jafner, Katie, and Matthew Lyon. 2003. *Where Wizards Stay Up Late: The Origins of the Internet*. London: Pocket Books (imprint of Simon & Schuster UK).

Jakobs, Kai, Rob Procter, and Robin Williams. 1996. Users and standardization—worlds apart? The example of electronic mail. *StandardView* 4 (4):183–191.

Jansen, Bernard J., Mimi Zhang, Kate Sobel, and Abdur Chowdury. 2009. Twitter power: Tweets as electronic word of mouth. *Journal of the American Society for Information Science and Technology* 60 (11):2169–2188.

Jardin, Xeni. 2005. Audience with the podfather. *Wired*, 14th May.

Jäschke, Robert, Leandro Marinho, Andreas Hotho, Lars Schmidt-Thieme, and Gerd Stumme. 2008. Tag recommendations in social bookmarking systems *AI Communications* 21 (4):231–247.

Java, Akshay. 2008. Mining social media communities and content. PhD diss., Computer Science and Electrical Engineering, University of Maryland.

Java, Akshay, Xiaodan Song, Tim Finin, and Belle Tseng. 2007. Why we Twitter: Understanding microblogging usage and communities. 9th WebKDD and 1st SNA-KDD 2007 Workshop on Web Mining and Social Network Analysis, 12th–15th August, at San Jose, California. Proceedings published by the Association for Computing Machinery.

Jazayeri, M. 2007. Some trends in Web application development. Future of Software Engineering (FOSE '07), 23rd–25th May, at Minneapolis, MN. Proceedings published by the Institute of Electrical and Electronics Engineers.

Jia, Xiaojing. 2010. Google cloud computing platform technology architecture and the impact of its cost. World Congress on Software Engineering (WCSE 2010), 19th–20th December, at Wuhan, China. Proceedings published by the Institute of Electrical and Electronics Engineers Computer Society.

JISC. 2009. *Higher Education in a Web 2.0 World*. JISC. Bristol, UK: JISC. March.

Jisun An, Meeyoung Cha, Krishna Gummadi, and Jon Crowcroft. 2011. Media landscape in Twitter: A world of new conventions and political diversity. International AAAI Conference on Weblogs and Social Media (ICWSM-11), 17th–21st July, at Barcelona, Spain. Proceedings published by AAAI Publications.

Johansmeyer, Tom. 2010. How industry marketers can save Twitter's ecosystem. *The Social Times*. 10th December. http://www.socialtimes.com/2010/12/how-industry-marketers-can-save-twitter%E2%80%99s-ecosystem/ (accessed 8th August 2011).

Johnson, Bobbie. 2010. The Web is reborn. *MIT Technology Review*, November/December, pp. 46–53.

Johnson, D. 2005. AJAX: Dawn of a new developer: The latest tools and technologies for AJAX developers. *JavaWorld.com*, 17th October.

Jones, Mike. 2010. LeWeb 2010: Q&A with Robert Scoble. YouTube. 9th December. http://www.youtube.com/watch?v=Fi_I20PaPyI&feature=BF&list=PL2E873884F73D3C4C&index=50

Joshi, Dhiraj, Andrew Gallagher, Jie Yu, and Jiebo Luo. 2012. Inferring photographic location using geotagged web images. *Multimedia Tools and Applications*: 56(1): 131–153.

Judge, Peter. 2011. Facebook open sources green data centre hardware. *eWeek Europe*, 8th April. http://www.eweekeurope.co.uk/news/facebook-open-sources-green-data-centre-hardware-26192

Kaar, Christian. 2007. *An Introduction to Widgets with Particular Emphasis on Mobile Widgets*. Technical Report Number 06/1/0455/009/02. Mobile Computing Dept. Hagenberg, Austria: University of Applied Sciences, October.

Kamps, Jaap, and Marijn Koolen. 2009. Is Wikipedia link structure different? Second ACM International Conference on Web Search and Data Mining (WSDM'09), 9th–12th February, at Barcelona, Spain. Proceedings published by the Association for Computing Machinery.

Karimzadehgan, Maryam, Manish Agrawal, and ChengXiang Zhai. 2009. Towards advertising on social networks. SIGIR 2009 Workshop on Information Retrieval and Advertising, 23rd July, at Boston, MA. Proceedings published by the Association for Computing Machinery.

Kart, Firat, L. E. Moser, and P. M. Melliar-Smith. 2008. Collaborative computing using the Atom Publishing Protocol. Third International Conference on Information Technology: New Generations, 7th–8th April, at Las Vegas, NV. Proceedings published by the Institute of Electrical and Electronics Engineers Computer Society.

Katzir, Liran, Edo Liberty, and Oren Somekh. 2011. Estimating sizes of social networks via biased sampling. 20th International Conference on World Wide Web (WWW'11), 28th March–1st April, at Hyderabad, India. Proceedings published by the Association for Computing Machinery.

Kazman, Rick, and Hong-Mei Chen. 2009. The metropolis model: A new logic for development of crowdsourced systems. *Communications of the ACM* 52 (7):76–84.

Keegan, William. 1998. Galbraith on crashes, Japan and walking sticks. *The Observer*, 21st June 1998, 32.

Kelly, Brian. 2006. What are open standards? UKOLN. http://www.ukoln.ac.uk/qa-focus/documents/briefings/briefing-11/html/ (accessed 14th July 2011).

Kennedy, Lyndon, Mor Naaman, Shane Ahern, Rahul Nair, and Tye Rattenbury. 2007. How Flickr helps us make sense of the world: Context and content in community-contributed media collections. 15th International Conference on Multimedia, 24th–29th September, at Augsburg, Germany. Proceedings published by the Association for Computing Machinery.

Kesan, Jay, and Rajiv Shah. 2008. Open standards in electronic governance: Promises and pitfalls. 2nd International Conference on Theory and Practice of Electronic Governance (ICEGOV), 1st–4th December, at Cairo, Egypt. Proceedings published by Association for Computing Machinery.

Kettell, Brian. 2002. *Valuation of Internet & Technology Stocks: Implications for Investment Analysis*. Oxford: Butterworth-Heinemann.

Khare, R. 2006. Microformats: The next (small) thing on the semantic Web? *IEEE Internet Computing* 10 (1):68–75.

Khare, Rohit, and Tantek Celik. 2006. Microformats: A pragmatic path to the Semantic Web. 15th International Conference on World Wide Web (WWW2006), 23rd–26th May, at Edinburgh, Scotland. Proceedings published by Association for Computing Machinery.

Kim, Eugene C. 2007. YouTube: Testing the safe harbors of digital copyright law. *S. Cal. Interdisc. Law Journal* 17 (1) (Fall 2007):139–171.

Kim, Jin. 2010. User-generated content (UGC) revolution? Critique of the promise of YouTube. PhD diss., University of Iowa.

Kim, Won, Ok-Ran Jeong, and Sang-Won Lee. 2010. On social Web sites. *Information Systems* 35 (2):215–236.

King, Rachael. 2007. When your social sites need networking. *BusinessWeek*, 18th June.

Kinsella, Sheila, Alexandre Passant, John G. Breslin, Stefan Decker, Ajit Jaokar, and V. Zelkowitz Marvin. 2009. The future of social web sites: Sharing data and trusted applications with semantics. In *Advances in Computers*. Waltham, MA: Elsevier.

Kirkpatrick, David. 2010a. Facebook's founder goes public. *Wired UK*, August.

Kirkpatrick, David. 2010b. *The Facebook Effect*. London: Virgin Books.

Kirstein, Peter T. 1999. Early experiences with the ARPANet and Internet in the United Kingdom. *IEEE Annals of the History of Computing* 21 (1):38–44.

Kittur, Aniket, Ed Chi, Bryan A. Pendleton, Bongwon Suh, and Todd Mytkowicz. 2007. Power of the few vs. wisdom of the crowd: Wikipedia and the rise of the bourgeoisie. Computer/ Human Interaction 2007, 28th April–3rd May, at San Jose, CA. Proceedings published by the Association for Computing Machinery.

Kittur, Aniket, and Robert E. Kraut. 2010. Beyond Wikipedia: Co-ordination and conflict in online production groups. 2010 ACM Conference on Computer Supported Cooperative Work (CSCW 2010), 6th–10th February, at Savannah, GA. Proceedings published by the Association for Computing Machinery.

Kleinberg, Jon. 2008. The convergence of social and technological networks. *Communications of the ACM* 51 (11):66–72.

Kleinberg, Jon, and Steve Lawrence. 2001. The structure of the Web. *Science* 294 (5548) (November 30, 2001):1849–1850.

Klemperer, P. 2006. *Network Effects and Switching Costs: Two Short Essays for the New Palgrave.* University of Oxford, Department of Economics. Published by Social Science Research Network (SSRN). http://papers.ssrn.com/sol3/papers.cfm?abstract_id=907502

Knoblock, Craig A. 1997. Searching the World Wide Web. *IEEE Expert: Intelligent Systems and Their Applications* 12 (1):8–14.

Kobayashi, M. forthcoming. Blogging Around the Globe: motivations, privacy concerns and social networking. In *Computational Social Network Analysis 2012*, edited by A. Abraham and A. E. Hassanien. Berlin: Springer Series on Computer and Communication Networks.

Kochan, Donald J. 2006. Blogosphere and the new pamphleteer. *Nexus Law Journal* 11 (May 2006):99–109.

Kolari, P., A. Java, T. Finin, J. Mayfield, and A. Joshi. 2006. Blog track open task: Spam blog classification. TREC Blog Track Notebook. Menlo Park, CA: American Association for Artificial Intelligence. http://citeseerx.ist.psu.edu/viewdoc/download?doi=10.1.1.92.6470&rep=rep1&type=pdf

Kolari, Pranam, Akshay Java, and Tim Finin. 2006. Characterizing the splogosphere. WWW'2006, 22nd–26th May, at Edinburgh, UK. Proceedings published by IW3C2.

Kolay, Santanu, and Ali Dasdan. 2009. The value of socially tagged URLs for a search engine. 18th International Conference on World Wide Web (WWW2009), 20th–24th April, at Madrid, Spain. Proceedings published by the Association for Computing Machinery.

Korn, Naomi, and Charles Oppenheim. 2007. *Web2.0 and IPR*. Bristol, UK: JISC.

Körner, Christian, Dominik Benz, Andreas Hotho, Markus Strohmaier, and Gerd Stumme. 2010. Stop thinking, start tagging: Tag semantics emerge from collaborative verbosity. 19th International Conference on World Wide Web (WWW2010), 26th–30th April, at Raleigh, NC. Proceedings published by the Association for Computing Machinery.

Kortuem, G., F. Kawsar, D. Fitton, and V. Sundramoorthy. 2010. Smart objects as building blocks for the Internet of Things. *IEEE Internet Computing* 14 (1) (January/February):44–51.

Koschmider, Agnes, Volker Hoyer, and Andrea Giessmann. 2010. Quality metrics for mashups. 2010 Annual Research Conference of the South African Institute of Computer Scientists and Information Technologists (SAICSIT Conf. 2010), 11th–13th October, at Bela Bela, South Africa. Proceedings published by Association for Computing Machinery.

Koutrika, Georgia, Benjamin Bercovitz, Robert Ikeda, Filip Kaliszan, Henry Liou, Zahra Mohammadi Zadeh, and Hector Garcia-Molina. 2009. Social systems: Can we do more than just poke friends? 4th Biennial Conference on Innovative Data Systems Research (CIDR), 4th–7th January, at Asilomar, CA. Proceedings published by the Association for Computing Machinery.

Kraan, Wilbert, and Li Yuan. 2010. *Cloud Computing in Institutions*. JISC CETIS. Bolton, UK: JISC CETIS (University of Bolton). March.

Krämer, Bernd, Kwei-Jay Lin, Priya Narasimhan, E. Maximilien, Hernan Wilkinson, Nirmit Desai, and Stefan Tai. 2007. A domain-specific language for Web APIs and services mashups. In *Service-Oriented Computing—ICSOC 2007*. Berlin/Heidelberg: Springer.

Krishnamurthy, Balachander. 2009. A measure of online social networks. First International Conference on COMmunication Systems And NETworks (COMSNETS 2009), 5th–10th January, at Bangalore, India. Proceedings published by the Institute of Electrical and Electronics Engineers Press.

Krishnamurthy, Balachander, Phillipa Gill, and Martin Arlitt. 2008. A few chirps about Twitter. 1st Workshop on Online Social Networks (WOSN 2008), 18th August, at Seattle, WA. Proceedings published by the Association for Computing Machinery.

Krishnamurthy, Balachander, and Craig E. Wills. 2008. Characterizing privacy in online social networks. First workshop on Online Social Networks (WOSN'08), 18th August, at Seattle, WA. Proceedings published by the Association for Computing Machinery.

Krishnamurthy, Balachander, and Craig E. Wills. 2010. On the leakage of personally identifiable information via online social networks. *SIGCOMM Computer Communication Review* 40 (1):112–117.

Kristaly, Dominic Mircea, Francisc Sisak, Ion Truican, Sorin-Aurel Moraru, and Florin Sandu. 2008. Web 2.0 technologies in Web application development. 1st International Conference on PErvasive Technologies Related to Assistive Environments (PETRA 2008), 15th–19th June, at Athens, Greece. Proceedings published by Association for Computing Machinery.

Kroeker, Kirk L. 2010. Engineering the Web's third decade. *Communications of the ACM* 53 (3):16–18.

Kruitbosch, Gijs, and Frank Nack. 2008. Broadcast yourself on YouTube: Really? 3rd ACM International Workshop on Human-Centered Computing (HCC '08), 26th–31st October, at Vancouver, British Columbia, Canada. Proceedings published by the Association for Computing Machinery.

Küpper, Axel, and Georg Treu. 2010. Next generation location-based services: Merging positioning and Web 2.0. In *Mobile Intelligence*, edited by L. T. Yang, A. B. Waluyo, L. T. J. Ma, and B. Srinivasan. Hoboken, NJ: John Wiley & Sons, Inc.

Kumar, Ravi, Jasmine Novak, Prabhakar Raghavan, and Andrew Tomkins. 2004. Structure and evolution of blogspace. *Communications of the ACM* 47 (12):35–39.

Kumar, Ravi, Jasmine Novak, Prabhakar Raghavan, and Andrew Tomkins. 2005. On the bursty evolution of blogspace. *World Wide Web* 8 (2):159–178.

Kumar, Ravi, Jasmine Novak, and Andrew Tomkins. 2006. Structure and evolution of online social networks. 12th ACM SIGKDD International Conference on Knowledge Discovery and Data Mining (KDD 2006), 23rd–30th August 2006, at Philadelphia, PA, USA. Proceedings published by ACM.

Kuuskeri, Janne, and Tuomas Turto. 2010. On actors and the REST. In *Web Engineering*, edited by B. Benatallah, F. Casati, G. Kappel and G. Rossi. Berlin/Heidelberg: Springer.

Kwak, Haewoon, Changhyun Lee, Hosung Park, and Sue Moon. 2010. What is Twitter, a social network or a news media? 19th International Conference on World Wide Web, 26th–30th April, at Raleigh, NC. Proceedings published by the Association for Computing Machinery.

Lacey, Sarah. 2008. *The Stories of Facebook, YouTube & Myspace*. Richmond, Surrey, UK: Crimson Publishing.

Lai, Eric. 2010. Twitter growth prompts switch from MySQL to 'NoSQL' database. *ComputerWorld*, 23rd February.

Laive, Patrick de. 2009. Shine a light on the Twitter ecosystem. *The Next Web*. 3rd November 2009. http://thenextweb.com/2009/03/11/web-conference-announces-twitter-ecosystem-session/ (accessed 8th August 2011).

Lakshman, Avinash, and Prashant Malik. 2010. Cassandra: A decentralised structured storage system. *SIGOPS Oper. Syst. Rev.* 44 (2):35–40.

Lam, Shyong (Tony) K., and John Riedl. 2009. Is Wikipedia growing a longer tail? Group'09, 10th–13th May, at Sanibel Island, FL. Proceedings published by the Association for Computing Machinery.

Lamb, Brian. 2004. Wide open spaces: Wiki ready or not. *EDUCAUSE Review* 39 (5) (September/October):36–48.

Lampe, Cliff, Nicole Ellison, and Charles Steinfield. 2006. A face(book) in the crowd: Social searching vs. social browsing. 20th Anniversary Conference on Computer-Supported Cooperative Work (CSCW 2006), 4th–8th November, at Banff, Alberta, Canada. Proceedings published by the Association for Computing Machinery.

Lampe, Cliff A.C., Nicole Ellison, and Charles Steinfield. 2007. A familiar face(book): Profile elements as signals in an online social network. SIGCHI Conference on Human Factors in Computing Systems, 28th April–3rd May, at San Jose, CA. Proceedings published by the Association for Computing Machinery.

Lange, Patricia G. 2008. Publicly private and privately public: Social Networking on YouTube. *Journal of Computer-Mediated Communication* 13 (1):361–380.

Langville, Amy N., and Carl D. Meyer. 2006. *Google's Page Rank and Beyond: The Science of Search Engine Rankings*. Princeton, NJ: Princeton University Press.

Laningham, S. 2006. Tim Berners-Lee: developerWorks interview: IBM. http://www-128.ibm.com/developerworks/podcast/

Lattanzi, Silvio, Alessandro Panconesi, and D. Sivakumar. 2011. Milgram-routing in social networks. 20th International Conference on World Wide Web (WWW'11), 28th March–1st April, at Hyderabad, India. Proceedings published by the Association for Computing Machinery.

Leadbeater, Charles, and Paul Miller. 2004. *The Pro-Am Revolution. Demos*. London: Demos. 24th November. http://www.demos.co.uk/publications/proameconomy

Leavitt, N. 2010. Will NoSQL databases live up to their promise? *Computer* 43 (2):12–14.

Lee, Edward. 2008. Warming up to user-generated content. *University of Illinois Law Review* 1459.

Lee, Jong Gun, Panayotis Antoniadis, and Kavé Salamatian. 2010. Faving reciprocity in content sharing communities: A comparative analysis of Flickr and Twitter. International Conference on Advances in Social Networks Analysis and Mining, 9th–11th August, at Odense, Denmark. Proceedings published by the Institute of Electrical and Electronics Engineers Computer Society.

Lefkow, Chris. 2010. US judge tosses out Viacom copyright suit against YouTube. *AFP Wire*, 23rd June.

Leiner, Barry M., Vinton G. Cerf, David D. Clark, Robert E. Kahn, Leonard Kleinrock, Daniel C. Lynch, Jon Postel, Larry G. Roberts, and Stephen Wolff. 2009. A brief history of the Internet. *SIGCOMM Computer Communication Review* 39 (5):22–31.

Lenhart, Amanda. 2006. User-generated content. Presentation made to *FTC Protecting Consumers in the Next Tech-Ade*, 6th November, at George Washington University. http://www.pewinternet.org/Presentations/2006/UserGenerated-Content.aspx

Lenhart, Amanda, Kristen Purcell, Aaron Smith, and Kathryn Zickuhr. 2010a. Social media and young adults. Pew Internet. Washington, DC: Pew Internet. http://www.pewinternet.org/Reports/2010/Social-Media-and-Young-Adults.aspx

Lenhart, Amanda, Kristen Purcell, Aaron Smith, and Kathryn Zickuhr. 2010b. Social media and mobile Internet use among teens and young adults. Pew Internet & American Life Project. Washington, DC: Pew Research Center. 3rd February 2010. http://pewresearch.org/pubs/1484/social-media-mobile-internet-use-teens-millennials-fewer-blog

Lerman, Kristina, and Laurie Jones. 2007. Social browsing on Flickr. International Conference on Weblogs and Social Media, 26th–28th March, at Boulder, CO. Proceedings published by conference organisers.

Leskovec, Jure. 2011. Analytics & predictive models for social media: WWW 2011 tutorial. Presentation made to WWW 2011, 28th March, at Hyderabad, India. http://snap.stanford.edu/proj/socmedia-www/index.html#info

Leskovec, Jure, Lars Backstrom, Ravi Kumar, and Andrew Tomkins. 2008. Microscopic evolution of social networks. 14th ACM SIGKDD International Conference on Knowledge Discovery and Data Mining (KDD'08), 24th–27th August, at Las Vegas, NV. Proceedings published by the Association for Computing Machinery.

Leskovec, Jure, Mary McGlohon, Christos Faloutsos, Natalie Glance, and Matthew Hurst. 2007. Cascading behavior in large blog graphs. SIAM International Conference on Data Mining, 26th–28th April, at Raddison University Hotel, Minneapolis, MN. Proceedings published by Society for Industrial and Applied Mathematics.

Lessig, Lawrence. 2004. *Free Culture: The Nature and Future of Creativity*. London: Penguin Books Ltd.

Levene, Mark. 2006. *An Introduction to Search Engines and Web Navigation*. Harlow, UK: Addison-Wesley.

Lévy, Pierre. 1997. *Collective Intelligence: Mankind's Emerging World in Cyberspace*. London: Perseus books.

Lévy, Pierre. 2010. The nature of collective intelligence. Royal Society. 28th September 2010. http://royalsociety.org/events-Web-Science-Presentations.aspx

Li, Gangmin. 2008. Economic sense of Metcalfe's Law. World Wide Web 2008, 21st–25th April, at Bejing, China. Proceedings published by IW3C2.

Li, Hui, Sourav S. Bhowmick, and Aixin Sun. 2009. Blog cascade affinity: Analysis and prediction. 18th ACM Conference on Information and Knowledge Management, 2nd–6th November, at Hong Kong, China. Proceedings published by the Association for Computing Machinery.

Li, Jia, Shih-Fu Chang, Michael Lesk, Rainer Lienhart, Jiebo Luo, and Arnold W. M. Smeulders. 2007. New challenges in multimedia research for the increasingly connected and fast growing digital society. 9th ACM International Workshop on Multimedia Information Retrieval (MIR), 28th–29th September, at Augsburg, Bavaria, Germany. Proceedings published by the Association for Computing Machinery.

Li, Xirong, Cees G. M. Snoek, and Marcel Worring. 2008. Learning tag relevance by neighbor voting for social image retrieval. 1st ACM International Conference on Multimedia Information Retrieval (MM'08), 26th–31st October, at Vancouver, British Columbia, Canada. Proceedings published by the Association for Computing Machinery.

Lidsky, David. 2010. The brief but impactful history of YouTube. *Fast Company*, 1st February.

Liebowitz, S. J., and S Margolis. 1994. Network externality: An uncommon tragedy. *Journal of Economic Perspectives* 8 (2) (Spring 1994):133–150.

Lih, Andrew. 2009. *The Wikipedia Revolution*. London: Arum Press Ltd.

Limpens, F., F. Gandon, and M. Buffa. 2008. Bridging ontologies and folksonomies to leverage knowledge sharing on the social Web: A brief survey. 23rd IEEE/ACM International Conference on Automated Software Engineering, 15th–16th September, at L'Aquila, Italy. Proceedings published by the Institute of Electrical and Electronics Engineers.

Limpens, Freddy. 2009. *Linking Folksonomies and Ontologies for Supporting Knowledge Sharing: A State of the Art*. EU Project, ISICIL. Intégration Sémantique de l'Information par des Communautés d'Intelligence en Ligne. Nice, France: INRIA Sophia-Antipolis. 16th July 2009. http://hal.archives-ouvertes.fr/docs/00/53/03/71/PDF/ISICIL-ANR-EA01-FolksonomiesOntologies-0906.pdf

Limpert, Eckhard, Werner Stahel, and Markus Abbt. 2001. Log-normal distributions across the sciences: Keys and clues. *BioScience* 51 (8) (May 2001):341–351.

Lin, Yu-Ru, Hari Sundaram, Yun Chi, Junichi Tatemura, and Belle L. Tseng. 2008. Detecting splogs via temporal dynamics using self-similarity analysis. *ACM Trans. Web* 2 (1):1–35.

Linaje, Marino, Juan Carlos Preciado, and Fernando Sanchez-Figueroa. 2007. Engineering Rich Internet Application user interfaces over legacy Web models. *IEEE Internet Computing* 11 (6):53–59.

Lipczak, Marek. 2008. Tag recommendation for folksonomies oriented towards individual users. European Conference on Machine Learning and Principles and Practice of Knowledge Discovery in Databases (ECML PKDD Discovery Challenge 2008), 15th–19th September, at Antwerp, Belgium. Proceedings published by University of Kassel.

Lipczak, Marek, and Evangelos Milios. 2010. The impact of resource title on tags in collaborative tagging systems. 21st ACM Conference on Hypertext and Hypermedia, 13th–16th June, at Toronto, Ontario, Canada. Proceedings published by the Association for Computing Machinery.

Liu, H. 2007. Social network profiles as taste performances. *Journal of Computer-Mediated Communication* 13 (1):252–275.

Livingstone, Sonia, Kjartan Ólafsson, and Elisabeth Staksrud. 2011. Social networking, age and privacy. ISSN 2045–256X, *EU Kids Online*. London: London School of Economics (Department of Media and Communications). http://www2.lse.ac.uk/media@lse/research/EUKidsOnline/EU%20Kids%20Online%20reports.aspx

Lohr, Steve. 2011. In a new Web world, no application is an island. *New York Times*, 26th March. http://www.nytimes.com/2011/03/27/business/27unboxed.html

Lorenzo, Giusy Di, Hakim Hacid, Hye-young Paik, and Boualem Benatallah. 2009. Data integration in mashups. *SIGMOD Record* 38 (1):59–66.

Maala, M. Zied, A. Delteil, and A. Azough. 2007. A conversion process from Flickr tags to RDF descriptions. 10th International Conference on Business Information Systems (BIS), 25th–27th April, at Poznan, Poland. Proceedings published by Springer Verlag.

Macskassy, Sofus A., and Matthew Michelson. 2011. Why do people retweet? Anti-homophily wins the day! International AAAI Conference on Weblogs and Social Media (ICWSM-11), 17th–21st July, at Barcelona, Spain. Proceedings published by AAAI Publications.

Madden, Mary. 2009. The audience for online video-sharing sites shoots up. Pew Internet & American Life Project. Washington, DC: P. R. Center. 29th July. http://www.pewinternet.org/Reports/2009/13--The-Audience-for-Online-VideoSharing-Sites-Shoots-Up.aspx

Madden, Mary, and Sydney Jones. 2008. Pew Internet Project data memo: Podcast downloading Pew Internet & American Life Project. Washington, DC: Pew Research Center, August.

Mahemoff, Michael. 2006. *Ajax Design Patterns*. Sebastopol, CA: O'Reilly Media Inc.

Makice, Kevin. 2009a. Maturation of the Twitter ecosystem. Presentation made to Tweetup, 22nd July 2009, at Mountain View, CA. http://www.slideshare.net/kmakice/maturation-of-the-twitter-ecosystem

Makice, Kevin. 2009b. *Twitter API: Up and Running*. Sebastopol, CA: O'Reilly Media Inc.

Malewicz, Grzegorz, Matthew H. Austern, Aart J. C. Bik, James C. Dehnert, Ilan Horn, Naty Leiser, and Grzegorz Czajkowski. 2009. Pregel: A system for large-scale graph processing. 28th ACM Symposium on Principles of Distributed Computing (PODC), 10th–12th August, at Calgary, Alberta, Canada. Proceedings published by Association for Computing Machinery.

Malinen, S. 2011. Strategies for gaining visibility on Flickr. 44th Hawaii International Conference on System Sciences (HICSS), 4th–7th January, at Hawaii. Proceedings published by the Institute of Electrical and Electronics Engineers.

Malloy, Betsy. 2006. Anonymous blogging and defamation: Balancing interests of the Internet. *Washington University Law Review* 84:1187.

Malone, Thomas W., Robert Laubacher, and Chrysanthos N. Dellarocas. 2009. Harnessing crowds: Mapping the genome of collective intelligence. 4732-09. Cambridge, MA: MIT. 3rd February. http://ssrn.com/paper=1381502

Mann, Charles C. 2006. Spam + Blogs = Trouble. *Wired*, September 2006. http://www.wired.com/wired/archive/14.09/splogs.html

Markines, Benjamin, Ciro Cattuto, and Filippo Menczer. 2009. Social spam detection. 5th International Workshop on Adversarial Information Retrieval on the Web (AIRWeb 2009), 20th–24th April, at Madrid, Spain. Proceedings published by the Association for Computing Machinery.

Marlow, Cameron, Mor Naaman, danah boyd, and Marc Davis. 2006. Position Paper, Tagging, Taxonomy, Flickr, Article, ToRead. WWW 2006, 23rd–26th May, at Edinburgh, Scotland. Proceedings published by the Association for Computing Machinery.

Martin, David. 2009. Update: Return of the Twitter quitters. *Nielsen Wire*. 30th April, 2009. http://blog.nielsen.com/nielsenwire/online_mobile/update-return-of-the-twitter-quitters/ (accessed 8th August 2011).

Martin, David, Hailin Wu, and Adil Alsaid. 2003. Hidden surveillance by Web sites: Web bugs in contemporary use. *Communications of the ACM* 46 (12):258–264.

Marwick, Alice E., and danah boyd. 2011. I tweet honestly, I tweet passionately: Twitter users, context collapse, and the imagined audience. *New Media & Society* 13 (1) (1st February):114–133.

Mathes, Adam. 2004. *Folksonomies—Cooperative Classification and Communication through Shared Metadata*. Computer Mediated Communication Report (LIS590CMC) Graduate School of Library and Information Science. Urbana, IL: University of Illinois, Urbana-Champaign. http://www.adammathes.com/academic/computer-mediated-communication/folksonomies.html

Maximilien, E. M., A. Ranabahu, and K. Gomadam. 2008. An online platform for Web APIs and service mashups. *Internet Computing, IEEE* 12 (5):32–43.

Maximilien, E. Michael, and Ajith Ranabahu. 2007. The programmable Web: Agile, social, and grassroot computing. International Conference on Semantic Computing (ICSC 2007), 17th–19th September, at Irvine, California. Proceedings published by the Institute of Electrical and Electronics Engineers Computer Society.

Maximilien, Michael, and Tyrone Grandison. 2008. Towards privacy propagation in the social Web. W2SP 2008: Web 2.0 Security and Privacy 2008, 22nd May, at Oakland, CA. Proceedings published by the Institute of Electrical and Electronics Engineers.

Mayer-Schonberger, Viktor. 2009. *Delete: The Virtue of Forgetting in the Digital Age*. Princeton, NJ: Princeton University Press.

McCandless, M. 1998. Web advertising. *Intelligent Systems and their Applications, IEEE* 13 (3):8–9.

McCarthy, Caroline. 2010. Facebook F8: One graph to rule them all. CNet, 21st April. http://news.cnet.com/8301-13577_3-20003053-36.html (accessed 2nd August 2011).

McCourt, Tom, and Patrick Burkart. 2003. When creators, corporations and consumers collide: Napster and the development of on-line music distribution. *Media, Culture & Society* 25 (3) (May 1, 2003):333–350.

McCown, Frank, and Michael L. Nelson. 2009. What happens when Facebook is gone? 9th ACM/IEEE-CS Joint Conference on Digital Libraries, 14th–19th June, at Austin, TX. Proceedings published by the Association for Computing Machinery.

McCullagh, Declan, and Anne Broache. 2007. Blogs turn 10—Who's the father? CNet, 20th March.

McDonnell, Michael, and Ali Shiri. 2011. Social search: A taxonomy of, and a user-centred approach to, social web search. *Program: Electronic Library and Information Systems* 45 (1):6–28.

McFedries, Paul. 2009. *Twitter: Tips, Tricks and Tweets*. Indianapolis, IN: Wiley Publishing Inc.

McGarr, Oliver. 2009. A review of podcasting in higher education: Its influence on the traditional lecture. *Australasian Journal of Educational Technology* 25 (3):309–321.

McGlohon, Mary, Jure Leskovec, Christos Faloutsos, Matthew Hurst, and Natalie Glance. 2007. Finding patterns in blog shapes and blog evolution. International Conference on Weblogs and Social Media (ICWSM), 26th–28th March, at Boulder, CO. Proceedings published by conference organisers.

McGregor, George, and Emma McCulloch. 2006. Collaborative tagging as a knowledge organisation and resource discovery tool. *Library Review* 55 (5):291–300.

McLaughlin, Laurianne. 2006. Podcasting 101: What the Web's new trend means to you. *Pervasive Computing* 5 (4) (October/December):7–11.

McLean, Jennifer. 2009. *State of the Blogosphere 2009 Introduction—Page 2*, 19th October. http://technorati.com/blogging/article/state-of-the-blogosphere-2009-introduction/page-2/ (accessed 17th September 2011).

McLellan, Drew. 2005. *Very Dynamic Web Interfaces*. O'Reilly Media Inc., 9th February. http://www.xml.com/pub/a/2005/02/09/xml-http-request.html (accessed 2nd August 2011).

McPherson, Miller, Lynn Smith-Lovin, and James M. Cook. 2001. Birds of a feather: Homophily in social networks. *Annual Review of Sociology* 27:415–444.

Medelyan, Olena, David Milne, Catherine Legg, and Ian H. Witten. 2009. Mining meaning from Wikipedia. *International Journal of Human-Computer Studies* 67 (9):716–754.

Mei, Lijun, W.K. Chan, and T.H. Tse. 2008. A tale of clouds: Paradigm comparisons and some thoughts on research issues. *IEEE Asia-Pacific Conference on Services Computing*, 9th–12th December, at Yilan, Taiwan, pp. 464–469. Proceedings published by IEEE.

Melia, Santiago, Jaime Gomez, Sandy Perez, and Oscar Diaz. 2010. Facing architectural and technological variability of Rich Internet Applications. *IEEE Internet Computing* 99 (PrePrints).

Melville, Prem, Wojciech Gryc, and Richard D. Lawrence. 2009. Sentiment analysis of blogs by combining lexical knowledge with text classification. 15th ACM SIGKDD International Conference on Knowledge Discovery and Data Mining (KDD-09), 28th June–1st July, at Paris, France. Proceedings published by the Association for Computing Machinery.

Mendes, P., M. Caceres, and B. Dwolatzky. 2009. A review of the widget landscape and incompatibilities between widget engines. 9th IEEE AFRICON '09, 23rd–25th September, at Nairobi, Kenya. Proceedings published by Institute of Electrical and Electronics Engineers.

Mercado Kierkegaard, Sylvia. 2005. How the cookies (almost) crumbled: Privacy & lobbyism. *Computer Law & Security Report* 21 (4):310–322.

Michahelles, Florian, Stephan Karpischek, and Albrecht Schmidt. 2010. What can the Internet of Things do for the citizen? Workshop at Pervasive 2010. *IEEE Pervasive Computing* 9 (4) (October–December):102–104.

Mikkonen, Tommi, and Antero Taivalsaari. 2008. Towards a uniform Web application platform for desktop computers and mobile devices. SMLI TR-2008-177. Sun Microsystems Laboratories (Finland). Menlo Park, CA: Sun Microsystems Inc. October. http://dspace.cc.tut.fi/dpub/handle/123456789/19127

Mikkonen, Tommi, and Antero Taivalsaari. 2011. Reports of the Web's death are greatly exaggerated. *Computer* 44 (5) (May 2011):30–36.

Millard, David E., and Martin Ross. 2006. Web 2.0: Hypertext by any other name? 17th Conference on Hypertext and Hypermedia, 22nd–25th August, at Odense, Denmark. Proceedings published by the Association for Computing Machinery.

Millen, David, Jonathan Feinberg, and Bernard Kerr. 2005. Social bookmarking in the enterprise. *Queue* 3 (9):28–35.

Millen, David R., Jonathan Feinberg, and Bernard Kerr. 2006. Dogear: Social bookmarking in the enterprise. SIGCHI Conference on Human Factors in Computing Systems (CHI '06), 22nd–27th April, at Montreal, Canada. Proceedings published by the Association for Computing Machinery.

Miller, Michael. 2007. *YouTube 4 You*. Indianapolis, IN: Que.

Miller, Paul, Rob Styles, and Tom Heath. 2008. Open Data Commons, a license for open data. Workshop on Linked Data on the Web (LDOW2008)(held as part of WWW 2008), 22nd April 2008, at Bejing, China. Proceedings published by IW3C2.

Miller, Rich. 2010a. Google's data center spending soars. Data Center Knowledge, 15th October. http://www.datacenterknowledge.com/archives/2010/10/15/googles-data-center-spending-soars/.

Miller, Rich. 2010b. The Facebook data center FAQ. Data Center Knowledge, 27th September. http://www.datacenterknowledge.com/the-facebook-data-center-faq/.

Miller, Rich. 2010c. Yahoo building next 'coop' in Switzerland. Data Center Knowledge, 8th October. http://www.datacenterknowledge.com/archives/2010/10/08/yahoo-building-next-coop-in-switzerland/ (accessed 27th January 2010).

Miller, Rich. 2010d. *Google Gift Means More Servers for Wikipedia*. Date Centre Knowledge, 18th February. http://www.datacenterknowledge.com/archives/2010/02/18/google-gift-means-more-servers-for-wikipedia/ (accessed 1st August 2011).

Miller, Rich. 2010e. *The Facebook Data Center FAQ*. Data Center Knowledge, 27th September. http://www.datacenterknowledge.com/the-facebook-data-center-faq/ (accessed 9th March 2011).

Mislove, Alan, Hema Swetha Koppula, Krishna P. Gummadi, Peter Druschel, and Bobby Bhattacharjee. 2008. Growth of the Flickr social network. First Workshop on Online Social Networks (WOSN 2008), 17th–22nd August, at Seattle, WA. Proceedings published by the Association for Computing Machinery.

Mislove, Alan, Massimiliano Marcon, Krishna P. Gummadi, Peter Druschel, and Bobby Bhattacharjee. 2007. Measurement and analysis of online social networks. 7th ACM SIGCOMM conference on Internet measurement, 24th–26th October, at San Diego, CA. Proceedings published by the Association for Computing Machinery.

Mitchell-Wong, J., R. Kowalczyk, A. Roshelova, B. Joy, and H. Tsai. 2007. OpenSocial: From social networks to social ecosystem. Digital EcoSystems and Technologies Conference, 2007 (DEST '07), 21st–23rd February, at Cairns, Australia. Proceedings published by the Institute of Electrical and Electronics Engineers.

Mitra, Siddharth, Mayank Agrawal, Amit Yadav, Niklas Carlsson, Derek Eager, and Anirban Mahanti. 2009. Characterizing Web-based video sharing workloads. 18th International Conference on World Wide Web (WWW'09), 20th–24th April, at Madrid, Spain. Proceedings published by the Association for Computing Machinery.

Mitzenmacher, M. 2001. A brief history of generative models for power law and lognormal distributions. 39th Allerton Conference on Communication Control and Computing, 3rd–5th October, at Champaign, IL. Proceedings published by University of Illinois at Urbana–Champaign, College of Engineering.

Mock, T. 2004. Music everywhere. *Spectrum, IEEE* 41 (9):42–47.

Moe, Hallvard. 2010. Everyone a pamphleteer? Reconsidering comparisons of mediated public participation in the print age and the digital era. *Media, Culture & Society* 32 (4) (1st July, 2010):691–700.

Mola-Velasco, Santiago M. 2011. Wikipedia vandalism detection. 20th International Conference Companion on World Wide Web, 28th March–1st April, at Hyderabad, India. Proceedings published by the Association for Computing Machinery.

Monica, Paul R. La. 2006. Google to buy YouTube. *CNNMoney.com*, 9th October.

Moore, Kathleen. 2011. 71% of online adults now use video-sharing sites. Pew Internet & American Life Project. Washington, DC: Pew Research Center. 26th July. http://pewinternet.org/Reports/2011/Video-sharing-sites.aspx

Moriyoshi, Ohara, P. Nagpurkar, Ueda Yohei, and K. Ishizaki. 2009. The data-centricity of Web 2.0 workloads and its impact on server performance. Paper read at Performance Analysis of Systems and Software, 2009. ISPASS 2009. IEEE International Symposium, 26th–28th April, Boston, MA.

Morville, Peter. 2005. *Ambient Findability*. Sebastopol, CA: O'Reilly Media, Inc.

Mowery, David C., and Timothy Simcoe. 2002. Is the Internet a US invention? An economic and technological history of computer networking. *Research Policy* 31 (8–9):1369–1387.

Mulligan, Geoff. 2010. The Internet of Things: Here now and coming soon. *IEEE Internet Computing* 14 (1) (January/February):35–36.

Murray, Brian, and James Cowart. 2001. *Web Bugs: A Study of the Presence and Growth Rate of Web Bugs on the Internet*. Fairfax, VA: Cyveillance Inc.

Murray-Rust, Peter. 2008. Open data in science. *Serials Review* 34 (1):52–64.

Naaman, Mor, Jeffrey Boase, and Chih-Hui Lai. 2010. Is it really about me? Message content in social awareness streams. ACM Conference on Computer Supported Cooperative Work (CSCW 2010), 6th–10th February, at Savannah, GA. Proceedings published by the Association for Computing Machinery.

Nagarajan, Meena, Amit Sheth, and Selvam Velmurugan. 2011. Citizen sensor data mining, social media analytics and development centric web applications. 20th International Conference Companion on World Wide Web (WWW'11) 28th March–1st April, at Hydrebad, India. Proceedings published by the Association for Computing Machinery.

Nagarajan, Meenakshi, Karthik Gomadam, Amit P. Sheth, Ajith Ranabahu, Raghava Mutharaju, and Ashutosh Jadhav. 2009. Spatio-temporal-thematic analysis of citizen sensor data: Challenges and experiences. In *Web Information Systems Engineering—WISE 2009*, edited by G. Vossen, D. Long and J. Yu. Berlin: Springer-Verlag.

Nagpurkar, P., W. Horn, U. Gopalakrishnan, N. Dubey, J. Jann, and P. Pattnaik. 2008. Workload characterization of selected JEE-based Web 2.0 applications. IEEE International Symposium on Workload Characterization (IISWC 2008), 14th–16th September, at Seattle, WA. Proceedings published by the Institute of Electrical and Electronics Engineers Computer Society.

Naone, Erica. 2008. Between friends. *MIT Technology Review*, April 2008, 43–47.

Naone, Erica. 2009. How Facebook copes with 300 million users. *MIT Technology Review*, 22nd September.

Narayanan, A., and V. Shmatikov. 2009. De-anonymizing social networks. 30th IEEE Symposium on Security and Privacy, 17th–20th May, at Oakland, CA. Proceedings published by the Institute of Electrical and Electronics Engineers.

Nardi, Bonnie A., Diane J. Schiano, and Michelle Gumbrecht. 2004. Blogging as social activity, or, would you let 900 million people read your diary? CSCW 2004 ACM Conference on Computer Supported Cooperative Work, 6th–10th November, at Chicago, IL. Proceedings published by the Association for Computing Machinery.

Naughton, John. 1999. *A Brief History of the Future: The Origins of the Internet*. London: Weidenfeld & Nicolson.

Nazir, Atif, Saqib Raza, and Chen-Nee Chuah. 2008. Unveiling Facebook: A measurement study of social network based applications. 8th ACM SIGCOMM Conference on Internet Measurement, 20th–22nd October, at Vouliagmeni, Greece. Proceedings published by the Association for Computing Machinery.

Nazir, Atif, Saqib Raza, Dhruv Gupta, Chen-Nee Chuah, and Balachander Krishnamurthy. 2009. Network level footprints of Facebook applications. 9th ACM SIGCOMM Conference on Internet Measurement Conference, 4th–6th November, at Chicago, IL. Proceedings published by the Association for Computing Machinery.

Negoescu, Radu Andrei, Alexander C. Loui, and Daniel Gatica-Perez. 2010. Kodak moments and Flickr diamonds: How users shape large-scale media. International ACM Conference on Multimedia (MM '10), 25th–29th October, at Firenze, Italy. Proceedings published by the Association for Computing Machinery.

Negoescu, Radu Andrei, and Daniel Gatica-Perez. 2008. Analyzing Flickr groups. International Conference on Content-based Image and Video Retrieval (CIVR'08), 7th–9th July, at Niagara Falls, Canada. Proceedings published by the Association for Computing Machinery.

Newitz, Annalee. 2005. Adam Curry wants to make you an iPod radio star. *Wired*, March. http://www.wired.com/wired/archive/13.03/curry.html

Newman, M. E. J. 2001. Clustering and preferential attachment in growing networks *Physical Review Series E* 64 (2):4.

Newman, M. E. J. 2003. Properties of highly clustered networks. *Physical Review Series E* 68 (2):026121.

Newman, M. E. J. 2005. Power laws, Pareto distributions and Zipf's law. *Contemporary Physics* 46 (5):323–352.

Newman, Mark, Albert-László Barabási, and Duncan J. Watts. 2006. *The Structure and Dynamics of Networks*. Princeton, NJ: Princeton University Press.

Nguyen, Ngoc, Radoslaw Katarzyniak, Adam Janiak, Pooyan Balouchian, and Atilla Elci. 2009. Data portability across social networks. In *New Challenges in Computational Collective Intelligence*, edited by R. Katarzyniak and A. Janiak. Berlin/Heidelberg: Springer.

Nie, Norman H., and D. Sunshine Hillygus. 2002. The impact of Internet use on sociability: Time-diary findings. *IT & Society* 1 (1):1–20.

Nissenbaum, Helen. 2010. *Privacy in Context*. Stanford, CA: Stanford Law Books.

Nov, Oded, and Sunil Wattal. 2009. Social computing privacy concerns: Antecedents and effects. 27th International Conference on Human Factors in Computing Systems (CHI 2009), 4th–9th April, at Boston, MA. Proceedings published by the Association for Computing Machinery.

Nyrhinen, Feetu, and Tommi Mikkonen. 2009. Web browser as a uniform application platform: How far are we? 35th Euromicro Conference on Software Engineering and Advanced Applications, 27th–29th August, at Patras, Greece. Proceedings published by the Institute of Electrical and Electronics Engineers Computer Society.

O'Reilly, Tim. 2003. The architecture of participation. *OnLamp.com*. 6th April. http://oreilly.com/pub/wlg/3017 (accessed 12th July 2011).

O'Reilly, Tim. 2004. The architecture of participation, June. http://oreilly.com/pub/a/oreilly/tim/articles/architecture_of_participation.html (accessed 12th July 2011).

O'Reilly, Tim. 2005a. Not 2.0? *O'Reilly Radar*. 5th August 2005. http://radar.oreilly.com/archives/2005/08/not-20.html (accessed 11th July 2011).

O'Reilly, Tim. 2005b. What is Web 2.0: Design patterns and business models for the next generation of software. O'Reilly Media. Sebastopol, CA: O'Reilly Media Inc. 30th September. http://oreilly.com/web2/archive/what-is-web-20.html

O'Reilly, Tim. 2006a. Web 2.0 compact definition: Trying again. *O'Reilly Radar*. 10th December. http://radar.oreilly.com/archives/2006/12/web-20-compact-definition-tryi.html (accessed 12th July 2011).

O'Reilly, Tim. 2006b. The open source paradigm shift. In *Open Source 2.0: The Continuing Evolution*. Sebastopol, CA: O'Reilly Media, Inc.

O'Reilly, Tim. 2008. Network effects in data. *O'Reilly Radar*. 27th October 2008. http://radar.oreilly.com/2008/10/network-effects-in-data.html (accessed 8th September 2011).

O'Reilly, Tim, Andrew Anker, Brian Behlendorf, Bob Morgan, and Allan Vermeulen. 2004. The architecture of participation. Kentfield, CA: The Conversations Network. Audio file. http://itc.conversationsnetwork.org/shows/detail328.html#

O'Reilly, Tim, and John Battelle. 2009. *Web Squared: Web 2.0 Five Years On*. Sebastopol, CA: O'Reilly Media Inc.

O'Reilly, Tim, and Tim Berners-Lee. 2009. A conversation with Tim Berners-Lee. O'Reilly Media Inc. 22nd Oct 2010. http://www.web2summit.com/web2009/public/schedule/detail/9286

O'Sullivan, Maureen. 2008. Creative Commons and contemporary copyright: A fitting shoe or "a load of old cobblers"? *First Monday* 13 (1) (7th January 2008).

Obradovič, Darko, and Stephan Baumann. 2008. Identifying and analysing Germany's top blogs. In *KI 2008: Advances in Artificial Intelligence*, edited by A. Dengel, K. Berns, T. Breuel, F. Bomarius and T. Roth-Berghofer. Berlin/Heidelberg: Springer.

Odlyzko, Andrew. 2000. *The History of Communications and Its Implications for the Internet*. Florham Park, NJ: AT&T.

Odlyzko, Andrew, and Benjamin Tilly. 2005. A refutation of Metcalfe's Law and a better estimate for the value of networks and network interconnections. Preprint. University of Minnesota, Digital Technology Centre.

OECD (Organisation for Economic Co-operation and Development). 2007. Participative Web: User-created content. DSTI/ICCP/IE(2006)7/FINAL. Paris: Organisation for Economic Co-operation and Development. 12th April. http://www.oecd.org/dataoecd/57/14/38393115.pdf

Ofcom. 2008. *Social Networking: A Quantitative and Qualitative Research Report*. Office of Communications (Ofcom). London: Ofcom. 2nd April.

Ofcom. 2010. *Traffic Management and 'Net Neutrality'*. London: Ofcom. 24th June.

Ofcom. 2011. *Communications Report: UK*. London: Ofcom. 4th August. http://stakeholders. ofcom.org.uk/market-data-research/market-data/communications-market-reports/cmr11/ downloads/

Ohara, M. 2010. Aggregating REST requests to accelerate Web 2.0 applications. *IBM Journal of Research and Development* 54 (1).

Oliva, Rogelio, John D. Sterman, and Martin Giese. 2003. Limits to growth in the new economy: Exploring the 'get big fast' strategy in e-commerce. *System Dynamics Review* 19 (2):83–117.

Olivarez-Giles, Nathan. 2011. Twitter, launched five years ago, delivers 350 billion tweets a day. *Los Angeles Times*, 15th July. http://latimesblogs.latimes.com/technology/2011/07/twitter-delivers-350-billion-tweets-a-day.html

Olsen, Russ. 2007. *Design Patterns in Ruby*. Boston: Addison Wesley.

Opsahl, Kurt. 2010. Social network privacy. Presentation made to W2SP 2010, 20th May, at Oakland, CA. http://w2spconf.com/2010/

Oqvist, Karen. 2009. *Virtual Shadows: Your Privacy in the Information Society*. London: British Computer Society.

Ousterhout, John, and Eric Stratmann. 2010. Managing state for Ajax-driven Web components. USENIX Conference on Web Application Development (WebApps '10), 23rd–24th June, at Boston, MA. Proceedings published by USENIX.

Overdick, Hagen. 2007. The resource-oriented architecture. IEEE Congress on Services (SCW '07), 9th–13th July, at Los Alamitos, CA. Proceedings published by the Institute of Electrical and Electronics Engineers Computer Society.

Owen, M, L Grant, S Sayers, and K Facer. 2006. *Social Software and Learning. FutureLab*. Bristol, UK: FutureLab. http://archive.futurelab.org.uk/resources/publications-reports-articles/ opening-education-reports/Opening-Education-Report199/

Palfrey, John, and Urs Gasser. 2007. Case study: Mashups interoperability and eInnovation. Berkman Publication Series The Berkman Center for Internet & Society (Harvard University). http://cyber.law.harvard.edu/interop/pdfs/interop-mashups.pdf

Pallis, G. 2010. Cloud computing: The new frontier of Internet computing. *IEEE Internet Computing* 14 (5):70–73.

Pallis, George, Demetrios Zeinalipour-Yazti, and Marios Dikaiakos. 2011. Online social networks: Status and trends. In *New Directions in Web Data Management 1*, edited by A. Vakali and L. Jain. Berlin/Heidelberg: Springer.

Panciera, Katherine, Aaron Halfaker, and Loren Ter Veen. 2009. Wikipedians are born, not made: A study of power editors on Wikipedia. GROUP'09, 10th–13th May, at Sanibel Island, FL. Proceedings published by the Association for Computing Machinery.

Pang, Bo, and Lillian Lee. 2008. Opinion mining and sentiment analysis. *Foundations and Trends in Information Retrieval* 2 (1–2):1–135.

Paolillo, J. C. 2008. Structure and network in the YouTube core. 41st Annual Hawaii International Conference on System Sciences (HICSS-41), 7th–10th January, at Waikoloa, Big Island, Hawaii. Proceedings published by the Institute of Electrical and Electronics Engineers Computer Society.

Park, James J., Laurence T. Yang, Changhoon Lee, Dina Hussein, Ghada Alaa, and Ahmed Hamad. 2011. Towards usage-centered design patterns for social networking systems. In *Future Information Technology*. Berlin/Heidelberg: Springer.

Parker, Conrad, and Silvia Pfeiffer. 2005. Video blogging: Content to the max. *IEEE MultiMedia* 12:4–8.

Parker, Sean. 2009. The new era of network effect. Presentation made to Web 2.0 Summit 2009, 23rd October 2009, at San Francisco, CA. http://www.youtube.com/watch?v=GZautIZJu2Y&feature=player_embedded

Parr, Ben. 2009. Twitpocalypse II: Twitter apps might break tomorrow. Mashable. 21st September. http://mashable.com/2009/09/21/twitpocalypse-ii-update/ (accessed 8th August 2011).

Passant, Alexandre, Julia Anaya, and Owen Sacco. 2011. Privacy-by-design in federated social Web applications. Web Science 2011, 14th–17th June, at Koblenz, Germany. Proceedings published by the Association for Computing Machinery.

Paterson, Richard, and Anthony Smith. 1998. *Television: An International History*. 2nd ed. Oxford: Oxford University Press.

Paulson, L. D. 2005. Building rich web applications with Ajax. *IEEE Computer* 38 (10):14–17.

Pautasso, Cesare. 2009. RESTful webservice composition with BPEL for REST. *Data & Knowledge Engineering* 68 (9) (September):851–866.

Pautasso, Cesare, Olaf Zimmermann, and Frank Leymann. 2008. Restful Web services vs. "big" web services: Making the right architectural decision. 17th International Conference on World Wide Web (WWW2008), 21st–25th April, at Beijing, China. Proceedings published by Association for Computing Machinery.

Pedersen, Mogens Kühn, and Vladislav V. Fomin. 2005. Open standards and their early adoption. Open Standards Research Report 1/2005. Copenhagen: Copenhagen Business School, November. http://ideas.repec.org/p/hhs/cbsinf/2006_008.html

Pedersen, Sarah, and Caroline Macafee. 2007. Gender differences in British blogging. *Journal of Computer-Mediated Communication* 12 (4):Article 16.

Pedro, Jose San, Stefan Siersdorfer, and Mark Sanderson. 2011. Content redundancy in YouTube and its application to video tagging. *ACM Trans. Inf. Syst.* 29 (3):1–31.

Pennock, David M., Gary W. Flake, Steve Lawrence, Eric J. Glover, and C. Lee Giles. 2002. Winners don't take all: Characterizing the competition for links on the web. *Proceedings of the National Academy of Sciences of the United States of America* 99 (8) (16th April, 2002):5207–5211.

Perreault, M., and D. Ruths. 2011. The effect of mobile platforms on Twitter content generation. International AAAI Conference on Weblogs and Social Media (ICWSM-11), 17th–21st July, at Barcelona, Spain. Proceedings published by AAAI Publications.

Phelan, Owen, Kevin McCarthy, Mike Bennett, and Barry Smyth. 2011. On using the real-time Web for news recommendation and discovery. 20th International Conference Companion on World Wide Web, 28th March–1st April, at Hyderabad, India. Proceedings published by the Association for Computing Machinery.

Pierce, Marlon E., Geoffrey Fox, Huapeng Yuan, and Yu Deng. 2006. Cyberinfrastructure and Web 2.0. HPC2006, 4th July, at Cetraro, Italy. Proceedings published by conference organisers.

Piero, Fraternali, Rossi Gustavo, and Sanchez-Figueroa Fernando. 2010. Rich Internet Applications. *IEEE Internet Computing* 14 (3) (May/June 2010):9–12.

Pilgrim, Mark. 2011. *HTML5: Up and Running*. Sebastopol, CA: O'Reilly Media Inc.

Ping, Yu, Kostas Kontogiannis, and Terence C. Lau. 2003. Transforming legacy Web applications to the MVC architecture. International Workshop on Software Technology and Engineering Practice (STEP '03), 21st September, at Portland, OR. Proceedings published by Institute of Electrical and Electronics Engineers Computer Society.

Pinkerton, Brian. 1994. Finding what people want: Experiences with the WebCrawler. 2nd International WWW Conference, 17th–20th October, at Chicago, IL. Proceedings published by the Association for Computing Machinery.

Pinkerton, Brian. 2000. WebCrawler: Finding what people want. PhD diss., Department of Computer Science & Engineering, University of Washington.

Pirolli, Peter, Jenny Preece, and Ben Shneiderman. 2010. Cyberinfrastructure for Social Action on National Priorities. *IEEE Computer* 43 (11):20–21.

Powell, Andy, and David Recordon. 2007. OpenID: Decentralised single sign-on for the Web. *Ariadne* (51) (April 2007).

Pressman, Roger S. 2000. *Software Engineering: A Practitioner's Approach*. 5th ed. London: McGraw-Hill.

Prieur, Christophe, Dominique Cardon, Jean-Samuel Beuscart, Nicolas Pissard, and Pascal Pons. 2008. The strength of weak co-operation: A case study on Flickr. Preprint. arXiv.

Probets, Steve, Julius Mong, David Evans, and David Brailsford. 2001. Vector graphics: From PostScript and Flash to SVG. 2001 ACM Symposium on Document Engineering (Doc Eng '01), 9th–10th November, at Atlanta, GA. Proceedings published by the Association for Computing Machinery.

Pujol, Josep M., Vijay Erramilli, Georgos Siganos, Xiaoyuan Yang, Nikos Laoutaris, Parminder Chhabra, and Pablo Rodriguez. 2010. The little engine(s) that could: Scaling online social networks. *SIGCOMM Computer Communication Review* 40 (4):375–386.

Putnam, Robert. 2000. *Bowling Alone: The Collapse and Revival of American Community*. New York: Simon & Schuster.

Quint, A. 2003. Scalable vector graphics. *IEEE Multimedia* 10 (3):99–102.

Rader, Emilee, and Rick Wash. 2008. Influences on tag choices in del.icio.us. 2008 ACM Conference on Computer Supported Cooperative Work, 8th–12th November, at San Diego, CA. Proceedings published by the Association for Computing Machinery.

RAJAR. 2010. RAJAR publishes findings of MIDAS 7. Press Release. December 2010. http://www.rajar.co.uk/docs/news/data_release_2010_Q4.pdf

Raman, T. V. 2009. Toward 2 W beyond Web 2.0. *Communications of the ACM* 52 (2):52–59.

Rattenbury, Tye, Nathan Good, and Mor Naaman. 2007. Towards extracting Flickr tag semantics. 16th International Conference on World Wide Web (WWW'07), 8th–12th May, at Banff, Alberta, Canada. Proceedings published by the Association for Computing Machinery.

Ravasz, E, and Albert-László Barabási. 2002. Hierarchical organisation in complex networks. *Physics Review E* 67 (2):026112

Razmerita, Liana, Martynas Jusevičius, and Rokas Firantas. 2009. New generation of social networks based on semantic web technologies: The importance of social data portability. Workshop on Adaptation and Personalization for Web 2.0 (UMAP'09), 22nd–26th June, at Trento, Italy. Proceedings published by CEUR Workshop Proceedings.

Recordon, David. 2009. Facebook in 2010: No longer a walled garden. O'Reilly, 4th March. http://radar.oreilly.com/2009/03/facebook-in-2010-no-longer-a-walled-garden.html (accessed 2nd August 2011).

Redden, Carla. 2010. Social bookmarking in academic libraries: Trends and Applications. *The Journal of Academic Librarianship* 36 (3):219–227.

Reed, David P. 1999. That sneaky exponential: Beyond Metcalfe's Law to the power of community building. http://www.reed.com/dpr/locus/gfn/reedslaw.html (accessed 18th July 2011).

Reed, David P. 2001. The law of the pack. *Harvard Business Review* (1st Feb 2001):23–24.

Reid, Robert H. 1997a. Marc Andreessen—Netscape. In *Architects of the Web*: John Wiley & Sons.

Reid, Robert H. 1997b. *Architects of the Web: 1,000 Days That Built the Future of Business*. New York: John Wiley & Sons, Inc.

Reisinger, Don. 2010. A review of Google's legal woes. UBM TechWeb, 21st June. http://www.internetevolution.com/author.asp?section_id=851&doc_id=193455&f_src=internetevolution_gnews (accessed 6th August 2011).

Rejaie, R., M. Torkjazi, M. Valafar, and W. Willinger. 2010. Sizing up online social networks. *IEEE Network* 24 (5):32–37.

Rettberg, Jill Walker. 2008. *Blogging*, (Digital Media and Society series.) Cambridge, UK: Polity Press.

Reynolds, Glenn. 2006. *An Army of Davids*. Nashville, TN: Thomas Nelson.

Rheingold, Howard. 2002. *Smart Mobs*. Cambridge, MA: Perseus.

Rhodes, John S. 1999. The human behind robot wisdom. WebWord.com. http://www.webword.com/interviews/barger.html (accessed 19th July 2011).

Ribeiro, B., W. Gauvin, B. Liu, and D. Towsley. 2010. On MySpace account spans and double pareto-like distribution of friends. INFOCOM IEEE Conference on Computer Communications Workshops, 15th–19th March, at San Diego, CA. Proceedings published by the Institute of Electrical and Electronics Engineers.

Richardson, Leonard, and Sam Ruby. 2007. *RESTful Web Services*. Sebastopol, CA: O'Reilly Media Inc.

Richardson, Matthew, Ewa Dominowska, and Robert Ragno. 2007. Predicting clicks: Estimating the click-through rate for new ads. 16th International Conference on World Wide Web (WWW 2007), 8th–12th May, at Banff, Alberta, Canada. Proceedings published by the Association for Computing Machinery.

Ritchie, Paul. 2007. The security risks of AJAX/Web 2.0 applications. *Network Security* 2007 (3) (March):4–8.

Rizvi, Raza. 2009. 100G Ethernet and beyond: Preparing for the exabyte Internet. JISC Technology & Standards Watch. Bristol: JISC. July 2009. http://www.jisc.ac.uk/whatwedo/services/techwatch/reports/horizonscanning/hs0901

Rodriguez, Marko A. 2009. A reflection on the structure and process of the Web of data. *Bulletin of the American Society for Information Science and Technology* 35 (6):38–43.

Romero, Daniel M., Brendan Meeder, and Jon Kleinberg. 2011. Differences in the mechanics of information diffusion across topics: Idioms, political hashtags, and complex contagion on twitter. 20th International Conference on World Wide Web, 28th March–1st April, at Hyderabad, India. Proceedings published by the Association for Computing Machinery.

Rosenbloom, Andrew. 2004. The blogosphere. *Communications to the ACM* 47 (12) (December):30–33.

Roth, Camille. 2007. Viable wikis: Struggle for life in the wikisphere. WikiSym'07, 21st–23rd October, at Montreal, Quebec, Canada. Proceedings published by the Association for Computing Machinery.

Rowe, M. 2009. Interlinking distributed social graphs. Linked Data on the Web Workshop (LDOW2009)(part of WWW2009), 20th April, at Madrid, Spain. Proceedings published by CEUR Workshop Proceedings (CEUR-WS.org).

Rowe, Matthew, and Fabio Ciravegna. 2010. Harnessing the social Web: The science of identity disambiguation. Paper read at Web Science Conf. 2010, 26th–27th April, at Raleigh, NC. Proceedings published by Web Science Trust.

Ruby, Sam. 2005. Agile Web 2.0 Development. intertwingly. 8th August 2005. http://www.intertwingly.net/blog/2005/08/08/Agile-Web-2-0-Development#web20 (accessed 14th July 2011).

Rushe, Dominic. 2011. Is this the start of the second dotcom bubble? *The Guardian*, 20th February. http://www.guardian.co.uk/business/2011/feb/20/is-this-the-start-of-the-second-dotcom-bubble.

Sagolla, Dom. 2006. Oh this is going to be addictive. Twitter Status Message, 21st March. http://twitter.com/#!/dom/status/38 (accessed 15th August 2011).

Sagolla, Dom. 2009. *140 Characters: A Style Guide for the Short Form*. Hoboken, NJ: John Wiley & Sons.

Sahlin, Doug, and Chris Botello. 2007. *YouTube for Dummies*. Indianapolis, IN: Wiley Publishing Inc.

Saltzer, J. H., D. P. Reed, and D. D. Clark. 1984. End-to-end arguments in system design. *ACM Transactions on Computer Systems* 2 (4):277–288.

Sang Lee, Taewon Hwang, and Hong-Hee Lee. 2006. Corporate blogging strategies of the Fortune 500 companies. *Management Decision* 44 (3):316–334.

Sanger, Larry. 2006. The early history of Nupedia and Wikipedia. In *Open Sources 2.0: The Continuing Evolution*, edited by C. DiBona, D. Cooper, and M. Stone. Sebastopol, CA: O'Reilly Media Inc.

Sankar, Krishna, Susan A. Bouchard, and Dennis Mancini. 2008. *Enterprise Web 2.0 Fundamentals*. Indianapolis, IN: Cisco Press.

Santos, Rodrygo L. T., Bruno P. S. Rocha, Cristiano G. Rezende, and Antonio A. F. Loureiro. 2009. *Characterizing the YouTube Video-Sharing Community*. Technical Report. Dept. of Comp. Sci. Belo Horizonte, Brazil: Federal University of Minas Gerais.

Sarno, David. 2009. Twitter creator Jack Dorsey illuminates the site's founding document. Part I. *LA Times*, February 18. http://latimesblogs.latimes.com/technology/2009/02/twitter-creator.html

Savage, Neil. 2010. New search challenges and opportunities. *Communications of the ACM* 53 (1) (January 2010):27–29.

Sayre, R. 2005. Atom: The standard in syndication. *IEEE Internet Computing* 9 (4):71–78.

Schaller, Andreas, Katrin Mueller, and Byung-Yong Sung. 2008. Motorola's experience in designing the Internet of Things. 1st International Conference, Internet of Things, 2008, 26th–28th March, at Zurich. Proceedings published by Springer.

Schiano, Diane, Bonnie Nardi, Michelle Gumbrecht, and Luke Swartz. 2004. Blogging by the rest of us. CHI 2004, 24th–29th April, at Vienna, Austria. Proceedings published by the Association for Computing Machinery.

Schmidt, Douglas C., Mohamed Fayad, and Ralph E. Johnson. 1996. Software patterns. *Communications of the ACM* 39 (10):37–39.

Schmidt, Jan. 2007a. Blogging practices in the German-speaking blogosphere. Research Centre New Communication Media. Bamberg, Germany: Research Centre New Communication Media. http://www.ssoar.info/ssoar/files/2008/239/fonkpaper0702.pdf

Schmidt, Jan. 2007b. Blogging practices: An analytical framework. *Journal of Computer-Mediated Communication* 12 (4):article 13. https://www.uni-bamberg.de/fileadmin/uni/fakultaeten/split_professuren/journalistik/Fonk/pdfs-Veroeffentlichungen/Blogging_practices.pdf

Schneider, David. 2011. Under the hood at Google and Facebook. *IEEE Spectrum* 48 (6) (June):63–67.

Scholz, Trebor. 2008. Market ideology and the myths of Web 2.0. *First Monday* 13 (3). http://firstmonday.org/htbin/cgiwrap/bin/ojs/index.php/fm/article/view/2138/1945 (accessed 11th July 2011).

Scoble, Robert, and Shel Israel. 2006. *Naked Conversations*. Hoboken, NJ: John Wiley & Sons Inc.

Scott, John. 1991. *Social Network Analysis*. London: SAGE Publications Ltd.

Searls, Doc. 2004. DIY radio with PODcasting. Doc Searls' IT Garage. 28th September. http://www.itgarage.com/node/462 (accessed 3rd August 2011).

Searls, Doc, and David Sifry. 2003. Building with blogs. *Linux J*. 2003 (107):4.

Segaran, Toby. 2007. *Programming Collective Intelligence*. Sebastopol, CA: O'Reilly Media Inc.

Seki, Kazuhiro, Huawei Qin, and Kuniaki Uehara. 2010. Impact and prospect of social bookmarks for bibliographic information retrieval. 10th Annual Joint Conference on Digital libraries, 21st–25th June, at Gold Coast, Queensland, Australia. Proceedings published by the Association for Computing Machinery.

Serdyukov, Pavel, Vanessa Murdock, and Roelof van Zwol. 2009. Placing Flickr photos on a map. 32nd International ACM SIGIR Conference on Research and Development in Information Retrieval, 19th–23rd July, at Boston, MA. Proceedings published by the Association for Computing Machinery.

Seshadri, Mukund, Sridhar Machiraju, Ashwin Sridharan, Jean Bolot, Christos Faloutsos, and Jure Leskove. 2008. Mobile call graphs: Beyond power-law and lognormal distributions. 14th ACM SIGKDD international conference on Knowledge discovery and data mining, at Las Vegas, NV. Proceedings published by the Association for Computing Machinery.

Shachaf, P., and N. Hara. 2010. Beyond vandalism: Wikipedia trolls. *Journal of Information Science* 36 (3):357–370.

Shadbolt, N., W. Hall, and T. Berners-Lee. 2006. The Semantic Web revisited. *Intelligent Systems, IEEE* 21 (3):96–101.

Shadbolt, Nigel. 2010. Why open government data? Lessons from data.gov.uk. 9th International Semantic Web Conference (ISWC), 7th–11th November, at Shanghai, China. Proceedings published by Springer.

Shamma, David A., Lyndon Kennedy, and Elizabeth F. Churchill. 2011. Peaks and persistence: Modeling the shape of microblog conversations. The 2011 ACM Conference on Computer Supported Cooperative Work (CSCW '11), 19th–23rd March, at Hangzhou, China. Proceedings published by the Association for Computing Machinery.

Shan, Tony C, and Winnie W Hua. 2006. Taxonomy of Java Web Application Frameworks. IEEE International Conference on E-Business Engineering, 24th–26th October, at Shanghai, China. Proceedings published by the Institute of Electrical and Electronics Engineers Computer Society.

Shankland, Stephen. 2008. Google spotlights data center inner workings. CNet, 30th May. http://news.cnet.com/8301-10784_3-9955184-7.html?tag=blog.1.

Shao, Guosong. 2009. Understanding the appeal of user-generated media: A uses and gratification perspective. *Internet Research* 19 (1):7–25.

Shaozhi, Ye, Lang Juan, and Wu Felix. 2010. Crawling online social graphs. 12th International Asia-Pacific Web Conference, 6th–8th April, at Buscan, Korea. Proceedings published by the Institute of Electrical and Electronics Engineers.

Shen, Kaikai, and Lide Wu. 2005. Folksonomy as a complex network. ARXIV Preprint.

Sheridan, John, and Jeni Tennison. 2010. Linking UK government data linked data on the Web (LDOW2010), 27th April, at Raleigh, NC. Proceedings published by CEUR Workshop Proceedings.

Sheth, A. 2009. Citizen sensing, social signals, and enriching human experience. *IEEE Computer* 13 (4) (July):87–92.

Shi, Xiaolin, Belle Tseng, and Lada Adamic. 2007. Looking at the blogosphere topology through different lenses. 2nd Int'l AAAI Conference on Weblogs and Social Media, 30th March–2nd April, at Boulder, Colarado. Proceedings published by Association for the Advancement of Artificial Intelligence (AAAI).

Shirky, Clay. 2005. Power laws, weblogs and inequality. In *Extreme Democracy*, edited by M. Ratcliffe and J. Lebkowsky. Published as a Creative Commons document. http://extremedemocracy.com/chapters/Chapter%20Three-Shirky.pdf

Shirky, Clay. 2008. *Here Comes Everybody: The Power of Organising without Organisations*. London: Allen Lane.

Shneiderman, Ben, Jennifer Preece, and Peter Pirolli. 2011. Realizing the value of social media requires innovative computing research. *Communications of the ACM* 54 (9) (September 2011):34–37.

Shuen, Amy. 2008. *Web 2.0: A Strategy Guide*: Sebastopol, CA: O'Reilly Media Inc.

Siegler, MG. 2010. Twitter slashes API rate limits in half across the board to deal with capacity issues. TechCrunch. 29th June. http://techcrunch.com/2010/06/29/twitter-api-limit/ (accessed 8th August 2011).

Siersdorfer, Stefan, Sergiu Chelaru, Wolfgang Nejdl, and Jose San Pedro. 2010. How useful are your comments?: Analyzing and predicting YouTube comments and comment ratings. 19th International Conference on World Wide Web (WWW2010), 26th–30th April, at Raleigh, NC. Proceedings published by the Association for Computing Machinery.

Silverthorne, Sean. 2007. How Wikipedia works (or doesn't). *Harvard Business Review*. http://hbswk. hbs.edu/item/5605.html (accessed 1st August 2011).

Simonite, Tom. 2011. Social indexing. *MIT Technology Review*, May/June.

Smart, P. R., P. C. Engelbrecht, D. Braines, M. Strub, and J. A. Hendler. 2009. Cognitive extension and the Web. Web Science '09, 18th–20th March, at Athens, Greece. Proceedings published by Web Science Trust.

Smith, Aaron. 2008. New numbers for blogging and blog readership. Pew Internet & American Life Project. Washington, DC: Pew Research Center. 22nd July, 2008. http://www.pewinternet.org/ Commentary/2008/July/New-numbers-for-blogging-and-blog-readership.aspx

Smith, Aaron. 2009. Online participation in the social media era. Presentation made to 36th Annual Symposium on Racing & Gaming, 10th December, at Tucson, AZ. http://www.pewinternet. org/Presentations/2009/RTIP-Social-Media.aspx

Smith, Aaron. 2011. Twitter update 2011. Pew Internet & American Life Project. Washington, DC: Pew Research Center. 1st June. http://pewinternet.org/%20Reports/2011/Twitter-Update-2011.aspx

Smith, Aaron, and Lee Rainie. 2010. 8% of online Americans use Twitter. Pew Internet & American Life Project. Washington, DC: Pew Research Center. http://pewinternet.org/Reports/2010/ Twitter-Update-2010.aspx

Snell, James. 2004. Resource-oriented vs. activity-oriented Web services. IBM DeveloperWorks, 12th October. https://www.ibm.com/developerworks/webservices/library/ws-restvsoap/ (accessed 9th August 2011).

Snell, James. 2005. An overview of the Atom 1.0 syndication format. IBM DeveloperWorks, 2nd August. http://www.ibm.com/developerworks/xml/library/x-atom10.html (accessed 9th August 2011).

Snell, James. 2006. Getting to know the Atom Publishing Protocol, Part 1: Create and edit Web resources with the Atom Publishing Protocol. IBM DeveloperWorks, 17th October. http:// www.ibm.com/developerworks/library/x-atompp1/ (accessed 9th August 2011).

Solis, Brian. 2011. Exploring the Twitterverse. BrianSolis.com. 3rd January. http://www.briansolis. com/2011/01/exploring-the-twitterverse/ (accessed 8th August 2011).

Solove, Daniel J. 2007. *The Future of Reputation: Gossip, Rumor, and Privacy on the Internet.* New Haven, CT: Yale University Press.

Song, Felicia. 2010. Theorizing Web 2.0—A cultural perspective. *Information, Communication & Society* 13 (2):249–275.

Song, Yang, Lu Zhang, and C. Lee Giles. 2011. Automatic tag recommendation algorithms for social recommender systems. *ACM Trans. Web* 5 (1):1–31.

Soto, José Felipe Ortega. 2009. Wikipedia: A quantitative analysis. PhD diss., Departamento de Sistemas Telemáticos y Computación, Universidad Rey Juan Carlos, Madrid.

Specia, L., and E. Motta. 2007. Integrating folksonomies with the semantic Web. *Lecture Notes in Computer Science* 4519:624–639. Berlin/Heidelberg: Springer.

Spinellis, Diomidis, and Panagiotis Louridas. 2008. The collaborative organisation of knowledge. *Communications of the ACM* 51 (8):68–73.

Stango, Victor. 2004. The economics of standards wars. *Review of Network Economics* 3 (1).

Stefanone, Michael A., and Chyng-Yang Jang. 2007. Writing for friends and family: The interpersonal nature of blogs. *Journal of Computer-Mediated Communication* 13 (1):123–140.

Sterne, Jonathan, Jeremy Morris, Michael Brendan Baker, and Ariana Moscote Freire. 2008. The politics of podcasting. *The Fibreculture Journal* (13). http://www.fibreculture.org/journal/issue13/ issue13_sterne.html (accessed 3rd August 2011).

Stöckl, Ralph, Patrick Rohrmeier, and Thomas Hess. 2008. Why customers produce user-generated content. In *Web 2.0: Neue Perspektiven für Marketing und Medien*, edited by B. H. Hass, G. Walsh and T. Kilian. Berlin/Heidelberg: Springer.

Stone, Biz. 2006. Let there be Twttr. *Biz Stone*. 13th July. http://www.bizstone.com/2006/07/let-there-be-twttr.html (accessed 15th August 2011).

Strahilevitz, Lior. 2005. A social networks theory of privacy. *Chicago Review of Law* 72 (3):919–988.

Strand, Ginger. 2008. Keyword: Evil. *Harper's Magazine*, March, 64–65.

Strange, Adario. 2007. What makes Techmeme tick? Inventor Gabe Rivera explains. *Wired*, 17th May.

Strohmaier, Markus, Christian Korner, and Roman Kern. 2010. Why Do Users Tag? Detecting users' motivation for tagging in social tagging systems. Fourth International AAAI Conference on Weblogs and Social Media, 23rd–26th May, at Washington DC. Proceedings published by Association for the Advancement of Artificial Intelligence (www.aaai.org).

Stross, Randall. 2010. World's largest social network: The Open Web. *New York Times*, 14th May. http://www.nytimes.com/2010/05/16/business/16digi.html

Stuckman, Jeff, and James Purtilo. 2009. Measuring the wikisphere. Proceedings of the 5th International Symposium on Wikis and Open Collaboration, 25th–27th October, at Orlando, FL. Proceedings published by the Association for Computing Machinery.

Stvilia, B., M. B. Twidale, L. C. Smith, and L. Gasser. 2008. Information quality work organisation in Wikipedia. *Journal of the American Society for Information Science and Technology* 59 (6) (21st February):983–1001.

Stvilia, Besiki, Michael B. Twidale, Les Gasser, and Linda C. Smith. 2005. *Information Quality Discussions in Wikipedia*. Technical Report ISRN UIUCLIS-2005/2+CSCW. University of Illinois at Urbana-Champaign. Champaign, IL: University of Illinois at Urbana-Champaign.

Su, Susan. 2011. Facebook now reaches 687 million users—Traffic trends and data at inside Facebook Gold, *Inside Facebook*, 10th June. http://www.insidefacebook.com/2011/06/10/facebook-now-reaches-687-million-users-traffic-trends-and-data-at-inside-facebook-gold-june-2011-edition/ (accessed 2nd August 2011).

Subrahmanyam, Kaveri, Stephanie M. Reich, Natalia Waechter, and Guadalupe Espinoza. 2008. Online and offline social networks: Use of social networking sites by emerging adults. *Journal of Applied Developmental Psychology* 29 (6) (2008/12//):420–433.

Suchanek, Fabian M., Milan Vojnovic, and Dinan Gunawardena. 2008. Social tags: Meaning and suggestions. 17th ACM Conference on Information and Knowledge Management (CIKM 2008), 26th–30th October, at Napa Valley, CA. Proceedings published by the Association for Computing Machinery.

Suh, Bongwon, Gregorio Convertino, Ed H. Chi, and Peter Pirolli. 2009. The singularity is not near: Slowing growth of Wikipedia. WikiSym'09, 25nd–27th October, at Orlando, FL. Proceedings published by the Association for Computing Machinery.

Sunstein, Cass R. 2006. *Infotopia: How Many Minds Produce Knowledge*. Oxford, UK: Oxford University Press.

Sunstein, Cass. 2007. *Republic.com 2.0*. Princeton, NJ: Princeton University Press.

Surowiecki, James. 2004. *The Wisdom of Crowds*. London: Little, Brown.

Surowiecki, James. 2006. Joshua Schachter, 32—Del.icio.us (Yahoo). *MIT Technology Review*, July/August.

Swarts, Jason. 2009. The collaborative construction of 'fact' on Wikipedia. SIGDOC'09, 5th–7th October, at Bloomington, IN. Proceedings published by the Association for Computing Machinery.

Szabo, Gabor, and Bernardo A. Huberman. 2010. Predicting the popularity of online content. *Communications of the ACM* 53 (8):80–88.

Talbot, David. 2010. Can Twitter make money? *MIT Technology Review* (April): 52–57.

Tapscott, Don, and Anthony D. Williams. 2007. *Wikinomics*. London: Atlantic.

Taraghi, Behnam. 2009. Will personal learning environments become ubiquitous through the use of widgets? 11th International Conference on Knowledge Management and Knowledge Technologies (I-KNOW '09), 7th–9th September, at Graz, Austria. Proceedings published by the Association for Computing Machinery International Conference Proceeding Series.

Terry, Douglas B. 1993. A tour through Tapestry. Conference on Organisational Computing Systems, 1st–4th November, at Milpitas, CA. Proceedings published by the Association for Computing Machinery.

Thelwall, Mike, David Wilkinson, and Sukhvinder Uppal. 2010. Data mining emotion in social network communication: Gender differences in MySpace. *Journal of the American Society for Information Science and Technology* 61 (1) (27th July 2009):190–199.

Thomas, Christopher, and Amit Sheth. 2011. Web Wisdom: An essay on how Web 2.0 and Semantic Web can foster a global knowledge society. *Computers in Human Behavior* 27 (4) (July):1285–1293.

Thomason, Adam. 2007. Blog spam: A review. Fourth Conference on Email and Anti-Spam (CEAS'2007), 2nd–3rd August, at Microsoft Research, Mountain View, CA. Proceedings published by the Association for Computing Machinery.

Thoreau, Henry David. 1854. *Walden, The Portable Thoreau.* London: Penguin.

Tojo, João, Jorge Sousa, and Paulo Gomes. 2008. Flickring our world: An approach for a graph based exploration of the Flickr community. 1st International Workshop on Collective Semantics: Collective Intelligence & the Semantic Web (CISWeb 2008), 2nd June, at Tenerife, Spain. Proceedings published by CEUR-WS.

Torkjazi, Mojtaba, Reza Rejaie, and Walter Willinger. 2009. Hot today, gone tomorrow: On the migration of MySpace users. WOSN'09, 17th August, at Barcelona, Spain. Proceedings published by the Association for Computing Machinery.

Travers, Jeffrey, and Stanley Milgram. 1969. An experimental study of the small world problem. *Sociometry* 32 (4).

Trébaol, Gildas. 2008. How to translate SVG documents for viewing them with any Flash player. 6th International Conference on Scalable Vector Graphics, 26th–28th August, at Nuremberg, Germany. Proceedings published by conference organisers.

Tsagkias, Manos, Martha Larson, and Maarten de Rijke. 2010. Predicting podcast preference: An analysis framework and its application. *Journal of the American Society for Information Science and Technology* 61 (2) (February):374–391.

Tsagkias, Manos, Martha Larson, Wouter Weerkamp, and Maarten de Rijke. 2008. PodCred: A framework for analyzing podcast preference. 2nd ACM Workshop on Information Credibility on the Web, 26th–30th October, at Napa Valley, CA. Proceedings published by the Association for Computing Machinery.

Tseng, Belle L., Junichi Tatemura, and Yi Wu. 2005. Tomographic clustering to visualize blog communities as mountain views. 14th International World Wide Web Conference (WWW' 2005), 10th–14th May, at Chiba, Japan. Proceedings published by the Association for Computing Machinery.

UKOLN. 2008. An introduction to Creative Commons. 34. UKOLN. 4th July 2008. http://www.ukoln.ac.uk/cultural-heritage/documents/briefing-34/

Umapathy, K. 2009. An investigation of W3C standardization processes using rational discourse. AIS SIGPrag Workshop, 15th December, at Phoenix, AZ. Proceedings published by Sprouts: Working Papers on Information Systems.

Valafar, Masoud, Reza Rejaie, and Walter Willinger. 2009. Beyond friendship graphs: A study of user interactions in Flickr. 2nd ACM Workshop on Online Social Networks (WOSN 2009), 17th August, at Barcelona, Spain. Proceedings published by the Association for Computing Machinery.

Valentino-DeVries, Jennifer. 2010. Facebook, Yahoo, other Web giants back YouTube in Viacom case. WSJ Blogs: Digits. 27th May. http://blogs.wsj.com/digits/2010/05/27/facebook-yahoo-other-web-giants-back-youtube-in-viacom-case/ (accessed 6th August 2011).

Valverde, Francisco, and Oscar Pastor. 2009. Facing the technological challenges of Web 2.0: A RIA model-driven engineering approach. In *Web Information Systems Engineering (WISE 2009)*, edited by G. Vossen, D. Long and J. Yu. Berlin/Heidelberg: Springer.

van Thuan, Do, Ivar Jørstad, and Do van Thanh. 2009. An analysis of widget security. In *Identity and Privacy in the Internet Age*, edited by A. Jøsang, T. Maseng, S. Knapskog and K. Holth. Berlin: Springer.

van Zwol, Roelof. 2007. Flickr: Who is looking? IEEE/WIC/ACM International Conference on Web Intelligence (WI '07), 2nd–5th November, at Silicon Valley, CA. Proceedings published by the Institute of Electrical and Electronics Engineers Computer Society Press.

Vander Wal, Thomas. 2005. Folksonomy definition and Wikipedia. vanderwal.net. 2nd Nov 2005. http://www.vanderwal.net/random/entrysel.php?blog=1750 (accessed 14th July 2011).

Vargas, Jose Antonio. 2010. The face of Facebook. *New Yorker*, 20th September.

Vázquez, Alexei, João Gama Oliveira, Zoltán Dezsö, Kwang-Il Goh, Imre Kondor, and Albert-László Barabási. 2006. Modeling bursts and heavy tails in human dynamics. *Physical Review E* 73 (3):036127.

Veer, E. A. Vander. 2010. *Facebook: The Missing Manual*. Edited by D. Frausto. Sebastopol, CA: O'Reilly Media Inc.

Venners, Bill. 2009. Twitter on Scala. Artima Developer. 3rd April. http://www.artima.com/scala-zine/articles/twitter_on_scala.html (accessed 8th August 2011).

Viégas, Fernanda B. 2005. Bloggers' expectations of privacy and accountability. *Journal of Computer-Mediated Communication* 10 (3):Article no. 12.

Viégas, Fernanda B., Martin Wattenberg, and Matthew M. McKeon. 2007. *The Hidden Order of Wikipedia*. Technical report No. 07-12. IBM Watson Research Center. http://domino.watson.ibm.com/cambridge/research.nsf/58bac2a2a6b05a1285256b30005b3953/d1c518c79f3bff26852574b30060d2a3!OpenDocument

Vieriu, Valentin, and Catalin Tuican. 2009. Adobe AIR: Bringing Rich Internet Applications to the desktop. Preprint (arXiv).

Vinoski, Steve. 2008. Serendipitous reuse. *IEEE Internet Computing* 12 (1):84–87.

Viswanath, Bimal, Alan Mislove, Meeyoung Cha, and Krishna P. Gummadi. 2009. On the evolution of user interaction in Facebook. 2nd ACM Workshop on Online Social Networks (WSON'09), 17th August, at Barcelona, Spain. Proceedings published by the Association for Computing Machinery.

Vlist, Eric van der, Danny Ayers, Erik Bruchez, Joe Fawcett, and Alessandro Vernet. 2007. *Professional Web 2.0 programming*. Indianapolis, IN: Wrox.

Voss, Jacob. 2005. Measuring Wikipedia. 10th International Conference of the International Society for Scientometrics and Informetrics (ISSI 2005), 24th–28th July, at Stockholm, Sweden. Proceedings published by Karolinska University Press.

Vossen, Gottfried. 2011. Web 2.0: From a buzzword to mainstream Web reality. In *e-Business and Telecommunications*, edited by M. S. Obaidat and J. Filipe. Berlin/Heidelberg: Springer.

Vossen, Gottfried, and Stephan Hagemann. 2007. *Unleashing Web 2.0*. Burlington, MA: Morgan Kaufmann.

W3C (World Wide Web Consortium). 2004. *Architecture of the World Wide Web, Volume One*. W3C, 15th December. http://www.w3.org/TR/webarch/ (accessed 9th August 2011).

W3C (World Wide Web Consortium). 2005. *World Wide Web Consortium Process Document*. W3C, 14th October. http://www.w3.org/2005/10/Process-20051014/ (accessed 9th August 2011).

W3C (World Wide Web Consortium). 2008. *Widgets 1.0: The Widget Landscape (Q1 2008)*. W3C. 14th April. http://www.w3.org/TR/widgets-land/

W3C (World Wide Web Consortium). 2009a. *Widgets 1.0: APIs and Events*. W3C. Published by W3C, 23rd April. http://www.w3.org/TR/2009/WD-widgets-apis-20090423/

W3C (World Wide Web Consortium). 2009b. *W3C Semantic Web Frequently Asked Questions* W3C, 12th November. http://www.w3.org/RDF/FAQ (accessed 5th July).

W3C (World Wide Web Consortium). 2009c. *W3C Semantic Web Frequently Asked Questions* W3C, 12th November 2009. http://www.w3.org/2001/sw/SW-FAQ#swgoals (accessed 17th August 2011).

W3C (World Wide Web Consortium) Incubator Group. 2010. *A Standards-Based, Open and Privacy-Aware Social Web*. Boston, MA: W3C. 6th December. http://www.w3.org/2005/Incubator/socialweb/XGR-socialweb-20101206/

Wagner, Christian, Sesia Zhao, Christoph Schneider, and Huaping Chen. 2010. The wisdom of reluctant crowds. Hawaii International Conference on System Sciences (HICSS-43), 5th–8th January, at Kauai, Hawaii. Proceedings published by the Institute of Electrical and Electronics Engineers Computer Society.

Walker, Jill. 2005. Feral hypertext: When hypertext literature escapes control. 16th ACM Conference on Hypertext and Hypermedia, 6th–9th September, at Salzburg, Austria. Proceedings published by the Association for Computing Machinery.

Walker, Rob. 2009. A successful failure: Fail whale. *New York Times Magazine*, 12th February.

Walls, Stephen M., John V. Kucsera, Joshua D. Walker, Taylor W. Acee, Nate K. McVaugh, and Daniel H. Robinson. 2010. Podcasting in education: Are students as ready and eager as we think they are? *Computers & Education* 54 (2):371–378.

Wang, Junjian, Huajun Chen, and Yu Zhang. 2009. Mining user behavior pattern in mashup community. Proceedings of the 10th IEEE International Conference on Information Reuse & Integration, at Las Vegas, NV. Proceedings published by the Institute of Electrical and Electronics Engineers Press.

Ward, Matt, Rob van Kranenburg, and Gaynor Backhouse. 2006. *RFID: Frequency, Standards, Adoption and Innovation*. JISC Technology & Standards Watch. Bristol: JISC. http://www.jisc.ac.uk/whatwedo/services/techwatch/reports/horizonscanning/hs0602.aspx

Waters, Roger. 2011. *Why the Wall Now?* http://www.roger-waters.com/why.php (accessed 5th July 2011).

Watters, Audrey. 2010. *The Age of the Exabyte*. Portland, OR: ReadWriteWeb. http://www.readwrite-web.com/reports/big-data/

Watts, Duncan J. 1999. *Small Worlds: The Dynamics of Networks between Order and Randomness*. Princeton, NJ: Princeton University Press.

Watts, Duncan J., and Steven H. Strogatz. 1998. Collective dynamics of 'small-world' networks. *Nature* 393 (6684):440–442.

Wayner, Peter. 2006. Surveying open-source AJAX toolkits. *InfoWorld*, 31st July.

Weaver, A. C., and B. B. Morrison. 2008. Social networking. *Computer* 41 (2):97–100.

Wei, Liu, Tan Songbo, Xu Hongbo, and Wang Lihong. 2008. Splog filtering based on writing consistency. IEEE/WIC/ACM International Conference on Web Intelligence and Intelligent Agent Technology (WI-IAT '08), 9th–12th December, at Sydney, Australia. Proceedings published by the Institute of Electrical and Electronics Engineers.

Weil, Debbie. 2006. *The Corporate Blogging Book*. London: Piatkus Books Ltd.

Weinberger, David. 2001. Reed's Law—An Interview. David Weinberger's Intranet Buzz. http://www.intranetjournal.com/articles/200101/ib_01_31_01a.html (accessed 16th September 2011).

Weinberger, David. 2003. *Small Pieces, Loosely Joined*. Oxford: Perseus.

Weinberger, David. 2007. *Everything is Miscellaneous*. New York: Times Books.

Weinman, Joe. 2007. Is Metcalfe's Law way too optimistic? *Business Communications Review* (August 2007):18–27.

Weiss, Aaron. 2005. WebOS: Say goodbye to desktop applications. *netWorker* 9 (4):18–26.

Wetzker, R., C. Zimmermann, and C. Bauckhage. 2008. Analyzing social bookmarking systems: A del.icio.us cookbook. ECAI Workshop on Mining Social Data (MSoDa), 21st July, at Patras, Greece. Proceedings published by conference organisers.

White, Bebo. 2007. The Implications of Web 2.0 on Web information systems. In *Web Information Systems and Technologies*. Berlin/Heidelberg: Springer.

Wilkinson, Dennis, and Bernardo Huberman. 2007a. Co-operation and quality in Wikipedia. WikiSym' 2007, 21st–23rd October, at Montreal, Quebec. Proceedings published by the Association for Computing Machinery.

Wilkinson, Dennis M., and Bernardo A. Huberman. 2007b. Assessing the value of co-operation in Wikipedia. arXiv. http://arxiv.org/abs/cs/0702140 (accessed 1st August 2011).

Williams, J. B., and J. Jacobs. 2004. Exploring the use of blogs as learning spaces in the higher education sector. *Australasian Journal of Educational Technology* 20 (2):232–247.

Willinger, Walter, Reza Rejaie, Mojtaba Torkjazi, Masoud Valafar, and Mauro Maggioni. 2009. Research on online social networks: time to face the real challenges. *SIGMETRICS Performance Evaluation Review* 37 (3):49–54.

Wilson, Christo, Bryce Boe, Alessandra Sala, Krishna P. N. Puttaswamy, and Ben Y. Zhao. 2009. User interactions in social networks and their implications. 4th ACM European Conference on Computer systems, 1st–3rd April, at Nuremberg, Germany. Proceedings published by the Association for Computing Machinery.

Wilson, Scott. 2010. W3C widgets and wookie. Presentation made to Building W3C Widgets Training Day (OSSWatch), February, at Oxford University, Oxford, UK. http://www.slideshare.net/scottw/open-source-junction-apache-wookie-and-w3c-widgets

Winer, Dave. 2001. Payloads for RSS. *The Two Way Web*. http://www.thetwowayweb.com/payloads-ForRss (accessed 3rd August 2011).

Wirdemann, Ralf, and Thomas Baustert. 2007. RESTful Rails Development: The REST and Ruby Tutorial. b-simple. Hamburg, Germany: b-simple. http://www.b-simple.de/documents

Wöhner, Thomas, and Ralf Peters. 2009. Assessing the quality of Wikipedia articles with lifecycle-based metrics. WikiSym '09, 25th–27th October, at Orlando, FL. Proceedings published by the Association for Computing Machinery.

Wortham, Jenna. 2011. YouTube founders revamping a site for link sharing. *New York Times*, 11th September. http://www.nytimes.com/2011/09/12/technology/youtube-founders-aim-to-revamp-delicious.html?_r=1&pagewanted=all.

Wu, Shaomei, Jake M. Hofman, Winter A. Mason, and Duncan J. Watts. 2011. Who says what to whom on Twitter. 20th International Conference on World Wide Web, 28th March–1st April, at Hyderabad, India. Proceedings published by the Association for Computing Machinery.

Wu, Wendy G., and Jie Li. 2007. RSS made easy: A basic guide for librarians. *Medical Reference Services Quarterly* 26 (1):37–50.

Xiang, Rongjing, Jennifer Neville, and Monica Rogati. 2010. Modeling relationship strength in online social networks. 19th International Conference on World Wide Web, 26th–30th April, at Raleigh, NC. Proceedings published by the Association for Computing Machinery.

Yan, Lu, Yan Zhang, Laurence T. Yang, and Huansheng Ning. 2008. *The Internet of Things: From RFID to the Next-Generation Pervasive Networked Systems*. Boca Raton, FL: Auerbach Publications.

Yang, Jiang, and Scott Counts. 2010. Predicting the speed, scale, and range of information diffusion in Twitter. 4th International Conference on Weblogs and Social Media (ICWSM-10), 23rd–26th May, at George Washington University, Washington, DC. Proceedings published by Association for the Advancement of Artificial Intelligence.

Yardi, Sarita, Scott A. Golder, and Michael J. Brzozowski. 2009. Blogging at work and the corporate attention economy. 27th International Conference on Human Factors in Computing Systems, 4th–9th April, at Boston, MA. Proceedings published by the Association for Computing Machinery.

Yeung, Ching-man Au, Nicholas Gibbins, and Nigel Shadbolt. 2009. Contextualising tags in collaborative tagging systems. 20th ACM Conference on Hypertext and Hypermedia (Hypertext 2009), 29th June–1st July, at Torino, Italy. Proceedings published by the Association for Computing Machinery.

Yeung, Ching-man Au, Ilaria Liccardi, Kanghao Lu, Oshani Seneviratne, and Tim Berners-Lee. 2007. Decentralisation: The future of online social networking. W3C Workshop on the Future of Social Networks 15th–16th January, at Barcelona. Proceedings published by the World Wide Web Consortium.

Yu, Jin, Boualem Benatallah, Fabio Casati, and Florian Daniel. 2008. Understanding mashup development. *IEEE Internet Computing* 12 (5) (September/October):44–52.

Yu, Louis, and Valerie King. 2010. The evolution of friendships in Chinese online social networks. IEEE International Conference on Privacy, Security, Risk and Trust, 20th August, at Minneapolis, MN. Proceedings published by the Institute of Electrical and Electronics Engineers.

Yu, Shuli, and C. Woodard. 2009. Innovation in the programmable Web: Characterizing the mashup ecosystem. In *Service-Oriented Computing—ICSOC 2008 Workshops*, edited by G. Feuerlicht and W. Lamersdorf. Berlin/Heidelberg: Springer.

Yuan, Li. 2010. The future of interoperability and standards in education. JISC CETIS Future of Interoperability Standards Meeting 2010, 12th January, at University of Bolton, UK. Proceedings published by JISC Centre for Educational Technology and Interoperability Standards (CETIS).

Zafarani, R., and H. Liu. 2009. Connecting corresponding identities across communities. ICWSM, 17th May, at San Jose, CA. Proceedings published by Association for the Advancement of Artificial Intelligence.

Zafeiropoulou, A. M., D. Millard, C. Webber, and K O'Hara. 2011. Privacy implications of location and contextual data on the social Web. ACM Web Science Conference 2011, 14th–17th June, at Koblenz, Germany. Proceedings published by the Association for Computing Machinery.

Zając, Jan M., Kamil Rakocy, and Andrzej Nowak. 2009. Dark side of the blogosphere. ASNA Conference, 27th–28th August, at Zurich. Proceedings published by University of Zurich.

Zakas, Nicolas C., Jeremy McPeak, and Joe Fawcett. 2006. *Professional Ajax, WROX*. Indianapolis, IN: Wiley.

Zeichick, Alan. 2008a. How Facebook works. *MIT Technology Review*, July/August.

Zeichick, Alan. 2008b. The end of Yahoo as we knew it. *netWorker* 12 (4):5–8.

Zhang, Bo, Yongcheng Xie, Xinxi Zhang, and Dan Wang. 2010. A weighted network model based on triad formation mechanism. *Intelligent Computation Technology and Automation, International Conference on* 1:390–392.

Zhang, Lei, and Wanqing Tu. 2009. Six degrees of separation in online society. WebSci'09: Society On-Line, 18th–20th March, at Athens, Greece. Proceedings published by Web Science Trust.

Zhang, Lei, Xian Wu, and Yong Yu. 2006. Emergent semantics from folksonomies: A quantitative study. In *Journal on Data Semantics VI*, edited by S. Spaccapietra, K. Aberer and P. Cudré-Mauroux. Berlin/Heidelberg: Springer.

Zhu, Jonathan J. H., Tao Meng, Zhengmao Xie, Geng Li, and Xiaoming Li. 2008. A teapot graph and its hierarchical structure of the Chinese web. 17th International Conference on the World Wide Web, at Beijing, China. Proceedings published by the Association for Computing Machinery.

Zickuhr, Kathryn. 2010. *Generations 2010*. Pew Internet & American Life Project. Washington, DC: Pew Research Center. 16th December. http://www.pewinternet.org/Reports/2010/Generations-2010.aspx

Zickuhr, Kathryn, and Aaron Smith. 2010. 4% of online Americans use location-based services. Pew Internet & American Life Project. Washington DC: Pew Research Center. 4th November. http://www.pewinternet.org/Reports/2010/Location-based-services.aspx

Zinko, Carolyne. 2009. What is Biz Stone doing? *San Francisco Chronicle*, 5th April. http://articles.sfgate.com/2009-04-05/living/17193250_1_twitter-biz-stone-ashton-kutcher.

Zittrain, Jonathan. 2008. *The Future of the Internet: And How to Stop It*. London: Allen Lane.

Zlatic, V., M. Bozicevic, H. Stefancic, and M. Domazet. 2006. Wikipedias: Collaborative web-based encyclopedias as complex networks. *Physical Review E* 74 (1 [part 2]):016115.

Index

DATE DUE

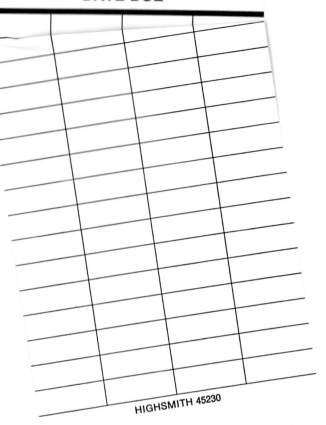

HIGHSMITH 45230